# The CONTOURS of POLICE INTEGRITY

To the memory of Carl B. Klockars

# *The* CONTOURS *of* POLICE INTEGRITY

Editors

## Carl B. Klockars
University of Delaware

## Sanja Kutnjak Ivković
Harvard Law School

## M. R. Haberfeld
John Jay College of Criminal Justice

**SAGE** Publications
*International Educational and Professional Publisher*
Thousand Oaks ▪ London ▪ New Delhi

*For information:*

Sage Publications, Inc.
2455 Teller Road
Thousand Oaks, California 91320
E-mail: order@sagepub.com

Sage Publications Ltd.
6 Bonhill Street
London EC2A 4PU
United Kingdom

Sage Publications India Pvt. Ltd.
B-42, Panchsheel Enclave
Post Box 4109
New Delhi 110 017  India

Printed in the United States of America

**Library of Congress Cataloging-in-Publication Data**

The contours of police integrity / editors, Carl B. Klockars,
Sanja Kutnjak Ivković, M.R. Haberfeld.
    p. cm.
Includes bibliographical references and index.
ISBN 0-7619-2585-6 (cloth)
ISBN 0-7619-2586-4 (pbk.)
   1.  Police ethics—Cross-cultural studies. 2.  Law enforcement—Cross-cultural studies. 3.  Police misconduct—Cross-cultural studies. I.  Klockars, Carl B. II.  Kutnjak Ivković, Sanja, 1965- III.  Haberfeld, M. R. (Maria R.), 1957-HV7924.C66 2003
174′.93632—dc21

               2003006152

This book is printed on acid-free paper.

03   04   05   06   10  9  8  7  6  5  4  3  2  1

| | |
|---|---|
| *Acquisitions Editor:* | Jerry Westby |
| *Editorial Assistant:* | Vonessa Vondera |
| *Typesetter:* | C&M Digitals (P) Ltd. |
| *Indexer:* | Pamela Van Huss |
| *Cover Designer:* | Michelle Lee Kenny |

# Contents

# CHAPTER 1

# The Contours of Police Integrity

Carl B. Klockars

Sanja Kutnjak Ivković

Maria R. Haberfeld

*T*he *Contours of Police Integrity* is a collection of essays from 14 different countries on the status of police integrity in each country. Each essay is written by an expert on his or her country's police. Most of the authors are senior officials in the police system of their country, leaders of police academies or police colleges, or directors of police research or training facilities. Some authors are academics with long histories of studying the police of their country. Still others are employed in governmental organizations with responsibilities for monitoring police behavior.

Despite differences in their backgrounds and training, these authors share a belief in the value of integrity. As students of police integrity, they seek to describe its present state, to understand its origins, and, where their assessments warrant change, to assess the prospects for reform. However, their analyses of the origins of police integrity (or the lack of it) and the prospects for change (or the lack of it) are as different as the countries themselves. This is so because the police are ineluctably part of the unique political, economic, legal, and cultural institutions of a country and cannot be understood apart from those distinctive institutions. This diversity becomes abundantly clear as one looks closely at the pages that follow. The material in this volume amply illustrates that the sources and solutions of problems regarding police integrity in Austria, Finland, Hungary, the Netherlands, Sweden, or Pakistan bear little resemblance to the sources and solutions of similar problems in Croatia, Poland, Slovenia, or Japan. Even in countries united by a common language, such as Canada, England, South Africa, and the United States, the causes of and prospects for police integrity are remarkably different.

It is also true that at some level of abstraction similarities in both the causes of and cures for problems with police integrity do most certainly appear. In fact, the greater the level of abstraction, the more distance one maintains from the objects of one's study, the more likely it is that similarities will appear. However, when the particulars of politics, economy, law, and culture are ignored to reveal similarities, discovery of those similarities is unlikely to prove very helpful to anyone.

These twin truths expose a paradox for anyone interested in a subject like the contours of police integrity. The paradox is that the closer one gets to a given police agency, the more likely it is that the contours of police integrity will seem to dissolve in the particular details of the agency. Alternatively, the more one steps away to discover the contours, the less useful one's discovery of contours is likely to be to anyone, and that is everyone, who lives in the real world, saturated as it is with political, economic, legal, and cultural facts.

This paradox, which provides that perceptions appear clearer the further one stands from what one observes, is genuine and besets all history, natural as well as social. However, there are two ways in which this paradox is normally resolved, both of which are employed in *The Contours of Police Integrity*. The first approach is to confine one's account to a local setting. This is the strategy adopted by all the authors of the essays in this collection. Each of the essays focuses in detail on the unique cultural, political, and historical conditions that influence police integrity in the country it describes.

The second approach to resolution of this paradox is to confess openly that any contours discovered are imposed by the discoverer and to let a discovery rise or fall on its internal logic, its correspondence to observable events, and its practical utility. As editors of this volume, we have, to a degree, imposed this resolution of the paradox of perception by requiring all of the authors to accept a common definition of integrity and a common operationalization of it.

We have proposed a modest theory of integrity and an equally modest theory of its measurement, and we have required that the authors represented here employ these theories as a condition of their participation in this volume. Doing so was necessary in order to speak of the contours of police integrity in any sensible way. Unless all the authors shared a common understanding of police integrity, it would be impossible to know whether they were all talking about the same thing, and unless they shared a common method of measuring it, any comments about its contours—its growth, its atrophy, its depth, or its dimensions—would be equally meaningless.

In this introduction to *The Contours of Police Integrity*, we therefore begin by describing the concept of police integrity and the method of its measurement we required of the authors whose work is included here. We then go on to summarize the profile of integrity it yielded in each nation and to display those profiles in comparison with one another. Not only will such comparisons increase our ability to discover contours, but they will also serve as a perspective from which to view the historically, culturally, and politically saturated accounts that follow.

## THE CONCEPT OF POLICE INTEGRITY

We proposed to the contributors to this volume that the term *police integrity* be defined as "the normative inclination among police to resist temptations to abuse the rights and privileges of their occupation." We have defined this term previously at some length (Klockars, Haberfeld, Kutnjak Ivkovich, & Uydess, 2002, pp. 2-7), but here we believe it is sufficient to confine our discussion to the six concepts within the term *police integrity* that are described below, each of which is of consequence methodologically as well as theoretically.

*Normativeness.* To speak of police integrity as *normative* makes three claims about it. The first claim denotes that police integrity is a belief rather than a behavior. When this belief is held by an individual, it is often called an *attitude* or *opinion*; when it is shared by a group, it is often called a *norm*. The second claim implies that the idea of police integrity is morally charged, that police conduct is to one degree or another right or wrong. This claim specifies, in the words of George Homans (1950), what people "should do, ought to do, are expected to do, under given circumstances" (p. 123). The third claim for describing integrity as normative indicates that it possesses a characteristic that is virtually inseparable from moral attitudes: It combines a belief with an inclination to behave in accordance with that belief. Just as a belief in honesty inclines one to avoid lying and a belief in fidelity obliges one to be faithful, integrity requires not only beliefs that certain behaviors are right or wrong but also actions that are in accord with those beliefs.

The failure to coordinate beliefs and actions is sometimes called *hypocrisy*. However, it is not certain what actions—beyond avoiding wrongful behavior—integrity demands. In the case of police integrity, does integrity require, in addition to the condemnation of misbehavior, support for the punishment of those who misbehave? Does it require an officer who witnesses corruption or brutality to intervene to stop it or come forward to report it? It is not difficult to imagine that the noble norm of integrity may even compete with other, equally noble norms in its discipline and reporting dimensions. When an officer is faced with the decision of whether or not to report the misconduct of a fellow officer, the norm of integrity may compete with or be tempered by norms that urge forgiveness, mercy, loyalty, reciprocity, tolerance, gratitude, compassion, and proportion, to name but a few. In fact, there may well be situations in which behavior that is wrong from one quite noble point of view may be right from an equally noble alternative perspective. Such situations are called *moral dilemmas* (see, e.g., Crank & Caldero, 2000; Delattre, 1996; Klockars, 1991). Because officer support for discipline and officer reporting of police misconduct may be as important or possibly even more important to the control of police misconduct than the belief in its

wrongness, this problem merits especially careful analytical attention.

***The Inclination to Resist.*** An even more general problem at the heart of the idea of integrity is that people who believe in honesty sometimes lie, people who believe in fidelity are sometimes disloyal, and people of integrity sometimes do things that they know are wrong. Attitudes, even those that are strongly held, are not always predictive of behavior.

Although criminologists may eventually succeed in specifying all of the major dimensions of the relationship between attitudes of integrity and misconduct, three dimensions that are signaled in our definition warrant exposure at this time. The first dimension is that not all avoidance of misconduct stems from an attitude of integrity. Although integrity describes the normative inclination to resist temptations to abuse the rights and privileges of the police office, it is not the only source of that resistance. Lack of imagination, lack of opportunity, fear of discovery and public humiliation, shame, punishment, and/or a simple unfavorable risk/reward calculus may suffice to ensure honest behavior irrespective of the sentiment of integrity. While attitudes are not always predictive of behavior, behavior is not always predictive of attitudes.

A second and allied dimension of the relationship between attitudes of integrity and police misconduct is that attitudes of integrity assert on those who hold them at least *some* pressure to avoid wrongful behavior. Because the relationship between an attitude of integrity and compliant behavior is not perfect, and a substantial amount of such behavior may stem from other sources, we have chosen to refer to integrity as the *inclination* to resist rather than the actual resistance to temptations.

A third dimension that may be exposed here is that the direction of the causal relationship between attitudes and behavior is not always clear. It may well be that requiring police to be honest may cause them to adopt belief in the virtues of integrity. Attitudes may cause behavior, but behavior may also cause attitudes.

If nothing else, these conceptual distinctions force us to be modest in our claims for the role integrity may play in suppressing misconduct. They remind us that integrity is only one of the factors that may influence police to be honest.

*Police as an Individual or a Group.* We emphasize the use of the word *police* (rather than *police officer*, *officer*, or some similar individualistic formulation) among the crucial components of our definition of police integrity for the sole purpose of signaling that integrity may describe a characteristic of an individual, a group, an organization, an agency, an institution, or, for that matter, any collection of police. When speaking about integrity, the seductions of lapsing into talk about individuals are almost irresistible. But they must be resisted if we wish to speak of police agencies, organizations, institutions, and cultures of integrity. Depending on the level of integrity under discussion, the dynamics and the relevant correlates of integrity will differ. How one understands and explains the psychology of integrity of an individual police officer will most certainly differ from one's understanding and explanation of the sociology, politics, or history of the evolution of a culture of integrity in a police agency.

*Temptations.* The *temptations* component of our definition of police integrity invites attention to the different environments in which police officers, police agencies, and police institutions operate. It urges one to inspect those environments for the particular temptations to misconduct they offer.

The most obvious of these temptations is *gain*, the defining reward for that type of police misbehavior called *corruption*. Societies, communities, and organizations will differ in the amount of gain and the frequency with which they offer it to officers in exchange for

their abusing their office. However, one should be careful to distinguish police misconduct that is motivated by the temptation of gain from that which is not. It is a common error to assume that all forms of police misconduct are the product of a similar, singular, or even ignoble temptation.

In cases of excessive force, for example, the excessive force

> need not (and usually will not) be the product of malicious or sadistic behavior. It can spring from good intentions as well as bad, mistakes and misreading, lack of experience, overconfidence, momentary inattention, physical or mental fatigue, experimentation, inadequate or improper training, prejudice, passion, an urge to do justice or demonstrate bravery, misplaced trust, boredom, illness, a specific incompetence, or a hundred other factors that might influence an officer to behave in a particular situation in a less than expert way. (Klockars, 1996, p. 8)

The most obvious implication of the assertion that police misconduct may be inspired by a range of quite different temptations is that methods of preventing and controlling police misconduct should be different for different types of misconduct. Methods of controlling corruption may be of no help whatsoever in controlling police offenses in which gain for the officer is not a consideration.[1]

The capacity to separate temptations into different categories also suggests that the contours of integrity may be very different in different police agencies. It may be assumed that police who steal, accept bribes, or take kickbacks also succumb to the temptations to lie in court, forge records, fabricate evidence, or make unwarranted searches or unjustified arrests, even though gain provides no motive for doing so. However, it is not difficult to imagine a police organization or subculture that is highly intolerant of officer theft, soliciting bribes, taking kickbacks, and other acts of corruption and at the same time is much more accepting of discourtesy, excessive force, perjury, forging records, fabricating evidence, or unwarranted or illegal searches.

Police integrity need not be a uniform phenomenon. However, to simplify measurement of it, we have confined our inquiry largely to police resistance of opportunities of police misbehavior for gain. This is not to say that in the future a survey measuring police resistance to excessive force, discourtesy to the public, discrimination against specific religious or ethnic groups, unwarranted or illegal searches, planting evidence, or any other police misconduct not necessarily motivated by gain could not be equally effective.

*Abuse of Office.* A core component of the idea of police integrity is the concept of *abuse of office.* Although in egregious situations of police misconduct the fact of abuse may be obvious, discussions of police misbehavior are often marked by two types of arguments that seek to deny or excuse its abusive character. The most common type of argument asserts that the behavior in question is actually innocent and that those who would criticize it simply fail to understand its true nature. Certainly the best known American occasions on which this type of claim is made involve situations in which police receive discounts, holiday gifts, and free food and liquor offered as gestures of goodwill, hospitality, and gratitude. The same type of argument is also offered in defense of police exercising their legal discretion not to arrest or issue summonses to friends, neighbors, fellow police officers, the clergy, or influential citizens and public officials for minor offenses.

These direct challenges to the idea that such behavior is abusive are complemented by a second type of argument, which concedes that certain behaviors may be abusive but argues that they may be excused. For example, many police and citizens are sympathetic to the argument that there is nothing wrong with police officers using foul, abusive, or threatening (but not racist) language in response to citizens who insult, defy, or

resist them. If the popularity of fictional officers on television dramas such as *NYPD Blue* or *Homicide* is any guide, there is also some portion of the public that has little objection to "street justice" in the form of moderate levels of physical violence visited on a wide variety of "lowlifes" who've "got it coming" (Klockars, 1986; Sykes, 1986).

Although such arguments may take many forms, the common theme in all is that police are human and therefore cannot be expected to behave without normal human emotions in situations in which they are insulted, defied, assaulted, deceived, shocked, repulsed, disgusted, or horrified by the conduct of those they police. It is, of course, precisely because the public does not want those it asks to handle such situations to react to them with normal human emotions that the police were created.

Both arguments should serve as a reminder that it is necessary to be careful to specify exactly what behavior is offered as evidence of a lack of integrity. What one police agency defines as bribery another may classify as hospitality, generosity, or appreciation. At the same time, the mere presence of those arguments should alert one to the prospect of substantial variations—not only in opinions about what constitutes integrity but in norms about how police officers, police agencies, and citizens ought to react to lapses in it.

*The Rights and Privileges of the Occupation.* By virtue of the fact that policing is a highly discretionary, coercive activity that routinely takes place in private settings, out of the sight of supervisors, and before witnesses who are often regarded as unreliable, it is, as the history of virtually every police agency in the world bears testimony, an occupation that is ripe with opportunities for misconduct of many types.[2] One type, *corruption,* the abuse of police authority *for gain,*[3] has been especially problematic. Contributing to the difficulties of controlling corruption are the reluctance of police officers to report corrupt activities of their fellow officers—a phenomenon sometimes identified as "the code," the "code of silence," or the "blue curtain" (Muir, 1977; Stoddard, 1979)—and the reluctance of police administrators to admit the existence of corruption, in addition to the fact that the typical corrupt transaction benefits the parties to it and thus leaves no immediate victim-complainant to call attention to it.

For all of these reasons, official statistics on corruption are of little or no value in assessing either the amount or the nature of corruption in any police agency. Whether an agency reports a large or small number of corruption incidents may bear little or no relationship to the actual level of corruption in that agency. An agency with very low levels of corrupt behavior may be very aggressive in detecting it, whereas an agency with high levels of corruption may make little or no effort to uncover it. At best, police agency reports on corruption should be understood as a reflection of the resources and energy applied to the problem[4] by the agency.

Moreover, the idea of integrity has a special relationship to corruption that invites theoretical and empirical understandings that might otherwise not be possible. Because the obstacles to the direct measurement of corruption are so great, the entire problem of measuring corruption must be rephrased if one is to make any progress toward its solution. It is in this effort that the concept of integrity proves most useful. If integrity is conceived of as the mirror opposite of corruption—the more integrity, the less corruption (and vice versa)—a measurement of corruption may be achieved indirectly through the measurement of integrity. The value of standing the problem of measuring corruption on its head in this way is that integrity is much more amenable to measurement than is corruption.

In fact, police themselves, as well as those charged with discovering police corruption, have pioneered this approach of focusing interest on integrity, rather than on corruption, with techniques used for what is called *integrity testing*. These are investigative efforts in which

police officers' integrity may be tested without there being probable cause to believe the officer has committed a violation. A common form of this technique requires prospective police officers to submit to lie detector tests as part of their pre-employment interview. Another technique is random drug testing—a practice common particularly in undercover drug investigation units. Other common forms of integrity testing involve having undercover police officers or their agents offer police officers bribes or place them in situations in which they believe they can commit certain crimes without being caught.

Although random drug testing is widely accepted by police as a mechanism for controlling drug abuse by police, both police officers and police administrators are often reluctant to accept or employ integrity testing methods that entice officers to commit corrupt acts. While most police agencies accept the idea of using the polygraph in pre-employment interviews, many refuse to use it in internal investigations. Although integrity testing methods can be highly effective, the more intrusive forms of the methods may provoke a fear of entrapment in police officers and may undermine the relationship of trust and respect that administrators wish to promote in their police agencies.

The distinctive theoretical character of the police form of police integrity testing, which drives the methods of integrity testing police are inclined to use, is its *individual* focus. Police are, after all, interested in identifying individually corrupt police officers—those who take illicit drugs, accept bribes, and otherwise exploit their police position for gain. However, if corruption is understood as an *organizational* or *occupational* problem and integrity as the character of a police *agency* and something police administrators should work to achieve, both the theory of integrity and the methods for measuring it must be transformed. Moreover, all of the components of an organizational or occupational view of integrity invite measurement. Furthermore, and most fortunately, it is unlikely that their measurement will provoke anything like the resistance that is nearly inevitable in testing the integrity of individual police officers.

## AN ORGANIZATIONAL
## VIEW OF INTEGRITY

Until relatively recently, at least in the United States, the administrative view of integrity has been to see integrity as largely reflective of the moral virtues of individual police officers[5] and to fight corruption in their agencies by carefully screening applicants for police positions, pursuing corrupt officers aggressively, and removing them from their police positions before their behavior spreads throughout the agency. Although no one questions the value of any of these efforts, ever since Goldstein's pioneering work in the mid-1970s (Goldstein 1975, 1977), this "bad apple" theory of police corruption has been recognized as inadequate.

What has begun to replace that theory is a recognition that enhancing police integrity is an organizational and administrative responsibility that goes well beyond the culling out of "bad apple" police officers. This approach appears to stress the importance of three distinct efforts, all of which are profoundly organizational in nature.

*Organizational Rule Making.* The first of these dimensions is the creation and communication of organizational rules. In nations in which police are highly decentralized (e.g., the United States), police organizations differ markedly in what behavior they permit and prohibit (McCormack, 1986; Muir, 1977). This is particularly true of marginally or *mala prohibita* corrupt behavior such as off-duty employment and receipt of favors, gratuities, small gifts, free meals, and discounts. The problem of organizational rule making is further complicated by the fact that, in many agencies, while an agency's *official* policy formally prohibits certain activities, the agency's *unofficial* policy, supported firmly but in silence by supervisors and administrators, is to permit and ignore such behaviors—provided that they are limited and conducted discretely.

The obligations of rule making require police agencies not only to develop policies and create both formal and informal rules that specify agency expectations of integrity but also to communicate those rules and the reasons for them to their employees. In a police agency of integrity, police officers ought to know the agency's rules that pertain to integrity, understand the agency's rationale for them, and come to believe in the rightness of both.

*Detecting, Investigating, and Disciplining Rule Violations.* The second organizational obligation in enhancing police integrity is the creation and maintenance of a whole range of activities that permit the detection, investigation, and discipline of misconduct. These include but are not limited to proactive and reactive agency internal investigations, inspections, audits, external reviews, reception of citizen complaints, integrity testing, and the general deterrence of misconduct by the disciplining of offending police offenders. The extent to which these and other techniques are employed in police organizations varies enormously. In a police agency of integrity, the occupational culture of the agency will support the discipline of officers who violate agency standards of integrity.

*Circumscribing the Code.* The third obligation of police organizations in enhancing police integrity is to circumscribe what has come to be called the code, the code of silence, or the blue curtain—the informal prohibition in the occupational culture of policing against reporting the misconduct of fellow police officers. Two special features of the code bear emphasis here.

First, exactly *what* behavior is covered by the code can vary enormously between police agencies. In some agencies, it may cover only relatively low-level corruption; in others, it may cover misconduct of even the most serious degree. Second, the code differs in not only what behavior it covers but *to whom* the benefit of its coverage is extended. In some police agencies, the code is largely limited to police partners who enjoy, vis-à-vis one another, a testimonial immunity that police liken to traditionally privileged relationships between husband and wife, physician and patient, and lawyer and client.

While many police administrators probably understand that circumscribing both whom and what the code covers should be an administrative priority (Barker & Wells, 1982), there is among police administrators, virtually all of whom have been line officers at some point in their careers, at least an appreciation if not an affection for the bonds of collegial loyalty and fraternal support that are part of the subculture of policing. To the extent that circumscribing the code requires the weakening of those bonds of loyalty and support, it is a task that more than a few police administrators approach with ambivalence.

## THE METHODOLOGY OF THE MEASUREMENT OF POLICE INTEGRITY

It is directly from this concept of police integrity, understood in its organizational terms, that we have designed the method of measuring it. The question on which we built our measurement instrument is "What is the level of intolerance for misconduct in the organization?" In order to answer it, we created the 11 hypothetical scenarios in Exhibit 1.1. Each scenario describes an instance of police misconduct, 10 of which are instances of corruption and 1 of which is the use of excessive force. The 10 corruption scenarios range from some that only seem to create the possibility of an appearance of abuse (e.g., Case 1, which is prohibited by official policy in some police agencies and permitted in others) to universally prohibited practices such as accepting bribes and stealing from a crime scene.

Because we sought to use this questionnaire in cross-cultural applications, we gave special attention to creating case scenarios that are as culturally neutral as possible, in the sense that they describe situations familiar to all citizens and represent acts that are roughly equivalent in all modern industrial societies.

Those who study instances of police abuse of authority for gain encounter their first problem in attempting to achieve cultural neutrality of this kind in the different meaning of money in different cultures. A bribe of U.S.$50 clearly has a different meaning for a U.S. police officer who earns $40,000 per year and an Eastern European police officer who earns the annual equivalent of U.S.$4,000. Conversion of U.S. currency to the currency of some other nation at prevailing exchange rates does not solve this problem, as the stimulus of a U.S.$50 bribe is different in the economic life of each officer.

In the scenarios we created that involved monetary gain, we attempted to resolve this problem by expressing the gain in terms of some local value equivalent. In Case 3, we describe the value of a bribe for ignoring a speeding violation as worth one half the value of the fine. In Case 5, we describe the value of a watch taken in an opportunistic theft as worth about 2 days' pay. Similarly, we describe in Case 6 an auto repair shop kickback scheme as producing a reward for the officer of 5% of the value of the repair.

In addition, in Case 4 we avoided specific mention of holidays that in the United States and some other cultures are occasions for giving gifts to police. Instead of using the word *Christmas*, we used the word *holiday* on the assumption that respondents in nations without a dominant Christian tradition (e.g., Israel and Pakistan) may still have holidays on which giving gifts to police is not uncommon.

While the above modifications in our scenarios attempted to make them, as near as possible, "culturally neutral," we found that even our best efforts at picking culturally common opportunities came up short. For example, in

Case 1. A police officer runs a private business in which he sells and installs security devices, such as alarms, special locks, etc. He does this work during his off-duty hours.

Case 2. A police officer routinely accepts free meals, cigarettes, and other items of small value from merchants on his beat. He does not solicit these gifts and is careful not to abuse the generosity of those who give gifts to him.

Case 3. A police officer stops a motorist for speeding. The officer agrees to accept a personal gift of half of the amount of the fine in exchange for not issuing a citation.

Case 4. A police officer is widely liked in the community, and on holidays local merchants and restaurant and bar owners show their appreciation for his attention by giving him gifts of food and liquor.

Case 5. A police officer discovers a burglary of a jewelry shop. The display cases are smashed and it is obvious that many items have been taken. While searching the shop, he takes a watch, worth about two days' pay for that officer. He reports that the watch had been stolen during the burglary.

Case 6. A police officer has a private arrangement with a local auto body shop to refer the owners of the cars damaged in the accidents to the shop. In exchange for each referral, he receives a payment of 5% of the repair bill from the shop owner.

Case 7. A police officer, who happens to be a very good auto mechanic, is scheduled to work during coming holidays. A supervisor offers to give him these days off, if he agrees to tune-up his supervisor's personal car. Evaluate the *supervisor's* behavior.

Case 8. At 2 A.M. a police officer, who is on duty, is driving his patrol car on a deserted road. He sees a vehicle that has been driven off the road and is stuck in a ditch. He approaches the vehicle and observes that the driver is not hurt but is obviously intoxicated. He also finds that the driver is a police officer. Instead of reporting this accident and offense he transports the driver to his home.

Case 9. A police officer finds a bar on his beat which is still serving drinks a half hour past its legal closing time. Instead of reporting this violation, the police officer agrees to accept a couple of free drinks from the owner.

Case 10. Two police officers on foot patrol surprise a man who is attempting to break into an automobile. The man flees. They chase him for about two blocks before apprehending him by tackling him and wrestling him to the ground. After he is under control both officers punch him a couple of times in the stomach as punishment for fleeing and resisting.

Case 11. A police officer finds a wallet in a parking lot. It contains the amount of money equivalent to a full day's pay for that officer. He reports the wallet as lost property, but keeps the money for himself.

**Exhibit 1.1**     Case Scenarios

attempting to translate our scenarios for distribution to a sample of police officers in Pakistan, both Case 7 and Case 8 had to be modified to reflect the fact that virtually no line police officers in Pakistan earned enough to own a car. (We substituted motorbikes for cars.) Similarly, in Poland, bars are not subject to closing hours. In the Polish survey, the offense in Case 9 was changed from a bar's late closing to serving underage drinkers—an offense that is taken quite seriously in Poland but widely ignored elsewhere in Europe.

We asked all respondents to assume that the officer in the scenario had been a police officer for 5 years, had a satisfactory work record, and had a history of no previous discipline. Needless to say, all respondents were promised confidentiality and all questionnaires were completed anonymously. Questions about the officer's history and background were kept to an absolute minimum. To measure the resistance to misconduct described in the scenarios, we chose three different approaches. We asked officers how *serious* they and other officers in their agency would evaluate the offense, what *discipline* they thought it should and would receive, and their and other officers in their agency *willingness to report* that behavior (see Exhibit 1.2). Each of these three measures attempts to estimate integrity in a different way.

*Seriousness.* The degree of seriousness officers attribute to various actions directly probes the strength of officers' normative inclinations to resist temptations to abuse their office. However, because it is the most abstract of the three approaches to measuring integrity, it is both the most difficult to interpret and the most subject to misunderstanding and manipulation. What, after all, are the differences among the claims that a behavior is somewhat serious, moderately serious, serious, or very serious misconduct? Why should officers not advertise and perhaps exaggerate their integrity by claiming that they think all violations of official policy to be very serious?

The only restraint on the estimation of how serious the officers evaluate misconduct to be is the internal pressure officers may feel for relative consistency in their answers. An officer who evaluates officer theft from a crime scene as very serious misconduct may feel obliged to indicate that accepting a free cup of coffee is less serious. In order to maximize this restraining effect, we provided officers with a fairly wide range of offenses to evaluate and asked them to evaluate them on the identical seriousness scale, ranging from a score of 1, indicating "not at all serious," to 5, indicating "very serious."

We also restrained officers' estimates of seriousness by asking them to estimate how serious most officers in their agency would regard this behavior to be. This estimate imposed a restraining effect in two ways. Unlike the estimate of how serious the officer being asked considers the behavior to be, the question about how serious most officers would regard the

behavior to be is a question of the officer's knowledge. Its accuracy is empirically verifiable by the very survey the respondent is taking. Also, because the question about the beliefs of most officers implicitly invites respondents to compare their evaluations with what they claim other officers' evaluations would be, it obliges respondents to imagine a reason for that difference. While most officers can imagine that they are morally superior to some officers or that some officers are their moral inferiors, to claim that they are substantially morally superior to most officers is a claim that most officers are not willing to make.

*Discipline.* The questions about what discipline each offense should and would receive also inquire about the implications of officers' normative inclination to resist temptation to abuse their office. The questions probe officer perceptions of the punishment that yielding to those temptations should and would receive. Dividing the question into parts by asking about what discipline should and what discipline would follow the misbehavior described in the scenarios divides the inquiry, like the inquiry about seriousness, into one question that is a matter of opinion and a second that is a matter of fact. However, unlike the questions about seriousness, the answers to both of these questions are limited to the disciplinary options available in the agency under study.

This proved to be a very difficult problem, given the differences in disciplinary systems to which officers were exposed. We elected to use a six-level disciplinary scale: 1. none; 2. verbal reprimand; 3. written reprimand; 4. period of suspension without pay; 5. demotion in rank; 6. dismissal. While we could have used a simpler scale (e.g., 1. no discipline; 2. some discipline; 3. dismissal) or a scale that did not specify agency-provided options, we thought that providing some detail on options was desirable. Although the six-level scale offered an adequate array of disciplinary options for most police agencies, it was defective in

1. How serious do YOU consider this behavior to be?

   Not at all serious                                                  Very serious

        1               2              3              4              5

2. How serious do MOST POLICE OFFICERS IN YOUR AGENCY consider
   this behavior to be?

   Not at all serious                                                  Very serious

        1               2              3              4              5

3. Would this behavior be regarded as a violation of official policy in your agency?

   Definitely not                                                   Definitely yes

        1               2              3              4              5

4. If an officer in your agency engaged in this behavior and was discovered doing so, what if any discipline do YOU think SHOULD follow?

   | | |
   |---|---|
   | 1. NONE | 4. PERIOD OF SUSPENSION |
   | 2. VERBAL REPRIMAND | 5. DEMOTION IN RANK |
   | 3. WRITTEN REPRIMAND | 6. DISMISSAL |

5. If an officer in your agency engaged in this behavior and was discovered doing so, what if any discipline do YOU think WOULD follow?

   | | |
   |---|---|
   | 1. NONE | 4. PERIOD OF SUSPENSION |
   | 2. VERBAL REPRIMAND | 5. DEMOTION IN RANK |
   | 3. WRITTEN REPRIMAND | 6. DISMISSAL |

6. Do you think YOU would report a fellow police officer who engaged in
   this behavior?

   Definitely not                                                   Definitely yes

        1               2              3              4              5

7. Do you think MOST POLICE OFFICERS IN YOUR AGENCY would report a fellow police officer who engaged in this behavior?

   Definitely not                                                   Definitely yes

        1               2              3              4              5

**Exhibit 1.2**     Case Scenario Assessment Options

numerous ways. First, the six options omitted some penalties (e.g., fines or delays in eligibility for promotion) that were regularly used in some agencies. Second, they also omitted some penalties (e.g., retraining, counseling, reassignment, or transfer) because they were not officially discipline or punishment. Third, one or more of the disciplinary options offered on our scale were not available in some countries. Fourth, our scale included one option, "demotion in rank," that was only applicable to officers who had achieved an advanced rank. And, finally, unlike the scales for measuring respondents' beliefs about the seriousness of the misconduct and their willingness to report it, our six-level disciplinary scale was not an interval scale and would not support basic mathematical calculations, such as means, sums, and differences, without compromising assumptions on which those calculations rest.

In some cases, disciplinary systems were so different that our six-level scale had to be replaced with an alternative scale. In the Croatian survey, for instance, we were compelled to offer respondents five rather than six options: 1. none; 2. public reprimand; 3. fine; 4. suspension without pay; 5. dismissal. One of these options, "public reprimand, " was unique to the Croatian system; another, "fine," was rarely used elsewhere; and two common disciplinary options, "verbal reprimand" and "demotion," were eliminated from the Croatian survey. Likewise, in Pakistan, it was necessary to use a six-level discipline scale that included the unique disciplinary practices of "stoppage of yearly increments" and "reduction in pay." Such differences must be kept in mind when we compare the discipline scores on various countries.

*Willingness to Report.* Questions about officers' willingness to report the misconduct of other officers, like questions about discipline, probe the implications of the normative inclination to resist temptations to abuse the rights and privileges of one's office. But whereas questions about discipline request information only about what others should or would do, the question about officers' willingness to report others asks officers directly about what they themselves would do. While other questions ask officers to predict their own opinions, the questions about reporting ask officers to predict their own behavior.

It should be appreciated, however, that this inquiry limits their choice of action to a single type of response—reporting. Other responses—shunning, avoiding, warning, counseling, threatening, embarrassing, or shaming—may also work to discourage or deter the behavior. Officers may, in fact, elect one or more of these informal means of handling the situation. However, we specifically ask about willingness to report because it involves an organizational response rather than a merely interpersonal response to the situation.

*The Error Properties of Officers' Estimates of Seriousness, Discipline, and Willingness to Report.* The six different questions about seriousness, discipline, and willingness to report are measures of the same phenomenon, integrity, but each of the six answers has different error properties. Officers who wish to "look good" to the public, to researchers, or merely to themselves may tend to exaggerate how "serious" they evaluate scenarios to be, although they may be restrained in their evaluations by their estimates of how serious they claim others will rank them. They may well underestimate the discipline that they say scenarios should receive because they want to minimize the severity of the punishments to which they are exposed, but this tendency to underestimate may also be tempered by officers' estimate of what they think would actually happen. Officers may overrate or underrate their willingness to report certain types of misconduct—an officer's ego may be gratified in some environments by standing up against misconduct and in other environments by advertising that he or she is not a "snitch." It is a distinct possibility that in agencies with weak codes of silence, the self-image of officers and the image of the agency will encourage officers to exaggerate their willingness to report. In agencies with very strong codes of silence, the self-image of officers and the image of the agency may advise officers to minimize their willingness to report. Employing these multiple measurements of the same phenomenon, each of which has different and countervailing error properties, is a long-standing strategy in the measurement of complex or subtle social phenomena.

## THE CONTOURS
## OF POLICE INTEGRITY

What can be learned about integrity, defined and measured in this way, from the contours it reveals in 14 different countries? Table 1.1 summarizes the responses from the sample in each counry with respect to the level of seriousness officers assign to certain offenses. The first point that this table illustrates is that despite substantial differences in absolute scores, the rank order in which police officers from most countries evaluated the seriousness of the misconduct in the scenarios is remarkably similar. This similarity in rank order is also reflected in Table 1.2 and in Table 1.3, which report similar summary scores for officers' views on discipline for and willingness to report the misconduct of other officers, respectively. However, there are some significant departures from this relatively uniform rank order that bear mention. The first of these departures is Case 8, the cover-up of a police DUI (driving under the influence) and minor accident. This offense is regarded as among the most serious of offenses in three countries and as among the least serious of offenses in four countries. This appears to reflect the general social seriousness with which driving under the influence of alcohol is regarded in different countries, an interpretation that is confirmed by difference in severity with which this offense would be punished in different countries. A similar difference in general cultural opinion also appears to be reflected in Case 10, which involves the use of excessive force on a car thief. In Hungary, it is regarded as the third most serious offense, worse than stealing from a crime scene or accepting a bribe; whereas in Pakistan, it is ranked as the tenth most serious offense and considered less serious than accepting a free cup of coffee. These differences are reflected in the punishment the officers accused of these offenses would receive in different countries. In Hungary, officers estimate that the use of excessive force, if discovered, would get one fired. In Pakistan, it would probably rate a verbal warning.

Although the overall similarity in the rank ordering of scenarios holds true across all three measures of integrity—seriousness, discipline, and willingness to report—it is the least stable in the data on officers' willingness to report other officers' misconduct. Here the problem appears to be that in some countries the code of silence is strong enough to confound the data on officers' willingness to report. In Croatia, Hungary, Pakistan, Poland, and South Africa the code of silence is so strong that in those countries officers are actually estimating just how *unwilling* most officers are to report the misconduct described in the scenarios.

There is much to be learned from the contours of the absolute scores reported in the summary tables. In each table, we have shaded scores of 4 or higher.[6] These scores mean an average expected discipline of a period of suspension without pay, a fine, or greater; a high level of seriousness; and a strong probability of being reported. We can see from the differences in the shaded areas on the three tables that officers in every country are inclined to estimate the absolute seriousness of offenses higher than they estimate discipline or willingness to report. This may be because officers' estimates of the seriousness of the misconduct are without behavioral consequences, and officers in all countries may feel free to exaggerate their estimates of the seriousness of the misconduct in the scenarios.

It appears that in each country the seriousness of officers' misconduct is, in large part, determined by the absolute level of discipline the organization is expected to visit on an offending officer. In almost every case, when the police organization is expected to punish a offense very severely, officers regard that offense as serious. Conversely, when organizations do not punish misbehavior severely, as is the case in Hungary, Pakistan, and South Africa, officers seem to have little ability to distinguish among the levels of seriousness with regard to misconduct.

Perhaps the most dramatic finding that emerges from examining the contours of

**Table 1.1**   Mean Scores and Rank Order of Police Officers' Views About Most Officers' Perceptions of the Seriousness of Misconduct, by Country

Each cell shows the mean score above the rank order (mean / rank).

| Case Number With Description | Austria 1,853 | Canada 455 | Croatia 1,649 | Finland 378 | Hungary 610 | Japan 182 | The Netherlands 795 | Pakistan 499 | Poland 1,477 | Slovenia 767 | South Africa 107 | Sweden 1,590 | U.K. 275 | U.S.A. 3,235 |
|---|---|---|---|---|---|---|---|---|---|---|---|---|---|---|
| Case 1 - Off-Duty Security System Business | 2.18 / 1 | 2.15 / 1 | 2.51 / 2 | 2.41 / 1 | 1.67 / 1 | n/a | 2.45 / 1 | 3.70 / 1 | 2.27 / 1 | 2.71 / 4 | 2.31 / 3 | 2.45 / 1 | 2.15 / 1 | 1.48 / 1 |
| Case 2 - Free Meals and Discounts on Beat | 3.35 / 3 | 2.80 / 2 | 2.79 / 4 | 2.90 / 2 | 1.95 / 2 | n/a | 3.87 / 4 | 4.19 / 3 | 3.27 / 5 | 2.52 / 3 | 2.02 / 1 | 3.74 / 2 | 2.95 / 3 | 2.31 / 2 |
| Case 3 - Bribe From Speeding Motorist | 4.93 / 10 | 4.80 / 10 | 3.91 / 9 | 4.96 / 11 | 2.53 / 4 | 4.93 / 10 | 4.93 / 10 | 4.64 / 11 | 4.38 / 9 | 4.57 / 10 | 4.02 / 11 | 4.92 / 10 | 4.93 / 9 | 4.81 / 10 |
| Case 4 - Holiday Gifts From Merchants | 3.26 / 2 | 2.86 / 3 | 2.09 / 1 | 3.72 / 3 | 2.45 / 3 | 3.42 / 4 | 3.86 / 3 | 4.26 / 4 | 2.91 / 3 | 1.94 / 1 | 2.06 / 2 | 3.83 / 3 | 2.39 / 2 | 2.64 / 3 |
| Case 5 - Crime Scene Theft of Watch | 4.93 / 11 | 4.89 / 11 | 4.38 / 11 | 4.96 / 10 | 2.65 / 5 | n/a | 4.98 / 11 | 4.58 / 10 | 4.52 / 11 | 4.80 / 11 | 3.95 / 10 | 4.97 / 11 | 4.99 / 11 | 4.88 / 11 |
| Case 6 - 5% Kickback From Auto Repair Shop | 4.27 / 7 | 4.32 / 8 | 3.50 / 7 | 4.44 / 6 | 3.21 / 6 | 4.79 / 9 | 4.16 / 5 | 4.33 / 5 | 3.70 / 6 | 4.10 / 8 | 3.05 / 4 | 4.56 / 6 | 4.42 / 8 | 4.26 / 7 |
| Case 7 - Supervisor Grants Holiday in Exchange for Car Tune-Up | 4.32 / 8 | 3.92 / 5 | 3.76 / 8 | 4.44 / 5 | 3.32 / 7 | 4.34 / 6 | 4.56 / 8 | 4.38 / 7 | 3.87 / 7 | 4.07 / 7 | 3.59 / 8 | 4.71 / 8 | 3.80 / 4 | 3.96 / 6 |
| Case 8 - Cover-Up of Police DUI Accident | 4.01 / 5 | 3.55 / 4 | 2.65 / 3 | 4.61 / 8 | 3.52 / 8 | 4.68 / 8 | 3.59 / 2 | 4.35 / 6 | 2.81 / 2 | 2.27 / 2 | 3.18 / 7 | 4.62 / 6 | 4.38 / 7 | 2.86 / 4 |
| Case 9 - Free Drinks to Ignore Late Bar Closing | 3.70 / 4 | 4.28 / 7 | 3.38 / 6 | 4.54 / 7 | 3.98 / 10 | 4.64 / 7 | 4.37 / 7 | 4.44 / 8 | 4.42 / 10 | 3.52 / 6 | 3.80 / 9 | 4.55 / 5 | 4.31 / 6 | 4.28 / 8 |
| Case 10 - Excessive Force on Car Thief | 4.25 / 6 | 4.18 / 6 | 2.82 / 5 | 4.32 / 4 | 3.97 / 9 | 4.26 / 5 | 4.21 / 6 | 3.89 / 2 | 3.21 / 4 | 2.72 / 5 | 3.16 / 6 | 3.97 / 4 | 4.23 / 5 | 3.70 / 5 |
| Case 11 - Theft From Found Wallet | 4.87 / 9 | 4.66 / 9 | 4.16 / 10 | 4.89 / 9 | 4.26 / 11 | 4.97 / 11 | 4.79 / 9 | 4.48 / 9 | 4.15 / 8 | 4.56 / 9 | 3.08 / 5 | 4.91 / 9 | 4.96 / 10 | 4.69 / 9 |

Note: Seriousness scale:   Not at all serious 1  2  3  4  5  Very serious

14

**Table 1.2** Mean Scores and Rank Order of Police Officers' Views About the Discipline the Misconduct Would Receive, by Country

*Country/Sample Size*

| Case Number With Description | Austria* 1,853 | Canada* 455 | Croatia** 1,649 | Finland*** 378 | Hungary**** 610 | Japan***** 182 | The Netherlands* 795 | Pakistan****** 499 | Poland* 1,477 | Slovenia* 767 | South Africa* 107 | Sweden* 1,590 | U.K.******* 275 | U.S.A.* 3,235 |
|---|---|---|---|---|---|---|---|---|---|---|---|---|---|---|
| Case 1 - Off-Duty Security System Business | 1.78 / 1 | 2.56 / 1 | 2.34 / 2 | 1.60 / 1 | 1.96 / 2 | n/a | 2.04 / 1 | 2.60 / 1 | 3.46 / 4 | 3.55 / 7 | 2.27 / 2 | 2.53 / 1 | 2.72 / 2 | 1.51 / 1 |
| Case 2 - Free Meals and Discounts on Beat | 2.51 / 2 | 2.71 / 2 | 2.43 / 5 | 1.67 / 2 | 1.94 / 1 | n/a | 3.12 / 2 | 2.80 / 3 | 3.48 / 5 | 2.56 / 3 | 2.17 / 1 | 3.49 / 2 | 3.00 / 3 | 2.37 / 2 |
| Case 3 - Bribe From Speeding Motorist | 4.42 / 10 | 4.53 / 9 | 3.74 / 9 | 3.52 / 10 | 3.32 / 6 | 5.82 / 10 | 5.02 / 10 | 3.28 / 9 | 5.26 / 10 | 5.12 / 10 | 3.93 / 10 | 5.24 / 9 | 5.52 / 9 | 4.86 / 9 |
| Case 4 - Holiday Gifts From Merchants | 2.52 / 3 | 2.72 / 3 | 1.78 / 1 | 2.20 / 3 | 2.98 / 5 | 2.75 / 4 | 3.25 / 5 | 2.91 / 4 | 3.27 / 3 | 1.87 / 1 | 2.29 / 3 | 3.76 / 3 | 2.64 / 1 | 2.82 / 3 |
| Case 5 - Crime Scene Theft of Watch | 4.87 / 11 | 5.37 / 11 | 4.29 / 11 | 3.65 / 11 | 2.87 / 4 | n/a | 5.80 / 11 | 3.60 / 11 | 5.31 / 11 | 5.53 / 11 | 4.33 / 11 | 5.72 / 11 | 5.91 / 11 | 5.57 / 11 |
| Case 6 - 5% Kickback From Auto Repair Shop | 3.64 / 8 | 4.40 / 8 | 3.35 / 8 | 2.91 / 7 | 3.78 / 8 | 4.81 / n/a | 3.90 / 8 | 3.01 / 6 | 4.04 / 9 | 4.60 / 8 | 3.10 / 6 | 4.80 / 8 | 4.96 / 6 | 4.46 / 8 |
| Case 7 - Supervisor Grants Holiday in Exchange for Car Tune-Up | 3.08 / 5 | 3.32 / 4 | 2.51 / 6 | 2.26 / 4 | 2.38 / 3 | 3.05 / n/a | 3.29 / 6 | 2.95 / 5 | 2.20 / 1 | 2.49 / 2 | 3.30 / 7 | 4.22 / 4 | 3.54 / 4 | 3.43 / 5 |
| Case 8 - Cover-Up of Police DUI Accident | 3.16 / 6 | 4.23 / 7 | 2.42 / 4 | 3.24 / n/a | 3.89 / 8 | 4.74 / n/a | 3.21 / 4 | 3.18 / 8 | 3.87 / 6 | 2.76 / 4 | 3.07 / 4 | 4.89 / 7 | 5.24 / 8 | 3.21 / 4 |
| Case 9 - Free Drinks to Ignore Late Bar Closing | 2.64 / 4 | 3.83 / 5 | 2.67 / 7 | 2.67 / 6 | 3.38 / 7 | 4.21 / n/a | 3.19 / 3 | 3.06 / 7 | 3.92 / 7 | 3.01 / 5 | 3.60 / 9 | 4.37 / 5 | 4.40 / 5 | 4.08 / 7 |
| Case 10 - Excessive Force on Car Thief | 3.46 / 7 | 4.20 / 6 | 2.40 / 3 | 2.58 / 5 | 5.54 / 10 | 4.01 / n/a | 3.38 / 7 | 2.66 / 2 | 3.18 / 2 | 3.13 / 6 | 3.09 / 5 | 4.56 / 6 | 5.19 / 7 | 4.00 / 6 |
| Case 11 - Theft From Found Wallet | 4.31 / 9 | 4.87 / 10 | 3.87 / 10 | 3.43 / 9 | 5.74 / 11 | 5.82 / 11 | 4.96 / 9 | 3.50 / 10 | 4.00 / 8 | 4.98 / 9 | 3.43 / 8 | 5.40 / 10 | 5.81 / 10 | 5.03 / 10 |

Notes: *Discipline would receive: (1) None; (2) Verbal reprimand; (3) Written reprimand; (4) Suspension without pay; (5) Demotion; (6) Dismissal
**Discipline would receive: (1) None; (2) Public reprimand; (3) Fine; (4) Suspension without pay; (5) Dismissal
***Discipline would receive: (1) None; (2) Verbal reprimand; (3) Written reprimand; (4) Dismissal
****Discipline would receive: (1) None; (2) Lenient written reprimand; (3) Serious written reprimand; (4) Reduction in salary; (5) Demotion in rank; (6) Dismissal
*****Discipline would receive: (1) None; (2) Verbal reprimand; (3) Written reprimand; (4) Reduction in pay; (5) Suspension without pay; (6) Dismissal
******Discipline would receive: (1) None; (2) Censure; (3) Stoppage of yearly increments; (4) Reduction in pay; (5) Demotion in rank; (6) Dismissal
*******Discipline would receive: (1) None; (2) Verbal warning; (3) Written warning; (4) Fine; (5) Demotion in rank; (6) Dismissal

**Table 1.3  Mean Scores and Rank Order of Police Officers' Views About Most Officers' Willingness to Report Misconduct, by Country**

Country/Sample Size

| Case Number With Description | Austria 1,853 | Canada 455 | Croatia 1,649 | Finland 378 | Hungary 610 | Japan 182 | The Netherlands 795 | Pakistan 499 | Poland 1,477 | Slovenia 767 | South Africa 107 | Sweden 1,590 | U.K. 275 | U.S.A. 3,235 |
|---|---|---|---|---|---|---|---|---|---|---|---|---|---|---|
| Case 1 - Off-Duty Security System Business | 2.00 / 1 | 2.03 / 2 | 2.31 / 4 | 2.59 / 1 | 1.83 / 3 | n/a | 2.12 / 1 | 2.78 / 11 | 2.29 / 2 | 2.53 / 5 | 1.97 / 2 | 1.91 / 1 | 2.16 / 1 | 1.46 / 1 |
| Case 2 - Free Meals and Discounts on Beat | 2.67 / 2 | 2.03 / 2 | 2.38 / 5 | 2.65 / 2 | 1.81 / 1 | n/a | 3.03 / 3 | 2.41 / 9 | 2.47 / 6 | 2.27 / 4 | 1.95 / 1 | 2.77 / 2 | 2.43 / 3 | 1.82 / 2 |
| Case 3 - Bribe From Speeding Motorist | 4.39 / 10 | 3.98 / 9 | 3.07 / 9 | 4.53 / 10 | 2.24 / 5 | 4.15 / 10 | 4.34 / 10 | 2.13 / 4 | 2.95 / 10 | 3.81 / 9 | 2.95 / 8 | 4.29 / 9 | 4.54 / 9 | 3.92 / 9 |
| Case 4 - Holiday Gifts From Merchants | 2.69 / 3 | 2.44 / 3 | 1.85 / 1 | 3.34 / 4 | 1.83 / 2 | 2.93 / 3 | 3.20 / 4 | 2.35 / 8 | 2.40 / 4 | 1.80 / 1 | 2.09 / 3 | 3.01 / 3 | 2.18 / 2 | 2.28 / 3 |
| Case 5 - Crime Scene Theft of Watch | 4.65 / 11 | 4.38 / 11 | 3.72 / 11 | 4.62 / 11 | 2.21 / 4 | n/a | 4.69 / 11 | 1.98 / 1 | 3.22 / 11 | 4.32 / 11 | 3.30 / 11 | 4.61 / 11 | 4.85 / 11 | 4.34 / 11 |
| Case 6 - 5% Kickback From Auto Repair Shop | 3.75 / 8 | 3.91 / 8 | 3.05 / 8 | 4.10 / 8 | 2.77 / 8 | 4.03 / 9 | 3.55 / 7 | 2.13 / 5 | 2.80 / 8 | 3.65 / 8 | 2.50 / 6 | 3.93 / 8 | 4.12 / 8 | 3.71 / 8 |
| Case 7 - Supervisor Grants Holiday in Exchange for Tune-Up | 3.45 / 7 | 3.50 / 6 | 2.73 / 7 | 3.75 / 5 | 2.35 / 6 | 3.50 / 4 | 3.80 / 8 | 2.31 / 7 | 2.42 / 5 | 3.09 / 7 | 3.18 / 10 | 3.79 / 6 | 3.41 / 4 | 3.29 / 6 |
| Case 8 - Cover-Up of Police DUI Accident | 3.19 / 5 | 2.91 / 4 | 2.20 / 3 | 4.09 / 7 | 2.65 / 7 | 3.96 / 8 | 2.88 / 2 | 2.15 / 6 | 2.31 / 3 | 1.97 / 2 | 2.87 / 7 | 3.90 / 7 | 3.85 / 7 | 2.28 / 4 |
| Case 9 - Free Drinks to Ignore Late Bar Closing | 2.76 / 4 | 3.62 / 7 | 2.58 / 6 | 3.81 / 6 | 2.82 / 9 | 3.83 / 7 | 3.42 / 6 | 2.10 / 3 | 2.95 / 9 | 2.79 / 6 | 3.17 / 9 | 3.67 / 5 | 3.68 / 6 | 3.47 / 7 |
| Case 10 - Excessive Force on Car Thief | 3.31 / 6 | 3.45 / 5 | 2.08 / 2 | 3.31 / 3 | 3.10 / 10 | 3.51 / 5 | 3.29 / 5 | 2.45 / 10 | 2.25 / 1 | 2.13 / 3 | 2.45 / 5 | 3.18 / 4 | 3.67 / 5 | 3.07 / 5 |
| Case 11 - Theft From Found Wallet | 4.37 / 9 | 4.00 / 10 | 3.41 / 10 | 4.35 / 9 | 3.47 / 11 | 4.59 / 11 | 4.19 / 9 | 2.06 / 2 | 2.80 / 7 | 3.94 / 10 | 2.43 / 4 | 4.46 / 10 | 4.69 / 10 | 3.96 / 10 |

Note: Most officers willing to report?

| Definitely not | | | | Definitely yes |
|---|---|---|---|---|
| 1 | 2 | 3 | 4 | 5 |

16

integrity concerns the worldwide prevalence of the code of silence. In 5 of the countries, not a single incident out of the 11 incidents described in the survey would be very likely to be reported. In 9 out of 14 countries, officers would not be certain to report a fellow officer who took a bribe from a speeding motorist. In fact, in every one of the countries surveyed, an officer could accept free drinks to overlook a bar that remained open past the official closing time or strike a prisoner in confinement without assuming that his or her police colleagues who witnessed the offense would be sure to report it. It appears that there are few places in the world in which a police officer will turn in a fellow police officer who accepts free meals and discounts, or holiday gifts.

Things could, of course, be different. In all countries where departments punish officers severely for their misconduct, officers regard that misconduct as serious and are inclined to report it. The relationship between officers' perceptions of the seriousness of misconduct, the expected level of discipline, and the willingness to report is not perfect, but there are very few cases that defy that relationship. On the other hand, there are no cases anywhere in which officers report behavior that the department does not punish severely. Clearly, it is up to police leaders to determine the quantity and quality of integrity in their departments.

## NOTES

1. This point was made forcefully by Herman Goldstein in his groundbreaking 1977 book, *Policing a Free Society* (p. 188).

2. Histories of police that document the abiding prevalence of corruption are too numerous to list here. The most thorough scholarly explorations of the temptations to corruption in contemporary policing include Manning and Redlinger (1993), Marx (1991), Punch (1986), Sherman (1978), and Rubinstein (1973).

3. The "for gain" dimension of corruption typically distinguishes it from other forms of police misconduct, such as brutality. There is, however, debate over whether the definition of police corruption should include various forms of the use of police authority for political, organizational, or strategic gain. See Goldstein (1975, 1977), Klockars (1983), Klockars and Mastrofski (1991), and Sherman (1978).

4. It is for this reason that much of what is known about corruption has been learned from high-profile investigations of police agencies with serious and systemic corruption problems; see, for example, the reports by The Pennsylvania Crime Commission (1974), The Knapp Commission (1972), and The City of New York Commission to Investigate Allegations of Police Corruption and the Anti-Corruption Procedures of the Police Department (1994).

5. The capacity to predict police integrity from psychological testing is extremely limited. See Taller and Hinz (1990), Delattre (1989), Malouff and Schutte (1980), Daley (1980), Morrison (1996), and Curran (1998).

6. In the cases of Croatia and Finland, we shaded scores of 3 or higher in Table 1.2, as those countries employed 4- or 5-point scales to record the data on officers' views of expected discipline rather than the 6-point scales used in other countries.

## REFERENCES

Barker, T., & Wells, R. O. (1982). Police administrators' attitudes toward definition and control of police deviance. *FBI Law Enforcement Bulletin, 51*(4), 8-16.

The City of New York Commission to Investigate Allegations of Police Corruption and the Anti-Corruption Procedures of the Police Department. (1994). *Commission Report.* New York: Author.

Crank, J. P., & Caldero, M. A. (2000). *The corruption of the noble cause.* Cincinnati, OH: Anderson.

Curran, S. F. (1998, October). Pre-employment psychological evaluation of law enforcement applicants. *The Police Chief,* pp. 88-94.

Daley, R. E. (1980). The relationship of personality variables to suitability for police work. *DAI, 44,* 1551-1569.

Delattre, E. J. (1989). *Character and cops: Ethics in policing.* Washington, DC: The American Enterprise Institute.

Delattre, E. J. (1996). *Character and cops: Ethics in policing* (3rd ed.). Washington, DC: The American Enterprise Institute.

Goldstein, H. (1975). *Police corruption: Perspective on its nature and control.* Washington, DC: The Police Foundation.

Goldstein, H. (1977). *Policing a free society.* Cambridge, MA: Ballinger.

Homans, G. C. (1950). *The human group.* New York: Harcourt Brace.

Klockars, C. B. (1983). *Thinking about police.* New York: McGraw-Hill.

Klockars, C. B. (1986). Street justice: Some micro-moral reservations. *Justice Quarterly, 3*(4), 513-517.

Klockars, C. B. (1991). The Dirty Harry problem. In C. B. Klockars & S. Mastrofski (Eds.), *Thinking about police* (2nd ed., pp. 413-423). New York: McGraw-Hill.

Klockars, C. B. (1996). A theory of excessive force and its control. In W. A. Geller & H. Toch, *Police violence: Understanding and controlling police abuse of force.* New Haven, CT: Yale University Press.

Klockars, C. B., Kutnjak Ivkovich, S., Haberfeld, M. R., & Uydess, A. (2002). *Enhancing police integrity: A final report to the national institute of justice.* Washington, DC: National Institute of Justice.

Klockars, C. B., & Mastrofski, S. (Eds.).(1991). *Thinking about police* (2nd ed.). New York: McGraw-Hill.

The Knapp Commission. (1972). *Report on police corruption.* New York: George Brazillier.

Malouff, J., & Schutte, N. S. (1980). Using biographical information to hire the best new police officers. *Journal of Police Science and Administration, 14,* 256-267.

Manning, P. K., & Redlinger, L. (1993). The invitational edges of police construction. In C. B. Klockars & S. Mastrofski (Eds.), *Thinking about police* (pp. 398-412). New York: McGraw-Hill.

Marx, G. (1991). Surveillance. Cambridge, MA: Harvard University Press.

McCormack, R. J. (1986). *Corruption in the subculture of policing: An empirical study of police-officer perceptions.* Unpublished doctoral dissertation, Fordham University, New York.

Morrison, R. D. (1996, April). Officer psychological profiling. *Law and Order,* pp. 93-94.

Muir, W. K. (1977). *Police: Streetcorner politicians.* Chicago: University of Chicago Press.

The Pennsylvania Crime Commission (1974). *Report on police corruption and the quality of law enforcement in Philadelphia.* Philadelphia: Author.

Punch, M. (1986). *Conduct unbecoming: The social construction of police deviance and control.* London: Tavistock.

Rubinstein, J. (1973). *City police.* New York: Ballinger.

Sherman, L. W. (1978). *Scandal and reform.* Berkeley: University of California Press.

Stoddard, E. (1979). Organizational norms and police discretion: An observational study of police work with traffic violators. *Criminology, 17,* 159-171.

Sykes, G. (1986). Street justice: A moral defense of order maintenance policing. *Justice Quarterly, 3*(4), 497-512.

Taller, J. E., & Hinz, L. D. (1990). *Performance prediction of public safety and law enforcement personnel.* Springfield, IL: Charles C Thomas.

# CHAPTER 2

# Ethics and the Police
## Studying Police Integrity in Austria

Maximilian Edelbacher

Sanja Kutnjak Ivković

## INTRODUCTION

Austria is a democratic republic and, since January of 1995, a member of the European Union. Covering an area of 84,000 square kilometers, Austria is a relatively small country that is situated in the heart of Europe (*Austria Facts and Figures*, 2000, pp. 6-8). Out of its 8 million inhabitants, 750,000 are foreign nationals (*Austria Facts and Figures*, 2000, p. 22). Austria's capital, Vienna, is situated in the Eastern part of the country and has a population of nearly 2 million, of which 350,000 are foreigners.

The Austrian Police are headed by the Federal Ministry of the Interior. They are divided into: (1) the federal police, which operate in the 14 largest cities; (2) the federal Gendarmerie, which operate in the rural areas; (3) the state police; and (4) the criminal police. The majority of police officers are employed by either the federal police (16,051) or the federal Gendarmerie (15,083) (Frič & Walek, 2001, p. 36).

Austria has a long and complex history that still affects the basic values and expectations of its citizens with regard to the state authority figures, including the police. In this chapter, we will explore these and other issues crucial for the understanding of police ethics and integrity from the Austrian perspective. We will begin by examining the question of defining ethics and corruption and follow with a detailed analysis of the key integrity-related factors. In the process, we will try to evaluate the effectiveness of the measures undertaken to deal with police corruption and to prevent and minimize its occurrence and promote integrity.

## ETHICS, CORRUPTION, AND THE POLICE

### A Definition of Ethics

To ensure a clear understanding of the basic terminology, we will briefly analyze the differences between morals and ethics, as these terms are often used interchangeably. As far as formal definitions are concerned, morals refers to what is judged as good conduct, whereas ethics refers to the study and analysis of what constitutes good or bad conduct (Sherman, 1985). The *Collins English Dictionary* (1979) defines *morals* as "principles of behavior in accordance with standards of right and wrong," whereas it defines *ethics* as "the philosophical study of the moral value of human conduct and of the rules and principles that ought to govern it."

In common usage, *morals* is used to refer to the sum of a person's actions in every sphere of life, whereas *ethics* is used to refer to certain specific types of behavior, usually related to a profession. Dictionary definitions provide support for this colloquial use of the terms: ethics is a social, religious, or civil code of behavior that is considered correct, especially that of a particular group, profession, or individual (*Collins English Dictionary,* 1979). A specific type of applied ethics is professional ethics. Just as other professions—for example, medicine and law—have their own sets of ethical standards or canons of ethics, the police can develop their own ethical code.

## A Definition of Corruption

It is impossible to assess the effectiveness of Austria's strategy to fight corruption in the police without identifying what police corruption is and what is considered police corruption in Austria. Accordingly, this section will examine the issue of defining police corruption and review several definitions.

Before we define *police corruption,* it is necessary for us to define *corruption.* General definitions of corruption seem to be difficult to produce. This may stem from conceptual reasons. The classic definition of corruption by Elliston and Feldberg (1985, p. 251) holds that a public official is corrupt

if that official accepts money or something else of value for doing something he or she is under a duty to do anyway, under a duty not to do, or for exercising legitimate discretion for improper reasons. However, many have decided that corruption defies generalization and instead tried to focus the discussion on the forms of corruption,[1] thereby trying to establish appropriate systems of classification.

In the absence of a consensus on the definition of corruption, others have opted for an empirical approach, which seeks to clarify the essence of corruption by looking at reality. The objective of this approach is to move toward a wider consensus as to which acts are harmful to the society and should, therefore, be prevented and punished. Thus, they seek to define corruption by reference to the law (Palmiotto & Alter, 2001, p. 3). They argue that only the legal realm can offer a solution, since a legal definition is more precise than a broad definition of corruption like "an abuse of power for private gain," which is difficult to translate into legal norms.

There are some problems inherent in this approach. Because legal traditions change over time and are intertwined with social, political, and cultural contexts, they tend to differ across countries; the decision on what to include in the definition of police corruption will vary from country to country and sometimes within the same country. Since countries do not necessarily agree on what forms of abuse of power constitute corruption and should be illegal, the international community has engaged in the elaboration of international legal instruments within different organizations, such as the Organisation for Economic Cooperation and Development (OECD), European Union (15 member countries), and the Council of Europe (42 member countries). The international community has recognized the need to prevent and combat corruption, as it is a phenomenon that transcends national boundaries and has harmful effects on societies. In addition to the detrimental impact on economic growth, corruption jeopardizes free trade, distorts competitiveness, and undermines the stability on which the free market system is based. Corruption further jeopardizes the credibility of governments and their institutions, and provides a fertile ground for the flourishing of organized crime.

An analysis of these international legal instruments shows, however, that they are also limited in geographical coverage, scope, and substance. With the exception of the Organisation for Economic Cooperation and Development, all other intergovernmental organizations under whose auspices the existing international legal instruments have been developed are regional. However, while the OECD Convention is the only instrument that has comprehensive geographical coverage, the scope of the instrument remains rather limited because it addresses only the supply side of the bribery of foreign public officials. A comprehensive international binding legal instrument is still lacking.

One of the most prominent definitions of police corruption is that proposed by Goldstein (1977, p. 188). Goldstein defines *police corruption* as the misuse of authority by a police officer in a manner designed to produce personal gain for the officer or for others. According to the definition by Palmiotto (2001, p. 37), and similar to the classic definition of corruption by Elliston and Feldberg (1985), police officers who engage in corrupt acts gain economically by providing services they should already be performing or by failing to perform services that are required by their position. Thus, a comprehensive definition of police corruption contains two essential elements: first, police officers gain direct or indirect advantages in exchange for official action or for-bearance; and, second, they misuse their authority by providing services or by failing

to perform services required by their position in exchange for the transfer of this benefit.

## DATA AND METHODS

A number of data sources are used in this chapter; they range from official statistics to an empirical study that we conducted. The Major Crime Bureau of the Federal Police provided official statistics on the complaints against the Federal Police of Austria. The Bureau was in charge of the investigations of these cases and responsible for the compilation of the statistics until the end of November of 2001. In December of 2001, a new unit, the Office for Special Investigations (*Büro für besondere Ermittlungen*), assumed this responsibility. The data about the court sentences, also based on the information provided by the Major Crime Bureau, refer to the cases initiated by complaints.

The questionnaire measuring police integrity, developed by Klockars and Kutnjak Ivkovich (1996), was distributed to the Austrian police in 1998. Vienna, a city of nearly 2 million people and the capital of the country, has a police force of 5,800 uniformed police officers and 1,100 criminal investigators. With the approval of the Police President of Vienna, questionnaires were distributed in the Major Crime Bureau, the First District, and the Thirteenth District. The Major Crime Bureau, which consists of 200 criminal investigators and 45 officers in the administration, deals with the major crime cases going on in Vienna (murder cases, robberies, fraud cases, burglaries, organized crime, prostitution, drug dealing). Out of the 50 distributed questionnaires, 15 questionnaires came back.

The First District, covering the city center, was included because of its central location, and the Thirteenth District was included because of its very active leadership. The police leadership of the First District refused to distribute the questionnaires. The then–Deputy Chief of the uniformed police wrote a letter to the Police President and explained that in his understanding the "questionnaire is dangerous" (Letter of the Deputy Chief, 1998). Consequently, although the Police President initially approved the distribution of the questionnaires, he changed his mind after receiving this letter.

Although no questionnaires were received from the First District, 50 questionnaires were sent to the Thirteenth District, which employs 160 uniformed police officers and 17 criminal investigators. Despite the Police President's intentions to stop the study completely, the respondents returned 79 questionnaires!

The second attempt to survey the Austrian police was conducted in 1998 and 1999. It was supported by the Minister of the Interior, Karl Schlögl, and the General Director of Security, Michael Sika, who advised the head of the Police Academy to allow the distribution of the questionnaires. Participants of an 11-week management seminar at the Police Academy distributed questionnaires in their respective police stations. This effort resulted in a substantial sample: A total of 1,853 sworn members of the police and Gendarmerie filled out the questionnaires.

Most of the respondents are experienced police officers; only 23% had been police officers for less than 10 years. The majority (56%) are at the rank of police officer and only 6% are women. In terms of their assignments, the respondents mostly work in patrol (51%) or in investigation (20.7%).

## FACTORS RELATED TO POLICE CORRUPTION AND ANTICORRUPTION MEASURES

There are a variety of opinions among experts on what constitute effective anticorruption strategies. Nevertheless, several common principles are shared by most. One such principle is the need to understand the complexity of the phenomenon and the strengths, weaknesses, and limitations of each of the components, which in turn necessitates the implementation of all of the various components concurrently. In addition, in light of the secretive nature of corruption and the related difficulty in obtaining evidence in reactive cases, there is general agreement about the importance of intelligence as a vital means to counter corruption. Although experts view both preventive measures and reactive measures as necessary components of the strategy, they disagree on the specific measures to be used. We will now discuss the anticorruption measures implemented by Austria and the factors related to police corruption.

### Laws and Official Rules

Law enforcement officers are educated to administrate the law with the purpose of fulfilling the authority of state power. Law enforcement agencies are bound to the principle of legality and the rule of law. The basis for police actions is the Security Police Law (1993).

As corruption takes different forms, it is important for the Austrian legislature to identify what constitutes a corrupt action and what the sanctions are. The development of a legal definition of *corruption* is the key for any effective anticorruption strategy. Police corruption can embrace a range of activities, including free or discounted meals, kickbacks, shakedowns, bribes, and protection of illegal activities.

The Austrian criminal law does not define the term *corruption*. In the absence of a definition, Austria has opted for a piecemeal approach in devising legal norms to combat corruption. Thus, there is often adoption of separate provisions, each dealing with a specific crime. The provisions address particular forms of corruption, such as bribery and extortion, sanctioned by criminal law. The Austrian Penal Code defines corruption, misuse of power, and acceptance of a bribe in Articles 302-310 (Foregger & Bachner Foregger, 2000, pp. 145-147). In essence, these Articles cover all problem areas except transnational cases.

In the empirical part of the study, we wanted to examine the extent of the respondents' knowledge or familiarity with the substantive rules of penal law and official disciplinary rules. Thus, we provided descriptions of 11 hypothetical cases. Ten of these cases describe violations of the Penal Code, while one case (Case 1 - Off-Duty Security System Business) describes behavior that is not a crime but merely a violation of disciplinary rules (see Table 2.1).

In 9 out of 11 cases, the majority of the respondents would "regard [this behavior] as a violation of official policy" in their agencies (see Table 2.1). However, the percentage of police officers who recognize these behaviors as violations of official rules differs greatly, from 15.1% for Case 1 (Off-Duty Security System Business) to 99.3% for Case 5 (Crime Scene Theft of Watch). Virtually everyone recognized rule violations in the two cases of theft (Case 5 - Crime Scene Theft of Watch; Case 11 - Theft From Found Wallet) and the case of a classic bribe (Case 3 - Bribe From Speeding Motorist), but a smaller percentage (but still above two thirds) declared the following cases as rule-violating behavior as well: the only case of excessive force (Case 10), the cover-up of police DUI accident case (Case 8), the kickback case (Case 6), the drinks-for-license-violation case (Case 9), and the only case involving supervisory misconduct (Case 7).

Approximately one half of the respondents did not identify the two cases with gifts and gratuities (Case 2 - Free Meals and Discounts on Beat; Case 4 - Holiday Gifts From Merchants) as violations of rules. Generally, the acceptance of a small gift, like the offer of a cup of coffee or of a pencil, would not be recognized as police corruption and would probably be tolerated by the police officers. Finally, the case that the majority of the respondents did not recognize as a violation of official rules describes off-duty employment (Case 1 - Off-Duty Security System Business), although, if such a case was reported and formal disciplinary proceedings initiated, the police officer involved would have to pay a fine and expect other disciplinary consequences as well.

A detailed analysis of the existing laws, both substantive and procedural, indicates that additional laws are needed to provide for more innovative evidence-gathering procedures (such as integrity testing, removal of the bank and professional secrecy statutes, strengthening of the money-laundering statutes, and the establishment of disclosure laws and whistleblower protection laws), since clear evidence of corruption can be hard to obtain and the traditional methods of evidence gathering often do not lead to satisfactory results. Currently, there are no disclosure laws and no laws providing for whistleblower protection, although the money-laundering provisions (which can contribute to the detection of corruption by providing the basis for financial investigations) are in place.

### Recruit Selection

There are established selection criteria for recruitment into the police or Gendarmerie. For example, a recruit for the Police Academy in Vienna has to have Austrian citizenship, no criminal record, and no administrative record (e.g., no DUI violations). Moreover, the recruit needs to pass the entrance test, be completely healthy, and satisfy the height and weight requirements. The goal is to strictly enforce these criteria. Because of the economic situation, it is not difficult to attract police recruits; more than

**Table 2.1**    Austrian Police Officers' Views About Whether the Misconduct is a Violation of Legal Rules

| Case Number and Description | Violation of Legal Rules | Percentage of Respondents Classifying Case as Violation |
| --- | --- | --- |
| Case 1 - Off-Duty Security System Business | Yes: Disciplinary Rules | 15.1% |
| Case 2 - Free Meals and Discounts on Beat | Yes: Penal Code | 52.1% |
| Case 3 - Bribe From Speeding Motorist | Yes: Penal Code | 99.1% |
| Case 4 - Holiday Gifts From Merchants | Yes: Penal Code | 47.1% |
| Case 5 - Crime Scene Theft of Watch | Yes: Penal Code | 99.3% |
| Case 6 - 5% Kickback From Auto Repair Shop | Yes: Penal Code | 80.3% |
| Case 7 - Supervisor Grants Holiday in Exchange for Car Tune-Up | Yes: Penal Code | 79.8% |
| Case 8 - Cover-Up of Police DUI Accident | Yes: Penal Code | 78.5% |
| Case 9 - Free Drinks to Ignore Late Bar Closing | Yes: Penal Code | 65.0% |
| Case 10 - Excessive Force on Car Thief | Yes: Penal Code | 83.5% |
| Case 11 - Theft From Found Wallet | Yes: Penal Code | 98.2% |

300 candidates are currently on the waiting list for admission to the police.

The process begins with the potential applicant filling out a questionnaire, submitting a curriculum vitae and a report about the nonexistence of both the criminal and administrative record, and then passing the written test and the medical examination. A background check is conducted, followed by the psychological test and an interview with the candidate. The project group within the Ministry examined this recruitment and selection system as a part of their overall corruption-related control efforts and proposed that candidates should be chosen for their invulnerability to corruption and that they should undergo integrity testing (*Internal Advice of the Ministry of the Interior*, 2001). One of the recommendations emphasized that the background investigation should be completed in all cases before the candidate is offered a position.

## Police Education and Training

Police education in Austria consists of several types of training, from the basic training offered to the incoming police officers to the more specialized types of training that requires a number of years of experience (e.g., training as a leading officer or as a criminal investigator). In addition, the Federal Police also recognize and reward advanced nonpolice education, such as legal education, which puts qualified people on a fast track to the highly ranked supervisory positions.

The basic education and training lasts 21 months and is offered in Vienna, Graz, Linz, Salzburg, and Innsbruck. Throughout their education and training, the students are required to serve 40 hours a week. The education and training is split into three parts.[2] The first part—theoretical education and training—takes 5 months. It is followed by

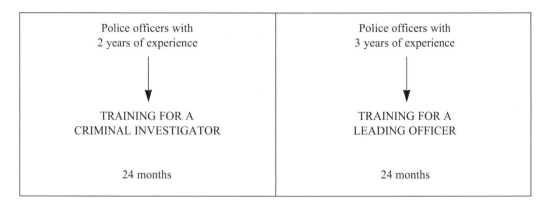

| Police officers with 2 years of experience | Police officers with 3 years of experience |
|---|---|
| ↓ | ↓ |
| TRAINING FOR A CRIMINAL INVESTIGATOR | TRAINING FOR A LEADING OFFICER |
| 24 months | 24 months |

**Figure 2.1**    Police Education and Training

the second part—2 months of practical training on the job. The third, main part of the training lasts 12 months. The education is comprised of a mixture of theory, law (e.g., constitutional law, administrative law, police security law), and other fields (e.g., criminalistics, conflict-management training). Finally, on favorable evaluation of their practical experiences, candidates take the final test. On passing the final test, rookies start to serve in one of the police districts. Thus, an 18-year-old woman or a 19-year-old man (after military service) can start the 21-month program and complete it as an inspector.

After a few years of experience, officers can choose a special unit or obtain further education and training. Three years of experience qualifies an officer to train to be a leading officer; 2 years of experience qualifies an officer to train to be a criminal investigator (see Figure 2.1).

A different path is available for individuals who are not older than 42 and have attended at least 12 years of school (including 4 years of primary education and 8 years of *Mittelschule*, or high school, and taken the *Matura*, or final test); they can attend the Police Academy for 2 years to become lieutenants.

A unique feature of the police system in Austria is the employment of legal experts. It is based on a historical tradition that can be traced back to the Austrian-Hungarian Monarchy. The police force in Austria employs about 200 legal experts. They start their service on completing a law degree at a university in Austria, practicing law at a court for a year, and completing education in a special practical and theoretical training on the job and in the Police Academy. Only legal experts can become top leaders in the police force. Contrary to the operating of the police, the Gendarmerie do not employ legal experts; the organization, based on the French model, is completely military, characterized by hierarchical decision making and military ranks.

### Leadership and Supervision

Since the days of the Austrian-Hungarian Monarchy, the principle of hierarchy in the organization of a bureaucratic system has been strictly followed and implemented. It is still strongly endorsed in the Second Republic (today's Austria). According to the old German and Austrian expectation of public servants' conduct—"to serve the Monarch requires a higher standard of conduct"—the leaders are always held to a higher standard of responsibility than are line officers in the bureaucracy; to be selected as a leader and educated for a leadership job by definition implies a higher standard of responsibility, which is, of course, accompanied by higher pay. Police utilize this general principle of higher standard of responsibility; police supervisors are thus expected to adhere to and are held to a different, higher standard of conduct than are line officers.

### Office of Internal Affairs

Since it is essential to develop a flow of information to overcome the inherent secrecy of corrupt offenses, efforts are made to encourage police personnel and citizens who know about instances of corruption to submit complaints to a credible and independent complaints office. Recognizing that intelligence is a central link not only in preventing corruption but also in reacting to the existing corrupt behavior, the Austrian police have established two complaints offices, the Office of Internal Affairs and the Office of Public Affairs. However, the Office of Internal Affairs and the Office of Public Affairs have multiple responsibilities and do not specialize in corruption.

The Office of Internal Affairs was established in November of 2001. It handles primarily high-level police corruption cases. Presently, the nature of its work is exclusively reactive. The processing of a complaint can be started based on an allegation from anyone, including a complainant who is anonymous. The accuracy of the allegation has to be investigated and the outcome of the investigation reported to the public prosecutor's office. The public prosecutor then makes a decision as to whether he or she will bring charges against the defendant and initiate court proceedings.

The Office of Public Affairs handles all other corruption-related cases; it reports its findings to the prosecutor's office or to the administrative authorities for further processing, if necessary. The prosecutor initiates the criminal proceedings, while the administrative authorities start the disciplinary process.

The investigations in these two offices are carried out with the purpose of gathering evidence and checking the accuracy of the information contained in the complaint. There are three possible outcomes of an investigation: the allegation can be determined to be unfounded (the incident of misconduct did not occur), not sustained (there is insufficient evidence to prove or disprove the allegation), or sustained (the allegation is supported by sufficient evidence). When the allegation is sustained, the administrative authorities open the disciplinary case. The punishment imposed depends on the seriousness of the corrupt act; in the most serious cases, the police officer can be terminated. In addition to termination, a prosecutor can bring criminal charges against the officer.

According to the official statistics for the Federal Police in Vienna (the Federal Police operate in 14 cities), in the 6-year period from 1996 to 2001, the overall number of complaints was stable at around 150 to 200 per year (see Table 2.2). When the number of corruption-related complaints is separated from the overall number of complaints, the numbers are substantially smaller: below 10 cases each year. The corruption-related cases constitute a small percentage of all the complaints (below 5%). Similarly, each year only very few police officers serving the Federal Police of Austria, Vienna are sentenced in the criminal court for corrupt behavior (see Table 2.3). In fact, police officers were sentenced in only five completed cases in the whole 6-year period.

The criminalization of corrupt practices is not intended merely as a punishment; it also serves a deterrent function, effectively issuing a warning to others not to become involved

**Table 2.2**     Complaints Against the Federal Police of Austria, Vienna

| Year | Number of Complaints | Number of Corruption-Related Complaints | Percentage of all Complaints |
|------|---------------------|------------------------------------------|------------------------------|
| 1996 | 211 | 2 | 0.95% |
| 1997 | 175 | 0 | 0.00% |
| 1998 | 155 | 3 | 1.94% |
| 1999 | 202 | 2 | 0.99% |
| 2000 | 190 | 8 | 4.21% |
| 2001 | 179 | 9 | 5.02% |

SOURCE: Annual Statistics of the Major Crime Bureau, Vienna.

**Table 2.3**     Completed Criminal Cases Against the Officers of the Federal Police of Austria, Vienna

| Year | Number of Completed Court Cases |
|------|--------------------------------|
| 1996 | 0 |
| 1997 | 0 |
| 1998 | 1 |
| 1999 | 0 |
| 2000 | 2 |
| 2001 | 2 (others not completed) |

SOURCE: Annual Statistics of the Major Crime Bureau, Vienna.

in corrupt practices. The penal action is intended to cause a change in the cost-benefit analysis of the public official (profit and opportunity are weighed against the risks of being detected and the likelihood and extent of any punishment). Indeed, when the risks are high, the punishment certain and severe, and the rewards low, the extent of police corruption should decrease. However, because of the limited resources for and difficulties in detecting corruption, no matter how draconian or rigorously enforced the penal measures, no society could realistically punish more than a small proportion of public officials who abuse their powers. Furthermore, clear evidence of corrupt practices can be extremely difficult to obtain, which also implies that the offenders frequently remain unpunished. Thus, if the level of police

integrity is to be improved, such improvement should be facilitated by administrative, regulatory, and reporting mechanisms.

## Police Subculture and the Code of Silence

Police subculture, in particular the "code of silence," is one of the most resistant forces to the adoption of and allegiance to a formal code of ethics. The code of silence, which develops as a consequence of a quasi-military character of the police organization, endorses standards of performance that can be in conflict with the official agency rules, code of ethics, and laws. Corrupt practices also might become viewed as acceptable (Austrian Police Academy, 1998/1999).

Police recruits are indoctrinated into this police subculture. They recognize that loyalty to their colleagues—other police officers—is important to ensure their personal safety and success on the job. Furthermore, recruits are dependent on the guidance of veteran officers and, since they want to be accepted by their colleagues, they accept the values of the police culture, including adherence to the code of silence. The code of silence, therefore, informally prohibits or discourages police officers from reporting the misconduct of their colleagues. However, what the code of silence covers and to whom it extends benefits tends to vary among police agencies and even within the same police agency.

In our empirical study, we wanted to examine the contours of police integrity among Austrian police officers and determine what behaviors are tolerated by the police culture. We used several measures of police integrity in our project: officers' evaluations of the seriousness of specific cases of police misconduct, opinions about appropriate and expected discipline, and expressed willingness to report the misconduct of their fellow officers (as described in the Data and Methods section above). We present the results of our survey in Table 2.4.

### Officers' Perceptions of the Seriousness of Cases of Misconduct

Police officers who participated in the survey perceived the described cases to range in terms of their seriousness from the least serious, Case 1 - Off-Duty Security System Business (mean value of 2.08) to the most serious, Case 5 - Crime Scene Theft of Watch (mean value of 4.96) (see Table 2.4). The case of off-duty outside employment, evaluated by the majority as the least serious, is the only case that describes rule-violating but not criminal behavior. In relative terms (i.e., compared to other cases in the questionnaire), the two cases involving the acceptance of gifts and gratuities (Case 2 - Free Meals and Discounts on Beat; Case 4 - Holiday Gifts From Merchants) were also evaluated as among the least serious examples of misconduct, although in absolute terms they are leaning toward the serious side of the scale (both means are above the midpoint of 3.0 on a 5-point scale).

Although all the remaining cases were perceived by the officers as very serious (they all have means close to or above 4.00 on a 5-point scale), there is a clear clustering of the cases into two groups. Those cases seen as less serious (cases with means from 3.91 to

4.49) include the only case of excessive force (Case 10 - Excessive Force on Car Thief), the single case describing the misconduct of a supervisor (Case 7 - Supervisor Grants Holiday in Exchange for Car Tune-Up), a case of collegiality gone too far (Case 8 - Cover-Up of Police DUI Accident), a kickback case (Case 6 - 5% Kickback From Auto Repair Shop), and a bribery case involving the overlooking of violation of a city ordinance (Case 9 - Free Drinks to Ignore Late Bar Closing).

Finally, a separate category includes cases with means very close to the serious end of the scale (4.93 or above). Theft of both money from a found wallet and a watch from a crime scene, followed by the fabrication of the related official report (Case 5 - Crime Scene Theft of Watch; Case 11 - Theft From Found Wallet), were evaluated as extremely serious. Also, respondents judged harshly the acceptance of a bribe from a speeding motorist (Case 3), an obvious violation of the penal code.

### Officers' Opinions About Appropriate and Expected Discipline in Cases of Misconduct

The surveyed police officers thought that no discipline should be applied in only one case, the case describing off-duty outside business (Case 1). This case is evaluated as the least serious of all 11 cases and, at the same time, it is the only case that is a violation not of criminal law but only of official rules. Moreover, only a minority of police officers labeled it as a rule-violating behavior (see the Laws and Official Rules section above). Despite the fact that this behavior *does* constitute a violation of the official rules, it is clear that the majority of police officers not only accept such behavior but also perceive that the message sent by the administration about such behavior is one of its unofficial permissiveness.

**Table 2.4**  Austrian Officers' Views About the Seriousness of Misconduct, the Discipline It Should and Would Receive, and Officers' Willingness to Report It

| Case Number and Description | Seriousness | | | | Discipline | | | | | | Willingness to Report | | | |
|---|---|---|---|---|---|---|---|---|---|---|---|---|---|---|
| | Own View | | Most Officers | | Should Receive | | | Would Receive | | | Own View | | Most Officers | |
| | $\bar{x}$ | Rank | $\bar{x}$ | Rank | $\bar{x}$ | Rank | Mode | $\bar{x}$ | Rank | Mode | $\bar{x}$ | Rank | $\bar{x}$ | Rank |
| Case 1 - Off-Duty Security System Business | 2.08 | 1 | 2.18 | 1 | 1.73 | 1 | None | 1.78 | 1 | None | 1.98 | 1 | 2.00 | 1 |
| Case 2 - Free Meals and Discounts on Beat | 3.57 | 2 | 3.35 | 3 | 2.50 | 2 | Written Reprimand | 2.51 | 2 | Written Reprimand | 2.74 | 2 | 2.67 | 2 |
| Case 3 - Bribe From Speeding Motorist | 4.95 | 10 | 4.93 | 10.5 | 4.56 | 10 | Suspension | 4.42 | 10 | Suspension | 4.63 | 10 | 4.39 | 10 |
| Case 4 - Holiday Gifts From Merchants | 3.50 | 3 | 3.26 | 2 | 2.48 | 2 | Written Reprimand | 2.52 | 3 | Written Reprimand | 2.80 | 3 | 2.69 | 13 |
| Case 5 - Crime Scene Theft of Watch | 4.96 | 11 | 4.93 | 10.5 | 5.07 | 11 | Dismissal | 4.87 | 11 | Suspension | 4.79 | 11 | 4.65 | 11 |
| Case 6 - 5% Kickback From Auto Repair Shop | 4.43 | 6 | 4.27 | 7 | 3.68 | 8 | Written Reprimand | 3.64 | 8 | Suspension | 3.94 | 8 | 3.75 | 8 |
| Case 7 - Supervisor Grants Holiday in Exchange for Car Tune-Up | 4.49 | 8 | 4.32 | 8 | 3.16 | 6 | Written Reprimand | 3.08 | 5 | Written Reprimand | 3.60 | 6.5 | 3.45 | 7 |
| Case 8 - Cover-Up of Police DUI Accident | 4.11 | 5 | 4.01 | 5 | 3.10 | 5 | Written Reprimand | 3.16 | 6 | Written Reprimand | 3.32 | 5 | 3.19 | 5 |
| Case 9 - Free Drinks to Ignore Late Bar Closing | 3.91 | 4 | 3.70 | 4 | 2.58 | 4 | Written Reprimand | 2.64 | 4 | Written Reprimand | 2.89 | 4 | 2.76 | 4 |
| Case 10 - Excessive Force on Car Thief | 4.48 | 7 | 4.25 | 6 | 3.44 | 7 | Suspension | 3.46 | 7 | Suspension | 3.60 | 6.5 | 3.31 | 6 |
| Case 11 - Theft From Found Wallet | 4.93 | 9 | 4.87 | 9 | 4.43 | 9 | Suspension | 4.31 | 9 | Suspension | 4.56 | 9 | 4.37 | 9 |

Although the surveyed police officers reported that some discipline should be exercised in all other cases, their choice of the actual disciplinary option for a particular case ranged from "written reprimand" to "dismissal" (see Table 2.4). The acceptance of gratuities and small gifts (Case 2 - Free Meals and Discounts on Beat; Case 4 - Holiday Gifts From Merchants), two cases evaluated to be among the least serious of the cases, were thought to deserve not a verbal reprimand (which would be the next disciplinary option) but a written reprimand. With the exception of the excessive use of force case (Case 10), all the cases of intermediate seriousness (Case 6 - 5% Kickback From Auto Repair Shop; Case 7 - Supervisor Grants Holiday in Exchange for Car Tune-Up; Case 8 - Cover-Up of Police DUI Accident; Case 9 - Free Drinks to Ignore Late Bar Closing) also describe behavior that, according to the respondents, merits (only) a written reprimand (see Table 2.4).

As cases were evaluated as more serious, the respondents reported an increase in the severity of appropriate discipline. In particular, the most serious cases were thought to deserve either suspension or dismissal. According to the officers, only the crime scene theft of a watch (Case 5)—the most serious case of them all—merits dismissal, whereas the other two most serious cases, theft of money from a found wallet (Case 11) and the acceptance of a bribe from a speeding motorist (Case 3), as well as the excessive force case (Case 10), merit suspension.

A comparison of means and modes of appropriate and expected discipline reveals the respondents' views about the fairness of the severity of the discipline. The results show that in a large number of cases (9 out of 11), the means and the modal values for the appropriate versus the expected discipline for the offenses are very similar, thus suggesting that the police officers evaluated the expected discipline as fair.

Even in the two cases with modal differences (Case 5 - Crime Scene Theft of Watch; Case 6 - 5% Kickback From Auto Repair Shop), these differences are not as large as they appear at the first glance (see Table 2.4). In particular, while the mode—the most frequently selected answer by the respondents—for appropriate discipline in Case 6 is "written reprimand" and for expected discipline is "suspension," the second most frequently selected answers in each question are interchanged ("suspension" for appropriate discipline and "written reprimand" for expected discipline, respectively). The difference in the percentages for the most frequently selected answer and the second most frequently selected answer is rather small (36.8% vs. 35.7% for appropriate discipline; 36.6% vs. 37.4% for expected discipline) in this case. The only case with a larger difference is Case 5, for which the respondents had a tendency to evaluate the expected discipline as somewhat too lenient; although 53% of the respondents picked dismissal and 40.2% picked suspension as an appropriate punishment, a smaller number picked dismissal and a larger number picked suspension for the expected punishment (44.4% and 48.0%, respectively).

*Officers' Expressed*
*Willingness to Report*
*Misconduct, or the Code of Silence*

We asked the respondents whether they would be willing to report a fellow police officer who had engaged in the rule-violating behaviors described in the questionnaire. For most cases, especially the more serious ones, the surveyed police officers as a group were more likely to say that they would report it than to say that they would not (for 7 out of 11 cases, the mean values are above the midpoint of 3.0) (see Table 2.4). Just as there were clusters of cases for the relative seriousness of the misconduct and discipline it

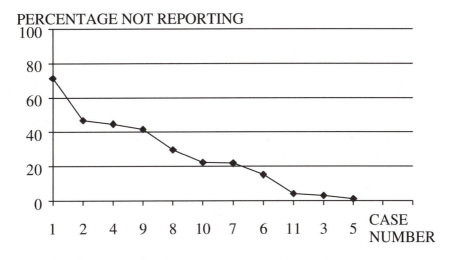

PERCENTAGE NOT REPORTING

**Figure 2.2**    Percentage of Officers Not Willing to Report Misconduct, by Case Number

deserved, there were three categories of cases for the relative willingness to report the misconduct.

In particular, for the four least serious cases (Case 1 - Off-Duty Security System Business; Case 2 - Free Meals and Discounts on Beat; Case 4 - Holiday Gifts From Merchants; and Case 9 - Free Drinks to Ignore Late Bar Closing), the respondents were likely to state that they would not report the misconduct (i.e., their mean values are below the midpoint and closer to the nonreporting side). On the other hand, the respondents were clearly much more willing to report (the mean values are close to or above 4.0 and thus close to the reporting end of the scale) the three most serious cases (Case 3 - Bribe From Speeding Motorist; Case 5 - Crime Scene Theft of Watch; Case 11 - Theft From Found Wallet) and the only other case deserving the more serious discipline of suspension (Case 6 - 5% Kickback From Auto Repair Shop). In the remaining few cases, the means are slightly above the midpoint.

A more revealing method of examining the same data is to analyze the percentage of police officers who said that they would not

report fellow police officers who engaged in the described behavior. We used this percentage as an estimate of the extent or strength of the code of silence.

A visual inspection of the data in Figure 2.2 shows that there are four clusters of cases. the code of silence strongly protects only the case of an officer's outside employment (Case 1 - Off-Duty Security System Business); close to three quarters of the respondents said that they would not report this (see Figure 2.2). While there is no other case regarding which the majority of the respondents opted for nonreporting, there are three cases for which the fraction was close to one half. These cases have one common feature—they are considered to be among the least serious cases (Case 2 - Free Meals and Discounts on Beat; Case 4 - Holiday Gifts From Merchants; and Case 9 - Free Drinks to Ignore Late Bar Closing). The next group of cases includes those that only one quarter or fewer respondents thought that they would not report. These are the cases judged to be of intermediate seriousness and they vary from a kickback to collegiality gone too far to use of excessive force (Case 6 - 5% Kickback From Auto

Repair Shop; Case 7 - Supervisor Grants Holiday in Exchange for Car Tune-Up; Case 8 - Cover-Up of Police DUI Accident; Case 10 - Excessive Force on Car Thief). Finally, the most remarkable is the last group, which only 5% or fewer of the respondents said that they would not report; not surprisingly, these are the three cases evaluated as the most serious and as deserving the most severe discipline (Case 3 - Bribe From Speeding Motorist; Case 5 - Crime Scene Theft of Watch; Case 11 - Theft From Found Wallet).

A separate analysis can be performed to examine whether the codes of silence of line officers and supervisors overlap completely. We separated the answers provided by the respondents in the supervisory positions from the answers provided by the line officers, and then compared their expressed willingness to report. According to the expectations of the higher standard of supervisory or leadership responsibility, we would expect that the code of silence would be wider for line officers (i.e., that they would be more likely than supervisors to say that they would not report).

Interestingly, while line officers are indeed more likely than supervisors to say that they would not report for each and every case in the questionnaire, the differences between the ranks, although statistically significant, are not of substantial importance in every case (see Table 2.5). The only two cases in which the Code seems to be substantially stronger for the line officers than for the supervisors are among the least serious cases: Case 1 (Off-Duty Security System Business) and Case 2 (Free Meals and Discounts on Beat). The two other potentially interesting differences exist for another of the least serious cases, describing the acceptance of gifts during holidays (Case 4 - Holiday Gifts From Merchants), and the case describing bribery to overlook a city ordinance violation (Case 9 - Drinks to Ignore Late Bar Closing).

In sum, the results of our empirical research reveal a complex police culture: At the same time, police culture is tolerant of certain types of misconduct (e.g., outside employment), intolerant of other types (e.g., acceptance of bribes from speeding motorists, thefts, kickbacks), and ambivalent about still other types (e.g., acceptance of free meals and discounts from merchants either on a regular basis or occasionally). Another layer of complexity springs from the results as well: While police officers perceived the majority of the cases as serious, with one exception, they did not advocate the use of harsh punishment, and, at the same time, most would not be willing to protect the rule violators in the majority of the cases. Also, the respondents generally had a good sense of what the majority of the police officers would say (the differences between their own opinions and their estimates of others' opinions, for both the seriousness of the misconduct and the officers' willingness to report it, were quite similar). Finally, when an analysis of the Code of Silence was performed separately for line officers and supervisors, the analyses yielded the conclusion that police officers, both line officers and supervisors, seem to be quite familiar with the extent of the Code of Silence.

## Police Officers' Salary

In the countries in which the government is unable to provide appropriate salaries for the police, corruption takes on a new importance in the economy: Police personnel may turn to corruption as a means of economic survival or as a means of economic advancement. In addition, low pay suggests that policing as a profession is not worthy of respect or that police functions can be performed by anyone. If these attitudes are communicated to the personnel, the element of idealism that brings some employees into the police is threatened and the moral tone of

**Table 2.5**   Austrian Officers' Views of Their Own Willingness to Report Misconduct, by Line Officers and Supervisors

| Case Number and Description | Line Officers' Own Reporting (N = 963) | | | | | Supervisors' Own Reporting (N = 754) | | | | | Value of Chi-Square Test |
|---|---|---|---|---|---|---|---|---|---|---|---|
| | Definitely not 1 | 2 | 3 | 4 | Definitely yes 5 | Definitely not 1 | 2 | 3 | 4 | Definitely yes 5 | |
| Case 1 - Off-Duty Security System Business | 62.2% | 15.6% | 14.3% | 3.8% | 4.0% | 45.2% | 17.4% | 13.0% | 8.2% | 16.2% | 104.08*** |
| Case 2 - Free Meals and Discounts on Beat | 32.2% | 24.5% | 25.4% | 8.1% | 9.9% | 15.2% | 19.3% | 22.2% | 17.7% | 25.6% | 151.39*** |
| Case 3 - Bribe From Speeding Motorist | 2.2% | 2.5% | 9.7% | 15.5% | 70.2% | 0.3% | 0.7% | 2.5% | 8.6% | 88.0% | 86.79*** |
| Case 4 - Holiday Gifts From Merchants | 30.0% | 20.5% | 23.7% | 13.1% | 12.8% | 18.1% | 20.2% | 22.5% | 15.3% | 23.9% | 56.30*** |
| Case 5 - Crime Scene Theft of Watch | 1.0% | 0.7% | 6.1% | 11.6% | 80.4% | 0.3% | 0.1% | 0.7% | 4.7% | 94.2% | 73.54*** |
| Case 6 - 5% Kickback From Auto Repair Shop | 7.8% | 11.5% | 23.1% | 18.6% | 39.1% | 3.2% | 7.1% | 13.3% | 16.7% | 59.7% | 86.26*** |
| Case 7 - Supervisor Grants Holiday in Exchange for Car Tune-Up | 11.1% | 14.7% | 26.5% | 17.3% | 30.3% | 5.8% | 10.7% | 18.9% | 20.1% | 44.4% | 54.50*** |
| Case 8 - Cover-Up of Police DUI Accident | 16.0% | 17.2% | 27.0% | 17.4% | 22.4% | 8.7% | 16.1% | 18.7% | 21.3% | 35.2% | 61.39*** |
| Case 9 - Free Drinks to Ignore Late Bar Closing | 25.1% | 22.5% | 23.1% | 14.6% | 14.7% | 15.7% | 19.1% | 26.4% | 19.2% | 19.6% | 33.81*** |
| Case 10 - Excessive Force on Car Thief | 12.2% | 14.3% | 23.8% | 20.2% | 29.6% | 6.6% | 10.4% | 18.1% | 21.9% | 43.0% | 48.65*** |
| Case 11 - Theft From Found Wallet | 1.5% | 4.8% | 10.7% | 14.5% | 68.4% | 0.3% | 1.1% | 4.6% | 12.0% | 82.0% | 59.41*** |

***sig. at .001; **sig. at .01; *sig. at .05

33

the force is thereby lowered, while at the same time a certain moral reward, which could otherwise partly compensate for any disparity in pay, is eliminated.

However, unlike their Eastern European counterparts, Austrian police officers do not need to resort to corruption in order to provide for basic necessities. Officers start their first year with a salary of €1,200 per month, which does not provide for a luxurious lifestyle but most certainly covers basic necessities. The starting police salary is comparable to starting salaries in the private sector that requires the same educational level.

## A Code of Ethics

The limitation that ethics places on behavior in Austria is based primarily on the old tradition of Christian education. There is a long tradition of Roman Catholic education and the development of the rule of law is based on the principles of the Roman Law, the old German Law, and the Roman Catholic Law. Although there has been no written police code of ethics, the creation of such a code was recommended in June of 2001, coupled with detailed suggestions about its content (Edelbacher, 2001).

The absence of or nonallegiance to a code of ethics is conducive to corruption in the police. The adherence to a code of ethics, emphasizing the principle of justice, public service work, the importance of the rule of law, objectivity, upholding the standard of behavior, and teamwork, can be important for a number of reasons. First, a code of ethics contributes to the image of policing as a profession, since it indicates a willingness to uphold certain standards of behavior. Second, a code of ethics helps officers to make decisions in a lawful, humane, and fair manner. Third, the code of ethics helps strengthen the self-respect of individual police officers; officers' self-pride comes from

knowing that they have conducted themselves in a proper manner. Fourth, a code of ethics contributes to a mutual respect among police officers and helps in the development of an esprit de corps, or a group striving toward a common goal. Indeed, an agreement over methods, means, and goals is a unifying element.

## The External Auditing Agency: The Austrian Office of the Ombudsman

The Austrian Office of the Ombudsman, established in the late 1970s, is an external auditing agency that reports directly to the Parliament. The Ombudsman is a multipurpose agency that reviews citizen complaints and serves as an avenue where the citizens can submit their complaints when they lack confidence in the police. Thus, the Ombudsman handles not only corruption cases but also all other types of complaints made by the public.

The hearing and the decision-making process regarding citizen complaints are both done in an open public view. Representation of both police personnel and citizens is guaranteed, with the purpose of establishing confidence in all the affected parties that their perspective and views will be heard and considered. Moreover, the most important cases are reported to the media.

The Ombudsman is also empowered to initiate its own investigations and to engage in fact-finding in the cases of citizen complaints. Since the Office of the Ombudsman sees its role as extending beyond that of finding out about the responsibility of a particular police officer in a case, it has the power to initiate its own investigations and to address the issue of corruption prevention as well. In its prevention efforts, it seeks to enlist the support of the public at large by raising public awareness.

## The Council for Human Rights

In the late summer of 2000, a dramatic accident happened. A black man of African origin, who had been residing in Austria illegally, had been scheduled for deportation to his native Nigeria. While being escorted by Austrian police officers, he died on the plane en route from Vienna to Sofia. The officers were later accused of serious human rights violations and criminally charged. The case is still being processed by a criminal court.

One of the consequences of the accompanying scandal was the establishment of the Council of Human Rights within the Ministry of the Interior. The purpose of the Council is to watch the activities of both the police and the Gendarmerie. In order to perform their control function, the 24 members of the Council have 24-hour access to the police stations and prisons. They are also given the legal right to participate in police activities if those activities involve an arrest of a suspect. Members of the Council of Human Rights are not allowed to participate when the police are interrogating the suspects, but they are allowed to speak to the suspects before and after the interrogation.

## The Media

The role of the media in corruption control has become increasingly more important as the media focus has shifted from reporting exclusively about existing cases of police misconduct to a more active engagement in investigative journalism. In the 1980s, the information obtained by journalists led to two scandals that had a substantial impact on the public's views about the integrity of public servants and the control of their conduct. The first scandal, in 1981, involved the building industry and political corruption; the second scandal, in 1988, involved insurance fraud and political corruption. As a consequence, two important political figures resigned. The response to the two scandals led to substantial changes in the political party financing system in Austria, which has become transparent and is now controlled by the Parliament. In general, the media are very critical of public servants and are always eager to find and report a story of corruption.

## Public Expectations

A political and social environment characterized by a high level of political corruption and little community interest to eliminate it presents an opportunity for police corruption; society contributes to police corruption by giving gratuities to police personnel in exchange for official action or forbearance and by tolerating misconduct. According to empirical studies, Austria seems to be among the countries characterized by a relatively low level of corruption in general. For the third year in a row, in 2001 the Transparency International Corruption Perceptions Index ranked Austria around 15th (Transparency International, 2001), behind countries such as Finland, Denmark, Singapore, Sweden, and Switzerland and before countries such as Germany, Japan, Spain, France, and Belgium. A second evaluation by Transparency International, which concentrated on taking bribes, ranked Austria even higher among those same countries—in fourth place.

As it turns out, not only does the public seem to be intolerant of corruption, especially police corruption, but it has quite a positive opinion about the police as well. The results of the most recent opinion poll, from 2001 (conducted by the Federal Bank of Austria since 1996), placed the police again as the number one institution of public trust; the results indicate that the level of public confidence in police competence exceeds the level of public confidence given to the politicians, journalists, prosecutors, and even judges (Federal Bank of Austria, 2001).

## Regional Factors: The War in the Balkans and Organized Crime

There is an old saying in Austria that "corruption starts in the Balkans and the Balkans starts in Vienna." This saying depicts the historical connection of the Balkan region to the Austrian-Hungarian Monarchy. Nowadays, Austria, a member of the European Union, borders countries of the former Eastern Block and is a gateway to the other countries in the European Union. Thus, it has to fulfill the Schengen criteria of border control (The First Schengen Treaty, 1985; The Second Schengen Treaty, 1994).

When the war in the Balkans ended in the mid-1990s, the completed peace negotiations incorporated the establishment of international presence in the area in the form of peace-keeping missions. These international organizations were immediately confronted with a high level of corruption in Bosnia-Herzegovina, Croatia, Kosovo, and the Republic of Serbia.

A large number of illegal immigrants try to cross the borders daily, which creates additional opportunities for corruption. The opening of the boundaries with the Eastern European countries has also resulted in the increased presence of organized crime, which shows a propensity to use corruption to achieve its ends. The known organized crime-related cases of police corruption typically include the selling of confidential police information to private investigators for their clients.

One case is particularly illustrative: A person believed to be involved in Ukrainian organized crime, in an effort to cover up his involvement, tried to bribe a German journalist to stop him from publishing a book about Vadim Rabinovic, one of the heads of organized crime in the Ukraine. A senior Austrian police officer, who served with the special unit for the fight against organized crime at the time, aided the corruption by communicating the offer of cash payment made by the alleged member of Ukrainian organized crime to the German journalist. He had established business relations with both parties to the deal. The German journalist did not accept the payoff and informed the Austrian police about the bribe offer.

## The Active Role of the Ministry

Austria's new government, established at the beginning of 2000, has as one of its main goals the establishment and implementation of more powerful mechanisms to fight corruption. Accordingly, the Ministry of the Interior considers police corruption to be a serious issue. To that effect, based on the recommendations by the European Union, in 2001 the Ministry established a project group that, after a thorough examination of the existing system, noted problems and recommended a number of measures aimed at reducing the corruption risk.

A number of recommendations targeted the selection process (the background investigation should be completed before the candidate is offered a position; candidates should be chosen for their invulnerability to corruption; candidates should undergo integrity testing), while others focused on the control once a candidate becomes a part of the police organization (e.g., merger of the existing two types of supervision, establishment of a designated police officer within a smaller unit, development of the innovative intelligence-gathering procedures (*Internal Advice of the Ministry of the Interior,* 2001). Another recommendation addressed the duty to disclose transactions above a certain limit (presently regulated by the Banking Law):

> Employees will be required to report financial transactions exceeding the amount

of €7,000,—(Euro). Even though it is not realistic to expect that any regulation requiring disclosure of a person's financial assets will result in voluntary confessions, they are an invaluable measure to obtain indicia of corrupt practices. They function as an early warning device, an indicator that a person whose financial picture and life-style are inconsistent with the salary of a public official should be required to explain the situation or be watched carefully. The constant fear of being required to account for should give rise to a state of anxiety which would have a deterrent effect. A second useful function is that it is a vehicle of prosecution. When the underlying corruption that generated the illegal income may not be provable. One of the most successful ways to produce evidence against corrupt persons is to conduct financial investigations to prove that they spend beyond the means of their income. (Article 41, Banking Law, 1994)

The Austrian Police also participate in various seminars on organized crime and corruption, some of which are either organized or held in Austria. For example, an international seminar on organized crime and economic crime, organized by the Council Presidency of the European Union, was held in Austria in 1998. This event was attended by experts from the law enforcement agencies from 27 European countries and the United States, as well as representatives of the United Nations, the European Commission, Europol, Interpol, and the Council General Secretariat. The aim of this seminar was to draw up guidelines and outline solutions for efficient implementation of Recommendations 6, 26, and 30 of the European Action Plan to Combat Organized Crime (Council Presidency of the European Union, 1998). These guidelines and recommendations relate to police corruption as well: to confiscate assets for corruption-related offenses, to declare admissible the use of cover investigators, and to issue common

guidelines for prevention of corruption to the members of the European Union (Council Presidency of the European Union, 1998).

## CONCLUSION

The official data on police corruption feature relatively few recorded cases each year. While the officially recorded cases constitute just the tip of the iceberg of all corruption cases, the iceberg does not seem to be as wide in Austria as it is in the countries characterized by widespread corruption. Indeed, empirical studies included in the Corruption Perceptions Index clearly show that the overall level of corruption in Austria is relatively low; Austria has consistently been ranked by the Transparency International as one of the top 20 least corrupt countries.

The results of our empirical study on police integrity indicate that the surveyed police officers generally seem to be intolerant of police corruption: They evaluated most of the cases described in our questionnaire as serious and said that they would not be very likely to tolerate such behavior. Police officers seemed to be especially intolerant of serious forms of corruption, while they are ambivalent about the acceptance of small gifts and gratuities. Both line officers and supervisors tended to be knowledgeable about the boundaries of the police culture, particularly about the behavior prohibited or tolerated by police culture.

This, however, does not mean that there is no police corruption in Austria, that there are no opportunities, or that there is no room for improvement. On top of the typical opportunities for corruption generated as a consequence of the nature of police work (e.g., constant contact with rule-violators, relative isolation, lack of credible witnesses), Austria is a gateway to the European Union from the Eastern European countries, which creates additional corruption opportunities. All these and future challenges notwithstanding, the active, preventive approach taken by the government and the Ministry of the Interior, coupled with the high degree of intolerance toward corruption among the members of the public at large, the active media, and strong sentiments for the transparency of public offices, seem to be healthy foundations of corruption control in Austria.

## NOTES

1. See, for example, *Report of the Secretary General on Existing International Legal Instruments Addressing Corruption* (2001), *Criminal Law Convention on Corruption* (Council of Europe, 1998), *Convention of the European Union on the Fight Against Corruption Involving Officials of the European Communities or Officials of Member States* (1997), and the *Convention on Combating Bribery of Foreign Public Officials in International Business Transactions* (OECD, 1997).

2. This description of the training is based on the curriculum developed by the Vienna Police School.

## REFERENCES

*Austria Facts and Figures.* (2000). Vienna: The Austria Federal Press Service.

Austrian Police Academy, The Fifth Working Group in Management. (1998/1999). Vienna.

Banking Law. (1994). Vienna.

*Collins English Dictionary.* (1979). Glasgow, UK: William Collins Sons.

*Convention of the European Union on the Fight Against Corruption Involving Officials of the European Communities or Officials of Member States.* (1997).

Council of Europe. (1998). *Criminal Law Convention on Corruption.*

Council Presidency of the European Union (1998). *International Seminar on Economic Crime.* November 3rd to 6th, 1998, Baden, Austria.

Edelbacher, M. (2001). Working paper on prevention of police corruption. Vienna: Ministry of the Interior.

Elliston, F., & Feldberg, M. (1985). *Moral issues in police work.* Totowa, NJ: Rowman & Allanheld.

Federal Bank of Austria. (2001). Vienna.

Foregger, E., & Bachner Foregger, H. (2000). *Penal Code.* Vienna: Staatsdruckerei.

Frič, P., & Walek, C. (2001). *Crossing the thin blue line: An international annual review of anti-corruption strategies in the police.* Prague, The Czech Republic: Transparency International ČR.

Goldstein, H. (1977). *Policing a free society.* Cambridge, MA: Ballinger.

*Internal Advice of the Ministry of the Interior.* (2001). Advice signed by the Ministry of the Interior, November 2001.

Kutnjak Ivkovich, S., & Klockars, C. B. (1996). *Police perceptions of disciplinary fairness and the formation of The Code of Silence.* Paper presented at the annual meeting of the Academy of Criminal Justice Sciences, Las Vegas, Nevada.

Letter of the Deputy Chief of the Uniformed Police to the Police President. (1998).

OECD. (1997). *Convention on Combatting Bribery of Foreign Public Officials in International Business Transactions.*

Palmiotto, M. J. (2001). *Police misconduct: A reader for the 21st century.* Upper Saddle River, NJ: Prentice Hall.

Palmiotto, M. J., & Alter, M. (2001, May). *Fighting police corruption: Strategies used by American police.* Paper presented at the annual International Police Executive Symposium, Szczytno, Poland.

*Report of the Secretary General on Existing International Legal Instruments Addressing Corruption.* (2001). U.N. Document E. CN. 15/2001/3.

*The First Schengen Treaty.* (1985).

*The Second Schengen Treaty.* (1994).

*Security Police Law.* (1993). Vienna.

Sherman, L. (1985). Becoming bent: Moral careers of corrupt policemen. In F. Elliston & M. Feldberg (Eds.), *Moral issues in police work.* Totowa, NJ: Rowman & Allanheld.

*Transparency International Corruption Perceptions Index.* (1999, 2000, 2001). Available at <http://www.transparency.org/ documents/index.htm#cpi>

# An Exploratory Study of Quebec's Police Officers' Attitudes Toward Ethical Dilemmas

MARC ALAIN

*According to this [rotten apple] theory, which bordered on official Department doctrine, any policeman found to be corrupt must promptly be denounced as a rotten apple in an otherwise clean barrel. It must never be admitted that his individual corruption may be symptomatic of underlying disease.*

— Knapp Commission report
(Knapp, 1972, p. 6)

*During the tenure of the Commission, the Department has begun to take significant steps to strengthen its corruption controls. The bulk of these reforms, however, have focused on improving and expanding detection and investigative efforts. While such reforms are essential, the Commission believes that effective control of police corruption must focus on prevention as much as detection; on the root causes and conditions of corruption as well as its symptoms.*

— Mollen Commission report
(Mollen, 1994, p. 148)

Twenty-two years separate these reports. For the more cynical among us, it would seem that the more things change, the more they remain the same. Things might have really changed, however. Undeniably, there has been some awakening to the idea that the "rotten apple" theory must also be combined with another idea—that once in a while it can be the barrel that rots the apples it contains. Thus for over a decade, in almost every public and private institution in democratic countries, for either good or rather twisted reasons (Lipovetsky, 1992), the question of ethics has become a major issue in police organizations as well as in policing in general. In this respect, Quebec's police organizations are no different from those in other countries.

## POLICING IN
## CANADA AND IN QUEBEC
## DURING THE LAST DECADE

Canada is a federal state; the Canadian Parliament is in Ottawa, and each of the 10 provinces also has its own parliament and provincial government. The two levels of government share jurisdictions in civilian matters and administration of criminal justice, but the federal level has exclusive responsibility for all matters regarding the code of penal procedure. The responsibility for police activity is also shared by the two levels. The two biggest provinces in Canada (Quebec and Ontario) have their own police forces (the Sûreté du Québec, established in 1870, and the Ontario provincial police, established in 1909), while the less populated provinces contract with the Royal Canadian Mounted Police (RCMP) for provincial penal responsibilities. In Ontario and Quebec, as is the case in the United States, police organization is decentralized and, other than the provincial police, delegated to the administrative supervision of city councils and municipalities.

We can sum up the last decade of policing in Quebec as being characterized by three concomitant phenomena: (1) a succession of inquiry commissions and investigations into police work and police organization; (2) a succession of reforms in laws governing police work and police functions; and (3) the replacement, within a short period of time, of experienced police officers by a contingent of younger, inexperienced officers.

### *Inquiry Commissions and*
### *Investigations Into Police Work*

From the end of the 1980s and throughout the 1990s, there was a cascade of public inquiry commissions and ensuing reports into police misconduct and deficiencies in police education and training, both in the investigation and patrol departments (the Keable Commission, 1986; the Griffin case investigation, 1990; the Barnabé case investigation, 1993; the Ferraro case investigation, 1995; the Suazo case investigation, 1995; the Bellemare report, 1996; the Poitras Commission, 1998; the Roberge Commission, 2001; the Dupont case investigation, 2001). Specific case investigations, such as those mentioned above, were generally appointed after a police intervention that resulted in the death of suspects or, in some cases (such as the Barnabé investigation), the death of innocents. In the Barnabé affair, for instance, two police officers from the Montreal police department were accused of beating to death a vagrant who made noise at the entry of a bar on one of Montreal's main streets. In the Griffin case, a black teenager was shot in the back by one officer while running away from another officer, who thought Griffin was a suspected robber. It was quickly discovered that Griffin had nothing to do with the alleged affair and, in the end, the case caused an uproar of protest within the Montreal black community that had led to the institution of a powerful lobby against police violence.

Commissions of inquiry, on the other hand, were directed either at whole departments, pointing at evidence of deficiencies in managerial practices (such as training, hiring, and promoting processes) or at individual and team work. The Keable Commission, in 1981, was the result of the turmoil generated by the October 1970 crisis in Quebec (Keable, 1981). A clandestine political movement, the FLQ (*Front de Libération du Québec*), kidnapped a local politician and the U.K. ambassador. The ambassador was liberated after a few days, but the politician was discovered dead in a car trunk. The federal government then passed the War Measures Act, which gives the police arresting power far superior to those usually granted. In the end, more than 400 citizens were arrested and detained, for periods varying between a few days and more than a month, without mandate or accusation. Ten years later, documents revealed how police organizations of that time used methods similar to those found mostly in dictatorial regimes. In October of 1970, for example, the police knew from intelligence sources how, when, and what the FLQ planned to do; instead of preventing these actions, the police did nothing, with the objective of infiltrating the movement and arresting its leaders: "Police in-action was justified by the desire to proceed to infiltration operations, as well as in order to protect already infiltrated sources" (Keable, 1981, p. 215).

What finally resulted was the enactment of the War Measures Act, which would lead to massive arrests of individuals throughout Quebec, the majority of whom had nothing to do with the political activities attributed to the FLQ. The Keable Commission even showed how, after 1970, the RCMP, as well as the Montreal police department and the provincial police, planned and executed illegal actions in order to blame the FLQ, actions such as stealing dynamite and setting houses on fire. If, on one hand, police involvement in political activities was exposed and seriously criticized, on the other hand, investigation methods continued to be plagued by generalized improvisation. This phenomenon led to the institution of the Bellemare Commission in 1996. The Commission exposed in its report how poorly equipped and educated Quebec's investigators were:

> We noted that, in general, the young investigators are characterized by a lack of analysis capabilities and lack of syntheses abilities. We also noted that too many arrests are processed without legal mandates and that investigators present themselves in court without having completed all the legal forms for the proof to be admitted. Too often, this behavior results in suspects

having to be released without charges being laid. (Bellemare, 1996, p. 25)

Nevertheless, investigators from the Sûreté du Québec (the provincial police force) carried on with the methods that had been so heavily criticized by the Bellemare Commission. It was later found that one investigative team falsified evidence in order to secure the accusation of an organized criminal network (this was known as "the Mattick affair"). This action resulted in the release of the accused and an investigation by the organization internal affairs division. The situation got progressively worse: The officers under investigation started to menace their colleagues from the internal affairs division to such an extent that some of them decided to resign. This development eventually caught the attention of the Minister of Public Security, who then had no other choice but to appoint yet another commission of inquiry, the Poitras Commission, which released a voluminous report in 1998 (Poitras, 1998). The Poitras Commission was appointed because of the misconduct of one investigative team, but the complete report went as far as to expose the whole organization of the Sûreté du Québec for its generalized reluctance to adapt its philosophy, mandate, operations, and accountability measures in accordance with what is expected of such an important organization (employing more than 4,000 police officers and almost 2,000 civilians) in a modern society. Interestingly, 2 years before, the Bellemare Report (Bellemare, 1996) addressed the same kinds of problems not only for the Sûreté du Québec but for all major police departments: Montreal (4,157 officers), Quebec City (451 officers), Laval (the northern suburb of Montreal; 436 officers), and Longueuil (the southern suburb of Montreal; 398 officers).

The question now stands: Did all these efforts change the police culture in Quebec?

Without necessarily emphasizing too heavily the possibility that police culture can really be changed (Crank, 1998), we agree with Brodeur (1984) that commissions of inquiry may not be the tools of change. For Brodeur, commissions of inquiry into police work are essentially political mechanisms aimed at letting the people know what went wrong at a given moment in a given organization. The capacity of commissions of inquiry to effectively modify an organization's structure and working methods is limited by the willingness of elected politicians to apply laws and rules to a police culture that may not readily accept either criticism or change. In Quebec, however, the politicians were quite vigorous in modifying the laws that govern police work; a little too vigorous, perhaps, as will now be seen in what follows.

### The Succession of Legal Reforms

The second phenomenon, which is directly linked with the problems described above, pertains to a succession of legal reforms, all aimed at modifying the everyday routine work of police officers and of police organization management. The present Police Act (Revised Statutes of Quebec, c. P13.1) was adopted in June of 2000; this Act replaced the two that preceded it, which governed police functions and overall police organization (and were revised, to varying extents, in 1979, 1988, 1990, and 1996). In the most recent version of the law, police status (the conditions required for the granting of police officer status, for example) and the legal structure of police organizations (mostly matters pertaining to the distribution ratio of police forces throughout the vast Quebec territory) were, for the first time, united in one single statute. More specifically, though, one new article in this last version of the Police Act can be seen as a direct consequence of the

Poitras Commission's inquiry into the Sûreté du Québec (Poitras, 1998). After 2 years of harsh deliberations, the Commission made over 170 recommendations, 2 of which[1] expressly push for the legislature to include an article in the reform of the Police Act that would ensure legal protection for any police officer who reports the behavior of a colleague that could potentially give rise to a disciplinary complaint.

Two years later, in 2000, Quebec's legislature went even further, with Article 260 of the newly reformed Police Act:

> Every police officer is required to inform the director of police of the conduct of another police officer likely to constitute a breach of discipline or professional ethics that may infringe upon rights or compromise the safety of the public, or likely to constitute a criminal offence. . . . Likewise, every police officer is required to take part or cooperate in any investigation concerning such conduct. (R.S.Q., c. P13.1, a. 260)

However, whether such a strong stand will have a perceptible impact on the traditional police culture of silence remains to be seen.[2] We can also point to a general contradiction between the global objective of giving police officers a professional statute and the myriad of new rules and operation standards that have gradually been added to their everyday routine work. If professionalism means relying on one's own capacity to make what are, to the best of one's knowledge, correct decisions, it is odd that professional police officers are being surrounded with more rules and more laws, which are diminishing their capacity for individual initiative. As described below, this phenomenon could be amplified when recruits cannot take advantage of the experience of senior officers who have had the possibility of dealing with this contradiction in real-life situations.

## The Massive Recruitment of Inexperienced Officers

The third and final aspect of the changes that have affected police organizations in Quebec is that during the second part of the 1970s, as well as for most of the 1980s, mostly because of a difficult economic situation, recruitment of new officers was cut to the bare minimum. In the 1990s, senior police officers retired en masse and recruits were hired in the same fashion to replace them. This posed the problem of who would supervise the recruits. As is still the case in Montreal, for instance, the officers who supervise recruits were often hired only 1 or 2 years before these recruits. It should not be surprising, then, that they can give their recruits a rather limited view of the more profound aspects of police work and the potential moral dilemmas they might encounter, since they themselves have not encountered these kinds of dilemmas.[3]

These three phenomena alone could explain some of the ambivalence of Quebec's police officers regarding their duties, social roles, and responsibilities. Yet, this situation has escalated in the last 15 years into one that internal and external observers have agreed qualifies as a general frustration within the police profession. In 1982, the Canadian Parliament enacted the Charter of Rights, which imposed new parameters for the most delicate aspects of police work. These parameters and obligations are considered by a vast majority of Quebec's police officers as additional restraints on their efforts to crack down on criminals (Nadeau, 2001). The combination of these obligations, the evolution of the Police Act, the myriad of commissions and investigations, and the officers' lack of experience may have created a state of uncertainty among Quebec's police officers. We will try to assess in the next sections how this uncertainty has affected the general police culture and officers' attitudes toward their duties, social role, and responsibilities. Accordingly, as we propose and amplify later in these pages, the isolation of police officers and the solidarity that proceeds from that isolation is a complex that has become an important feature of Quebec's police culture (Reiner, 1992).

## EXPLORING POLICE VALUES: THE USE OF SURVEY TOOLS

Exploring police officers' attitudes and values in the United States with the use of survey tools started with the pioneering work of Milton Rokeach (Rokeach, Miller, & Snyder, 1971). The first aim of Rokeach and his team was essentially to assess the differences between the values of police and the values of the public the officers policed; however, as their research went on, their explorations were gradually aimed at assessing differences in values and attitudes from one police officer to another (Caldero, 1997). Within this era, police managers grasped the idea of surveying the officers in their own organizations in order to better understand them before or during change implementation, such as the shift from traditional policing to the community policing model (Greene, Bergman, & McLaughlin, 1994). These efforts, however, are generally kept within each organization, for managerial purposes. It is then rather difficult to pretend that these various surveys could really represent the values and attitudes of a random sample of a given population of police officers. This problem was well addressed by Weisburd and his team (Weisburd, Greenspan, Hamilton, Williams, & Bryant, 2000) in their study of the attitudes of U.S. police officers regarding the problem of abuse of authority. They surveyed a representative sample of 925 randomly selected American police officers in 121 departments. The tool developed for this study consists of

92 questions, of which 25 can be regrouped to create six themes.[4] Specifically, police officers' attitudes regarding the notion of abuse of authority are clearly related to at least one other important aspect of police culture: The "code of silence." Weisburd and colleagues (Weisburd, Greenspan, Hamilton, Bryant, & Williams, 2001) demonstrated that respondents who think that instances of abuse of authority are related to a tougher stand on crime are also those who think that in some instances these abuses are permissible and should not be reported.

Although we used Weisburd's tool combined with the one developed independently by Carl Klockars and his team (Klockars, Kutnjak Ivkovich, Harver, & Haberfeld, 2000), our analysis will rest on the results obtained from this second tool. This second survey tool has been used in several countries in comparative studies (Klockars, Kutnjak Ivkovich, Harver, & Haberfeld, 1997; Kutnjak Ivkovich, Klockars, & Harver, 1995; Punch, Huberts, & Lamboo, 2000). The survey asks the respondents to assess 11 hypothetical cases of police misconduct so as to measure how serious they find each case, as well as to measure the degree to which they would be willing to report such conduct.

## METHODOLOGY, SAMPLING, AND RESULTS

### Sampling Methodology and Levels of Representation

According to the latest available figures (Ministry of Public Security, 1999), Quebec's total police force is estimated at nearly 13,000 men and women (part time and full time) and is equitably divided into three types of organizations: Quebec's provincial police (the Sûreté du Québec, which operates in rural areas and is also responsible for investigations at the provincial level), the

Montreal Police Department (the Service de Police de la Ville de Montréal, which operates in Quebec's largest city), and, finally, a shrinking number of smaller urban police organizations.[5] Because confidential information was shared with the researchers on the condition that no specific organization would be identified in their published work, we present only aggregate results for the whole sample.

The two questionnaires were first translated into French and then pretested with three small focus groups of sworn police officers who attended specialized courses at Quebec's National School of Police (the only police academy in Quebec). As a result of comments from these focus groups that the different themes were too easily identifiable (therefore creating the risk that it would be easier for respondents to answer according to the "expected" attitude rather than according to their own attitude), the questions of this first survey were shuffled randomly and the two tools were then fused into one questionnaire. Questions about the professional characteristics of respondents (number of years of service, rank, etc.) were also adapted to the realities of Quebec's police organizations. While negotiations with department officials and union representatives were being conducted to ensure maximum cooperation from all parties,[6] 333 police cadets attending their mandatory training course at the Police School agreed to answer the final version of the questionnaire. In this chapter, however, we will only report results obtained from the sworn officers sample.

When permissions were granted and cooperation ensured, 600 questionnaires were distributed to police managers, instructing them to distribute the questionnaires according to a predefined data-collection plan, where different quotas were apportioned in accordance with rank, duties, and number of years' experience in the whole officer population. Of these 600 questionnaires,

**Table 3.1** Comparison of the Characteristics of the Sample and the Whole Population

| Function and Rank | Sample's Percentages (n) | Police Officer Population's Percentages (n) |
| --- | --- | --- |
| Patrol officer | 39.4 (172) | 54.7 (7 028) |
| Investigator | 31.9 (139) | 12.3 (1 577) |
| First- and mid-level supervisor | 27.3 (119) | 31.3 (4 015) |
| Top-level supervisor | 1.4 (6) | 1.7 (221) |
| Total | 100.0 (436) (*n* missing=19) | 100.0 (12 841) |
| *Length of Experience* | | |
| Less than 6 years | 10.2 (45) | 24.1 (3 066) |
| 6 to 10 years | 18.3 (81) | 19.9 (2 527) |
| 11 to 15 years | 27.7 (122) | 17.4 (2 215) |
| 16 to 20 years | 16.8 (74) | 7.9 (1 002) |
| Over 20 years | 27.0 (119) | 30.7 (3 905) |
| Total | 100.0 (441) (*n* missing=14) | 100.0 (12 715) |

Note: These data are from the 1999 census conducted by Quebec's Ministry of Public Security.

455 were returned, which is a response rate of 75.8%. But, as Table 3.1 shows, we must recognize how this sample might not be representative of the whole population with regard to the different characteristics' strata.

There is clearly an overrepresentation of investigators in our sample, as there is also an underrepresentation of younger officers. Since we cannot pretend that our results could be extended to the whole population, we propose to explore as deeply as possible the attitudes of a randomly selected group of Quebec's police officers. We must also acknowledge that this group might reflect the attitudes of somewhat older officers, mostly from the administrative and investigator ranks.[7]

## Comparing the Attitudes of Quebec's Officers and America's Officers

Although this was not a specific objective of our research, a brief comparison will give us the opportunity to better understand our sample, as well as serve the general purpose of this book, which is to assess how officers from different cultures react to somewhat similar situations in everyday police practice. Table 3.2 illustrates the similarities and differences between the original U.S. sample and the Quebec sample.

As Punch and colleagues (2000, p. 8) have noted, there is, in our case, a strong consistency cross-nationally in the rank ordering of the seriousness of the various forms of police misconduct exemplified in the scenarios. This is particularly true with the last three scenarios of the scale. Furthermore, we noticed something that was also noted by Punch and colleagues (2000)—the phenomenon of officers underestimating how seriously others would consider the offenses in the scenarios, as well as the fact that, in the respondents' view, the agency's response ("would receive") is always harsher than the disciplinary measure they themselves would give ("should receive"). We can see, however, that Quebec's officers show a general tendency toward believing the conduct in the cases slightly more serious than their American colleagues do, and this observation is also true for the "discipline" and

**Table 3.2** Comparison of U.S. and Quebec Officers' Views of the Seriousness of the Misconduct, the Discipline It Should and Would Receive, and Their Willingness to Report It

| Case Number and Description | Seriousness — Own | | | Seriousness — Others | | | Discipline — Should Receive | | | Discipline — Would Receive | | | Willingness to Report — Own | | | Willingness to Report — Others | | |
|---|---|---|---|---|---|---|---|---|---|---|---|---|---|---|---|---|---|---|
| | Score | Rank | Median | Score | Rank | Median | Score | Rank | Median | Score | Rank | Median | Score | Rank | Median | Score | Rank | Median |
| Case 1 - Off-Duty Security System Business | 1.46 | 1 | 1 | 1.48 | 1 | 1 | 1.34 | 1 | 1 | 1.51 | 1 | 1 | 1.37 | 1 | 1 | 1.46 | 1 | 1 |
| *(Quebec)* | *2.15* | *1* | *2* | *2.01* | *1* | *2* | *1.97* | *1* | *2* | *2.52* | *1* | *3* | *1.96* | *1* | *1* | *1.86* | *1* | *1* |
| Case 2 - Free Meals and Discounts on Beat | 2.60 | 2 | 2 | 2.31 | 2 | 2 | 2.13 | 2 | 2 | 2.37 | 2 | 2 | 1.94 | 2 | 1 | 1.82 | 2 | 1 |
| *(Quebec)* | *3.26* | *3* | *3* | *2.86* | *3* | *3* | *2.47* | *2* | *2* | *2.80* | *2* | *3* | *2.32* | *2* | *1* | *1.96* | *2* | *1* |
| Case 3 - Bribe From Speeding Motorist | 4.92 | 10 | 5 | 4.81 | 10 | 5 | 4.92 | 9 | 5 | 4.86 | 9 | 4 | 4.19 | 9 | 5 | 3.92 | 9 | 4 |
| *(Quebec)* | *4.97* | *10* | *5* | *4.87* | *10* | *5* | *4.76* | *9* | *4* | *4.75* | *9* | *4* | *4.60* | *10* | *5* | *4.04* | *10* | *5* |
| Case 4 - Holiday Gifts From Merchants | 2.84 | 3 | 3 | 2.64 | 3 | 3 | 2.53 | 3 | 2 | 2.82 | 3 | 3 | 2.36 | 4 | 2 | 2.28 | 3.5 | 2 |
| *(Quebec)* | *3.17* | *2* | *3* | *2.85* | *2* | *3* | *2.53* | *3* | *3* | *2.87* | *3* | *3* | *2.57* | *3* | *1* | *2.30* | *3* | *1* |
| Case 5 - Crime Scene Theft of Watch | 4.95 | 11 | 5 | 4.88 | 11 | 5 | 5.66 | 11 | 6 | 5.57 | 11 | 6 | 4.54 | 11 | 5 | 4.34 | 11 | 5 |
| *(Quebec)* | *5.00* | *11* | *5* | *4.93* | *11* | *5* | *5.63* | *11* | *6* | *5.60* | *11* | *6* | *4.82* | *11* | *5* | *4.42* | *11* | *5* |
| Case 6 - 5% Kickback From Auto Repair Shop | 4.50 | 7 | 5 | 4.26 | 7 | 5 | 4.40 | 8 | 4 | 4.46 | 8 | 4 | 3.95 | 8 | 5 | 3.71 | 8 | 4 |
| *(Quebec)* | *4.67* | *8* | *5* | *4.42* | *8* | *5* | *4.51* | *8* | *4* | *4.58* | *8* | *4* | *4.33* | *8* | *5* | *3.88* | *8* | *4* |
| Case 7 - Supervisor Grants Holiday In Exchange for Car Tune-Up | 4.18 | 6 | 5 | 3.96 | 6 | 4 | 3.59 | 5 | 4 | 3.43 | 5 | 3 | 3.45 | 6 | 4 | 3.29 | 6 | 3 |
| *(Quebec)* | *4.23* | *5* | *4* | *4.12* | *6* | *4* | *3.45* | *4* | *3* | *3.31* | *4* | *3* | *3.93* | *6* | *5* | *3.60* | *7* | *5* |
| Case 8 - Cover-Up of Police DUI Accident | 3.03 | 4 | 3 | 2.86 | 4 | 3 | 2.81 | 4 | 3 | 3.21 | 4 | 3 | 2.34 | 3 | 2 | 2.28 | 3.5 | 2 |
| *(Quebec)* | *3.68* | *4* | *4* | *3.44* | *4* | *3* | *3.57* | *5* | *4* | *4.11* | *6* | *4* | *2.78* | *4* | *1* | *2.52* | *4* | *2* |
| Case 9 - Free Drinks to Ignore Late Bar Closing | 4.54 | 8 | 5 | 4.28 | 8 | 5 | 4.02 | 7 | 4 | 4.08 | 7 | 4 | 3.73 | 7 | 4 | 3.47 | 7 | 4 |
| *(Quebec)* | *4.55* | *7* | *5* | *4.28* | *7* | *4* | *3.74* | *6* | *4* | *3.83* | *5* | *4* | *3.94* | *7* | *5* | *3.48* | *6* | *3* |
| Case 10 - Excessive Force on Car Thief | 4.05 | 5 | 5 | 3.70 | 5 | 4 | 3.76 | 6 | 4 | 4.00 | 6 | 4 | 3.39 | 5 | 4 | 3.07 | 5 | 3 |
| *(Quebec)* | *4.35* | *6* | *5* | *3.99* | *5* | *4* | *3.88* | *7* | *4* | *4.20* | *7* | *4* | *3.59* | *5* | *5* | *3.07* | *5* | *3* |
| Case 11 - Theft From Found Wallet | 4.85 | 9 | 5 | 4.69 | 9 | 5 | 5.09 | 10 | 6 | 5.03 | 10 | 6 | 4.23 | 10 | 5 | 3.96 | 10 | 4 |
| *(Quebec)* | *4.86* | *9* | *5* | *4.70* | *9* | *5* | *4.92* | *10* | *5* | *5.03* | *10* | *6* | *4.45* | *9* | *5* | *4.02* | *9* | *5* |

Note: These are the responses of officers from America and Quebec (in italics) to questions about the 11 cases in the survey designed by Klockars and colleagues (2000).

"willingness to report" items. There is, here again, a strong consistency among the three items: As was observed earlier by Klockars and colleagues (1997), as well as Dixon (1999) in another context, the more serious officers consider a scenario to be, the more heavily they believe it should be disciplined and the more respondents think they would be willing to report the behavior.

There are, however, some peculiar differences between the responses given by the two samples. We can start with what is probably the easiest one to explain: Quebec's respondents consider Case 1 (Off-Duty Security System Business) more serious than do America's respondents. As was the case in Croatia (Punch et al., 2000, p. 9), the Quebec Police Act forbids a police officer to engage in any business that would constitute a potential conflict of interest. Operating a private security system business is cited in the law as an example of such forbidden conduct. The "Discipline" column is also marked with interesting differences, but here explanations cannot be put forward so easily. We can observe that regarding the scenarios considered by the respondents to be less serious (the first four scenarios), Quebec's officers are less lenient, whereas the same officers are more lenient than their American counterparts regarding the more serious scenarios (Case 3 - Bribe From Speeding Motorist and Case 11 - Theft From Found Wallet). If we take the third and fourth scenarios (Case 4 - Holiday Gifts From Merchants and Case 8 - Cover-Up of Police DUI Accident), we can see that Quebec's respondents are tougher with regard to disciplinary measures, while they are also less prone to report these two instances than are America's respondents. It seems that for these two instances, the respondents' conceptualization of discipline is not that strongly related to their willingness to report. Police officers with whom we had the opportunity to discuss these results told us that whatever kind of disciplinary measure officers would receive for forbidden conduct, they would agree with the measure as long as it was proportional to the seriousness of the alleged conduct. However, these same officers were also very prone to say that it would be crucial that both the forbidden conduct and the disciplinary measure remain unknown and thus protected from public scrutiny. We hereby propose, however, that an empirical explanation of these particularities might only be extracted from a much deeper investigation into Quebec's police culture. And because the research presented here is mainly in its exploratory stage, it would be untenable to advance to such a level of analysis. We will, however, try to assess how three control variables might give us some clues. In the next section, series of bivariate analysis for each of the 11 scenarios are presented.

But before we move on, examining these first results may give us some clues about the attitudes of this sample of police officers. The first important element revealed in Table 3.2 pertains to the fact that Quebec's respondents do not consider the seriousness of misconduct in exactly the same way that their American counterparts do: Even though the ranking order is almost the same in the two samples, Quebec's respondents are generally more severe. A second important element we noted was that while less serious conduct would be disciplined slightly more heavily by the respondents from Quebec, in the cases of more serious conduct these respondents tended to be less severe than were respondents from America. One potential explanation for this element is the fact that those scenarios considered less serious (such as Cases 1, 2, 4, and 8) are also those most often cited by the managers and ranked officers as the most frequent cases of misconduct punished by the organization. Potentially more damaging forms of misconduct are seen by Quebec's respondents to be so improbable that they consider it worthless to even engage in a minimal dialogue about these types of problems. In addition, these police officers seem uncertain as to whether there are moral justifications for the more severe forms of misconduct. The next section should give us additional clues, such as how general characteristics are or are not related to officers' perceptions of the seriousness of misconduct, the disciplinary measures it deserves, and the officers' willingness to report it.

## Controlling for Police Hierarchy and Officers' Number of Years of Experience and Functions

Table 3.3 presents results obtained from a bivariate analysis using the nonparametric Spearman rank correlation coefficient. But first, it must be known that in Quebec both hierarchy and police functions tend to vary together (Spearman rank correlation coefficient between the variable "hierarchy" and the variable "function" is .60, significant at $p < .001$). In other words, one will change function as he or she gets higher in the structure hierarchy, as well as he or she gets more experienced. We can thus analyze how these three elements affect the respondents' propensity to judge misconduct, to discipline it, and to report it.

A first general observation emerges from the analyses of the data presented in Table 3.3: The three control variables correlate more in the cases of the more benign scenarios and two of the more severe scenarios (Cases 3 and 11) than they do with those of the scenarios that fall in the middle of the rank ordering. One tempting explanation derives from the one proposed in the previous section: Cases 1, 2, and 4, for instance, can be described as basic examples of police corruption, examples that are often used by ranked officers to tell their troops what is expected of them. We hereby propose that attitudes correlate with the control variables because

of the necessity felt by ranked officers to serve as role models.

Another general observation can also be made: The propensity to report misconduct is almost invariably correlated with the three control variables, and this observation might serve as a message to Quebec's police organizations. In this case, the coefficients are positive everywhere; in other words, the more the respondent is ranked and placed in a higher hierarchical position, the more the respondent expresses his or her will to report misconduct. One can also note that "fairness" is negatively associated with the control variables in the first four scenarios (Cases 1, 2, 4, and 8). Since the variable "fairness" is constructed by subtracting the scores for the variable "should receive" from the variable "would receive," the negative correlation indicates that the higher a respondent is in the hierarchy and in terms of the number of years of experience, the less willing he or she is to express that discipline measures are not fair. This observation can also serve as yet another message: If punishment of corrupt behavior is considered by patrol officers as unfair, it may be a sign that the administration and supervising staff are also considered by the same patrol officers as somehow detached from the ground's preoccupations.[8]

We saw, in this chapter's first section, how Quebec's police organizations are characterized by the youth of their officers. This fact might be another part of the explanation for what we observe in Table 3.3. Perhaps the scenarios described in the survey, especially those that are considered less serious, may be more typical of the senior ranked officers' cultural frame of reference. It would be as if these corrupt behaviors were those they were confronted with at the start of their careers. We can also see in Cases 9 and 10 that the three control variables are not so heavily correlated with the attitudes in the scenarios. If the control variables in these cases are less often correlated with the

**Table 3.3**  Quebec Police Officers' Views About the Seriousness of the Misconduct, Whether It Violates Policy, the Discipline It Should and Would Receive, Officers' Willingness to Report It, and Fairness, With Three Control Variables

### Case 1 - Off-Duty Security System Business

|  | Hierarchy | Experience | Function |
|---|---|---|---|
| Seriousness - Own | (.11) | .11* | .20*** |
| Seriousness - Others | (.01) | (.07) | (.08) |
| Violation of Policy | (-.07) | -.11* | (.07) |
| Discipline - Should | (-.12) | (.02) | .14** |
| Discipline - Would | (-.10) | -.12* | (.04) |
| Report - Own | .21** | .11* | .26*** |
| Report - Others | (.03) | (.003) | (-.05) |
| Fairness | -.23*** | -.18*** | -.13* |

### Case 11 - Theft From Found Wallet

|  | Hierarchy | Experience | Function |
|---|---|---|---|
| Seriousness - Own | (.05) | (.04) | (.06) |
| Seriousness - Others | (-.03) | (.08) | (.04) |
| Violation of Policy | (.04) | (-.03) | (-.05) |
| Discipline - Should | .18* | .23*** | .21*** |
| Discipline - Would | (.08) | .16*** | .14** |
| Report - Own | .16* | (.09) | .20*** |
| Report - Others | (-.03) | (-.04) | -.12* |
| Fairness | (-.13) | (-.08) | -.11* |

### Case 10 - Excessive Force on Car Thief

|  | Hierarchy | Experience | Function |
|---|---|---|---|
| Seriousness - Own | (.04) | (.08) | .13** |
| Seriousness - Others | (.01) | (.05) | (.03) |
| Violation of Policy | (.03) | (.03) | .18*** |
| Discipline - Should | 14* | (.08) | .18*** |
| Discipline - Would | (.03) | (.05) | .13** |
| Report - Own | .20** | .18*** | .27*** |
| Report - Others | (-.02) | (-.06) | (-.08) |
| Fairness | (-.12) | (-.04) | (-.05) |

### Case 3 - Bribe From Speeding Motorist

|  | Hierarchy | Experience | Function |
|---|---|---|---|
| Seriousness - Own | (-.01) | (-.01) | (-.004) |
| Seriousness - Others | (-.02) | (-.05) | (.09) |
| Violation of Policy | (.06) | (-.01) | (.03) |
| Discipline - Should | .14* | .17*** | .19*** |
| Discipline - Would | (.04) | .11* | .10* |
| Report - Own | .20** | .10* | .26*** |
| Report - Others | (-.03) | (-.03) | -.11* |
| Fairness | -.14* | (-.05) | -.11* |

### Case 7 - Supervisor Grants Holiday in Exchange for Car Tune-Up

|  | Hierarchy | Experience | Function |
|---|---|---|---|
| Seriousness - Own | (.03) | (.04) | (.03) |
| Seriousness - Others | (.04) | (.06) | (.01) |
| Violation of Policy | (-.08) | (.04) | (.04) |
| Discipline - Should | (.05) | .12* | (.05) |
| Discipline - Would | (.11) | .17*** | (.03) |
| Report - Own | (.06) | .16*** | .10* |
| Report - Others | (.07) | (-.03) | (.01) |
| Fairness | (.05) | (.08) | (.01) |

### Case 5 - Crime Scene Theft of Watch

|  | Hierarchy | Experience | Function |
|---|---|---|---|
| Seriousness - Own | (-.07) | (-.03) | (.05) |
| Seriousness - Others | (-.10) | (-.03) | (-.01) |
| Violation of Policy | (.02) | (-.001) | (.07) |
| Discipline - Should | (.10) | .12* | (.02) |
| Discipline - Would | (.08) | .15*** | (-.08) |
| Report - Own | .14* | (.03) | .19*** |
| Report - Others | (.02) | (.01) | -.10* |
| Fairness | (-.04) | (.06) | -.10* |

### Case 2 - Free-Meals and Discounts on Beat

|  | Hierarchy | Experience | Function |
|---|---|---|---|
| Seriousness - Own | (.12) | .19*** | .26*** |
| Seriousness - Others | (-.07) | .14** | .10* |
| Violation of Policy | (.05) | (.04) | .23*** |
| Discipline - Should | .15* | .20*** | .25*** |
| Discipline - Would | (.03) | (.07) | .13** |
| Report - Own | .22*** | .25*** | .31*** |
| Report - Others | (-.01) | -.11* | (-.07) |
| Fairness | -.14* | -.14** | -.10* |

### Case 6 - 5% Kickback From Auto Repair Shop

|  | Hierarchy | Experience | Function |
|---|---|---|---|
| Seriousness - Own | (.09) | (.04) | (.03) |
| Seriousness - Others | (-.07) | (.0001) | (-.03) |
| Violation of Policy | (.04) | (-.001) | (.08) |
| Discipline - Should | (.05) | .11* | (.09) |
| Discipline - Would | (-.05) | (.09) | (.08) |
| Report - Own | .18** | .15** | .21*** |
| Report - Others | (-.03) | (-.06) | (-.05) |
| Fairness | -.21** | (-.01) | (-.03) |

### Case 4 - Holiday Gifts From Merchants

|  | Hierarchy | Experience | Function |
|---|---|---|---|
| Seriousness - Own | (.09) | .14** | .19*** |
| Seriousness - Others | (-.07) | (.03) | (.004) |
| Violation of Policy | (.04) | (.09) | .14** |
| Discipline - Should | (.05) | .12* | .11* |
| Discipline - Would | (-.10) | (.03) | (.03) |
| Report - Own | .18** | .17*** | .23*** |
| Report - Others | (-.03) | (-.09) | (-.02) |
| Fairness | -.21** | -.11* | (-.09) |

### Case 9 - Free Drinks to Ignore Late Bar Closing

|  | Hierarchy | Experience | Function |
|---|---|---|---|
| Seriousness - Own | (-.03) | (-.04) | (.07) |
| Seriousness - Others | -.22*** | (-.08) | (-.05) |
| Violation of Policy | (.10) | (.03) | .17*** |
| Discipline - Should | (-.01) | (.03) | (.07) |
| Discipline - Would | (-.11) | (.03) | (.003) |
| Report - Own | (.11) | (.07) | .22*** |
| Report - Others | (.04) | (.04) | (-.05) |
| Fairness | -.17* | (.02) | (-.08) |

### Case 8 - Cover-Up of Police DUI Accident

|  | Hierarchy | Experience | Function |
|---|---|---|---|
| Seriousness - Own | (-.05) | -.12* | (-.06) |
| Seriousness - Others | (-.07) | -.11* | (-.07) |
| Violation of Policy | (.001) | (-.07) | (.07) |
| Discipline - Should | (.11) | (-.01) | .14** |
| Discipline - Would | (-.01) | -.12* | (.07) |
| Report - Own | .17* | (.06) | .22*** |
| Report - Others | (-.01) | (.06) | (.01) |
| Fairness | -.15* | -.11* | (-.06) |

*p <= .05 ; **p < = .01 ; ***p < = .001
Note: Spearman's rank correlation; nonsignificant coefficients are in parentheses.

attitude variables, we can interpret that any of the other elements not taken into account here may constitute the explanation or that it reflects a more solid consensus among respondents. This last type of explanation fits Case 5 (Crime Scene Theft of Watch) best: Because this scenario is ranked as the most serious misconduct, it is logical to assess that respondents are more consensual in their attitudes toward this behavior, whether we look at it from the perspective of its seriousness, the degree to which it should be punished, or the number of officers willing to report it.

## CONCLUSION

We have shown, in this exploratory study, how officers from a small sample randomly selected from throughout Quebec's police agencies differ in their cultural attitudes and in characteristics regarding the degree to which they would report and punish unethical or corrupt behavior from a colleague. While younger and less experienced officers are less prone to report and to punish relatively minor misconduct, a consensus among officers emerges where the types of misconduct are more serious.

One could offer here the somewhat cynical explanation that the more experienced a police officer gets, the more he or she is likely to have developed a capacity to answer these kinds of questions in the "expected" way. We might, however, look at things in a rather more pragmatic way. The more compliant officers are more experienced, and our data show that these officers also occupy a higher position in the hierarchy. The literature has long since shown that the higher a police officer gets in the hierarchy, the less he or she tends to adhere to the core culture of the police institution (Frank, McConkey, Huon, Hesketh, & McGrath, 1995a; Manning & Redlinger, 1991; Reiner, 1992). Even more

pragmatically, though, the fact also remains that these officers have fewer contacts with the population and the more common everyday police duties than do younger officers, so it might be easier for them to put in a broader perspective situations such as those described in the scenarios of the survey tool. Our results seem to confirm Reiner's (1992) idea that the solidarity/isolation complex is not shared equally by all officers. Therefore, some thought and effort should be devoted to the whole socialization process as an essential part of strategies aimed at better controlling police misconduct.

The question now stands: Is Quebec's strategy for such control likely to attain its goals? The fact is that this strategy remains solely oriented toward repressive action, whether we look at it from the angle of the article in the Police Act (which makes it compulsory for police officers to report instances of misconduct on the part of colleagues) or from the existence, since 1990, of Quebec's Police Ethics Commissioner (which is an administrative tribunal independent of police organizations that is responsible for the treatment of citizens' complaints). In other words, is ethics a concept that can only be enforced and imposed? Kennison (2002) and Lewis (1999) have shown the detrimental effects of such a one-sided strategy: the reenforcement of a somewhat cynical and suspicious attitude toward the law, its institutions, and the public by police officers and, more dramatically, the ambivalence of those same police officers to act when it is clearly needed, fearing the unintended consequences of having to face up to the responsibility for their actions. It should not be thought that police officers would never report misconduct; we had numerous occasions, during the first stages of this research, to discuss these matters at length with the officers in the focus groups. From their perspective, it remains essential to deal as swiftly as possible with police who have the kind of attitude that might lead to corruption, but, on the other hand, the officers made it clear that they would always favor a process that would remain mostly unknown to the public so as to minimize the risk that one individual's faults would be seen by the public as the organization's failures. Therefore, repressive action and measures must be accompanied by more preventive and educative measures aimed at the police as well as the public. Thus the chances are that both the police and the public will see that at least something is being done to break down their cynical view that nothing can change (Frank et al., 1995a).

In conclusion, this exploratory study points to three avenues of further investigation. First, future research efforts should be devoted to better understanding how to create specific training for recruits in handling officers' ethical dilemmas, using situations that are as close as possible to real police work. Frank, McConkey, Huon, Hesketh, & McGrath (1995b) and Nadeau (2001) show,

from qualitative research in two different countries, the small extent to which officers actually think ethical training is close enough to real situations. Second, as Alpert and Macdonald (2001) and Newburn (1999) suggest, researchers must pay attention to how police organizations cope with problems such as the excessive use of force; little is known about how different police structures in different countries and different operating contexts manage these problems. Research in this field could help identify the best practices and strategies. Third, since our data lead us to the conclusion that the less experienced officers seem to be those who get more easily impregnated with the traditional core culture of the police institution, research may also help to identify the best ways to cope effectively with this phenomenon, thus ensuring an effective replacement of retiring officers by other officers already at a higher stage with regard to morals and work ethics.

## NOTES

1. The following is from the report of the Public Inquiry Commission appointed to inquire into the Sûreté du Québec (1998):

99.

The Government amend the *Police Act* or the *Act respecting police organization* in order to expressly provide for the right of an officer to expose the misconduct of a colleague, a superior, even the Director General, if this is likely to challenge the bonds of trust between the Government and the officer in question or to give rise to a disciplinary complaint;

100.

The *Police Act* or the *Act respecting police organization* provide that any harassment, intimidation or reprisals, or attempt or conspiracy in this connection, of and against an officer having made a denunciation or members of his family be strictly prohibited. (p. 69)

2. More than 2 years after its enactment, Article 260 of the Police Act had been cited only once in court (*Meunier v. Monty*, C.S. Montreal 500–05–052318–993, May 30, 2001) and even in this specific instance the article is only referred to indirectly, in comparison with the preexisting Common Law regarding the matters at hand.

3. This kind of problem was also noted by Frank, McConkey, Huon, Hesketh, and McGrath (1995) in their study of the individual perspective on police ethics in the police departments of South Australia, Queensland, and New South Wales.

4. The six themes are as follows: (1) general attitudes toward the use of force; (2) use of force behavior in officers' departments; (3) the code of silence; (4) the impact of demeanor, race, and socioeconomic status on police behavior; (5) the impact of measures intended at controlling abuses of authority; and (6) the impact of community policing on instances of abuse of authority.

5. Before the January 2002 reform, the 1999 estimate counted 126 of these sometimes very small police departments. The 2002 municipal reform forced villages and small cities to unite their police departments into fewer than 40 bigger organizations in order to diminish the costs associated with duplication and overlapping jurisdictions.

6. Cooperation was not necessarily granted, however: Of the three main components of Quebec's police structure, one was reluctant to the point that the whole sample cannot be said to be representative in terms of an equal three-thirds apportionment. One of the conditions requested by all the participating organizations was that we would never publish any results that exposed the differences between these organizations; a similar assurance was given by Klockars and his colleagues (2000, p. 5) in their work—and even then some agencies declined to participate.

7. On the other hand, as Crank and Caldero (2000) and Zhao, He, and Lovrich (1998) clearly suggest, attitudes from these segments of a police population might very well represent the core attitudes of even the younger police officers, confirming here earlier findings by Wilson (1968), who wrote that "within it [the police department] discretion increases as one moves down the hierarchy" (p. 7). An important argument in favor of such an assumption is the fact that when we compared police cadets' attitudes with those of sworn officers, out of six general themes (from attitudes toward the abuse of force to the importance of the code of silence) only one showed significant differences on chi-square tests. This theme explores the relationship between the implementation of community policing and the control of abuse of authority; here, police cadets showed more enthusiasm than did their more experienced counterparts.

8. We (Alain, 2000, 2001) had numerous occasions to verify this assertion in qualitative fieldwork. One one hand, the administrators too often refuse to adapt the structure and the rules to fit more adequately the realities of what is happening in the patrol officer's routine, while, on the other hand, police culture is also too often paralyzed and resistant to change.

---

# REFERENCES

Alain, M. (2000). Les heurts et les bonheurs de la coopération policière international en Europe, entre la myopie des bureaucrates et la sclérose culturelle policière. *Déviance et Société, 24*(3), 237-253.

Alain, M. (2001). The trapeze artist and the ground crew: Police cooperation and intelligence exchange mechanisms in Europe and in North America. A comparative empirical study. *Policing and Society, 11*, 1-27.

Alpert, G. P., & MacDonald, J. M. (2001, June). Police use of force: An analysis of organizational characteristics. *Justice Quarterly, 18*(2), 393-409.

Bellemare, J. (1996). *Les pratiques policières en matière d'enquêtes criminelles au sein des corps de police du Québec.* Sainte-Foy, Quebec: Les Publications du Québec.

Brodeur, J.-P. (1984). *La délinquance de l'ordre*. Montreal: Hurtubise HMH.

Caldero, M. (1997, March). *Value consistency within the police: The lack of a gap*. Paper presented at the annual meeting of the Academy of Criminal Justice Sciences, Louisville, KY.

Crank, J. P. (1998). *Understanding police culture*. Cincinnati, OH: Anderson.

Crank, J. P., & Caldero, A. (2000). *Police ethics: The corruption of noble cause*. Cincinnati, OH: Anderson.

Dixon, D. (1999). *A culture of corruption: Changing an Australian police service*. Sydney: Hawkins.

Frank, M. G., McConkey, K. M., Huon, G. F., Hesketh, B. L., & McGrath, G. M. (1995a). Perceptions of ethical dilemmas. *Ethics and policing* (Study-1, Report series no. 125.1). Payneham, AU: National Police Research Unit.

Frank, M. G., McConkey, K. M., Huon, G. F., Hesketh, B. L., & McGrath, G. M. (1995b). Individual perspectives on police ethics. *Ethics and policing* (Study-2, Report series no. 125.2). Payneham, AU: National Police Research Unit.

Greene, J. R., Bergman, W. T., & McLaughlin, E. J. (1994). *Implementing community policing: Cultural and structural change in police organization*. In D. P. Rosenbaum (Ed.), *The challenge of community policing*. Thousand Oaks, CA: Sage.

Keable, J. (1981). *Rapport de la Commission d'enquête sur les opérations policières en territoire québécois*. Sainte-Foy, Quebec : Les Publications du Québec.

Kennison, P. C. (2002). Policing diversity–managing complaints against the police. *The Police Journal, 75*, 117-135.

Klockars, C. B., Kutnjak Ivkovich, S. H., Harver, W. E., & Haberfeld, M. R. (1997). *The measurement of police integrity: Final report*. Washington, DC: National Institute of Justice.

Klockars, C. B., Kutnjak Ivkovich, S., Harver, W. E., & Haberfeld, M. R. (2000). *The measurement of police integrity*. Washington, DC: National Institute of Justice.

Knapp, W. (1972). *The Knapp Commission report on police corruption*. New York: Georges Braziller.

Kutnjak Ivkovich, S., Klockars, C. B., & Harver, W. E. (1995). *Cross-cultural study of police corruption: Perceptions of offense seriousness; police perceptions of disciplinary fairness and code of silence*. Paper presented at the 47th annual meeting of the America Society of Criminology. Boston, Massachusetts.

Lewis, C. (1999). *Complaints against police: The politics of reform*. Sydney: Hawkins.

Lipovetski, G. (1992). *Le crépuscule du devoir*. Paris: Gallimard.

Manning, P. K., & Redlinger, L. J. (1991). *Invitational edges*. In C. B. Klockars & S. D. Mastrovski (Eds.), *Thinking about police*. New York: McGraw-Hill.

Ministry of Public Security. (1999). *Statistiques des corps de police du Québec*. Sainte-Foy, Quebec: Les Publications du Québec.

Mollen, M. (1994). *Commission report: Commission to Investigate Allegations of Police Corruption and the Anti-Corruption Procedures of the Police Department*. New York: The City of New York.

Nadeau, J. (2001). *L'utilisation du soutien social par les policiers-patrouilleurs vivant du stress chronique au travail*. Unpublished master's thesis, Faculty of Social Sciences, Université Laval, Quebec.

Newburn, T. (1999). Understanding and preventing police corruption: Lessons from the literature. *Police research series* (Paper 110). London: Policing and Reducing Crime Unit.

Poitras, L. (1998). *Pour une police au service de l'intégrité et de la justice*. Sainte-Foy, Quebec: Les Publications du Québec.

Punch, M., Huberts, L., & Lamboo, T. (2000). *Perceptions on integrity of Dutch police officers in comparative perspective.* Paper presented at the IIPE conference Ethics in the New Millennium, Ottawa.

Reiner, R. (1992). *The politics of the police.* Toronto: University of Toronto Press.

Roberge, D. (2001). *Rapport d'enquête sur la mort suspecte de Achille Volant et de Moïse Régis.* Sainte-Foy, Quebec: Les Publications du Québec.

Rokeach, M., Miller, M., & Snyder, J. (1971). The value gap between police and policed. *Journal of Social Issues, 27*(2), 155-171.

Weisburd, D., Greenspan, R., Hamilton, E. E., Bryant, K. A., & Williams, H. (2001). *The abuse of police authority: A national study of police officer's attitudes.* Washington, DC: The Police Foundation.

Weisburd, D., Greenspan, R., Hamilton, E. E., Williams, H., & Bryant, K. A. (2000). *Police attitudes toward abuse of authority: Findings from a national study.* Washington, DC: National Institute of Justice.

Wilson, J. Q. (1968). *Varieties of police behavior.* Cambridge, MA: Harvard University Press.

Zhao, J., He, N., & Lovrich, N. P. (1998). Individual value preferences among American police officers: The Rokeach theory of human values revisited. *Policing: An International Journal of Police Strategies and Management, 21,* 22-36.

CHAPTER 4

# Police Integrity in Croatia

Sanja Kutnjak Ivković

Carl B. Klockars

## INTRODUCTION

Croatia embarked on the road to independence in the early 1990s. The journey has been far from smooth: The country has experienced a defensive war against the aggression of the Serb-dominated Yugoslav Army and various paramilitary troops; the influx of refugees from Bosnia and Herzegovina; a decade-long governance of a strong, right-wing-oriented political party; the strengthening of nationalism; a legacy of continuous mismanagement of the economy; the transition to a market economy; and a high unemployment rate. All these factors shape the environment in which the Croatian police operate, and these factors have a strong impact on the state of police integrity.

The Croatian police are among the youngest police in Europe; they were established in the early 1990s. Before 1991, the police role in Croatia was performed by the old, communist-style Yugoslav militia. On the eve of the war in Croatia in the early 1990s, when Croatia was still a republic within the former Yugoslavia, the Croatian Ministry of the Interior was the only legitimate

armed force. Facing a clash between the need to establish an army in order to defend the country in case of an increasingly likely war and the legal impossibility of doing so, the Croatian Parliament passed the necessary statutory changes to facilitate the establishment of the National Guard Corps (NGC) as a police service within the Ministry of the Interior. Police officers constituted a large portion of the staff of the NGC and, for a period of almost 2 years, the police performed both the defense role and the role of the regular police (Kutnjak Ivkovich, 2000).

The Croatian police, a part of the Ministry of the Interior, are headed by the Chief of Police (Police Law, 2001). The organization of the police is centralized; that is, it is a pyramidal structure with the police headquarters at the top, followed by 20 police administrations, followed by approximately 200 police stations at the bottom of the organizational chart. The police presently employ approximately 20,000 sworn officers, or 4.28 police officers per 1,000 inhabitants.

Police integrity in Croatia is molded by a complex network of heterogeneous factors.

This chapter analyzes the societal factors external to the police agency and the impact they have on police integrity, as well as internal factors—those indigenous to the police themselves—and their resulting effects. The second part of this chapter provides an empirical analysis of survey data measuring the level of police integrity among the Croatian police.

## SOCIETAL FACTORS IN CORRUPTION CONTROL

### The War

The war that started in Croatia in mid-1991, followed by the war in the neighboring Bosnia and Herzegovina in the spring of 1992, has had severe economic, social, and ethical consequences. To begin with, in addition to the lives lost[1] and tens of billions of dollars in war damages,[2] the war had other serious economic consequences: a substantially increased portion of the GNP devoted to the war-related purposes;[3] sizeable resources allocated to the support of refugees and displaced persons from Croatia, Bosnia, and Herzegovina;[4] a sharp decline in the standard of living;[5] and a high unemployment rate.[6]

The war-related expenses occupied a prominent role on the list of expenditures in the state budget, and the police probably experienced the scarcity of resources for the items that were not crucial. The areas that were likely affected included control of police misconduct, training for both police officers and supervisors, quality of supervision, and salaries. Furthermore, the impoverishment of the society made the citizens and the police officers more in need of, and willing to, "cut corners."

In terms of social and ethical consequences, the war resulted in the displacement of a large number of inhabitants, disrupted the established system of social values, created a sense of solidarity in both the police and the larger society, and enhanced the existing nationalist sentiment. These effects of the war were felt by the police and the public. Old social values from the Communist regime were relinquished and new ones were not established. Furthermore, the war relaxed the standard of acceptable police behavior. The reality of destruction of life and property on a mass scale, as well as war-related atrocities, diverted public focus away from street-level corruption and police deviance.

The war also caused substantial organizational changes within the police. For a period of at least a year, the police were assigned a dual role—the military role and the regular police role, the fulfillment of which required (1) rapidly mobilizing a large number of recruits to fight the war (most of whom, because of the legal boundaries, had to be hired as employees of the Ministry of the Interior) and (2) choosing recruits to fill a large number of suddenly available police positions, especially at the detective rank.[7] Consequently, the recruitment criteria were relaxed and refocused, training was either shifted or omitted completely, police officers were promoted into the supervisory ranks without substantial experience, discipline of police officers was relaxed, and the code of silence (an informal prohibition against reporting fellow police officers for police misconduct) was strengthened.

## THE TRANSITION PROCESS AND THE EXTENT OF CORRUPTION

The mismanagement of the state-controlled economy under the Communist regime, coupled with the war-related problems, illegal practices by the ruling elite in the process of transition,[8] and the bankruptcy of a large number of the state-run companies, created a complex economic environment in which corruption could flourish. Derenčinović (2000) described the postwar situation as it relates to corruption:

> The weakening of solidarity among the people is more or less a normal phenomenon after a period of very intensified solidarity and the above-average sense of social closeness during the aggression on the Republic of Croatia and the homeland war. The time of enthusiasm, optimism, and affirmation of positive feelings of mutual solidarity of people drawn by the same global goals, is regularly followed by shorter or longer periods of skepticism, indifference, and egoism. This [experience] is intensified by the majority of the population who participated in the achievement of these global goals by the feeling of being tricked, i.e., marginalized in favor of war profiteers, tycoons, and other now important and previously marginal segments of society. This is coupled with the weaknesses, both objective and subjective, in the operation of the police and courts, and especially the inability of these institutions to establish the previous equilibrium, normal social order, and the system in which the good ones are rewarded and the bad ones are held responsible and punished. (p. 363)

In the introduction to his 1999 monograph on corruption, Josip Kregar, President of the Croatian Chapter of the Transparency International, summarized the level of corruption in the Croatian society in the following way:

> Croatia is a corrupt country. Corruption is widespread; it is a part of the political system and neither economy nor public services can operate without it; it is supported by cultural norms, we have no systematic defense nor institutions assigned to deal with it; there exists neither a serious standard nor a common belief in honesty [or integrity] as a basis for politics, law, [and] public service institutions. (p. 11)

There are indeed a number of indicators that corruption in Croatia may be widespread. In 1999, the first time that it was included in the Transparency International Corruption Perceptions Index, Croatia ranked 74th out of 99 countries, with the score of 2.7. The 2000 and 2001 indexes placed Croatia more than 20 positions higher (the 51st and 47th position, respectively) and closer to the middle of the scale (Transparency International, 1999, 2000, 2001). This rapid improvement reflects the fact that the political scenery in Croatia had changed in those 2 years (the 2000 elections ended the decade-long rule of a right-wing government). Indeed, the new government seems to be more willing to deal with the obstacles that have prevented the admission into the European Union (including corruption), the volume of foreign investments has increased, and government reform and efforts have been at least partly successful in improving macroeconomic indicators. Although the government has shown a stronger resolve to deal with corruption, as Derenčinović (2001) has stated, "at the same time, improvements on the Transparency International Index are followed neither by the quality changes in the policies on corruption prevention, improvements in the conflict-of-interest legislation, investigative journalism, nor resistance in other segments of civil society" (p. 238).

Croatia also participated in the 1997 International Crime Victim Survey (ICVS). The respondents, citizens of Zagreb (the capital), were asked about their recent crime-related experience. One of the survey questions asked the respondents whether they had been asked to pay a bribe last year; 15% of the respondents said that they did (Kutnjak Ivkovich, 2001). This finding indicates that the extent of corruption in Croatia is substantially higher than it is in Western democracies (less than 5% of respondents in the United States, Canada, the United Kingdom, the

Netherlands, Switzerland, Austria, and Malta reported having done the same). The ICVS puts Croatia in the category of those Eastern European countries more prone to corruption.

Derenčinović (2000, 2001) conducted another empirical study that can be used as an illustration of the extent of corruption in Croatia. A convenience sample of 76 citizens from the capital perceived corruption to be prevalent: 65.8% reported it to be "very widespread" and an additional 32.9% reported it to be "widespread" (Derenčinović, 2000, p. 359). In fact, 40.8% wrote that they had a personal corruption-related experience, and 30.3% reported that they had paid a bribe (Derenčinović, 2000, p. 367).

## *Legal Rules and Their Enforcement*

In the post-Communist period, the war and the lack of time and resources effectively postponed an extensive reform of the criminal law. The existing laws, dating back to the Communist regime, were continuously changed and updated to fit the new social and political conditions, resulting, for example, in a revised version of the Criminal Code in 1996. The extensive reform, completed in 1997, yielded two new statutes crucial for corruption control: the new Criminal Procedure Code (1997) and the Criminal Code (1997).

The changes in the Criminal Code (1997) were quite substantial with respect to certain issues. It guaranteed citizens a more extensive set of rights through the introduction of a stricter set of regulations of official conduct, but the changes it instituted with respect to corruption were limited because the basic criminal offenses ("Abuse of Office and Official Authority" and "Acceptance of a Bribe") existed in the previous versions of the code.

A separate section in the Criminal Code is devoted to the crimes against official duty. One of the basic offenses is titled "Abuse of Office and Official Authority" (Article 337). It serves as the grounds for criminally charging any public official who abuses the office, oversteps the limits of official authority, or fails to perform official duty with the aim of obtaining pecuniary gain or other nonpecuniary benefit. Furthermore, in Article 347, the code explicitly prohibits the acceptance of a bribe ("gift or some other benefit") by any public official (which implicitly includes police officers) either for the violation of official duties (i.e., not doing something the official was supposed to do or doing something the official was not supposed to do) or for conduct in accordance with official duties (i.e., not doing something the official was not supposed to do or doing something the official was supposed to do).

According to the experts from the European Union, the old criminal procedure legislation was woefully inadequate for successful intrusion into the dark numbers of corruption and into organized crime in general (Sačić, 1998, p. 14). Revisions of the rules of criminal procedure potentially relevant for corruption had to be far more extensive. The new criminal procedure legislation provides a special set of rules, titled "Temporary Restriction on the Constitutional Rights and Freedoms for the Purpose of Collecting Data and Evidence in Criminal Proceedings" (Article 181, Criminal Procedure Code, 1997). These rules apply to a narrow subset of explicitly enumerated offenses, including acceptance of a bribe and abuse of office, as well as any offense punishable by at least 5 years of imprisonment if reasonable suspicion exists that it has been prepared or already committed by a criminal organization. The range of measures introduced by this law, with the purpose of providing more efficient and effective resources to the police, include surveillance, wiretapping, the use of undercover operations, and sting operations. These measures significantly expand the

**Table 4.1**    Corruption-Related Cases in Croatia From 1992 to 1997

|  | *1992* | *1993* | *1994* | *1995* | *1996* | *1997* | *Total* |
|---|---|---|---|---|---|---|---|
| Initiated | 594 | 594 | 598 | 543 | 535 | 452 | 3,316 |
| Sentenced | 142 | 107 | 115 | 84 | 76 | 46 | 570 |
| (Percentage Initiated) | (23.9%) | (18.0%) | (19.2%) | (15.5%) | (14.2%) | (10.2%) | (17.2%) |
| Suspensioned Sentence (Percentage Sentenced) | 107 (75.4%) | 89 (83.2%) | 84 (73.0%) | 55 (65.5%) | 57 (75.0%) | 38 (82.6%) | 430 (75.4%) |

Note: The data in this table are based on information in Derenčinović, 2001 (pp. 228-231).

mechanisms legally available to the police to collect evidence and information in the course of conducting criminal investigations, especially in instances in which the inquiry into criminal acts could otherwise not be carried out or would be burdened with disproportionate difficulties.

Thus, this expanded availability of investigative methods, coupled with the existing criminal-law regulation, can serve as a stable ground for punishment of public officials and citizens who engage in corruption. A more important issue, however, is to what extent these novel investigative methods are used and the criminal rules enforced in reality. The answer to this question is of crucial importance for corruption control; if norms of the criminal law are not enforced, then the message sent by the criminal justice system undermines their importance in the eyes of both society at large and public officials' potential partners in corrupt transactions.

The number of reported corruption-related cases was stable over the 6-year period preceding the reform of criminal laws. Approximately 500 to 600 cases have been initiated each year (see Table 4.1). Out of the total of 3,316 cases, the prosecutors brought charges in only 39% of the cases (1,408) (Derenčinović, 2001, p. 229). The stated reason for the state prosecutors' decision not to prosecute was either that the conduct did

not constitute a crime prosecutable ex officio (49.7%) or that there was no reasonable suspicion that the defendant committed the crime (38.9%) (Derenčinović, 2001, p. 229). Less than half of those prosecuted were finally convicted (40.2%). In sum, the defendant was sentenced in less than a quarter of all the reported cases (as shown in the second row in Table 4.1) and in the majority of these cases, the defendant received a suspended sentence (as shown in the third row in Table 4.1).

Thus, in a country perceived to be corrupt, where, according to the ICVS estimates, 15% of the respondents were asked to pay a bribe last year, corruption-related cases are initiated each year against less than 0.02% of the adult population. Although this discrepancy seems large, its existence should not be surprising. After all, corruption seems to share the fate of other "invisible offenses"[9] (invisible to traditional law enforcement methods, that is), in which neither of the parties involved has an interest in reporting the offense.

If corruption-related cases are reported at all, they reach the sentencing stage in only a minority of cases (17.2% overall), and then the sentences are relatively mild (a suspended sentence is the outcome in the overwhelming majority of the cases). The sentencing policies that are actually enforced by the courts are far from the legislative sentencing policies established in the statutes; most of the sentences meted out are close to the legal minimums, while the harshest punishment is rarely, if ever, applied (Derenčinović, 2001, p. 233).

Public opinion polls record the discrepancy between the actual extent of corruption and the officially recorded corruption, especially at the highest levels of the government. According to 60% of the respondents in a study conducted by the magazine *Globus* in 1997, the state did not have the resolve to deal with corruption at high levels (Butković, 1997, p. 15). At one point, even the late President Tudjman had to suspend 33 highly ranked members of his ruling party (the Croatian Democratic Union) because they were under investigation for embezzlement. The scandals continued, especially after the Croatian Democratic Union was strongly defeated in the 2000 elections.

## The Role of the
## Public in Corruption Control

The public has a dual role in corruption control. First, through various methods of direct and indirect democracy (e.g., by selection of political leaders, holding public officials accountable, passing ambiguous laws, and/or creating scandals), the public determines the acceptable level of corruption in the society. Second, citizens usually constitute the other side in corrupt transactions with officials.

The role they played during the war endowed the police and the army in Croatia with a very positive, idealized image not only during the war but, to a certain degree, in the postwar period as well. According to the *World Values Survey* conducted in Croatia in 1995, 78.4% of the respondents reported "a great deal" or "quite a lot" of confidence in the armed forces, and 60.4% of the respondents reported the same confidence in the police (*World Values Survey*, 1995).

However, the postwar experience of disillusionment described by Derenčinović (2000, p. 363), coupled with the lack of serious determination to control the level of corruption, has affected public opinion about the police. The confidence in the armed forces and the police had weakened by 1999. While the *European Values Survey* conducted in 1999 indicated that 62.2% of the respondents said that they had "a great deal" or "quite a lot" of confidence in the armed forces, only 46.4% said the same for the police (*European Values Survey—Croatia*, 1999).

If the society at large accepts networking and corruption as rules rather than exceptions to the rules, sticking to these unofficial rules may be an important determinant of an individual's success. Čehok and Veič (2000) have explained this situation as follows:

> The word is that it is necessary to have contacts, even for the simplest interaction with the state administration and public services, and even if the cases involve requests that have to be approved [and may not be denied], like the issuance of various documents. Many people share the opinion that, based the contact with the "right" people, it is possible to do anything, even things that are otherwise impossible to achieve or things that are otherwise forbidden. The existence of such a state of affairs and such a shared perception among the people are the bases for the acceptance of an award for the services (bribe) and [the existence of] the favors market. (p. 107)

Empirical studies indicate that a substantial portion of Croatia's citizens are willing to engage in corruption. Indeed, 15% of the respondents surveyed in the International Crime Victimization Surveys reported being asked to pay a bribe last year (Kutnjak Ivkovich, 2001), and over 30% of the respondents in another study (using a convenience sample) said that they paid a bribe to a public official (Derenčinović, 2000, p. 367). At the same time, none of the respondents in the latter study said that they reported the transaction to the police.

## The Role of the Media in Corruption Control

The media can serve as a powerful ally in the process of corruption control, an alternative source of information about corruption, a viable outlet for the spread of the anticorruption deterrent message, and a force for change in public opinion. Western agencies evaluated that, "despite these provisions [guaranteeing freedom of thought and expression and freedom of the press and other media], the media [in Croatia] were controlled and journalists were harassed by the government throughout 1999" (*Freedom in the World 1999-2000: Croatia*, 2000). The situation may have changed since the establishment of the new government in 2000, although no empirical studies are available to assess this possibility.

Although Croatia has recently been evaluated as only "partially free" in terms of political and civil rights (*Freedom in the World 1992-2000: Croatia*, 2000), the media have played a watchdog role in Croatia. First, they served as a source of information in 1.5% of Croatia's Internal Affairs division's completed cases in 2000. Second, like the story published in *Globus* at the end of 2001 (Ivanović, 2001), they drew the attention of the public, politicians, and police to the discourse about corruption and to the actual cases of corruption in Croatia.

## INTERNAL FACTORS IN CORRUPTION CONTROL

### The Enforcement of Legal Rules

Because the police in Croatia are a national police, the conduct of police officers is regulated by the acts of Parliament. Criminal norms prohibiting corrupt behavior of public officials apply to the police. The existing criminal norms provide sufficient grounds for the prosecution and punishment of various forms of police corruption, including corruption of authority, kickbacks, shakedowns, protection of illegal activity, and internal payoffs.[10] The new rules of criminal procedure allow the police to use surveillance, wiretapping, and undercover operations (if certain conditions are met) and thus enhance their ability to detect and investigate corruption committed by their own.

Any citizen has the right to submit a complaint, if the citizen perceives that his or her rights have been violated by the police (Article 6, Police Law, 2001) and, based on Article 112 of the Criminal Code, police officers can be charged criminally if they abuse their office with the purpose of preventing citizens from submitting complaints (Pavišić & Veić, 1996, pp. 83-84). The task of detecting and investigating misconduct by police officers is placed in the hands of their supervisors and the Office of Internal Control within the Ministry of the Interior. The Office of Internal Affairs investigates only a small subset of the initiated cases (e.g., more complex cases, cases against police officers in the police headquarters), while the bulk of the cases are investigated by the heads of the respective police administrations.

The overwhelming majority of investigations by Internal Affairs are reactive. Out of all the cases received, coordinated, or investigated by Internal Affairs in 2000, 81.6% were initiated based on either internally or externally generated complaints. If at the end of the investigation there is reasonable suspicion that the police officer committed a crime, the case is forwarded to the criminal police for criminal investigation.

Unfortunately, it is impossible to extract the data about the number of police officers investigated for corruption-related offenses from the overall number of initiated disciplinary proceedings provided to us by the Ministry (see Table 4.2). Each year, between 2,000 and 5,000 disciplinary proceedings are initiated against police officers. The number of

**Table 4.2**     Disciplinary Proceedings Initiated Against Police Officers in Croatia From 1992 to 1999

|  | *1992* | *1993* | *1994* | *1995* | *1996* | *1997* | *1998* | *1999* |
|---|---|---|---|---|---|---|---|---|
| Number of Officers Charged With Serious Violations | 1,666 72.7% | 1,988 68.8% | 2,040 41.6% | 1,847 36.5% | 1,279 35.6% | 1,114 — | 1,161 — | 1,293 — |
| Number of Officers Charged With Minor Violations | 625 27.3% | 902 31.2% | 2,870 58.4% | 3,214 63.5% | 2,394 65.4% | N/A | N/A | N/A |
| Total Number of Officers Charged | 2,291 100% | 2,890 100% | 4,914 100% | 5,061 100% | 3,673 100% | N/A | N/A | N/A |

Source: Croatian Ministry of the Interior.

cases concerning serious violations has been stable over the years, while the number of cases with minor violations increased substantially after the war ended (e.g., from 625 cases in 1992 to 3,214 cases in 1995; see Table 4.2), probably reflecting stricter enforcement of official rules in the postwar period.

As the ratio of disciplinary proceedings initiated for serious violations to the proceedings initiated for minor violations has decreased, the number of disciplinary proceedings in which the police officer was found in violation (i.e., "total discipline cases") followed a different path: it increased slightly at the beginning and then started to decrease. Interestingly, the rate of dismissal remains relatively stable (around 10%) and the most frequent discipline meted out is a fine (see Table 4.3).

Sačić (1998) analyzed the nature of corruption-related *criminal cases,* in which there was an arrest, in the period immediately preceding the legislative reform. In this period of almost 3 calendar years (from January 1, 1995 to December 1, 1997), the overall number of corruption-related cases with arrests was, on average, below 600 per year (see Table 4.4). Among the corruption-related offenses, the overwhelming majority

(81%) included the basic one—the abuse of office and official authority.[11] Although police officers were defendants in only 10.4% of all the corruption-related cases (Sačić, 1998, p. 10), for the crime of bribe acceptance, a quarter of the defendants were police officers. In absolute terms, 46 police officers had been charged with accepting a bribe in the 3-year period.

How do these annual official statistics— 15 police officers charged with the acceptance of a bribe and thousands of initiated disciplinary cases—compare with the actual extent of corruption? Since the actual extent of corruption is not known, in the following we rely on estimates of its extent. The only study that offers such an estimate, albeit indirectly, is the International Crime Victimization Survey. Its results indicate that 6.84% of citizens said that they have been asked to provide a bribe to a police officer last year (see Kutnjak Ivkovich, 2001).

Assuming that these estimates can be extended to the general population over age 18 (approximately three quarters of the 4.7 million inhabitants of Croatia), the figure of 6.84% corresponds to approximately 240,000 citizens saying that they paid a bribe to a police officer last year. It is clear that

**Table 4.3**    Outcomes of Disciplinary Proceedings and Criminal Cases Initiated Against Police
Officers in Croatia From 1992 to 1999

|  | *1992* | *1993* | *1994* | *1995* | *1996* | *1997* | *1998* | *1999* |
|---|---|---|---|---|---|---|---|---|
| Public Reprimand | 251 18.6% | 401 20.0% | — | 336 23.4% | 62 6.4% | 33 4.1% | N/A | N/A |
| Fine | 915 67.9% | 1,428 71.3% | 1,768 92.4% | 983 68.5% | 799 82.3% | 703 87.7% | 796 89.6% | 880 81.9% |
| Dismissal | 182 13.5% | 173 8.7% | 145 7.6% | 115 8.1% | 110 11.3% | 66 8.2% | 80 9.0% | 64 6.0% |
| Total Discipline | 1,348 100% | 2,002 100% | 1,913 100% | 1,434 100% | 971 100% | 802 100% | 888 100% | 1,074 100% |
| Criminal Cases | 118 | 209 | 287 | 168 | 186 | 129 | 136 | 101 |

Source: Croatian Ministry of the Interior.

**Table 4.4**    Croatian Corruption-Related Cases With Arrest From January 1, 1995 to December
1, 1997

| *Criminal Offense* | *Frequency* | *Percentage* |
|---|---|---|
| Acceptance of a Bribe | 133 | 7.6% |
| Offering of a Bribe | 162 | 9.2% |
| Illegal Intermediation | 5 | 0.3% |
| Abuse of Office and Official Authority | 1,422 | 81.0% |
| Abuse in Performance of Governmental Duties | 13 | 0.7% |
| Other | 20 | 1.2% |
| Total | 1,755 | 100.0% |

Source: Sačić, 1998 (p. 10).

very few police officers who accept a bribe are criminally charged or punished administratively for doing so. In addition to the usual arguments that make the development of corruption cases difficult (the secretive nature of corrupt transactions, lack of motivation by the participants to report the misconduct, absence of complaints, difficulty in satisfying the standard of proof, and reluctance of the criminal justice system to punish police officers), it is clear that there are other reasons that render the utilization of the existing palette of criminal offenses quite infrequent.

## Supervision

First-line supervisors play a crucial role in corruption control. Their everyday contact with line officers provides them with the best position to learn about subordinates' misconduct, react to it, and monitor their future behavior. If they fail to react adequately, regardless of the reasons behind it (e.g., their own involvement in corruption; lack of ability, skill, or opportunities to supervise), they convey to their subordinates that corruption is unofficially tolerated.

One of the potential problems supervisors in Croatia may face is their relative inexperience. As a consequence of the war, some of the less experienced police officers have been promoted, or those police officers who were promoted did not obtain sufficient training before assuming their new, supervisory roles. Furthermore, the supervisors who participated in the war typically fought shoulder to shoulder with their subordinates; as a result, the relationship with their subordinates is unusually close and they would likely think twice before opening the official channels of investigation into their subordinates' misconduct.

The administration wanted to weaken the impact of the excuse "Let it go, it is the war!"[12] very early; in mid-1992 it fired 600 people for misconduct (Jarnjak, 1992, pp. 4-5). In recent years, even stronger attempts have been made to strengthen the sense of responsibility in the police, especially supervisory responsibility. As a consequence, over one quarter of the cases coordinated and investigated by Internal Affairs in 2000 focused on the (mis)conduct of supervisors. Although it might be tempting to relate the 2000 election of the new government to this shift in focus, the lack of empirical data precludes precise inferences.

## POLICE CULTURE

Because of the conditions surrounding their formation, the Croatian police started from an unusual position: They inherited neither the equipment nor the staff from their predecessor, the Yugoslav militia. While Serbs in prewar Croatia constituted approximately 12% of the population, the estimates are that over 70% of militia officers in the old Ministry of the Interior were ethnic Serbs (Jarnjak, 1995). The numbers seem to be even higher for detectives: The estimates are that over 80% of detectives were of Serbian origin (Lovrić, 1993). When the war broke out, a substantial number of ethnic Serbs abruptly left their posts.

The resulting rapid hiring of new employees created a truly exceptional circumstance: The experienced police officers who needed to socialize recruits into police culture did not constitute the overwhelming majority. For example, several detectives (whom we interviewed in the course of carrying out the empirical study on police integrity in 1996) noted that they had very few experienced colleagues on the force to teach them how to investigate crimes (Kutnjak Ivkovich, 1996, unpublished field notes).

Thus, it seems that the seemingly natural transmission of the old culture to the incoming police officers did not take place. Instead, a new police culture has developed. A significant factor in its shaping was the war, as a result of which the standards of what is considered normal behavior changed and the tolerance for less serious forms of misconduct increased. Although there were no previous attempts to measure the extent of the code of silence (i.e., how wide the code is and what behavior is covered by it) in a scientific and empirical way, the comparison of the official crime cases and disciplinary cases with the estimates of the actual extent of corruption can serve as a rough illustration: It indicates that the code of silence—tolerance of corrupt behavior—can be expected to be widespread.

### Recruitment, Selection, and Training

The quality of recruitment, selection, and training was adversely affected by the war. In order to fill the ranks rapidly and send people to fight the war, the recruitment criteria were unofficially relaxed and the training was either shortened or omitted completely[13]

(Kutnjak Ivkovich, 2000). Although the direct impact of these factors of police integrity and the level of corruption is not known, the Ministry was concerned about the impact and promised a thorough evaluation of its ranks.

The Ministry dismissed several hundred police officers for serious misconduct in the period from 1992 to 1999 (see Table 4.3). The dismissal of a large group of 3,000 police officers in August of 2001, on the other hand, was justified as a measure of reducing the size by dismissing insufficiently qualified police officers, rather than as a measure of cleaning the ranks. However, only a detailed case-by-case analysis might reveal whether the police officers dismissed were ones it was thought should be dismissed because of the level of their misconduct.

### Salary

It is commonly believed that if the salary of a police officer does not reach a certain minimum that provides for a decent living, or, put differently, if the salary does not extend to cover the most basic needs, police officers may be tempted to engage in corruption, especially if the opportunities appear in abundance and they perceive that corruption is widespread and acceptable. However, it is unclear, in a society that has grown tolerant of corruption, whether, once police officers' basic needs are met, increasing their salaries will automatically increase their resistance to corruption.

The effects of the war and the postwar transition are reflected in the police salary structure: The annual salary range in 1993 was from U.S.$1,560 for beginning police officers to U.S.$3,360 for a higher inspector (Osrečki, 1993). As time passed, salaries tended to increase. In 1996, the average annual salary for police officers ranged from U.S.$2,400 to U.S.$3,600 (Osrečki, 1995). This nevertheless placed average salaries for the police below average salaries for those in industry, which ranged from U.S.$4,200 to U.S.$4,800 (Marković, 1997, p. 5).

### MEASURING THE LEVEL OF TOLERANCE OF CORRUPTION

The analysis of the complex set of factors affecting police integrity in Croatia *indicates* that police culture could be rather tolerant of corruption. However, none of the previous studies tried to actually *measure* the level of police integrity among the Croatian police. Using the survey instrument developed by Kutnjak Ivković and Klockars as a part of a larger cross-cultural study of police integrity (Kutnjak Ivkovich & Klockars, 1996), we are seeking to measure the level of tolerance of, or the level of resistance to, police corruption among Croatian police officers.

The questionnaire, which provides descriptions of 11 hypothetical scenarios, measures the integrity level of the police by examining officers' perceptions of the seriousness of misconduct, their level of support for disciplinary consequences for it,[14] and their expressed willingness to report misconduct. The scenarios range from less serious misconduct, such as the acceptance of free drinks, half-price meals, and small gifts from merchants, to the more serious forms, such as the acceptance of bribes, kickbacks, and opportunistic thefts (Kutnjak Ivkovich & Klockars, 1998, 2000).

### The Sample

The Croatian sample is a stratified national sample of 41 police stations, selected in a manner that reflected as closely as possible the national distribution of police by region, size, type, and district. Questionnaires were completed by 1,649 Croatian police officers from these stations in 1995 (Kutnjak Ivkovich & Klockars, 1998).

Because the Croatian police are a young police force, it is not surprising that most of the police officers in our stratified representative sample (74%) had been police officers for less than 5 years and that most (85%) had served at their present police station for less than 5 years. Most police officers reported that they performed patrol (41%) or traffic (21%) duty. Most served in small (25-75 officer) or medium-sized (76-200 officer) police agencies. About 19% of the respondents were employed in the supervisory ranks.

### The Results

The overall finding that follows from examining the data in Table 4.5 is that all three measures of police integrity—the officers' perceptions of the seriousness of misconduct, the expected discipline for it, and the officers' willingness to report it—indicate that the occupational culture among the surveyed Croatian police tends to be generally tolerant of police corruption.

### Seriousness

The respondents perceived the 11 cases to range in terms of seriousness from the least serious, Case 4, describing the acceptance of holiday gifts, to the most serious, Case 5, describing the theft of a watch from a crime scene (see Table 4.5). The officers' average evaluations of the seriousness of the misconduct in the scenarios enable us to classify the cases into three groups.

The five *least serious cases*—Case 4 (Holiday Gifts From Merchants), Case 1 (Off-Duty Security System Business), Case 8 (Cover-Up of Police DUI Accident), Case 2 (Free Meals and Discounts on Beat), and Case 10 (Excessive Force on Car Thief)—all have means below or just above the midpoint of our scale (3.00). Interestingly, while the behavior in the two cases involving the acceptance of gratuities (Case 2 and Case 4) violates

the official rules, the estimates of the seriousness of these two cases differ by almost one full point; the *occasional* acceptance of gifts on *holidays* is perceived to be substantially less serious than the acceptance of free meals and discounts on a *regular* basis. Case 8 (Cover-Up of Police DUI Accident), another case not evaluated as serious, describes behavior that does not involve the quid pro quo arrangement characteristic of bribery-style corruption; rather, it involves an act of excessive (but misplaced) collegiality and solidarity with a fellow police officer. One of the two cases evaluated as the least serious ones (Case 1) describes a police officer running his own private security system business. The official rules, which regulate the conduct of police officers, at the time prohibited outside employment by police officers, but, because of the difficult economic situation, the topic of outside employment was brought to the table (see Veić, 1996, p. 131) and suggestions were made to allow such employment if it was previously approved by the Ministry. Finally, the case perceived as the most serious one in the group is Case 10, describing the use of excessive force on a car thief after a chase.

Out of the three cases that can be classified as perceived as *cases of intermediate seriousness* (the values of means are mostly between 3 and 4), one describes misconduct by a supervisor (Case 7 - Supervisor Grants Holiday in Exchange for Car Tune-Up). The two remaining cases are typical quid pro quo arrangements, in which a police officer either overlooks a city ordinance violation (Case 9 - Free Drinks to Ignore Late Bar Closing) or uses the official position of being a police officer to obtain an illegal kickback (Case 6 - 5% Kickback From Auto Repair Shop).

The three *most serious cases* all have means substantially closer to 5 (the "very serious" end of the scale). These three cases, plain violations of criminal law, include two cases of theft (Case 5 - Crime Scene Theft of Watch and Case 11 - Theft From Found

Wallet), followed by a forgery of official documents in order to hide the crime. The case evaluated to be the more serious of the two cases (Case 5) puts the police officer in the position to abuse his official duty *in order* to commit the theft (i.e., he steals from a crime scene he is examining). The least serious case in the group (Case 3 - Bribe From Speeding Motorist), and perhaps the most frequent in police practice,[15] is the only case in the questionnaire in which police officers perceived that most of the police officers in their agencies would evaluate this case as less serious than they did (see Table 4.5).

## *Violation of Official Rules*

Although all the cases in the questionnaire describe rule-violating behavior, the majority of the respondents evaluated only six out of eleven cases as violations of official rules (see Table 4.5). Not surprisingly, the five other cases are the ones that respondents evaluated as the five least serious cases.

Only 16.2% of the respondents said that the least serious case, Case 4 (Holiday Gifts From Merchants), is a violation of official rules. Moreover, as many as 43.4% of the respondents felt that Case 2 (Free Meals and Discounts on Beat), the case describing the acceptance of gratuities on a regular basis, was a violation of official rules as well (see Table 4.5). This discrepancy is not surprising in light of the previously reported evaluations of seriousness—Case 2 was perceived to be more serious than Case 4.

While between one third and one half of the respondents described the other three least serious cases (Case 1 - Off-Duty Security System Business; Case 8 - Cover-Up of Police DUI Accident; Case 10 - Excessive Force on Car Thief) as violations, approximately two thirds of the respondents said the same for the three cases of intermediate seriousness (Case 6 - 5% Kickback From Auto

Repair Shop; Case 7 - Supervisor Grants Holiday in Exchange for Car Tune-Up; Case 9 - Free Drinks to Ignore Late Bar Closing). Finally, the overwhelming majority of the respondents (89% or more) evaluated the three most serious cases as violations of official agency rules.

With the exception of the three most serious cases, why can only two thirds of the respondents recognize these cases as violations of official rules? There are several (possibly overlapping) explanations. First, it is possible that a substantial minority of police officers do not know the official rules. Although extensive training was not provided during the war years to each newly hired police officer, in-service training and on-the-job experience since those early years should have provided police officers with sufficient opportunities to learn "the basic rules." However, the results of Veić's study indicate that a substantial portion of the officers still may have problems with at least some of the rules (Ivanović, 2001, p. 12). Second, it is possible either that some of the official rules are not enforced at all (thus creating an unofficial rule that overrides the official rule) or that some of the rules are not enforced on a regular basis (thus creating ambiguity about them). It is clear from Table 4.5 that the official rules prohibiting the behavior in Case 4 (acceptance of holiday gifts) are not enforced systematically: Only 16.2% of the respondents recognize the behavior as a violation of official rules and, on average, they expect no discipline to follow such misconduct and believe that the police officer should not be punished for such behavior. The cases with more potentially conflicting messages about the importance of official rules include cases for which approximately one half of the respondents evaluated the described behaviors as violations (e.g., Case 2 - Free Meals and Discounts on Beat; Case 8 - Cover-Up of Police DUI Accident).

**Table 4.5**  Croatian Police Officers' Views of the Seriousness of the Misconduct, the Discipline It Should and Would Receive, and Officers' Willingness to Report It

| Case Number and Description | Seriousness | | | | Violation | Discipline | | | | | | Willingness to Report | | | |
|---|---|---|---|---|---|---|---|---|---|---|---|---|---|---|---|
| | Own View | | Most Officers | | X̄ | Should Receive | | | Would Receive | | | Own View | | Most Officers | |
| | $\bar{x}$ | Rank | $\bar{x}$ | Rank | % def. yes | $\bar{x}$ | Rank | Mode | $\bar{x}$ | Rank | Mode | $\bar{x}$ | Rank | $\bar{x}$ | Rank |
| Case 1 - Off-Duty Security System Business | 2.57 | 2 | 2.51 | 2 | 2.92 (39.7%) | 2.03 | 2 | None | 2.34 | 2 | None | 1.90 | 2 | 2.31 | 4 |
| Case 2 - Free Meals and Discounts on Beat | 3.01 | 4 | 2.79 | 4 | 3.08 (43.4%) | 2.24 | 5 | Public Reprimand | 2.43 | 5 | Public Reprimand | 2.15 | 5 | 2.38 | 5 |
| Case 3 - Bribe From Speeding Motorist | 4.47 | 9 | 3.91 | 9 | 4.61 (89.0%) | 3.64 | 9 | Suspension | 3.74 | 9 | Suspension | 3.16 | 9 | 3.07 | 9 |
| Case 4 - Holiday Gifts From Merchants | 2.13 | 1 | 2.09 | 1 | 2.11 (16.2%) | 1.60 | 1 | None | 1.78 | 1 | None | 1.67 | 1 | 1.85 | 1 |
| Case 5 - Crime Scene Theft of Watch | 4.72 | 11 | 4.38 | 11 | 4.79 (93.8%) | 4.27 | 11 | Dismissal | 4.29 | 11 | Dismissal | 3.96 | 11 | 3.72 | 11 |
| Case 6 - 5% Kickback From Auto Repair Shop | 3.86 | 7 | 3.50 | 7 | 3.99 (69.0%) | 3.23 | 8 | Suspension | 3.35 | 8 | Suspension | 3.14 | 8 | 3.05 | 8 |
| Case 7 - Supervisor Grants Holiday in Exchange for Car Tune-Up | 4.09 | 8 | 3.76 | 8 | 3.76 (62.4%) | 2.73 | 7 | Public Reprimand | 2.51 | 6 | None | 2.72 | 7 | 2.73 | 7 |
| Case 8 - Cover-Up of Police DUI Accident | 2.79 | 3 | 2.65 | 3 | 3.20 (45.5%) | 2.17 | 4 | Public Reprimand | 2.42 | 4 | Public Reprimand | 2.09 | 3.5 | 2.20 | 3 |
| Case 9 - Free Drinks to Ignore Late Bar Closing | 3.85 | 6 | 3.38 | 6 | 3.93 (67.2%) | 2.57 | 6 | Public Reprimand | 2.67 | 7 | Fine | 2.66 | 6 | 2.58 | 6 |
| Case 10 - Excessive Force on Car Thief | 3.03 | 5 | 2.82 | 5 | 3.28 (47.9%) | 2.14 | 3 | None | 2.40 | 3 | Public Reprimand | 2.09 | 3.5 | 2.08 | 2 |
| Case 11 - Theft From Found Wallet | 4.55 | 10 | 4.16 | 10 | 4.64 (89.2%) | 3.82 | 10 | Fine | 3.87 | 10 | Fine | 3.63 | 10 | 3.41 | 10 |

## Appropriate and Expected Discipline

The officers' opinions about appropriate and expected discipline are related to their evaluations of the seriousness of the misconduct in each of the scenarios: Generally, the more serious the case is evaluated to be, the more serious the perceived appropriate discipline it merited. For the five least serious cases (Case 4 - Holiday Gifts From Merchants; Case 2 - Free Meals and Discounts on Beat; Case 1 - Off-Duty Security System Business; Case 8 - Cover-Up of Police DUI Accident; Case 10 - Excessive Force on Car Thief), the respondents expected and approved of the officer receiving either no discipline or a public reprimand (see Table 4.5). For the cases of intermediate seriousness (Case 6 - 5% Kickback From Auto Repair Shop; Case 7 - Supervisor Grants Holiday in Exchange for Car Tune-Up; Case 9 - Free Drinks to Ignore Late Bar Closing), the surveyed police officers selected either a public reprimand or suspension as the adequate discipline. Finally, the opinions about the appropriate discipline for the three most serious cases differ—whereas the most adequate punishment for theft of money from a found wallet (Case 11) is perceived as a fine and for acceptance of a bribe from a speeding motorist (Case 3) is perceived as suspension, only the case of theft of watch from a crime scene (Case 5) is perceived to merit the officer's dismissal.

There are three cases in which the appropriate modal discipline and expected modal discipline diverge, indicating that the respondents did not perceive the expected discipline to be of adequate severity. While in the only case describing the misconduct by a supervisor (Case 7 - Supervisor Grants Holiday in Exchange for Car Tune-Up) the respondents perceived the expected discipline as too lenient, in Case 9 (Free Drinks to Ignore Late Bar Closing) and Case 10 (Excessive Force on Car Thief) they evaluated the expected discipline as too harsh.

## Officers' Willingness to Report Misconduct

The respondents were asked not only about their own willingness to report the misconduct described in the questionnaire but also about their perceptions of others' willingness to report it. The results indicate that estimates of the respondents' willingness to report misconduct seem to be directly related to their perceptions of the seriousness of misconduct—the more serious the officers perceived the case to be, the less likely they were to say that they would not report it (see Table 4.5).

Another analysis can be performed to examine the extent of the code of silence in more detail by examining for each case the percentage of police officers who said that they definitely would not report it. Not surprisingly, the extent of the code is the widest for the least serious cases and the narrowest for the most serious ones (see Figure 4.1). In other words, tolerance seems to be the strongest for the cases perceived to be the least serious. In particular, while the majority of the surveyed police officers (65% or more) said that they would not report the five least serious cases (Case 4 - Holiday Gifts From Merchants; Case 2 - Free Meals and Discounts on Beat; Case 1 - Off-Duty Security System Business; Case 8 - Cover-Up of Police DUI Accident; Case 10 - Excessive Force on Car Thief), between one third and one half said that they would not report the cases of intermediate seriousness (Case 6 - 5% Kickback From Auto Repair Shop; Case 7 - Supervisor Grants Holiday in Exchange for Car Tune-Up; Case 9 - Free Drinks to Ignore Late Bar Closing). Finally, with the exception of Case 3, one quarter or fewer said that they would not report the most serious cases (Case 5 - Crime Scene Theft of Watch; Case 11 - Theft From Found Wallet).

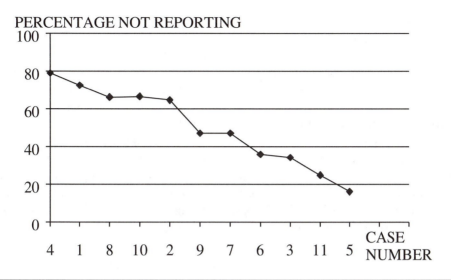

PERCENTAGE NOT REPORTING

**Figure 4.1**   Percentage of Officers Not Willing to Report Misconduct, by Case Number

## CONCLUSION

Croatia's transition to a democratic society has been burdened by the war; a complex set of external factors—including the war itself, continued mismanagement of the economy, bankruptcy of a large number of state-run companies, illegal practices by the ruling political structure, the war in neighboring Bosnia and Herzegovina, and the void created by the relinquishment of Communist values and the lack of new social rules—have contributed to the creation of an atmosphere conducive to corruption. The effects of the war and the military role successfully played by the Croatian police seem to have generated a positive public opinion about the police. In 1995, when the effects of the war were still being felt and the Croatian military and the police participated in the two short-lasting but large-scale military operations ("Flash" in May and "Storm" in August), over two thirds of the respondents who participated in the opinion poll expressed a substantial level of confidence in both the military and the police (*World Values Survey—Croatia*, 1995).

At the same time, not knowing that the operation Storm was being planned, we surveyed police officers with the purpose of measuring the extent of tolerance of police corruption. We used three measures (the officers' perceptions of the seriousness of the misconduct in the scenarios, the appropriate discipline for such behavior, and their willingness to report it) to measure the same underlying phenomenon—police tolerance of corruption—and all of the results of our study point in the same direction; they indicate that the occupational culture of the surveyed Croatian police seems to be generally tolerant of police corruption.

While other indicators, such as the International Crime Victimization Survey and the Transparency International Corruption Perceptions Index, show that in the late 1990s corruption seemed to be tolerated more in Croatia than in a number of other Eastern European countries, there are signs that the situation may be gradually improving. In particular, these elements—the end of a decade-long domination of a right-wing-oriented political party, greater willingness of the new government to deal with the obstacles to Croatia's admission into the European Union, government reforms, the increased volume of foreign investments, the recognition of corruption as an acceptable topic for research and investigative journalism—have the potential of contributing to the task and could be responsible for Croatia's rapid climb on the Transparency International Corruption Perceptions Index in 2000 and 2001. On the policing side, the expansion of the set of available investigative methods and the indicators of the increased account-

ability of supervisors could potentially have an effect on the actual level of police corruption.

However, this difficult and cumbersome journey is merely beginning, and the success of control efforts depends on a number of complex, heterogeneous factors. One of the crucial factors is education of the society at large about the negative consequences of corruption. As long as the public tolerates corruption and its individual members are willing to bribe public officials, the relatively high level of corruption will persist.

## NOTES

1. Perić reported on May 4, 1993 that since the beginning of the war, 6,592 people had died and 23,824 had been wounded (1995, p. 166).

2. Kovačević, Kovačević, Lončarić-Horvat, Kandžija, and Blažević (1993, p. 170) estimated that the total value of the direct and indirect war damages through the end of 1991 was U.S.$18.7 billion.

3. For example, over 5% of the GNP (over U.S.$1 billion) was devoted to the military expenditures in 1997 (Rakman, 1998, p. 8). Similarly, the CIA's *The World Factbook* (2000, p. 124) reports that 5% of the GDP (U.S.$950 million) was assigned for military expenditures in 1999.

4. The estimated expenses for the 600,000 registered refugees and displaced persons in 1992 were close to U.S.$1.5 billion (Perić, 1995, p. 160).

5. The average annual salary in Croatia (in German marks) dropped from DM 8,000 in 1990 to DM 2,100 in 1991 and 1992 (Marković, 1997, p. 5). The estimated average annual salary has been increasing gradually. In 1998 it had reached DM 5,000 (*The World Factbook*, 2000, p. 124).

6. The unemployment rate in 1993 was 17% (Perić, 1995, p. 166) and continues to be relatively high—for example, it was 15.9% in 1997 (*The Time Almanac 2000*, 2000, p. 202) and 18.6% in 1998 (*The World Factbook*, 2000, p. 124).

7. Ivan Jarnjak, the former Minister of the Interior, estimated that approximately 80% of the detectives on the force were of Serbian origin and that most left at the beginning of the war (Lovrić, 1993). There are estimates that over 70% of the old Yugoslav militia officers were ethnic Serbs (Jarnjak, 1995).

8. For example, a study by Kroll Associates indicated that "the Croatian program of privatization is infected by corruption" (Butković, 1997, p. 15).

9. See Moore (1983) for more on the invisible offenses.

10. For a typology of police corruption, see Barker and Roebuck (1973).

11. While the absolute numbers of reported corruption-related cases reported by Derenčinović (2001) and Sačić (1998) differ, a feature common to both data sources is that abuse of office and official authority is the most common type of crime (75.9% according to Derenčinović and 81.0% according to Sačić), followed by offering a bribe (10.7% and 9.2%, respectively) and acceptance of a bribe (6.7% and 7.6%, respectively).

12. Ivan Jarnjak, the former Minister of the Interior, argued that during the war, "for many mistakes, for laziness, the golden excuse was the following, 'Let it go, it is the war!' That excuse is no longer valid" (Jarnjak, 1992, pp. 4-5).

13. *Globus* provided summary results of a recent test on criminal law (Ivanović, 2001, p. 12). The Dean of the Police Academy described that "90% of police officers did not know what 'catching the offender in the act of committing the crime' means; 70% did not hear for some of the rules of the *Criminal Code*, notwithstanding that they do not know how to apply them, although they cannot perform their job without this knowledge" (Ivanović, 2001, p. 12).

14. The Croatian version of the questionnaire had five disciplinary options: 1. no discipline; 2. public reprimand; 3. fine; 4. period of suspension; and 5. dismissal.

15. The experts who participated in the survey by the Czech Chapter of Transparency International estimated that one of the three most frequent forms of corruption in Hungary and Poland, two other Eastern European countries, is "fining a driver and failing to give a ticket" (Frič & Walek, 2001, pp. 43, 49).

## REFERENCES

Barker, T., & Roebuck, J. (1973). *An empirical typology of police corruption: A study in organizational deviance.* Springfield, IL: Charles C Thomas.

Butković, D. (1997, September). Tajni izvještaj o Hrvatskoj. *Globus*, pp. 14-15.

Čehok, I., & Veić, P. (2000). *Etika policijskog zvanja.* Zagreb, Croatia: Ministarstvo unutarnjih poslova Republike Hrvatske.

Criminal Code. (1997). Zagreb, Croatia: Narodne novine 110/97.

Criminal Procedure Code. (1997). Zagreb, Croatia: Narodne novine 110/97.

Derenčinović, D. (2000). *Kaznenopravni sadržaji u suprotstavljanju korupciji.* Unpublished doctoral dissertation, University of Zagreb, Croatia.

Derenčinović, D. (2001). *Mit(o) korupciji.* Zagreb, Croatia: NOCCI.

*European Values Survey—Croatia.* (1999). Zagreb, Croatia: Faculty of Catholic Theology.

*Freedom in the World 1999–2000: Croatia* (2000). Available from http://www.free-domhouse.org/survey/2000/reports/country/croatia.html.

Frič, P., & Walek, C. (2001). *Crossing the thin blue line: An international annual review of anti-corruption strategies in the police.* Prague: Transparency International ČR.

Ivanović, R. (2001, December). Korupcija u policiji? *Globus*, pp. 10-16.

Jarnjak, I. (1992). Izvaci s tiskovne konferencije. *Halo 92, 11,* 4-5.

Jarnjak, I. (1995). Hrvati rado nose odoru. *Halo 92, 44,* 7.

Kovačević, J., Kovačević, J., Lončarić-Horvat, O., Kandžija, V., & Blažević, B. (1993). *Ratne štete i reparacije.* Zagreb, Croatia: Školska knjiga.

Kregar, J. (1999). *Nastanak predatorskog kapitalizma i korupcija.* Zagreb, Croatia: Rifin.

Kutnjak Ivkovich, S. (2000). Challenges of policing democracies: The Croatian experience. In D. K. Das & O. Marenin (Eds.), *Challenges of policing democracies.* Amsterdam: Gordon and Breach.

Kutnjak Ivkovich, S. (2001, April). *Opinions about the police in democratic countries and countries in transition: An analysis of the International Crime Victim Survey data.* Paper presented at the annual meeting of the Academy of Criminal Justice Sciences, Washington, DC.

Kutnjak Ivkovich, S., & Klockars, C. B. (1996, March). *Police perceptions of disciplinary fairness and the formation of the code of silence.* Paper presented at the annual meeting of the Academy of Criminal Justice Sciences, Las Vegas, Nevada.

Kutnjak Ivkovich, S., & Klockars, C. B. (1998). The code of silence and the Croatian police. In M. Pagon (Ed.), *Policing in Central and Eastern Europe: Organizational, managerial, and human resource aspects*. Ljubljana, Slovenia: College of Police and Security Studies.

Kutnjak Ivkovich, S., & Klockars, C. B. (2000). Comparing police supervisor and line officer opinions about the code of silence: The case of Croatia. In M. Pagon, (Ed.), *Policing in Central and Eastern Europe: Ethics, integrity, and human rights*. Ljubljana, Slovenia: College of Police and Security Studies.

Lovrić, J. (1993). Policija znači život. *Halo 92, 16, 3.*

Marković, L. J. (1997, December 21). Panika medju poslodavcima. *Vjesnik*, p. 5.

Moore, M. H. (1983). Invisible offenses: A challenge to minimally intrusive law enforcement. In G. M. Caplan (Ed.), *Abscam ethics: Moral issues and deception in law enforcement*. Cambridge, MA: Ballinger.

Osrečki, K. (1993). Rekli su . . . Izvaci s tiskovne konferencije. *Halo 92, 25, 8.*

Osrečki, K. (1995). Jesmo li štedljivi? *Halo 92, 53,* 18-19.

Pavišić, B., & Veić, P. (1996). *Komentar Krivičnog zakona Republike Hrvatske*. Zagreb, Croatia: Ministarstvo unutarnjih poslova Republike Hrvatske.

Perić, I. (1995). *Godine koje će se pamtiti*. Zagreb, Croatia: Školska knjiga.

Police Law. (2001). Zagreb, Croatia: Narodne novine 129/01.

Rakman, I. (1998, January 4). Hrvatska će još neko vrijeme morati natprosječno izdvajati za obranu. *Vjesnik*, p. 8.

Sačić, Ž. (1998). Korupcija i njeno suzbijanje u svijetu i Hrvatskoj. *Policija i sigurnost, 7*(1-2), 1-16.

*The Time Almanac 2000.* (2000). Boston: Information Please.

Transparency International. (1999, 2000, 2001). *Transparency International Corruption Perceptions Index* (1999, 2000, 2001). Available from http://www.transparency.org/documents/index.htm#cpi

Veić, P. (1996). Neka otvorena pitanja "Policijskog zakonodavstva" Republike Hrvatske—de lege ferenda. *Policija i sigurnost, 2,* 117-136.

*The World Factbook.* (2000). Washington, DC: Brassey's.

*World Values Survey—Croatia.* (1995). Zagreb, Croatia: Erasmus Guild.

# CHAPTER 5

# Policing Integrity
## Britain's Thin Blue Line

### Louise Westmarland

International images of the unarmed British police officer, as a "paid member of the public in uniform" as opposed to part of a quasi military organization, "is that of the friendly bobby, sympathetic and understanding and impeccably behaved" (Uildriks & van Mastrigt, 1991, p. 10). Home Office statistics show, however, that in the reporting period from 2000 to 2001, 18,911 complaints against the police in England and Wales were recorded. Of these, around 10% were for "incivility," although only 87 cases were substantiated upon investigation (Povey & Cotton, 2001). Indeed, Cain (1992) argues that there has a been an "unscientific myopia" surrounding what is known about the police that "precludes . . . the raising of questions about what the police might be" (p. 3). Waddington (1999) suggests that "what the police *do,* as opposed to have the potential to do, is *exercise authority*" (p. 20). Authority and power are exercised over the population

by the police, either as an organization or through individual officers' actions, and so concerns will always exist about the way authority and power are enacted. As Waddington (1999) argues, the exercise of police authority curtails personal freedom and, as the English have traditionally been very attached to this aspect of their lives, all social classes were originally opposed to the introduction of a military-style police force. Despite this, since 1829, when a formal, paid force was established, "the police in Britain [have] quickly acquired responsibilities for regulating a broad, indeed indefinite, spectrum of routine activity" (p. 22).

More recently, in a survey of the English language literature on police corruption, Newburn (1999) argued that concern about the standards of police ethics and integrity in the United Kingdom has been increasing due to a "series of public scandals" (p. 1). Reiner (2000), in his discussion of a lack of public

AUTHOR'S NOTE: With thanks to the research force, the participants, and in particular to the Chief and Deputy Chief Constables and to Judith Marshall for help with data analysis.

confidence in the police, explains how the Guildford Four, the Maguire Seven, and Birmingham Six were all groups of innocent people who were exonerated and released after serving long jail sentences for alleged offenses relating to terrorist activities in Northern Ireland. Other similar abuses of police power, concerning the fabrication or suppression of evidence, "shook public opinion" (p. 66) in the early 1990s. Professional integrity is of particular importance at present in Britain because of the recent introduction of the Human Rights Act (1998), which was implemented in 2000. This Act of Parliament introduced a number of new, more explicitly "ethical" issues for officers to consider, such as the right to family life, privacy, and freedom from "discrimination." Indeed, it has raised previously unexplored dilemmas for officers in Britain to such an extent that Neyroud and Beckley (2001) have described it as a "new agenda in policing" (p. 54).

This presumes that the "old" agenda was rather different and highlights a period when Holdaway (1996) said that police authority was "tested to the limit by black youths demonstrating on the streets" (p. 105). Crises of confidence and levels of distrust were also revealed in the early 1980s by studies such as the Islington Crime Survey in London (Jones, MacLean, & Young, 1986, p. 205). It was said to be particularly problematic among groups such as the young and ethnic minorities, and this led to recommendations regarding police training policies. As the Policy Studies Institute reported in 1983, the police in London were regarded favorably by the majority of the public until they had actually been in contact with the force. As a result of encounters with police officers, however, citizens found that some officers were "rude and bullying towards members of the public" (Heward, 1994, p. 243). Since then, in response to such criticism, the police have been attempting to improve their image on two fronts; first, by pacifying their

protagonists regarding their interactions with the public, and second, through the transformation of their internal personnel affairs. The extent to which integrity and, more specifically, corruption have been tackled will be taken up in the discussion that follows.

## POLICE ORGANIZATION IN THE UNITED KINGDOM

The United Kingdom, which is sometimes called the British Isles, is made up of a number of geographically separate and legislatively different areas. With regard to criminal justice and policing systems, four main jurisdictions exist—England, Wales, Scotland, and Northern Ireland. In Northern Ireland, the recent changes introduced as a result of the peace process have led to some structural changes in the police force, which was formerly know as the Royal Ulster Constabulary (RUC). According to Mawby (1999), prior to the Patten Report and its implementation, there had been in the province a comparatively "paramilitary nature of policing since the mid-1970s" (p. 44). In contrast, policing is organized along much less paramilitary lines in England and Wales, which share a common system of rules, regulations, and legislation; however, law and policing structures in Scotland differ from these. It is therefore intended that, for the purposes of this chapter, the largest and most coherent system in the United Kingdom, that of England and Wales, is being referred to unless otherwise stated.

In England and Wales, the police are organized into a number of "forces" that amount to 43 separate departments, of which a large southeastern one is the focus of this chapter. In a total that includes all 43 forces, the most recent Home Office statistics show that there were 127,231 police officers in September of 2001 (Povey & Rundle, 2001). This is an increase of 2% over the previous year and represents an attempt by the British government to fulfill an election mandate to increase police numbers significantly over the next few years. Each police force has 3,708 officers and is subdivided into a number of smaller divisions. In the United Kingdom, each department is relatively autonomous; it is governed by a local committee made up of elected and co-opted members, with inspections and audits carried out by the Home Office on behalf of central government. Funding is almost equally shared (51%/49%) between local and national government sources. Each department is headed by a chief constable, usually assisted by two or three deputies at the chief executive level, depending on the size of the department. Police departments vary in size from under 1,000 officers to over 7,000 officers.

Governing the police at the local level is done through a series of Police Authorities, which are committees made up of some elected and some co-opted representatives. The appointment of some very senior officers, while largely controlled by the local Police authority, may in some circumstances be influenced by the central government. As Mawby (1999) argued, this "balance between central and local control over policing clearly impinges upon the nature of police accountability and legitimacy" (p. 42). Their accountability to the community they serve, however, is not necessarily to the "citizen" as a consumer of the product they offer. As Morgan and Newburn (1997) have explained, the police in the United Kingdom are responsible for crime control, law enforcement, and Britain's only 24-hour general emergency service (p. 75). Explaining what they do is of course different from explaining how it should be done, as Johnston (2000) argued, which is wider than the traditional "'force versus service' debate" (p. 43). Issues such as the definition of "discrimination" and the "right to a fair trial" may be especially difficult for police officers in Britain because they have not been

accustomed to having to consider such concepts so explicitly. Indeed, integrity is a problematic concept to define and describe, but in practice many professional groups with the power to make decisions, not least of all the police, have to confront it. Moreover, Newburn (1999) has argued that there has been a history in the United Kingdom of malpractice and misconduct. Many of the instances he quoted from Britain, however, tend to be related to the "noble cause" or practices associated with the outcome of cases rather than to those with an acquisitive motive. In comparison with the examples he cited from the United States, Australia, and other jurisdictions, British police officers appear to be much more "noble" than are their colleagues in other countries. Similarly, in a comprehensive examination of police integrity published by the Her Majesty's Inspectorate of Constabulary (HMIC, 1999), which is the governmental audit and policy arm of the Home Office for the police in the United Kingdom, few references are made to major corruption in terms of gambling, protection rackets, or other money-making endeavors. Rather, most of the discussion in the HMIC report regarding "integrity" is about public perceptions of the police, the acceptance of gratuities, and the investigation and prosecution of offenders.

Nevertheless, research has been published on the existence of acquisitive corruption in the United Kingdom, even though a quantitative study of such corruption has not been conducted and is considered "almost impossible to achieve"(HMIC, 1999, p. 8). A case-by-case documentary history of police corruption carried out by Morton (1993), however, covers the period from the development of the modern police in 1829, and subsequent tracts of history until the introduction of a significant piece of legislation, the Police and Criminal Evidence Act, in 1984. These new regulations, in combination with the

Prosecution of Offenses Act (1985), provided "very considerable safeguards for suspects," "substantially curtailed the way the police throughout the country could conduct their enquiries," and "removed opportunities for direct corruption" (Morton, 1993, p. 167). New safeguards that were developed as a result of these laws include the tape recording of interviews and the timetabling and monitoring of those in police custody. This is not to say that these new laws, which are usually referred to as "PACE," have necessarily solved the problem, and Morton has explained how police corruption can be viewed as a cultural issue, as a part of British life that has always existed (1993, p. 338).

Over the 150 years of the British police before the introduction of the PACE, there was what Morton (1993) has described as a history of "bent coppers," of police officers "bent for self" and "bent for the job." He presents extensive evidence for these assertions, beginning with a description of a number of cases around 1830 that led to the "integrity and trustworthiness of the New Police" being defended by a journal author at the time (1993, p. 31). Morton's main evidence centers on the period from 1945, the so-called golden age of policing (Benyon & Bourn, 1986, p. 7), up to the late 1950s and early 1960s when, particularly in London, numerous protection rackets and money-making schemes were discovered. According to Morton (1993), this was followed by a period, the 1970s, that was dominated more by malpractice resulting in miscarriages of justice than by high earnings for corrupt officers. In this history of "bent coppers," Morton described at length cases in the United Kingdom of corrupt practices without personal gain, although he argues that there is very little distinction between those with and without gain, given that personal advantage is often gained through "noble cause" practices.

One of the main actors in the cleaning up of the Metropolitan Police in London was Sir Robert Mark in the 1970s. As the commissioner of the force, he instigated a number of sweeping reforms, which included setting up a special department to deal with police corruption. In Mark's (1978) view, the problem was not so much the uniformed patrol officers in Britain as the Criminal Investigation Department (CID). Gaining control of this department, he argued, would lead to the control of corruption. He claimed that a number of factors had combined to allow police corruption to become endemic and that the "function of policing being one of regulation and control, [it] involves an inevitable temptation to corruption, sometimes petty, sometimes serious" (p. 97). To illustrate this argument, he claimed the example of "sensible" laws that make gaming legal and remove the need to criminalize commonplace activities such as prostitution and abortion and the stigma attached to homosexuality. These new attitudes toward various aspects of social life had "virtually eliminated corruption from the uniformed branch of the police" by the late 1970s (Mark, 1978, p. 98).

Of course the police are in a difficult position as a publicly accountable service because they have to appear to be upholding the highest moral and ethical standards of behavior. Legitimate enforcers of the law have to be above subjective judgements affected by biases such as visible minority ethnicity, gender, or class. This is a matter of some concern in a number of specific areas, such as informer handling, and more generally in terms of the rights of the arrestee and bystanders' privacy. In addition, the Police Act (1997) now obliges the police in the United Kingdom to develop codes of practice with respect to issues such as intrusive surveillance, the new national crime squad, information technology, and criminal records (Uglow & Telford, 1997). Reiner (2000) expressed the view that "given the low visibility and hence inevitable discretion of much routine police work the key changes

**Table 5.1** The British Association of Chief Police Officers' Recommendations for an Ethical Code of Behavior

| *Ethical Principles* | *Implementation Difficulties* |
|---|---|
| Act with fairness, carrying out my responsibilities with integrity and impartiality. | Notion of "fairness" is partial and open to interpretation. |
| Perform my duties with diligence and a proper use of discretion. | *Discretion* is a problematic concept for which to provide rules or guidance. |
| Uphold fundamental human rights, treating every person as an individual and displaying respect toward them. | If everyone is treated as an individual, it may lead to some people being dealt with less "fairly" or equally than others. |
| Support my colleagues in the performance of their lawful duties and, in doing so, actively oppose and draw attention to any malpractice by any person. | Asking police officers to report others' misdeeds or corrupt practices may not fit easily within the solidarity culture. |
| Exercise force only when justified and then only use the minimum amount of force necessary to effect my legal purpose and restore the peace. | It is difficult to quantify the minimum amount of force necessary in any given situation. |

SOURCE: Westmarland (2000).

Note: The complete set of principles, including aspects of personal responsibility, is listed below.

must be in the informal culture of the police, their practical working rules" (p. 183). In quoting Wilson (1968, p. 7), Reiner (2000) argued that the police are a unique organization, in that "discretion increases as one moves down the hierarchy" (p. 86). In effect, therefore, those in the lowest ranks in supervisory terms have the most power in operational situations, and Waddington (1999) asks whether "police rules made by superiors serve to insulate them from criticism by pushing responsibility *down* the hierarchy" (p. 129).

There have been recent attempts to change this situation and to improve the poor image of detectives, which a number of cases of police corruption in the United Kingdom have highlighted. These efforts are not helped by situations in which police officers who sometimes are poorly supervised and are vulnerable to temptation "come into regular contact with criminals," situations in which "the dangers of informers and police officers becoming corrupt are high" (Clark, 2001, p. 38). Police managers and senior

policy makers have drawn up codes of conduct or "principles" for guidance in such situations, but officers may still have difficulty with adhering to a set of professional ethical standards (see Table 5.1).

The following list of the guidelines developed by a group of senior police officers in the United Kingdom illustrates that these codes of conduct can state the obvious in places (e.g., performance of duties with diligence), while demanding the impossible in others (e.g., always displaying self control, understanding, and courtesy).

1. Act with fairness, carrying out my responsibilities with integrity and impartiality.

2. Perform my duties with diligence and proper use of discretion.

3. Display self-control tolerance, understanding, and courtesy appropriate to the circumstances in my dealings with all individuals, both outside and inside the police service.

4. Uphold fundamental human rights, treating every person as an individual and display respect towards them.

5. Support my colleagues in the performance of their legal duties and, in doing so, actively oppose and draw attention to any malpractice by any person.

6. Respect the fact that much of the information I receive is confidential and may only be divulged when my duty requires me to do so.

7. Exercise force only when justified and then only use the minimum amount of force necessary to effect my lawful purpose and restore the peace.

8. Act only within the law, in the understanding that I have no authority to depart from due legal process and that no one may place a requirement upon me to do so.

9. Use resources entrusted to me to the benefit of the public.

10. Accept responsibility for my own self-development, continually seeking to improve the way in which I serve the community.

11. Accept personal responsibility for my own acts or omissions. (Neyroud & Beckley, 2001, p. 191).

Furthermore, police recruits tend to be socialized by more experienced officers who teach them to be aware of a number of "insider" cultural rules. One of the most important of these is the need to produce "results" such as arrests. As Fielding (1988) said, new recruits are "aware that 'arrests' are one of the concrete things which serve the organization's need to assess performance" (p. 151). Even experienced officers are afforded status according to their arrest rate (Westmarland, 2001a, pp. 108-109). Furthermore, due to the solitary nature of the work, police officers can often cover up their mistakes and embellish their successes. Another important aspect of "cop culture" is

officers' need to collude with other officers when they tell distorted versions of events, especially within the rarefied world of the Criminal Investigation Division (CID). It is an environment that Young (1991) described as "a closed and somewhat elite family group, whose strengths include the inside support of other members of that society" (p. 81). To blow the whistle on a close colleague in this situation could mean being ostracised from the work and social groupings of the others on the team. Fear of such exclusion, despite having reservations about the values and culture of the group, according to Morgan (1987) is "an even more powerful force than wishing to join it and be accepted" (p. 48). One of the dangers of this type of "solidaritist" behavior, however, is the pressure on individual officers to conform, despite any feelings they might have that something ethically or morally dubious has occurred.

In effect, Mark (1978) argued this was the case in the 1970s regarding the causes of corruption in the Metropolitan Police's CID prior to his reforms to clean up the force. Due to the CID regarding themselves as an elite, better paid and more autonomous than were uniformed officers, a culture developed that facilitated "three kinds of wrongdoing" (p. 122). Mark said that the first kind of wrongdoing was "institutional corruption," involving the suppression of information as a favor to the suspect in return for recruiting them as informers. According to Mark (1978), this was simply a cover for other much more dubious practices, namely accepting bribes. The second type of wrongdoing was involvement with more serious crimes, such as bank robbery, drugs, and illegal pornography, where "sweeteners" would be accepted. The third type of wrongdoing was the acceptance that the British criminal justice system was itself so corrupt as to make rule bending acceptable and necessary in order to work fairly (Mark, 1978, pp. 122-123).

Much later, in the 1990s, the Association of Chief Police Officers in Britain attempted to solve some of these problems by developing a working party to create a code of ethics for serving police officers. As Table 5.1 illustrates, however, a number of difficulties arise in the practical implementation of these integrity objectives (see Westmarland, 2000, for a fuller discussion of this). For each principle, fundamental problems arise in terms of definitions and meaning. A simple example is the problem with defining "reasonable force" for instance.

These principles not only are somewhat utopian but also seem to be aimed specifically at "operational" officers, particularly those in relatively junior posts within the organization. Many of the demands (such as reporting colleagues' misdeeds) are seemingly incompatible with police occupational culture. Others, such as the principles referring to the use of force or discretion, are already encoded within police rules and regulations or the law, where problems with defining terms like *reasonable* have never been resolved. Indeed, although codes of ethics are usually written by members of a profession or organization, as Kleinig (1996) has argued, they are usually written as the result of pressure from outside (p. 237). As they appear to be driven by those who have reason to be critical of the police, they can be regarded as part of the controlling function of management groups. On the other hand, in his discussion of ethics and police leaders, Alderson (1998) argued that police officers should not carry out orders that are unlawful. He suggests a code of ethics for senior ranking officers, which is reproduced below.

POLICE LEADERSHIP: A DECLARATION

I will seek to inculcate high ethical humanitarian standards into carrying out of duties by officers under my command, whilst at the same time accepting their need to use force, sometimes deadly force, in the lawful performance of their duty, the need to use powers granted to us by governments so that we may protect the people, their freedoms, and their property, in accordance with the spirit of the implied social contract.

I will not ask, demand of, or cause any officer under my command to carry out duties and actions which are contrary to the laws of my country, or to those laws of International covenants and treaties such as the Universal Declaration of Human Rights and its protocols, and the European Convention on Human Rights and Fundamental Freedoms which have been adopted by my government.

All this I promise in the cause of justice, freedom and the common good. (pp. 71-72)

It is evident from these two types of ethical guidance for U.K. police officers that contrasting requirements seem to exist for those in operational positions and those in managerial roles. In effect, one set of rules is about the types of values and beliefs officers should use to guide their behavior on the streets, and the latter set of principles is for managers in the "suites." These are about the orders given to their junior co-workers and, in a wider sense, they are about justice in a societal and international sense. These two sets of guidelines may have contradictory aims, however, and could be viewed as subscribing to a separate set of norms for each group.

## DEFINITIONS OF CORRUPTION AND INTEGRITY

Other attempts to encourage integrity and prevent corruption in the U.K. police have included a handbook of good practice (HMIC, 1999), an "anti-corruption strategy" for London's Metropolitan Police Service (see Westmarland, 2002, for a discussion of this strategy), and training on human rights. In order to be compliant with the new Human Rights legislation, forces in the United

Kingdom were obliged to carry out extensive in-service training. National committees were also established, one of which was to work toward deciding whether a code of ethics should be introduced. This type of action, however, is generally aimed at procedural or legal issues rather than "moral" conduct, which might be described as personal ethical issues, such as theft or deception leading to monetary gain. Indeed, Newburn (1999) argued that there are numerous ways of defining *corruption* that can discriminate between these two types of motivation. He begins with an outline of the various terms commonly used to describe various forms of corrupt behavior, such as "kickbacks," "shake-downs," and "flaking" or "padding" (p. 4). Drawing on Roebuck and Barker's (1974) typology, added to by Punch (1985), Newburn (1999) explained that many competing definitions, both broad and narrow, exist in the literature. Some useful distinctions Newburn has drawn from this literature include the difference between a police officer's action when stealing from the scene of a crime and when stealing from friends or family (the former being corruption, the latter being thievery) (Manning & Redlinger, 1977).

Other cases of corruption cited by Newburn (1999) draw on the misuse of authority or breach of trust arguments (Klockars, 1977), and the importance of considering not only the means by which the action was carried out but also the result or "ends" gained. Therefore, those actions that do not include the officer's profiting financially, receiving material goods, or advancing in any way may not be regarded by some as corruption per se. Where such behavior results in some perceived gain by the organization or some group within it, this is normally described as "noble cause" corruption. In summary, however, Newburn (1999) has argued that the means and ends should be considered of equal importance in any attempt to define corruption and further, that

the goals of the corrupt behavior might be well supported by the organization and no illegal conduct might be involved in the corrupt behavior. Hence the corrupt officer may be working with or against organizational goals and practices, with one or more colleagues, and/or for "private or organizational advantage" (p. 8).

In order to prevent these abuses, there are attempts by the Home Office, as the police audit and regulation body, to provide guidance and advice on integrity. Corruption is pervasive in police agencies and societies, it has a long history and is a problem throughout all ranks, but some areas are more "at risk" than others—and financial abuses are not the only abuses that it is important to consider (Newburn, 1999, p. 14). Indeed, the HMIC report mentioned above claims to "examine 'integrity' in its broadest sense, encompassing subjects such as fairness, behavior, probity, equal treatment and a range of operational and management issues. It is not about corruption in a narrow sense, rather how public confidence is secured and maintained" (HMIC, 1999, p. 3). Such image-conscious statements are reported to have begun in the early 1990s in Britain. Heward (1994) has reported that in 1992, throughout the British Chief Constables' national conference, delegates were aiming to find ways to regain public confidence by enhancing their image with "new speak." Talk of "negative personal experiences" replaced that of being framed, assaulted, or racially abused by the police. Miscarriages of justice, such as the case of the Birmingham Six (in which police officers were found to have fabricated crucial confession evidence; Belloni & Hodgson 2000, p. 7), became known as "high profile reversals" and, rather than the press being regaled by "old fashioned coppers in braid" demanding more rubber bullets, the new breed of chief constables were anxious to show their new sector policing, domestic violence, or equal opportunities initiatives. In addition, quality of service delivery and performance indicators are examples of this image management package, which Heward (1994) described as being designed to "empower consumers" (p. 242). The effectiveness of the past 10 years of such attempts will be assessed, to some extent, in the survey of British police officers that is discussed below.

## MEASURING INTEGRITY

In the next part of this chapter, findings from a survey of British police officers are discussed. Three areas of concern are explored in turn. The first is the issue of violations of the rules, particularly minor violations, or what are sometimes described as "invitational edge" or "slippery slope" misdemeanors (Sherman, 1985). The second area of concern is the concept of the "blue code" of silence, including how and why officers might choose to report colleagues who break or bend the rules. Newburn (1999) has argued that police managers "support" or at least collude in this secrecy by allowing officers to rely on the "existence of discretion and low visibility in the job" (pp. 18-19). In effect, he has argued that officers have a combination of limited managerial control, access to places in which they cannot be observed by the public, and "peer group secrecy" engendered by loyalty and occupational culture. A third issue tackled here is so-called noble cause corruption (Klockars, 1983), and whether such violations can be considered less serious acts when they involve acquisitive motives or violent outcomes.

The data for this chapter were gathered from questionnaires that were delivered through the internal mail system of a large police force in the southeast of England. It is one of the largest police departments in Britain and is located close to, and in places borders, the London Metropolitan Police. Other parts of the force area are more rural, but include major towns and cities and affluent commuter belt areas within their borders. Printed questionnaires were distributed in the force area within three subdivisions, largely on the eastern side of the geographic area covered by the force. After permission was granted to distribute the questionnaires, a meeting was held with senior officers in each of the relevant subdivisions at which the aims of the study were explained. In addition, there were numerous communications about the study with the deputy chief constable of the force, to make sure the language and terms—for instance, relating to discipline procedures—were compatible with usage in the United Kingdom in general and in this police department in particular. In total, 275 questionnaires were returned, representing a response rate of 27.5%, as 1,000 were distributed initially. The completed questionnaires were returned to the university for analysis by post, either from individual officers or through a communal collection point in the police station.

In the sample there were 216 men and 43 women, with the remainder declining to answer the question about gender. Hence the 16% of the sample said to comprise women is a reasonable representation of the gender composition of the U.K. police in general. At the end of 2001, there were 127,231 serving police officers in England and Wales, of which women comprised 17%. Around 10% of the survey respondents were probationers, with between 1 and 2 years of service. There were 171 police constables, 40 sergeants, and 24 officers with the rank of inspector or above. As might be expected, the vast majority of the sample were patrol officers, with 151 placing themselves in this category. In addition, 55 of the respondents were working as detectives, 23 were in special operations, 13 were in administration, and 19 were disposed to classify themselves as "other." Overall, 64 respondents classified themselves as being in a supervisory position, which means that about three quarters of the sample (74%) were working in positions in which, to take Reiner's (2000) view, there exists "the low visibility and inevitable discretion of much routine police work" (p. 183). Hence this survey draws a significant proportion of its evidence from officers most likely to be in what Sherman (1996) has termed the "heat of battle," discretionary decision-making situations.

## POLICE ETHICS IN
## THE UNITED KINGDOM

According to the questionnaires, U.K. officers think that a number of misdemeanors are fairly insignificant and not very serious. Although various activities are seen as perhaps against force policy or "definitely against it," as Table 5.2 shows, many officers think it "not at all serious" or "not serious." For instance, with regard to Case 2, which involves an officer accepting meals and gifts, most respondents think that it is contrary to force policy but are less certain about whether or not the misconduct is "serious."

With regard to one of the scenarios (Case 9), officers were asked about the behavior of a colleague who accepts a couple of drinks in return for not reporting that the pub was open later than it should have been. Although the goods that are offered are technically similar to those in the misconduct classed as not serious, more of the respondents think this misconduct is very serious (62.5%) or serious (26.5%). Also, in contrast to their responses to the other scenarios where meals or drinks are accepted, only 4% say that they would definitely not report it, and in this case they think that only 2% of their colleagues would not report it (see Table 5.3). Thus, for some reason, the misconduct in Case 9 is seen as more serious as that in other, similar cases. This may be linked to the issue of the pub being seen as a "public" space, one that is "more visible" than the "private" spaces that Newburn

(1999) has explained are an essential part of "peer group secrecy" and more amenable to the "blue curtain of secrecy" (Sherman, 1978, p. 47, quoted in Newburn, 1999, p. 19).

Similarly, Case 7, the scenario concerning the supervisor's allocation of leave for favors rendered, is a seemingly minor administrative violation. Of the respondents who rated the behavior of the supervisor, 30% think that it is a very serious offense and 41.5% think that it is a serious offense. In this case, 32% say that they would definitely report it. This case seems to have been judged more serious than some of the cases that were seemingly more "acquisitive," perhaps because the sample included such a large proportion of nonsupervisors (74%). The two cases of "noble cause" corruption (Klockars, 1983), which involve officers' deviation from the rules in the interests of their perception of "justice" or fairness rather than for personal gain, are Case 8, in which a police officer covers up for another officer who was in an drunk driving accident, and Case 10, in which police officers punch a suspected car thief after he has been caught. In addition to being classed as "corrupt" behavior, Case 8 could also be seen as an illustration of the "blue code," or protection of and covering up for police by their fellow officers. Hence, officers might view their actions as justified in terms of protecting the reputation of their local police department or the organization as a whole. They might reason that it would be better that officers guilty of misconduct did not lose their jobs and thus make the force less effective due to fewer human resources.

As Newburn (1999) has suggested, the "ends" resulting from the corrupt behavior might be supported by the organization and by individual colleagues (p. 7). With regard to Case 8, although almost 90% think it serious or very serious misconduct (at 22.5% and 66%, respectively), only 50% would definitely report it and they think that only 30% of their colleagues would report it. Regarding the second case in this noble cause/blue code

**Table 5.2**   British Officers' Views About the Seriousness of the Misconduct in the Scenarios

| | Not serious | 2 | 3 | 4 | Very Serious |
|---|---|---|---|---|---|
| Case 1<br>Off-Duty Security System Business<br>N = 267 | 41% | 24% | 17% | 11% | 5% |
| Case 2<br>Free Meals and Discounts on Beat<br>N = 271 | 10.5% | 18% | 29% | 27% | 14% |
| Case 3<br>Bribe From Speeding Motorist<br>N = 271 | 0% | 0% | 0% | 3% | 95% |
| Case 4<br>Holiday Gifts From Merchants<br>N = 270 | 21% | 33% | 29% | 12% | 4% |
| Case 5<br>Crime Scene Theft of Watch<br>N = 270 | 0 | 0 | 0 | 0 | 98.5% |
| Case 6<br>5% Kickback From Auto Repair Shop<br>N = 271 | 0 | 2% | 4% | 27% | 65% |
| Case 7<br>Supervisor Grants Holiday in Exchange<br>  for Car Tune-Up<br>N = 270 | 0.4% | 4% | 22% | 41.5% | 30% |
| Case 8<br>Cover-Up of Police DUI Accident<br>N = 271 | 1% | 2.5% | 6.5% | 22.5% | 66% |
| Case 9<br>Free Drinks to Ignore Late Bar Closing<br>N = 271 | 0 | 2% | 8% | 26.5% | 62.5% |
| Case 10<br>Excessive Force on Car Thief<br>N = 270 | 1% | 4% | 10.5% | 17.5% | 65.5% |
| Case 11<br>Theft From Found Wallet<br>N = 270 | 0 | 0 | 0 | 1% | 97% |

category, Case 10, 65.5% of the respondents consider the behavior of the officers who hit their captive arrestee very serious misconduct, and 54% say they think they would report this behavior or they would definitely report it, at 23% and 31%, respectively. Overall, 5% think that they would definitely not report it and 4% think that their colleagues would not report this sort of behavior.

**BENT FOR "SELF"**

In the survey, there are four scenarios that fit the "acquisitive" corruption model, as they involve a reasonable amount of financial gain. These include an officer's taking money from a found wallet (Case 11), a speeding motorist who gives money to the officer in return for not being reported (Case 3), an officer's taking a percentage to refer crashes to a particular body repair shop (Case 6), and an officer's taking a watch from a shop that has been burgled (Case 5). Certain distinctions can be made between these types of acquisitive actions, however, in terms of motive. It could be argued that the officer who takes the watch does so in the knowledge that the shopkeeper is insured and that one more item on the list will not make any difference. In this case, however, almost all the respondents, 97%, thought that the behavior was very serious misconduct, with 95% saying that they would definitely report it and they think that 85.5% of their colleagues would also report this behavior. Another example of an acquisitive action, the officer who takes money from a found wallet (Case 11), is regarded as very serious misconduct by a high proportion (97%) of respondents. Slightly fewer respondents (88%) think that they would definitely report this, however, and even fewer (74%) think that others would report such actions.

With regard to the officer who was receiving a percentage of the repair bill from a vehicle body shop (Case 6), 65% think this is very serious misconduct and 27% think it is serious misconduct. This said, only 61% think they would definitely report it and 20% think they would report it. Similarly, in the scenario about the officer who takes half the fine in return for not reporting the offense (Case 3), 95% think that this is very serious misconduct; however, only 81.5% think that they would definitely report it and 63% think their colleagues would also report this sort of behavior.

Overall, therefore, the types of behavior regarded as most serious were the four cases of acquisitive corruption. Of these scenarios, the respondents perceived the increasing seriousness of the officers' misconduct in this order: taking a watch at a burglary (Case 5), taking money from a found wallet (Case 11), taking a bribe from a speeding motorist (Case

3), and taking a kickback from a repair shop (Case 6). In each case, the exact amount of money cannot be ascertained, although the watch was described as worth 2 days' pay for an officer and the speeding fine would certainly only amount to a part, perhaps a maximum of one half, of an officer's day's pay, unless there were exceptional circumstances, such as excessive speed or previous convictions. Hence, the respondents' perceptions of the seriousness of the offenses in this survey are not necessarily related to the amount of financial gain for the officer involved. The scenario involving the theft of money from a found wallet (Case 11), for instance, was said to be equal to an officer's day's pay, and so it should, if this measure is used, be perceived by officers as half as serious as the watch incident in Case 5. It is clearly too simple to analyse actions, motives, and integrity in these terms, but it is interesting that the misconduct the officers in the U.K. sample have selected as most serious, and the misconduct they are most likely to report, involves the acquisition of money or apparently valuable property.

The findings from this survey suggest that in the United Kingdom there are three scenarios in which the respondents thought the officers' misconduct was very serious. These were Case 3, an officer taking a bribe of half the value of the speeding fine in exchange for not issuing a citation (95%); Case 5, an officer taking a watch at the scene of a burglary (98.5%); and Case 11, an officer taking money from a found wallet (97%). In each of these three scenarios, there is a high level of positive response to the question of whether the respondents would report the misconduct: 81.5% think that they would definitely report an officer's taking a bribe from a motorist, 95% think that they would report the officer's theft of a watch, and 88% think that they would report an officer's taking of money from a found wallet. The only other scenarios that came near to these three, in terms of respondents' perceptions of the seriousness of

**Table 5.3** British Officers' Views About Their Willingness to Report the Misconduct

|  | Definitely not | 2 | 3 | 4 | Definitely yes |
|---|---|---|---|---|---|
| Case 1<br>Off-Duty Security System Business<br>N = 265 | 45% | 20% | 14% | 7% | 10% |
| Case 2<br>Free Meals and Discounts on Beat<br>N = 271 | 22% | 28% | 25% | 12% | 12% |
| Case 3<br>Bribe From Speeding Motorist<br>N = 271 | 0 | 0.7% | 4% | 13% | 81.5% |
| Case 4<br>Holiday Gifts From Merchants<br>N = 270 | 37% | 30% | 18% | 9% | 5% |
| Case 5<br>Crime Scene Theft of Watch<br>N = 271 | 0 | 0 | 0.4% | 3% | 95% |
| Case 6<br>5% Kickback From Auto Repair Shop<br>N = 271 | 2% | 5% | 12% | 20% | 61% |
| Case 7<br>Supervisor Grants Holiday in Exchange<br>  for Car Tune-Up<br>N = 270 | 6% | 14% | 21% | 26% | 32% |
| Case 8<br>Cover-Up of Police DUI Accident<br>N = 271 | 6% | 6% | 15% | 22% | 50% |
| Case 9<br>Free Drinks to Ignore Late Bar Closing<br>N = 271 | 4% | 8% | 23% | 21% | 43% |
| Case 10<br>Excessive Force on Car Thief<br>N = 269 | 5% | 8% | 15% | 17% | 53% |
| Case 11<br>Theft From Found Wallet<br>N = 270 | 0 | 0.4% | 1.5% | 9% | 88% |

the misconduct and their likelihood of reporting it, were Case 6, the scenario about the officer taking a percentage from the vehicle repair shop (65% think it is very serious misconduct and 61% think that they would report it), and Case 8, the scenario about the drunk driving colleague (66% think it is serious misconduct). Here, the "breach of trust"

argument is clearly illustrated. Officers who steal from their friends, families, or others when they are not on duty are "merely thieves," but those who steal in the course of their work are corrupt (Newburn, 1999, p. 6).

Further, it could be argued that the punishment an officer might receive affects the respondent's likelihood of reporting the officer's misconduct. Reporting might lead to a punishment for the guilty officer that his or her fellow officers may feel they wouldn't want to initiate. So, for example, in the case of the officer receiving the cut from the body repair shop, 50.5% think that the punishment would and should be dismissal, which might affect their willingness to report their colleague (see Tables 5.4 and 5.5). This consideration appears to be overridden, however, when the offense becomes serious enough, as in the case of the watch, wallet, and speeding fine scenarios, where in the latter case, 78.5% think dismissal an appropriate punishment and 76% think dismissal would follow the discovery of such misconduct. Similarly, in the watch scenario, 93% think dismissal should be the consequence and 92% think it would be the case. In the wallet scenario, 90% of respondents think that dismissal is the appropriate punishment for the offense and 87% think this would be the outcome.

So, these "worst case" scenarios illustrate high levels of agreement between officers' perceptions of the seriousness of the misconduct and their willingness to report it, despite the likelihood that their colleague would be dismissed and that the responsibility for it may lie with the person blowing the whistle. It may be that the respondents feel that the behavior is so reprehensible that they would have no qualms about what they had to do to stop it or see it punished. They may also feel that someone with the poor moral standards of their guilty colleague should not serve as a police officer.

As explained earlier, there are some minor "administrative" misdemeanors on the questionnaire that respondents think they would not report. Typically, the punishments or sanctions the respondents suggest in these cases are minor and tend to be similar to what the officers think should happen to the person concerned. In other words, respondents think that the misdemeanors would attract a fine or a verbal or written warning, which seems to be generally in line with what they think

should happen. Where the ambiguity arises, however, is in the marginal cases where the "crime" is less clear in terms of its outcome. One example is Case 8, in which the drunk driver stopped at the scene of an accident is a police officer, and the other is Case 10, in which two officers assault a captive suspect. It is unclear from the brief scenarios whether any of the officers knew each other previously and, of particular importance in the drunk driver scenario, whether they were from the same police force. It is debateable whether the respondents' answers reflect their feeling that they are protecting someone "on their side," as the blue code argument would suggest. What is interesting, however, is the percentage of respondents in the U.K. survey who think they would definitely not report such behavior: In the drunk driver case, this is 6% of the officers, and regarding their colleagues' reporting, this is 2.5%. Similarly, in the assault on the captive suspect, 5% think they would definitely not report it and 4% think their colleagues would be unlikely to do so.

A possible explanation for these levels of nonreporting is that the punishment the officers think would follow their reporting the misconduct of a fellow officer is regarded as excessive. In the case of the drunk driver, for example, 59% of the respondents think the officer would be dismissed; for the assault, 61% think this would be the outcome. In the case of the drunk driver, 48% think this should be the punishment, a difference of 10%; whereas for the assault, 52% think this should happen, a difference of only 4%. This small difference between what the officers perceive the punishment should and would be may have influenced their decision about reporting, but this is an area that needs more investigation. Punishment perceived as suitable and as probable by officers for some versions of what might arguably be described as "noble cause" corruption may be seen by other officers as too harsh. As noted earlier, the most serious and punishable offenses, in

**Table 5.4**    British Officers' Views About the Discipline the Misconduct Would Receive

|  | *None* | *Verbal* | *Written* | *Fine* | *Demotion* | *Dismissal* |
|---|---|---|---|---|---|---|
| **Case 1** Off-Duty Security System Business | 28.4% | 12% | 27% | 16% | 0.7% | 9% |
| **Case 2** Free Meals and Discounts on Beat | 6% | 30% | 37% | 13% | 3% | 7% |
| **Case 3** Bribe From Speeding Motorist | 0.7% | 0.4% | 6% | 12% | 1% | 76% |
| **Case 4** Holiday Gifts From Merchants | 16% | 34% | 28% | 12% | 4% | 0.7% |
| **Case 5** Crime Scene Theft of Watch | 0.4% | 0.7% | 0% | 2% | 1% | 92% |
| **Case 6** 5% Kickback From Auto Repair Shop | 0.7% | 2.5% | 10% | 23% | 5% | 50.5% |
| **Case 7** Supervisor Grants Holiday in Exchange for Car Tune-Up | 6% | 18.5% | 29% | 9.5% | 27% | 5% |
| **Case 8** Cover-Up of Police DUI Accident | 0.4% | 1.5% | 9% | 16% | 7% | 59% |
| **Case 9** Free Drinks to Ignore Late Bar Closing | 1.5% | 6% | 22% | 23% | 9% | 32% |
| **Case 10** Excessive Force on Car Thief | 0.7% | 5% | 8% | 11% | 5% | 61% |
| **Case 11** Theft From Found Wallet | 0.4% | 0.7% | 1.5% | 2% | 3% | 87% |

the view of the officers who responded, are the actions and behaviors that could result in financial gain for the individual. Even the behavior of the officer who took home the drunk driver—whom it could be argued might pose the threat of killing someone if he is not identified, punished, and dismissed—is nevertheless considered less serious misconduct by the respondents than taking a watch worth 2 days' pay. Similarly, the officer who takes a bribe not to report a speeding motorist is seen as committing a very serious offense, and respondents may also be taking into account that what he did could be seen as acting against road safety. Nevertheless, the case of an officer taking money worth a day's

pay from a found wallet and the case of an officer taking a bribe from a car repairer are considered worse offenses than the behavior of an officer who covers for a colleague who has had an accident while driving drunk. Of course, the behavior being judged is that of the officer who covers up for the offender, not that of the offender. If the question had been posed about direct reporting of an officer who had had an accident while driving drunk, the results may have been different. Nevertheless, consistent responses that the offense is very serious and that the officers would definitely report it are reserved for these four acquisitive crimes. Thus the findings from the United Kingdom suggest that

**Table 5.5**    British Officers' Views About the Discipline the Misconduct Should Receive

|  | *None* | *Verbal* | *Written* | *Fine* | *Demotion* | *Dismissal* |
|---|---|---|---|---|---|---|
| **Case 1**<br>Off-Duty Security System Business | 41% | 18% | 25% | 6% | 4% | 0.4% |
| **Case 2**<br>Free Meals and Discounts on Beat | 14.5% | 34% | 34% | 8% | 1.5% | 4% |
| **Case 3**<br>Bribe From Speeding Motorist | 0% | 0% | 5% | 9% | 3.3% | 78.5% |
| **Case 4**<br>Holiday Gifts From Merchants | 30% | 38% | 20% | 4% | 0.7% | 2% |
| **Case 5**<br>Crime Scene Theft of Watch | 0% | 0% | 0.4% | 1.5% | 0.4% | 93.1% |
| **Case 6**<br>5% Kickback From Auto Repair Shop | 0% | 2% | 10.5% | 23% | 8% | 50.5% |
| **Case 7**<br>Supervisor Grants Holiday in Exchange<br>for Car Tune-Up | 2% | 19% | 29% | 8% | 30.5% | 5.5% |
| **Case 8**<br>Cover-Up of Police DUI Accident | 1% | 5% | 10% | 18% | 10.5% | 48% |
| **Case 9**<br>Free Drinks to Ignore Late Bar Closing | 0.7% | 8% | 25.5% | 26% | 7% | 27% |
| **Case 10**<br>Excessive Force on Car Thief | 2% | 8% | 10.5% | 13.5% | 8% | 52% |
| **Case 11**<br>Theft From Found Wallet | 0% | 0% | 1% | 2.5% | 1.5% | 90% |

officers view acquisitive crime—that is, the taking of money or property—by police officers as very serious misconduct and as unacceptable behavior even where the amounts of money are relatively small. Further, this is the type of behavior that respondents say they would be likely to report. Other behavior, such as officers' use of excessive force, is regarded as serious by the respondents, but they say they would be less likely to report it. This could be due to their belief that the punishment would be excessive or that, we might speculate, the occurrence of such behavior is so common as not to warrant reporting.

## CONCLUSION

Police ethics is being viewed with increasing interest throughout the world by academics and practitioners. Alderson (1998) has described this period in the United Kingdom as one of "scholarly interest in police affairs" (p. 11). As others have argued (see Newburn, 1999, and Neyroud and Beckley, 2001, for a fuller discussion), issues surrounding ethics can be placed within traditional academic debates concerning accountability, legitimacy, and even equal opportunities and diversity. In effect, how police officers treat their colleagues and members of the public has always had an ethical or moral dimension, but this was not really explicitly stated until "ethical policing" became an issue. In his description of "principled policing," for example, Alderson (1998) has argued that throughout history and across many societies, versions of what it is to be "ethical" exist. More fundamentally, in Kleinig's (1996) analysis of such questions, he asked what moral basis exists for the powers we afford the police and whether there might be some preferable system available (p. 11).

Thus, despite evidence from this study of high levels of reported integrity in the British police, as the first British survey to examine rank and file police officers' beliefs about morals and ethics, it leaves many questions unanswered. Although it provides initial insight into the respondents' attitudes and views on certain behavior, it is debatable whether the officers' "integrity" can be assessed from their answers to the questions that were asked. This is partly because the participants were asked about what they think they or their colleagues might do in certain situations, rather than about what they had done in the past. Further, their predictions of the punishment they think the officers in the scenarios should, and probably would, receive were based on the limited details given for each scenario. Respondents' actual reactions might very well depend on their relationship to and feelings about the person violating the rules. In some cases, a close professional "buddy" might not be reported, and some unexplored circumstance, such as behavior out of character due to some sort of life crisis the officer may be experiencing, might be a factor. Hence, the working partnership that develops between officers over time could affect how the officer would reply, as would individual circumstances and context. Regarding some scenarios, where respondents say that they think the misconduct is very serious but a

significant number say they would not report it, it could be supposed that either circumstances or comradeship, or perhaps other forms of resolution (such as telling the officer to give the money back, for instance) might have been envisaged.

It is therefore difficult to draw precise conclusions from this survey because it presents scenarios that individual officers may not have experienced, and yet the data that have resulted from it are interesting in at least two respects. First, in some cases the respondents say that although they believe that certain misconduct is very serious, they wouldn't always report it and, in most cases, they think their colleagues would be even less likely to do so. The second interesting aspect of the data from the United Kingdom that should be emphasized is that corrupt behavior involving financial gain is viewed by the respondents as more serious than are other misdemeanors, such as assaulting an arrestee. Data indicating that more officers think they would report a colleague who had stolen a watch than one who had carried out such an assault or taken a drunk colleague home from the scene of an accident are also the first of their type in the United Kingdom. In effect, the respondents reveal that they can tolerate colleagues' receiving small gifts and even assaulting suspects, but that when officers get greedy, or are in their view simply stealing, their behavior crosses the line of acceptability.

Such actions, we might argue, are understandable in some circumstances. Problems arise within all professional groups when the behavior of certain individuals crosses acceptable boundaries. Like other occupational groups, police officers occasionally use unethical, illegal, or improper actions to achieve their ends (Klockars, 1983; Macintyre & Prenzler, 1999). Police officers often have to make decisions about which course of action to take, without the benefit of time for reflection or peer consultation.

They often work alone and can find themselves in a powerful position regarding the outcome of incidents and the lives of people they encounter. As Kleinig (1996) has argued, professionals such as doctors, lawyers, and university professors work within systems that afford certain freedoms, and it is assumed that they will "exercise good judgement and discretion" (p. 256).

Indeed, some commentators, such as Davis (1991), have questioned whether public servants such as police officers should be required to abide by proscribed ethical standards. The argument is that the people the police are investigating will not abide by any sort of moral or ethical codes, so to encourage police officers to do so will diminish their effectiveness. In effect, such commentators are saying that using "dirty" methods is essential to catch criminals (Villiers, 1987) and that the public accepts, and in some cases expects, a certain amount of police "rule bending" (Klockars, 1983). Unlike other organizations, however, the police have to consider their role as the enforcers of society's mandate to control and detect crime and those committing illegal acts. In this role, they have to be aware of how their actions are perceived and that the way the mandate is enacted is as important as the outcome. It is clear that the police have to be seen to be acting in a fair and just manner because they are the body that arbitrates over so many circumstances where discretionary judgements about these matters are made. In addition, as Neyroud and Beckley (2001) have suggested, the demands created by published performance indicators in the United Kingdom mean that there has been a "rise of managerialism that has taken place at the expense of personal autonomy" (p. 94), potentially creating new ethical dilemmas for the police in the United Kingdom and elsewhere in the world.

## REFERENCES

Alderson, J. (1998). *Principled policing: Protecting the public with integrity.* Winchester, UK: Waterside.

Belloni, F., & Hodgson, J. (2000). *Criminal justice. An evaluation of the criminal justice process in Britain.* Hampshire, UK: Macmillan Press.

Benyon, J., & Bourn, C. (Eds.). (1986). *The police: Powers, procedures and proprieties.* Oxford: Pergamon.

Cain, M. (1992). Trends in the sociology of policework. In K. R. E. McCormick & L. A. Visano (Eds.), *Understanding policing.* Toronto: Canadian Scholars' Press.

Davis, M. (1991). Do cops really need a code of ethics? *Criminal Justice Ethics,* 10(Summer/Fall), 14-28.

Fielding, N. (1988). *Joining forces: Police training, socialisation and occupational competence.* London: Routledge.

Flanagan, T. J., & Vaughn, M. S. (1996). Public opinion about police abuse of force. In W. A. Geller & H. Toch (Eds.), *Police violence: Understanding and controlling police abuse of force.* New Haven & London: Yale University Press.

Heward, T. (1994). Retailing the police: Corporate identity and the Met. In R. Keat, N. Whitely, & N. Abercrombie (Eds.), *The authority of the consumer.* London: Routledge.

Her Majesty's Inspectorate of Constabulary (HMIC). (1999). *Police Integrity: England, Wales and Northern Ireland. Securing and Maintaining Public Confidence.* London: Author.

Holdaway, S. (1996). *The racialisation of British policing*. London: Macmillan.

Home Office. (2001). *Police service strength* (Home Office Statistical Bulletin). London: HMSO.

Johnston, L. (2000). *Policing Britain*. Longman: Essex.

Jones, T., MacLean, B., & Young, J. (1986). *The Islington Crime Survey: Crime, victimization and policing in inner-city London*. Aldershot, UK: Gower.

Kleinig, J. (1996). *The ethics of policing*. Cambridge, UK: Cambridge University Press.

Klockars, C. B. (1983). The Dirty Harry problem. In C. B. Klockars (Ed.), *Thinking about police*. New York: McGraw-Hill.

Macintyre, S., & Prenzler, T. (1999). The influence of gratuities and personal relationships on police use of discretion. *Policing and Society, 9*(2), 181-201.

Manning, P. K., & Redlinger, L. J. (1983). Invitational edges. In C. B. Klockars (Ed.), *Thinking about police*. New York: McGraw-Hill.

Mark, R. (1978). *In the Office of Constable*. London: Collins.

Mawby, R. I.(1999). *Policing across the world: Issues for the twenty-first century*. London: UCL Press.

Morgan, D. (1987). *"It Will Make a Man of You": Notes on national service, masculinity and autobiography. Studies in sexual politics*. Manchester, UK: University of Manchester Press.

Morgan, R., & Newburn, T. (1997.) *The future of policing*. Oxford: Clarendon.

Morton, J. (1993). *Bent coppers. A survey of police corruption*. London: Little, Brown.

Newburn, T. (1999). *Understanding and preventing police corruption: Lessons from the literature*. London: Home Office Policing and Reducing Crime Unit.

Newton, T. (1998). The place of ethics in investigative interviewing by police officers. *The Howard Journal, 37*(1), 52-69.

Neyroud, P., & Beckley, R. (2001). *Policing, ethics and human rights*. Devon, UK: Willan.

Povey, D., & Cotton, J. (2001). *Police complaints and discipline, 21/01* (Home Office RDS). London: HMSO.

Povey, D., & Rundle, S. (2001). *Police service strength. England and Wales, 30 September 2001*. (Home Office Statistical Bulletin 23/01, Home Office RDS). London: HMSO.

Reiner, R. (2000). *The politics of the police* (3rd ed.). Oxford: Oxford University Press.

Sherman, L. W. (1985). Becoming bent: Moral careers of corrupt policemen. In F. A. Elliston & M. Feldberg (Eds.), *Moral issues in police work*. Totowa, NJ: Rowan and Allanheld.

Sherman, L. W. (1996). Learning police ethics. In M. C. Braswell, B. R. McCarthy, & B. J. McCarthy (Eds.), *Justice, crime and ethics* (2nd ed.). Cincinnati, OH: Anderson.

Uglow, S., & Telford, V. (1997). *The Police Act 1997*. Bristol, UK: Jordans.

Uildriks, N., & van Mastrigt, H. (1991). *Policing police violence*. Boston: Kluwer Law.

Villiers, P. (1987). *Better police ethics*. London: Kegan Paul.

Waddington, P. A. J. (1999). *Policing citizens: Authority and rights*. London: UCL Press.

Westmarland, L. (2000, Fall). Telling the truth the whole truth and nothing but the truth? Ethics and the enforcement of law. *Journal of Ethical Sciences and Services, 2*(3), 193-202.

Westmarland, L. (2001a). *Gender and policing: Sex, power and police culture*. Devon, UK: Willan.

Westmarland, L. (2001b). Blowing the whistle on police violence: Gender, ethnography and ethics. *British Journal of Criminology, 41*(2), 523-535.

Westmarland, L. (2002). Challenges of policing London: A conversation with the metropolitan police commissioner, Sir John Stevens. *Police Practice and Research: An International Journal, 3*(3), 247-260.

Wilson, J. Q. (1968). *Varieties of police behavior.* Cambridge, MA: Harvard University Press.

Young, M. (1991). *An inside job: Policing and police culture in Britain.* Oxford: Oxford University Press.

# CHAPTER 6

# Sustaining Police Integrity in Finland

Anne Puonti

Sami Vuorinen

Sanja Kutnjak Ivković

## INTRODUCTION

A recent article title in the leading Finnish newspaper announced: "A Police Officer Convicted of Assault Should Not Have Been Re-employed. Assistant Parliamentary Ombudsman: 'Police Officers Must Be Pronouncedly Blameless'" (Reinboth, 2002a, p. A7). The article was about a police officer who hit his wife and was consequently convicted of assault and fired, but who was able to get a post some time later as an officer in another police department. This situation raised a public debate. Ten days later, the same newspaper contained an interview with the National Police Commander titled "Supreme Police Command Fears the Status of the Police Is Bloodied Because of the Assaulter" (Reinboth, 2002b, p. A8). These titles nicely illustrate how Finns generally feel about police officers: They should be more upright than the average Finn. The Supreme Police Command fears that a single case of misconduct will harm the image of the police. It expresses its willingness to abolish the first stains that threaten the good image of the police, so as to prevent a situation where there are so many stains that new ones go unnoticed. A corrupt or otherwise illegally behaving police officer is, indeed, a rare phenomenon in Finland. Let's look at a description of a morally dubious police officer, Tapsa, found in a semiautobiographical Finnish novel of a criminal:

> His speech was already drunkard's sputter, but you could figure it out. Tapsa was all too grasping and greedy for booze for a

AUTHOR'S NOTE: We would like to extend our sincere gratitude to Hannu Kiehelä, Head of the Research Unit at the Police College of Finland, for collecting the survey data and making the data set available to us.

police officer. He did not possess the strict and ascetic self-discipline so typical of guardians of laws. In fact, Tapsa may have turned out to be a professional criminal in other circumstances. He enjoyed spending money, booze, and women; he did not have tight moral rules; and he hated to wake up early in the morning for work. His bad economic situation, deriving from his drinking, was of help in this [loosening of his morals]. (Tulimeri, 1994, p. 56; our translation)

In this excerpt, we can read a description of the opposite between the lines as well: what the author, a convicted professional criminal, thinks a decent police officer is like. The text suggests that a police officer normally keeps a distance, is sober, is self-disciplined, is moral, is not greedy, and is punctual at work. According to the surveys made on how Finns see the police, the image of a trustworthy police officer seems, indeed, to be the prevalent conception (Lappi-Seppälä, Tala, Litmala, & Jaakkola, 1999). The statistics on the crimes committed by police officers are in accordance with this conception: Charges against police officers are very rare in general and corruption cases against police officers were not tried in courts at all during 2000 and 2001 (Office of the Prosecutor General, Finland, 2002).

We will examine several sources of data to view the integrity of police officers and police corruption from different perspectives. However, the general situation concerning corruption cannot be excluded, as the general situation is definitely reflected in the police. The purpose of this chapter is to describe the integrity of Finnish police practice. We shall approach this target through the four different perspectives represented in the following questions:

1. What is the level of corruption in Finnish society in general, and how is it reflected in the activity of police officers and civil servants?

2. What is the status of the police institution in Finnish society?

3. How common are corruption and other abuses of power in the Finnish police, and what is the exposed and suspected misconduct like?

4. How do police officers view police corruption, and what is the overall level of police integrity?

Finally, we will consider the reasons for the reportedly low rates of police corruption and high rate of police integrity in Finland, as well as ponder the threats and challenges that Finnish society may face in the future, despite the present calm situation.

## DATA AND METHODS

The Police Department of the Ministry of the Interior acts as the Supreme Police Command in Finland. The number of Finnish police officers in relation to population is the smallest in Europe: There is 1 police officer per 650 inhabitants in Finland, compared to the average European Union (EU) figure of 1 officer per 300 people. There are 90 local police departments in Finland, which operate under the Provincial Police Command in the State Provincial Offices of the five provinces. The national police departments (such as the National Bureau of Investigation and the Security Police) report directly to the Supreme Police Command. The Province of Åland has its own independent police department. In addition to the 90 local police departments, there are national police units, which operate directly under the Ministry of the Interior. These are comprised of the National Bureau of Investigation, Security Police, National Traffic Police, the Police School, Police College, and the Police Technical Center. The biggest police department in Finland, the Helsinki Police Department, operates directly under the

Ministry of the Interior as well. At the end of December of 1998, the police administration employed a total of 10,633 persons, 7,891 of whom were police officers. Approximately 7% of the police officers were women. The Local Police employed 6,818 police officers, the National Traffic Police employed 680 officers, the National Bureau of Investigation employed 511 officers, the Security Police employed 169 officers, and the police institutes employed 132 officers. The corresponding figure for the Police Technical Center was 57 police officers.[1]

Police duties are social public authority duties. Therefore, it is justified to base the analysis of police integrity on the general level of corruption in the Finnish society. The main sources of information regarding government corruption in Finland are comparative studies made by Transparency International[2] and the reports of the Organisation for Economic Cooperation and Development (OECD) Secretariat for anticorruption work (OECD, 2001). Transparency International's Corruption Perceptions Index (CPI) consists of several sources, which use different sampling frames and various methodologies.[3]

Research has been carried out in several countries to assess the level of trust in social institutions.[4] It is reasonable to claim that the level of trust people feel is based on the actions of these institutions. The most recent survey on people's confidence in their social institutions was conducted in Finland in 1998 (Lappi-Seppälä et al., 1999). A random sample of 1,281 respondents, from 15 to 74 years of age, was asked by phone, "How much do you trust the following institutions . . .?" One of the 17 institutions named was the police (Lappi-Seppälä et al., 1999, pp. 8-15). The survey was similar to two international surveys, the World Values Survey and the European Values Survey (Listhaug & Wiberg, 1995).

We assess corruption and fraudulence among Finnish police officers on the basis of official statistics and the outcome of the International Crime Victim Survey (ICVS). All the information concerning reports about offenses committed by police officers is collected regularly by the Office of the Prosecutor General, the highest prosecuting official in Finland. In 2001, reports of such offenses were made in 392 cases (Office of the Prosecutor General, Finland, 2002).

The ICVS, by interviewing representative samples of adults, assesses victimization (with regard to violence and property crime) and reporting crimes to the police. Finland participated in all four sweeps of the survey (1989, 1992, 1996, and 2000). In 2000, the sample was 1,818 people (Aromaa & Heiskanen, 2000, p. 2). The following question regarding corruption was asked in 1996 and 2000: "In some countries, there is a problem of corruption among government or public officials. During 1995[1999], has any governmental official, for instance a custom officer, a police officer or inspector in your country asked you to, or expected you to pay a bribe for his or her services?" (Aromaa & Heiskanen, 2000, p. 21).

To assess the integrity level of the Finnish police officers, we employ the survey methodology developed by Klockars and Kutnjak Ivković (Kutnjak Ivkovich & Klockars, 1996), the purpose of which is to measure police officers' attitudes toward police corruption and integrity. In the survey carried out in Finland, the police officers were presented with 17 descriptions of police behavior that may depart from official policy. In addition to the 11 hypothetical scenarios focusing almost exclusively on police corruption (ranging from an officer accepting a free cup of coffee to stealing money from a found wallet), the questionnaire included 6 hypothetical scenarios describing other forms of police misconduct, such as illegitimate use of deadly force, use of excessive force, and verbal abuse of citizens.[5] With the purpose of measuring the same underlying phenomenon—police integrity—the respondents were asked the same set of seven questions after each scenario; the questions inquired about the seriousness of the misconduct, knowledge of official rules, the appropriate and expected discipline for the misconduct, and the officers' willingness to report it.

The questionnaires were distributed electronically in 1999. Responses were received from 378 respondents from four police districts, the police personnel of the Ministry of the Interior, recruits from the Police School, and the personnel of the Police School. The majority of the respondents had been police officers for over 10 years; only 24.9% reported that they had been police officers for 10 years or less. Despite their overall long experience in policing, the officers' length of employment in their present police agency was somewhat shorter, in that 60% had been employed in their current police agency for less than 10 years (with 36.2% employed in their present agency for 5 years or less). In terms of agency sizes, the respondents were almost uniformly split among very large agencies (29.0%), large agencies (24.0%), medium-sized agencies (24.9%), and smaller agencies (22.2%). Eight out of ten respondents occupied nonsupervisory positions, and most of the respondents worked in patrol/order maintenance (64.1%) or investigations (25.7%).

## ANALYSIS OF DATA ON THE INTEGRITY OF THE FINNISH POLICE

### The Overall Level of Corruption and Expectations of Integrity

Many separate reports and researches suggest that the level of corruption is low in Western European countries and in North America. Lashmar (2001, p. 150) noticed that in these so-called Western countries corruption is typically manifested as the bribery of regional or foreign officials.

Laitinen (1989, pp. 78-98) has formulated a ranking of the types of gifts or bribes offered to Finnish civil servants. His list is based on a survey posted to selected clusters of state and municipal officials. The most common gifts or bribes the respondents named were (1) a lunch or dinner, (2) an evening's entertainment, (3) goods, (4) "exceptionally" large discounts in purchases, (5) domestic or foreign trips, and (6) other favors. More than 80% of the civil servants he studied had been offered a gift or bribe at least once, most often from building contractors and other enterprises. However, he did not hear recounts of monetary bribes like those revealed in connection with some organizational crimes handled by the courts. Laitinen could not find out how many of the civil servants had actually accepted bribes. The civil servants themselves did not consider bribery a problem; they thought that the public discussion in the 1980s about the boundaries between permissible and unacceptable gifts and advantages was "severe and meticulous" (Laitinen, 1989, p. 105).

Transparency International's annual Corruption Perceptions Index (CPI) reflects the degree to which corruption is perceived to exist among public officials and politicians. For the last 2 years, the level of perceived corruption in Finland's public service has been rated as the lowest of the 91 countries studied.

In September of 2001, Finland was the first party to the Convention on Combating Bribery of Foreign Public Officials in International Business Transactions to be visited by an evaluation team from the OECD Working Group. The team noticed a high level of transparency in and accessibility of the Finnish government. This was particularly evident during consultations with the private sector and civil society, both of which praised the Finnish government for its openness. The efficient monitoring of civil servants by two independent bodies (the Office of the Parliamentary Ombudsman and the Office of the Chancellor of Justice) was acknowledged as well (OECD, 2001).

## Expectations of Police Integrity

The aforementioned integrity of the public officials is typical throughout the Finnish governing system. Officials are expected to be honest. Because of the status of police officers as users of public power, the legitimacy of all their actions is extremely important. For instance, according to the Act issued on police training (A 1272/1997, 15§), "a person to be selected to the Police School has to be suitable for taking care of the duties of the police." In practice, a minor disciplinary record will bar a person from a career in the police force.[6] The applicants for the Police School have to receive a certificate of their suitability and impeccability from the local police chief. Another example of the application of the rule of suitability is the specific instance of a police officer who had been convicted of several assaults losing his job because of the offense. After a while, he applied for a new post as a police officer and managed to get temporary employment. However, his hiring raised a stir and his employment was not renewed. The demand for blamelessness in civil servants working in security tasks is tighter than it is for civil servants working in other tasks (Helminen, Kuusimäki, & Salminen, 1999, p. 329)

The legitimacy of the police, as well as the legitimacy of other institutions, can be measured through surveys. As discussed earlier, in Finland the last measure of confidence in social institutions was carried out in 1998 (Lappi-Seppälä et al., 1999). According to that survey, the Finnish police enjoy the confidence of the people. The survey

showed that 92% of the respondents in a representative sample of Finnish society noted that they trust the police. Only 1% of respondents provided the information that they do not trust the police at all. The level of confidence was very high when compared both with the level of confidence in other domestic state and municipal institutions and with the level of confidence in the police felt by citizens in other countries. According to the survey, another security institution, the military forces, enjoys almost as high a level of confidence as the police (88%). The people's confidence in the other social institutions measured in the survey did not reach near the level of their confidence in their security institutions.

From the survey, we can see that the police have a stable and significant status in Finnish society. The police inspire the people with confidence. The people's confidence in the police is greater than their confidence in most other social institutions (Lappi-Seppälä et al., 1999, p. 25). The high level of confidence proves that the police have fulfilled the most important expectations and requirements of the people. The most significant principles in all official service are integrity and incorruptibility.[7] Repeated violation or neglect of these principles would undoubtedly lower the confidence the people feel in the police.

On the international front, in the surveys made during the past two decades no institution has ever in any country reached high levels of public confidence equal to those achieved by the Finnish police in the 1998 survey. Generally, the confidence in the police has been highest in Nordic countries. The surveys show that the level of the people's confidence in the police is high in Denmark (89%), in Norway (88%), and in Iceland (85%) (Listhaug & Wiberg, 1995). According to the CPI,[8] these countries are at the same time among the least corrupted countries in the world as well.

In sum, it seems that there is a connection between low corruption and a high level of confidence in security institutions: People's confidence in security institutions is especially high in the countries of low corruption such as Finland. Indeed, the fact that people consider security one of the most important duties of the government could explain the relationship between high public confidence in the police and low corruption. An unstable and corrupted society is typically also insecure. On the other hand, because Finnish people feel safe, they think that the police are reliable and that police officers give them protection.

It is estimated that around 40% of crimes are reported to the police in Finland. Moreover, the international comparison based on the 1992 ICVS shows that crimes are reported to the police less frequently in Finland than in other European countries (van Dijk & Mayhew, 1993). This observation seems a little surprising. Why do people who trust the police not report crimes—even when they themselves are the victims? Aromaa & Heiskanen (2000, p. 14) believe that this difference in crime reporting behavior reflects differences in the crime structures across countries. Apparently, in many European countries the prevailing crimes are serious in nature, the ones that people are most willing to report. In Finland, on the other hand, the less serious crimes are prevalent in the crime structure and people's willingness to report them may therefore be low, especially when compensation for the crime is available through an insurance company.

In addition to the CPI and OECD reports, a number of other reports show that the corruption level in Finland is low. For example, according to the results of the 2000 ICVS, less than 1% (0.2%) of people (4 respondents) reported that a Finnish official had asked or expected a bribe for his or her services. The 1996 question regarding corruption yielded even fewer affirmative answers (0.1%). None of the civil servants demanding bribes were police officers (Aromaa & Heiskanen, 2000, pp. 19-20).

## Police Perceptions About Police Integrity

The results of the integrity survey support the overall image of the Finnish police as a police force intolerant of corruption; the results on all of the measures of police integrity—officers' perceptions of the seriousness of misconduct, knowledge of official rules, opinions about appropriate and expected discipline for the misconduct, and expressed willingness to report it—point in the same direction.

### The Seriousness of the Misconduct

The respondents evaluated Case 1 (Off-Duty Security System Business) as the least serious misconduct and Case 5 (Crime Scene Theft of Watch) as the most serious misconduct (see Table 6.1). Although the respondents differentiated among the corruption-related cases in terms of their seriousness, the majority of the cases are evaluated as very serious. In fact, with the exception of the two cases describing the acceptance of gifts and gratuities (Case 2 and Case 4) and the case with off-duty employment (Case 1), the mean evaluations of seriousness are all above 4.5 on a 5-point scale, even for cases considered to be of intermediate seriousness.

It is not surprising that off-duty employment (Case 1) is evaluated as the least serious case among the cases, since it describes behavior that is in accordance with official rules. The surveyed police officers estimated the two cases describing the acceptance of gifts and gratuities (Case 2 and Case 4) among the least serious. There is almost a 1-point differential between these two cases, with the acceptance of free meals and

**Table 6.1**  Finnish Police Officers' Views of the Seriousness of the Misconduct, Knowledge of Official Rules, the Discipline Misconduct Should and Would Receive, and Officers' Willingness to Report It

| Case Number and Description | Seriousness Own View x̄ | Own View Rank | Most Officers x̄ | Most Officers Rank | Violation % Definitely Yes x̄ | Should Receive x̄ | Should Receive Rank | Should Receive Mode | Would Receive x̄ | Would Receive Rank | Would Receive Mode | Willingness Own View x̄ | Own View Rank | Most Officers x̄ | Most Officers Rank |
|---|---|---|---|---|---|---|---|---|---|---|---|---|---|---|---|
| Case 1 - Off-Duty Security System Business | 2.19 | 1 | 2.41 | 1 | 2.88 (36.4%) | 1.47 | 1 | None | 1.60 | 1 | None | 2.20 | 1 | 2.59 | 1 |
| Case 2 - Free Meals and Discounts on Beat | 2.98 | 2 | 2.90 | 2 | 3.24 (45.0%) | 1.63 | 2 | Verbal Reprimand | 1.67 | 2 | Verbal Reprimand | 2.37 | 2 | 2.65 | 2 |
| Case 3 - Bribe From Speeding Motorist | 4.96 | 10 | 4.96 | 10.5 | 4.98 (99.7%) | 3.59 | 10 | Dismissal | 3.52 | 10 | Dismissal | 4.56 | 10 | 4.53 | 10 |
| Case 4 - Holiday Gifts From Merchants | 3.73 | 3 | 3.72 | 3 | 3.94 (71.7%) | 2.27 | 3 | Verbal Reprimand | 2.20 | 3 | Verbal Reprimand | 3.16 | 3 | 3.34 | 4 |
| Case 5 - Crime Scene Theft of Watch | 4.99 | 11 | 4.96 | 10.5 | 4.99 (99.7%) | 3.73 | 11 | Dismissal | 3.65 | 11 | Dismissal | 4.66 | 11 | 4.62 | 11 |
| Case 6 - 5% Kickback From Auto Repair Shop | 4.54 | 6 | 4.44 | 5.5 | 4.63 (93.4%) | 2.92 | 7 | Written Reprimand | 2.91 | 7 | Written Reprimand | 4.10 | 7 | 4.10 | 8 |
| Case 7 - Supervisor Grants Holiday in Exchange for Car Tune-Up | 4.50 | 4 | 4.44 | 5.5 | 4.50 (90.7%) | 2.42 | 4 | Verbal Reprimand | 2.26 | 4 | Verbal Reprimand | 3.75 | 5 | 3.75 | 5 |
| Case 8 - Cover-Up of Police DUI Accident | 4.69 | 8 | 4.61 | 8 | 4.85 (96.7%) | 3.21 | 8 | Written Reprimand | 3.24 | 8 | Written Reprimand | 4.11 | 8 | 4.09 | 7 |
| Case 9 - Free Drinks to Ignore Late Bar Closing | 4.63 | 7 | 4.54 | 7 | 4.75 (97.3%) | 2.67 | 6 | Written Reprimand | 2.67 | 6 | Written Reprimand | 3.85 | 6 | 3.81 | 6 |
| Case 10 - Excessive Force on Car Thief | 4.53 | 5 | 4.32 | 4 | 4.74 (96.7%) | 2.59 | 5 | Written Reprimand | 2.58 | 5 | Written Reprimand | 3.36 | 4 | 3.31 | 3 |
| Case 11 - Theft From Found Wallet | 4.95 | 9 | 4.89 | 9 | 4.96 (99.7%) | 3.44 | 9 | Dismissal | 3.43 | 9 | Dismissal | 4.42 | 9 | 4.35 | 9 |
| Case 12 - Failure to Arrest Friend With Felony Warrant | 4.37 | | 4.41 | | 4.74 (95.5%) | 2.61 | | Written Reprimand | 2.64 | | Written Reprimand | 3.72 | | 3.83 | |
| Case 13 - Unjustifiable Use of Deadly Force | 4.77 | | 4.72 | | 4.87 (97.3%) | 3.60 | | Dismissal | 3.66 | | Dismissal | 4.78 | | 4.75 | |
| Case 14 - Striking Prisoner Who Hurt Partner | 4.51 | | 4.41 | | 4.85 (98.2%) | 2.76 | | Written Reprimand | 2.77 | | Written Reprimand | 3.69 | | 3.60 | |
| Case 15 - Verbal Abuse of Motorist | 4.05 | | 3.90 | | 4.55 (91.4%) | 1.87 | | Verbal Reprimand | 1.88 | | Verbal Reprimand | 2.67 | | 2.66 | |
| Case 16 - False Report of Drug Possession on Dealer | 4.70 | | 4.60 | | 4.83 (96.7%) | 2.74 | | Written Reprimand | 2.80 | | Written Reprimand | 4.03 | | 3.94 | |
| Case 17 - Sgt. Who Fails to Halt Beating of Child Abuser | 4.52 | | 4.36 | | 4.86 (99.1%) | 2.75 | | Written Reprimand | 2.73 | | Written Reprimand | 3.89 | | 3.73 | |

discounts on the beat (Case 2) evaluated as substantially less serious than the acceptance of holiday gifts from merchants (Case 4). According to the Transparency International Czech Republic's annual review of anti-corruption strategies (Frič & Walek, 2001, p. 41), these two cases describe the most frequent forms of police corruption in Finland (i.e., receiving free service and buying goods or services for discounted prices). There seems to be clear consensus in Finnish society with respect to what constitutes serious corruption, and the bar has been set high. Since the survey was conducted, the line between acceptable and unacceptable conduct has been further reinforced at the lower end: The Finnish Supreme Court recently reinforced a zero-tolerance rule when it decided in 2000, in a high visibility case, that even the acceptance of a free lunch (worth U.S.$10) by a judge is unacceptable and thus reaffirmed the judge's conviction (Finnish Supreme Court Decision 2000:40).

Finnish police officers perceive the remaining six cases, which focus on other forms of police misconduct (see Table 6.1), to be serious as well. Even for a case involving rude behavior toward a citizen (Case 15 - Verbal Abuse of Motorist)—the least serious in the group—the mean value is above 4 on a 5-point scale where 5 indicates very serious misconduct.

### Violation of Official Rules

The respondents were asked whether the behavior described in the questionnaire violates official agency rules. Since 16 out of the 17 cases describe behavior that constitutes violations, the respondents' positive answers indicate that the police are making official rules and their enforcement a very clear and important priority. On the other hand, negative answers would not necessarily indicate that the police officers do not know the official rules, but, possibly, that the unofficial rules created in the agency based on the actual behavior of the administration (e.g., enforcement or lack of enforcement, punishment for rule-violating behavior) overshadow the official ones, or at least create a confusion among the police officers as to what the actual, enforced rules are.

As the results in Table 6.1 show, with the exceptions of three cases (Case 1, Case 2, and Case 4), the surveyed police officers overwhelmingly evaluated these behaviors as violations of official rules; the means in 14 cases are all above 4.5 on a 5-point scale. A slightly more revealing method is, instead of looking at averages, to look at the percentage of the police officers who felt strongly that the described behavior is a violation of the official agency rules (i.e., the respondents who selected 4 or 5). Indeed, it seems to be clear to virtually every police officer surveyed that the behaviors described are violations of official rules: over 90% of the respondents think that each of these behaviors is definitely a violation of the official rules (see Table 6.1).

The three most interesting cases are those evaluated to be the least serious. Regarding the least serious case—Case 1 (Off-Duty Security System Business)—only 36.4% of the respondents classified this behavior as a violation of the official agency rules. While this case describes the behavior that is in accordance with the official rules (i.e., police officers are officially allowed to have a second job), police officers have the obligation to declare any secondary employment.[9] This declaration need not be in a specific form; even an oral announcement fulfills the letter of the law. Since the wording of the case did not provide information on whether the imaginary police officer had declared the second job, some respondents—probably most of those who said that this behavior violates the official rules—may have interpreted it to mean that the officer had not declared the job.

While slightly less than one half of the respondents (45.0%) evaluated routine acceptance of free meals, cigarettes, and other items of small value from merchants on the beat as a violation of the rules (Case 2), three quarters of the respondents (71.7%) reported the same about the acceptance of gifts of food and liquor on holidays (Case 4). The modest value of the regular gifts from merchants probably makes them more likely to be tolerated, interpreted perhaps as the "perks of the job," while the acceptance of food and liquor (which can either be consumed on the spot or taken home), especially in the aftermath of the aforementioned Supreme Court decision (Finnish Supreme Court Decision 2000:40), may be understood as more serious rule violations. It is also possible that the line drawn by the police administration, the courts, the media, and the public—through punishment of violators and their denunciation—is brighter with respect to somewhat larger or more expensive items (e.g., a bottle of whiskey or a free meal in a first-class restaurant) than with respect to the smaller ones (e.g., a free cup of coffee or a pack of cigarettes). However, let us emphasize that Case 2 and Case 4 are both relatively mild cases of corruption. Overall, the line with respect to the more serious forms of corruption seems to be quite clear.

### Discipline

Unlike the questionnaire distributed in the United States, which had six disciplinary options (ranging from no discipline to dismissal), the Finnish version contained only four disciplinary options (no discipline, verbal reprimand, written reprimand, and dismissal). Thus, the range of options was relatively narrow and the gap between the officer's receiving dismissal, the most serious disciplinary option, and a written reprimand, the first more lenient option next to dismissal, is wider than in the U.S. version.

Consequently, it need not be surprising that the respondents think that only the three most serious corruption cases (Case 3, Case 5, and Case 11) and the unjustifiable deadly force case (Case 13), deserve dismissal, while they think that most of the cases of intermediate seriousness deserve a written reprimand, the second most serious disciplinary option (see Table 6.1). The only case in which the respondents did not consider any discipline to be appropriate is Case 1 (the off-duty employment). The respondents further think that the most appropriate discipline for the remaining least serious cases (Case 2 and Case 4) is a verbal reprimand, a punishment they also think should be applied to the case of supervisor corruption (Case 7) and the case of the officer's verbal abuse of citizens (Case 15). It is clear that the respondents' opinions about the appropriate discipline are directly related to their perceptions of the seriousness of the misconduct in the cases: The more serious the case is perceived to be, the harsher the punishment respondents think appropriate for it.

While the message sent by the society at large about the inappropriateness of corrupt behavior and the level of seriousness with which the society treats cases involving corruption seems to be clear, a lack of recent cases and related information may have made it difficult for the respondents to determine the exact punishment that the police agencies would mete out in the actual cases of police corruption. The modal expectations of the actual discipline match those of the appropriate discipline in all 17 cases (see Table 6.1), indicating that the respondents perceived the expected discipline to be fair in terms of its severity.

### Willingness to Report

The last two questions inquired about the respondents' own willingness to report misconduct and their estimate of the willingness of most of the police officers in their agencies to report it. The respondents' willingness to report seems to be directly related to their estimates of the seriousness of the misconduct: The more serious they estimated the misconduct to be, the less likely they were to say that they would not report it. With the exception of the three least serious corruption cases (Case 1, Case 2, and Case 4) and the verbal abuse case (Case 15), the means are all above the midpoint of the reporting scale (3.0). Although these findings suggest that the respondents would be more likely to report misconduct than not, their willingness to report is not the same for all cases; the means for the three most serious corruption cases (Case 3, Case 5, and Case 11) and the unjustifiable deadly force case (Case 13) are much closer to the reporting end of the scale (all three means are above 4.4) than are the means for the cases of intermediate seriousness (which are between 3.5 and 4.5).

Another way of looking at the same data is to examine the percentage of police officers who think that they definitely would not report certain types of misconduct. This percentage could serve as an estimate of the extent of the code of silence. The data indicate that the code seems to be the strongest for the least serious cases. In particular, close to two thirds of the police officers said that they would not report a fellow police officer who runs an off-duty security system business (Case 1), misconduct evaluated by most respondents as the least serious, not violating the official rules, and deserving no discipline. Similarly, the majority of the police officers also think that they definitely would not report a fellow officer who accepts free meals and discounts on the beat (Case 2), while only a strong minority (30.4%) of the police officers think that they would not report a fellow police officer who accepts holiday gifts from merchants. Police officers who verbally abuse citizens (Case 15) and police officers engaging in excessive force on a car thief (Case 10)

could expect that only a strong minority of their fellow officers would not report them (44.9% and 28.7%, respectively).

Thus, the extent of the code of silence seems to be rapidly shrinking as the cases become more serious than the off-duty security business, acceptance of free meals and discounts, or verbal abuse of citizens (see Figure 6.1). With the exception of Case 10 (Excessive Force on Car Thief), the code narrows to below 20% for most cases that describe other forms of police misconduct and remains closer to 10% for corruption cases respondents perceive as of intermediate seriousness. The three most serious cases of police corruption (Case 3, Case 5, and Case 11) have the highest chance of being reported, and for the case of unjustifiable use of deadly force (Case 13) the extent of the code of silence seems to be very narrow, since less than 6.5% of the respondents think that they definitely would not report it (and only 1.2% believe that they would not report the unjustifiable use of deadly force).

### Indications From the Official Data

The police crime statistics suggest that the Finnish police force is not corrupt. There has not been a single case in which a police officer would have demanded or accepted a bribe reported during the past 2 years. Table 6.2 shows the crime reports made against police officers in Finland in 2000 and 2001. The items in Table 6.2 are cases in which someone has reported to the police that he or she thinks a police officer has committed a crime. The reports of an offense in Table 2 include the suspected crimes or malpractice cases of police officers both on and off duty.

In addition to offense reports, people can give both oral and written feedback on police services. All citizens are entitled to make a complaint. An administrative complaint is lodged either with a superior police authority or with an authority responsible for the

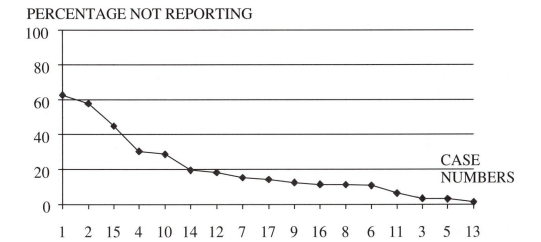

PERCENTAGE NOT REPORTING

**Figure 6.1**    Percentage of Officers Not Willing to Report Misconduct, by Case Number

| **Table 6.2** | Crime Reports Against Police Officers in Finland in 2000 and 2001 | | |
|---|---|---|---|
| | | *2000* | *2001* |
| Assault (also aggravated and minor) | | 92 | 85 |
| Dereliction of Duty (willful, negligence) | | 80 | 97 |
| Misuse of Power (also aggravated) | | 10 | 8 |
| Bribery, Corruption | | 0 | 0 |
| Defamation, Discrimination | | 8 | 8 |
| False Statement | | 2 | 5 |
| Traffic Offenses | | 58 | 47 |
| Other Offenses | | 20 | 31 |
| Other Investigation | | 88 | 111 |
| Total | | 358 | 392 |

Source: Office of the Prosecutor General, Finland (2002).

supervision of legality. In Finland, the supreme guardians of the law are the Parliamentary Ombudsman and the Chancellor of Justice. Within the police administration, complaints are mainly dealt with at the Police Departments of the State Provincial Offices and at the Police Department of the Ministry of the Interior. The police chiefs in the State Local Districts and the chiefs of the national police units can also handle the complaints made against their subordinates. If the erroneous action or neglect is of such a serious nature that there is reason to suspect that an offense in office has been committed, the authority responsible for the investigation of the complaint can make a report of an offense. Offenses committed by a police officer are investigated following a procedure referred to in the Criminal Investigations Act, with the public prosecutor acting as the head of the investigation.

Every report of an offense will be investigated. In 2001, a pretrial investigation in which a police officer was the suspect was started in 392 cases. In many reported cases, the pretrial investigation indicated that the police officer had not committed an offense after all. The row labelled "Other Investigation" in Table 6.2 indicates reported cases in which it was obvious that no crime had been committed. In some cases, the report had been made without a good reason. Maybe the reporting person thought that he or she had not been treated appropriately; in his or her opinion the police officer had used too much force or made an impertinent remark. In some cases, the suspects make crime investigation more difficult by accusing the police detective of committing a crime while investigating the criminal case (Vuorinen, 2002, p. 77). In a majority of the police crime investigation cases, approximately 80% to 90% of the legal proceedings against police officers are dropped. The investigation ends when the prosecutor, as the supervisor of the investigation, is convinced that an offense has not been committed.

If we exclude cases included in the "other investigation" category, then a total of 281 offenses with a police officer as a suspect were reported in 2001. In the scale of police personnel in Finland, that means 35 reported offenses per 1,000 police officers.[10] In approximately 60 cases, prosecuting discretion was exercised. In only a very few cases will a police officer be prosecuted and in even fewer cases will he or she be convicted.

## REFLECTIONS ON
## THE EXPLANATIONS
## FOR LOW CORRUPTION

Generally, corruption is not a severe problem in Finnish society. According to all the indicators analyzed above, the Finnish police have a high standard of conduct. Even the newspaper headlines and the book excerpt quoted in the Introduction seem to connect the malpractice of police officers to their personal lives, to the personal problems and characteristics of individual police officers. However, there is a system of support for these individuals during crises to prevent the situation from developing into something more serious, such as corruption or some other unwanted conduct. The health-care system works relatively efficiently in Finland in regard to physical as well as mental problems. Well-being at work is a central theme in occupational health care, and there are groups in Finnish police departments in which police officers can discuss the strenuous events they face at work.

Next to the personal characteristics of police officers, the integrity of the police is dependent on their societal and cultural context. Even though we think that the personal output of individual police officers is an integral part of good police practice, we will focus almost solely on the societal factors, on which, in our opinion, the integrity of the police relies. The police are a central social institution. We claim that the police culture has emerged as a part of its social background. Cultural factors have a significant impact on how the police operate in a certain country.

One important cultural factor to consider is the general level of corruption in a country. The fact that corruption does not occur as a large-scale societal phenomenon in Finland does not indicate, however, that there is no corruption. However, corruption has not erupted as a major problem in Finnish society at any point in history. A key question is "Why not?"—especially in light of the fact that there is no separate system to control corruption in Finland. Instead of the single components of police culture, we will examine the social elements that illustrate why Finnish civil servant activity, and police activity as one part of it, is scarcely corrupt.

We shall look for explanations in three directions: the general conditions of high integrity in Finnish society, the control mechanisms applied to corruption, and the preventive measures taken toward corruption in Finland. These explanations are not exhaustive, but they may give an impression of the reasons for the present good ranking in the international comparisons.

### General Conditions in
### Finland of High Integrity

The principles of transparency and openness have been promoted in public administration in Finland. This we consider one of the general conditions to guarantee the high integrity of civil servants. As one

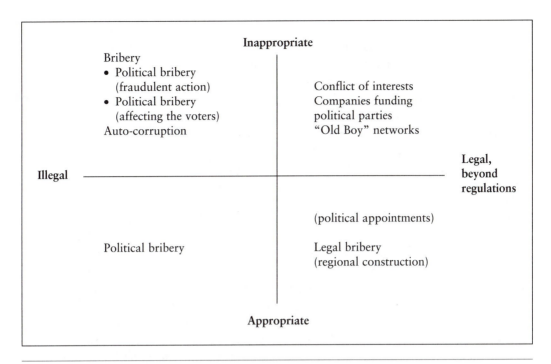

**Figure 6.2**     A Heuristic Representation of Corruptive Phenomena

SOURCE: Isaksson (1997, p. 152).

example of succeeding in this effort, the OECD report (2001) verifies that

> The highest level of transparency and co-operation on the part of the Finnish government characterized the on-site visit. The lead examiners are confident that the Finnish government fully disclosed all available relevant information in its possession regarding the implementation of the Convention and the Revised Recommendation, and that any deficiencies in the information obtained were due to internal shortcomings in the data collection.

Freedom of expression and access to public information are basic rights protected by the Constitution (Section 12). The citizens have access to a majority of public documents and the public decision making is fairly explicit. People are aware that they should complain if they have been mistreated or if they suspect that a civil servant has not acted according to the law.

In Finnish public discussion concerning corruption, it is not merely the aspects of legality or illegality of actions that count. The aspects of appropriateness and inappropriateness are frequently raised publicly, especially by the media. The focus on legality is complemented by the focus on the appropriateness of the conduct.

Isaksson (1997, p. 13) includes both bribery *and seeking to influence others through inappropriate means* within his definition of corruption. He has formulated a matrix of four fields with the axes of appropriateness and legality (see Figure 6.2). This model, the multidimensional definition of corruption, illustrates the Finnish conception of corruption based on what is moral in more ways than one.

First, social institutions are trusted in Finland, as we have pointed out above. When all civil service activity is evaluated in terms of this trust, the threshold of evaluating actions as blameworthy is lowered. This may mean that actions of civil servants that under no circumstances can be considered crimes may be denounced as immoral. For example, the fact that the former director of the Bank of Finland accepted huge pensions while still working in the European Central Bank raised a heated public discussion. In this respect, Finnish citizens demand impeccable conduct of their civil servants.

The severity or insignificance of the actions raised into public discussion on corruption reflects the nature of corruption in the society. Isaksson's figure, which encompasses the definitions of illegal actions and inappropriate actions side by side, suggests that there is scant corruption in Finland. Emile Durkheim (1895/1982, pp. 82-84) noted that the most severe actions that violate the moral beliefs of the society are defined as crimes. If the number of defined crimes decreases, the definition will become stricter and actions that earlier were defined as condemnable will be defined as criminal. However, when the criminal regulation of corruption is no longer defined merely within the community, the inappropriate actions illustrated by Isaksson are not defined as crimes, as Durkheim would suggest. Using the definition of inappropriate actions indicates that the discussion of corruption in Finland focuses on relatively petty immoral actions. When the definition of corruption is linked to individuals' moral beliefs, and not only to the regulation of criminal activity, it strengthens the foundation being laid for anticorruption work.

## Control Mechanisms Applied to Corruption

The grounds for the societal order are given in the Constitution (Section 2, Paragraph 3). The Constitution states that in all public activity, the law shall be strictly obeyed. Section 118 states that civil servants are responsible for the legality of their actions. It also states that everyone who has suffered a violation of his or her rights or sustained loss through an unlawful act or omission by a civil servant or other person performing a public task shall have the right to request that the civil servant or other person in charge of a public task be sentenced to punishment and that the public organization, official, or other person in charge of a public task can be held liable for damages.

When the injured party thinks that a suspected crime was not investigated thoroughly, he or she has the opportunity to complain to those who supervise public agencies and civil servants, the Parliamentary Ombudsman and the Chancellor of Justice. The same possibility is open to each citizen who thinks that he or she has not been treated properly in the society. Complaints about police officers are made regularly in Finland.

What are the specific methods of controlling corruption in Finland then? There is no special organization to fight corruption. The general policy against corruption is satisfactory. There is no specific control system for bribery either. Anyone can report an observed bribery case to the police. When a police officer or other civil servant severely violates his or her official duties, the liability of the offender is settled through the criminal system. A criminal or illegal act that fulfills the essential elements of malfeasance can lead to dismissal of the official in addition to the determination of a punishment.

A corruption case is investigated by the regular police organizations, just as is any other offense. Cases that have wide national significance, coverage, or international connections are investigated by the National Bureau of Investigation. Prosecutors take part in targeting investigations involving the most serious offenses. In a case in which a police officer is suspected of bribery, a public prosecutor will be in charge of the investigation instead of a Chief Inspector from the police.

There is no separate corruption control system within the police. Generally, there is an atmosphere of trust in individual police officers at the police departments. It is also assumed that when misconduct takes place, it will be revealed through colleagues, supervisors in higher positions, or clients. A civil servant who has violated his or her duties can be cautioned as an administrative sanction. But being cautioned is not an actual disciplinary sanction that would be marked in the register. Still, a caution may be taken into account if the civil servant later in his or her career is guilty of malpractice. Blame expressed by a superior in a note is a lenient sanction that is not regulated by the law (Helminen et al., 1999, pp. 334-337; Law on Civil Servants 24§).

The role of the media cannot be forgotten either: The media reveal cases with pleasure, and it is not unknown in Finland that a crime investigation starts from a piece of news on TV or in a newspaper. During the 1990s, the political atmosphere in Finland was emancipated and the role of the free press became more visible. However, the media cannot act as the definers of corruption. They state what is morally right or wrong: As Isaksson (1997, p. 40) points out, the media are only one "authority" among others, and they are just as imperfect as the others. He reminds us that the politicians, police, and high officials are also capable of using the media to promote their own interests and suppress those of their enemies (Isaksson, 1997, p. 40).

Despite the fact that there is no specific organization to control corruption, recent court cases indicate that the courts have taken up a role of defining policy concerning corruption. Even though cases are few, they often have a delineating nature. The line between illegal and legal was drawn, for example, in a case in which a water rights court judge was convicted for accepting a lunch worth 10 € (U.S.$10) during a visit to a scene (Finnish Supreme Court Decision 2000:40). The Supreme Court decision made it clear that taking a low-priced bribe is not more acceptable than taking a high-priced one.

In another case, a highly ranked civil servant was convicted for traveling to the United States at the expense of a private association. The trip was claimed to be a partly work-related field trip (Finnish Supreme Court Decision 1997:37). As a consequence of this decision, the old regulations (dated October 27, 1983) concerning cases in which a private company or association pays for the duty-related traveling expenses of a civil servant were found to be out of date and new, strict, and detailed regulations (known as directions) were created. According to the new directions, a trip can be paid for by a private enterprise only when it does not endanger the public's trust in the objectivity of the civil servant in the performance of his or her official duties. The decision to approve private funding is made by the head of the office, who also will give the warrant for the trip (The Directions of the Ministry of Finance, Finland, 2001).

The court cases indicate that when a problem is noted, efforts are made to resolve it. Action initiated against corruption has traditionally been scarce, but when such action is required, the Finnish system is ready for it. The system that deals with corruption in Finland (i.e., the control system) was created not out of a specific need but as a part of the legal crime control system. The specific measures taken toward corruption were established on the basis of international requirements such as the OECD Convention on Combating Bribery of Foreign Public Officials in International Business Transactions. The European Union has adopted an active role in the fight against corruption. This has given Finns an additional challenge to develop civil-servant activity and judicial regulation in Finland as well. The Parliament of the European Union, for instance, suggests public hearings on corruption at the parliaments of the member countries and preventive measures to exclude corrupted actors from the competitive biddings at the market (Isaksson, 1997, p. 125).

*Preventive Measures*
*Taken Toward Corruption*

The prevention of corruption cannot be totally separated from the general conditions and general control of the society. The prevention of corruption relies partly on the deterrent provided by the control system. Because corruption is low in Finland, it is highly improbable that one would meet a corrupt official in Finland. Also, when the risk of being caught offering a bribe is obvious, it is not sensible to do so.

However, the system's prevention of corruption relies more on educational factors than on the deterrence provided by the control system (Andenaes, 1974). The moral code is strengthened when the criminal and disciplinary norms unambiguously mark the boundary between permissible and forbidden behavior. It is important to draw a line between these so that civil servants will be able to avoid misconduct. It has been a tradition in Finnish civil servant training to emphasize the ethical foundation of civil servant culture.

Many professionals, such as lawyers, accountants, and auditors, have professional ethical norms. The ethical norms are not very explicit in public sector organizations. They have been taken for granted in many organizations, but currently ethical issues are being raised in public discussion more frequently, especially in the universities. The explicit establishment of ethical norms specific to different fields of administration is being planned. Isaksson (1997, pp. 189-191) has suggested that an ethical code also be prepared for each of the different groups of civil servants. At the moment, the ethical

norms of the police are being worked on. When separate ethical guidebooks are lacking, ethical norms are intertwined with the legislation and other regulations. The law sets the standard for good quality word, but it is the employee who decides how he or she carries out the work.

The criminal deterrence provided by the control system is not the main feature of bribery prevention in Finland. However, education and information (e.g., ethical codes) undoubtedly prevent corruption in a way that resembles such deterrence. We see educational principles and a high level of education as important explanatory factors for the high integrity of Finnish civil service. Most civil servants in public administration are highly educated and even some police officers have a university degree.[11]

To assure a high level of integrity in civil service, it is important to recruit the best available persons for the tasks. In Finnish police recruitment, the situation has been excellent for several years now. In 1999, a total of 2,536 persons applied for police basic training. Of these applicants, 312 people were selected (12% of the applicants). In practice, a variety of features are taken into account in the selection, such as the applicant's studies and the success in them, work experience, language skills, and other specific merits. Ultimately, the selection is based on an entrance examination in which the applicant's suitability to become a police officer is assessed.

## THREATS AND CHALLENGES

Although the exposed corruption cases are few, even these few cases indicate that there is a working control system for corruption in Finland. It would be arrogant to claim that the threat of corruption does not concern Finland because there are so few cases that come to trial. However, we are very confident that the remoteness of corruption cases in Finland reflects the real situation and is not explained by hidden corruption. Regardless of this, the threat of corruption should be taken seriously.

Laitinen (1989, p. 52) has claimed that as a result of the changes that took place in the contents and structure of the administration during the 1980s, Finnish society seems to have become more favorable to corruption than it had been previously. Laitinen noted that corruption tends to increase along with rapid growth and modernization, due to changing values, new sources of wealth and power, and the expansion of government (Alvesalo & Laitinen, 1994, p. 44). He also claimed that the "corruptive interface," that is, contacts between economic and administrative institutions, increased during the 1980s, which suggests that corruption would also increase. Similarly, Isaksson (1997, p. 135) warned that the increase in interaction between business and public authorities means an increase in the possibilities and potential situations for corruption. However, the statistics do not indicate any rise in the corruption figures. In fact, the statistics show the opposite, so it is natural to ask for the reasons for such a fine situation.

As we think that the integrity of the police is intertwined with the general situation regarding corruption in the society, we propose that the police have to face the same risks that form challenges for other institutions in Finnish society. Isaksson (1997, p. 149) claimed that the abuse of power is often related to the broad discretionary power of civil servants and to their lack of supervision. According to him, this means that the risk for abuse has to be recognized. He has suggested a situational prevention of corruption. The possibilities for corruption are realized in the situations where decisions are made. Joutsen (1975, pp. 48-49) says that an opportunity for corruption arises when (1) the actor has a chance to

communicate his or her corrupt intent to the second actor, (2) there is a chance that the second actor will accept the offer, and (3) the actors believe that there is a good chance that the transaction will not be disclosed. The situations that present civil servants with opportunities for corruption have to be controlled.

Isaksson (1997, p. 178) has speculated, however, that it may already be too late for such situational measures. In addition to the situational measures, he calls for the transparency, openness, and publicity of the decision making to minimize the risk of corruption. When hiding corruption is made difficult, it should diminish. Citizens are encouraged to take an active role in monitoring what the elected decision makers are actually doing. Openness and transparency are accepted principles in Finnish administration, but they can never be overemphasized. Furthermore, Isaksson has suggested that an implementation of more detailed administrative guidelines would consolidate the situation. These guidelines might improve the present practice of the courts that consider the events in the afterlight, case by case (Isaksson, 1997, p. 193).

Isaksson (1997, p. 12) has claimed that the societal change, with increasing competition, privatization, incorporation, and management by results in public administration, may increase the inclination to corruption as the procedures, ethics, and practices of business invade politics and public administration. There is a risk that profitability becomes value number one, unchallenged.

Considering the profitability of corruption, the salary of police officers is one matter that could be seen as a threat to officer resistance to corruption. Despite the fact that the police work is male-dominated (which in Finland are generally better paid occupations than female-dominated occupations), the salary is relatively low, especially for new police officers. The monthly salary of a newly graduated police officer is about U.S.$1300 to U.S.$1700, including *shift benefits* (i.e., the extra salary paid for night and evening shifts). This is comparable with the salaries of several underrated, women-dominated occupations. The police officers arranged a very exceptional demonstration in 2001 to highlight this. If the disparity between the salaries of police officers and those of other, comparable semiprofessional workers continues to increase, it may be seen as a threat to officers' integrity in that it may lower the moral standard of police officers and make accepting bribes more attractive.

The OECD evaluation report (OECD, 2001) brought up some central issues concerning the threats Finland may face today in light of the internationalization and globalization of most fields of activity. Internationalization concerns the police as well as other institutions. The risk the OECD report brings up could be formulated as a "vicious circle": The public administration does not face corruption in the present healthy situation, which may lead it to neglect training, informing, and public discussion about corruption. It is not currently considered important. When communication and information on corruption are minimal, the risk increases that corruption cases, either international or domestic, will not be recognized or reported. Therefore, the threat of corruption must be taken seriously.

The structure of corruption control in Finland is based on a low level of corruption. As we noted, this control is efficient given the present situation. We also believe that the anticorruption structure in Finland has some flexibility. But is the structure flexible enough? If the number of corruption cases suddenly increased, would the police, the prosecutors, and the courts be able to react adequately to it? For instance, at the beginning of 1990s, there was a dramatic

expansion of economic crime in Finland.[12] In 1995, the Finnish government initiated an action plan to control economic crime. The plan seemed to be successful, but the damages would have been smaller if the control measures had been taken a couple of years earlier. It is important to remember that there are no signs of rising corruption in Finland in sight. Still, we are wondering whether the Finnish bodies charged with controlling corruption are awake or relying on the flattering statistics.

## CONCLUSION

The Constitution, legislation against corruption, and an effective organization to investigate, prosecute, and judge forthcoming cases comprise some of the cornerstones in the fight against corruption in Finland. They also act as preventive measures against corruption. Although an active corruption control system is lacking, corruption control may be even more efficient as a part of the normal legal control than as a separate system, as it is not necessary for a witness to make subtle distinctions between legal and illegal actions before reporting a suspicious deed. Reporting inappropriate matters is allowed as well. This may reduce minor deceit and prevent more extensive misconduct from the start.

We have found on the basis of several sources that corruption is scarce in Finland. Although our approach is not, or at least is not intended to be, uncritical, all sources available suggest that corruption is not a severe problem in Finland. In addition, the level of integrity of the Finnish police is high. The police are relied on, and they seldom commit crimes. We have claimed that because the police operate as one part of the public authorities, the integrity of the police cannot be separated from the general level of corruption in the society. The same factors that have resulted in the low level of corruption in general in the Finnish society have an influence on the level of integrity of the police.

We have focused on bringing out the social factors that have influenced the low level of corruption. The factors we brought out are the general conditions, the corruption control mechanisms, and the structures that prevent corruption.

Finnish legislation is not innovative regarding corruption, and a system of mechanisms for controlling corruption is lacking. However, when evaluating the significance of this lack of control mechanisms, we have to keep in mind that corruption has never been a problem in Finland. It is evident that instituting control mechanisms is not the Finnish way of fighting corruption. Rather, in Finland it is the preventive measures that alert officials to the problems so that they can actively consider them and, without delay, issue guidelines for decent behavior.

Although corruption is low in Finland, the risk of it cannot be underestimated. The prevention of corruption cannot be based merely on legislation and control: The factors in society that enhance the lure of corruption must be analyzed and managed as well. Furthermore, the situation should be reflected in public discussions. For Finland to be able to keep its present healthy situation, with so little corruption in the society and the integrity of the police as one part of it, the continuation of its openness, publicity, and transparency is essential.

## NOTES

1. For further information, see http://www.poliisi.fi/english/index.htm.

2. For further information on Transparency International, see http://www.transparency.org.

3. A full description of these methodologies is available at http://www.ifs.univie.ac.at/~uncjin/wcs.html.

4. See, for example, Lipset and Schneider (1983), United States; Döring (1990), Europe; Klingemann and Fuchs (1995), United States, Canada, Europe.

5. These six cases are a part of the new questionnaire designed by Klockars and colleagues (2001).

6. The Finnish Minister of the Interior, Ville Itälä, commented publicly on January 1, 2002 on a case in which a person who had been convicted for assaults was employed as a police officer (see Introduction). Itälä pointed out that in order for the police to maintain the confidence of the people, there has to be a strict demand for blamelessness in the police force. According to Itälä, a person with a record of conviction for assault is not suitable for police work.

7. See the Finnish Virkamieslaki [Act on Civil Servants] (19.8.1994/750) 14–17§.

8. See http://www.transparency.org/dokuments/cpi/2001/cpi2001.html.

9. An officer's second job can be officially rejected only when it endangers the trust in the police officer's performance of his or her official duties (Act on Civil Servants 18–19§).

10. Comparing the activity with the crime statistics in Finland is problematic. In 2000, the police reported 763,000 crimes, which means 150 crimes per 1,000 people (Sirén, 2001, pp. 7–10).

11. Detailed information of the educational background of police officers is not available. The average age of the recruits when they start police training is 23.5 which suggests that most of them have already gained another occupational/college training or work experience.

12. In 1992, the police reported 295 debtor's offense cases. In 1996, the number of cases reported was 853. Accounting offenses increased following the same pattern (Vuorinen, 2001, p. 101).

## REFERENCES

Alvesalo, A., & Laitinen, A. (1994). *Perspectives on economic crime.* Turku, Finland: Publications of the Faculty of Law, Criminal Law and Judicial Procedure, University of Turku.

Andenaes, J. (1974). General prevention–illusion or reality? In *Punishment and deterrence.* Ann Arbor, MI: University of Michigan Press.

Aromaa, K., & Heiskanen, M. (2000). *Crime risks in Finland 2000: Finnish results of the 2000 sweep of the International Crime Victims Survey.* Helsinki: National Institute of Legal Policy.

Döring, H. (1990, April). Aspekte des Vertraues in Institutionen. *Zeitschrift für Soziologie,* pp. 73-89.

Durkheim, E. (1982). *Sosiologian metodisäännöt* (S. Randell, Trans.). Helsinki: Tammi. (Original work published 1895)

van Dijk, J. J. M., & Mayhew, P. (1993). Criminal victimization in the industrialised world: Key findings of the 1989 and 1992 International Crime Surveys. In A. Alvazzi del Frate, U. Zvekic, & J. J. M. van Dijk (Eds.), *Understanding crime: Experiences of crime and crime control* (pp. 1-51). Rome: United Nations Interregional Crime and Justice Research Institute (UNICRI).

Finnish Supreme Court Decision 1997:37.

Finnish Supreme Court Decision 2000:40.

Frič, P., & Walek, C. (2001). *Crossing the thin blue line: An international annual review of anti-corruption strategies in the police.* Prague: Transparency International ČR.

Helminen, K,. Kuusimäki, M., & Salminen, M. (1999). *Poliisioikeus* (Police law). Helsinki: Lakimiesliiton Kustannus.

Isaksson, P. (1997). *Korruptio ja julkinen valta* (Corruption and public authority). Tampere, Finland: Research Institute of Social Sciences, University of Tampere.

Joutsen, M. (1975). *The potential for corruption.* Helsinki: National Research Institute of Legal Policy.

Klingemann, H.-D., & Fuchs, D. (Eds.). (1995). *Citizen and the state.* Oxford, UK: Oxford University Press.

Klockars, C. B., Kutnjak Ivkovich, S., Haberfeld, M. R., & Uydess, A., with contributions by W. A. Geller (2001). *Enhancing police integrity: Three case studies.* Final report submitted to the National Institute of Justice.

Kutnjak Ivkovich, S., & Klockars, C. B. (1996, March). *Police perceptions of disciplinary fairness and the formation of the code of silence.* Paper presented at the annual meeting of the Academy of Criminal Justice Sciences, Las Vegas, Nevada.

Laitinen, A. (1989). *Vallan rikokset* (Crime of the powerful). Helsinki: akimiesliiton kustannus.

Lappi-Seppälä, T., Tala, J., Litmala, M., & Jaakkola, R. (1999). *Luottamus tuomioistuimiin. Haastattelututkimus väestön asenteista 1998* (Trust toward courts. An interview study of the attitudes of the public in 1998). Helsinki: National Institute of Legal Policy.

Lashmar, P. (2001). Regional report: West Europe and North America. In *Global Corruption Report 2001*. Prague: Transparency International. Available at http://www.globalcorruptionreport.org.

Lipset, M., & Schneider, W. (1983). *The confidence gap*. New York: Macmillan.

Listhaug, O., & Wiberg, M. (1995). Confidence in political and private institutions. In H.-D. Klingemann & D. Fuchs (Eds.), *Citizen and the state* (pp. 298-322). Oxford, UK: Oxford University Press.

OECD (Organisation for Economic Cooperation and Development). (2001, December 18). Report on the Application of Convention and 1997 Recommendation. Finland: Phase 2 (draft report). Retrieved from www.oecd.org/pdf/M00029000/M00029564.pdf.

Office of the Prosecutor General, Finland (2002, January 25). Memo.

Reinboth, S. (2002a). A police officer convicted of assault should not have been employed. Assistant parliamentary ombudsman: "Police officers must be pronouncedly blameless." *Helsingin Sanomat*, p. A7.

Reinboth, S. (2002b, January 29). Supreme Police Command fears the status of the police is bloodied because of the assaulter. *Helsingin Sanomat*, p. A8.

Sirén, R. (2001). Rikollisuuden rakenne ja kehitys (The structure and development of crime in Finland). In *Crime and criminal justice in Finland 2000* (pp. 7-10). Helsinki: National Research Institute of Legal Policy.

Tulimeri, J. (1994). Kaikki rahasta (Anything for money). In T. Arolainen (Ed.), *Talousrikollisen tunnustukset* (The confessions of a white-collar criminal). Helsinki: WSOY.

The Directions of the Ministry of Finance, Finland (2001).

Vuorinen, S. (2001). Talousrikollisuus (Economic crime). In *Crime and criminal justice in Finland 2000* (pp. 97-109). Helsinki: National Research Institute of Legal Policy.

Vuorinen, S. (2002). *Talousrikosten tutkinta* (Investigating economic crime). Helsinki: National Research Institute of Legal Policy.

# CHAPTER 7

# Police Integrity in Hungary

## How the Police Have Adapted to Political Transition

FERENC KRÉMER

## INTRODUCTION

To understand the integrity-related challenges the Hungarian police are facing in the 21st century, we need to focus on the transition process from Communism to the more democratic structures occurring in the society at large. Prior to the 1990s, the police served the ruling Communist regime. As a consequence, animosity developed between the police and the public. Despite denials of its existence by the official regime, police corruption was widespread and only added to the widening of the gap between the police and the citizens. In 1990, after the collapse of Communism, the expectations of the police—the enforcement tool of the previous regime—and their role became ill-defined. More important, the transition created numerous novel opportunities for corruption, while the standards of proper police conduct remained low.

## A BRIEF BACKGROUND OF THE HUNGARIAN POLICE

The Hungarian police is a national police force. At the top of its pyramid-like structure is the National Headquarters (ORFK). At the bottom of the pyramid are municipal police departments (which serve small and neighboring villages) and police departments of districts of cities. The next organizational unit is at the county level. Every county has its own headquarters that oversees the police departments. However, the police officers working in the county headquarters have better salaries and working conditions than those who are employed in the city police departments.

The Budapest police department is structured like those in the counties—that is, the headquarters (BRFK) is above the district police departments. Now, more than a decade after the transition began, this centralized structure gives relatively little formal autonomy to police departments,[1] which is similar to how they functioned during the last half of the 20th century. A second important organizational characteristic of the Hungarian police force is its paramilitary nature.

### The Hungarian Police in Figures

In 1999, the number of sworn officers in the Hungarian police was 26,628. The proportion of ranking officers was 31%, which is quite a large number when compared to the size of other European police forces. Ranking officers have been educated at the college level since 1971, and they are employed in different managerial duties. The proportion of female police officers is relatively low at 11.4%. However, currently, the proportion of women students attending the Hungarian Police College is nearly 50%.

Year by year, those serving in the Hungarian police have become younger. In 1999, the average age of a police officer was 32.4 years, whereas in 1986 the average age of police officers was 36.6 years, in 1990 it was 35.6 years, and in 1995 it was 35.8 years. There are no data about the proportion of minorities employed in the police. In Hungary, the largest and most important minority group is the gypsies; since 1990, however, the Constitution has prohibited the differentiation of individuals as minorities. It has been estimated that there are a very small number of gypsy police officers. One of the possible causes for this may stem from the animosity that has historically existed between the police and the gypsies.

## The Hungarian Police in the Communist Era (1949–1990)

Under Communism, the Hungarian police were characterized by their secrecy, their willingness to serve the oppressive regime, and their high degree of discretion. Thus, it is difficult to obtain data about the police during the Communist era because of the lack of data, whether in published documents or studies. For example, in a book on corruption published in 1986, the concept of police corruption was not even mentioned (Kránitz, 1986). Lengyel (1998) described the situation with respect to corruption in general:

[Under communism, the] law was applied to everyone and to no one at the same time.

The ruling elite was above the law. The men-in-the-street, the "homo kadaricus," lived in a special position among the laws. One was always able to get around norms and was always able to break them. In society everyone made his or her way by refined corruption, and everyone talked about it, but a political corruption affair was never prosecuted or was never in the open. (p. 112)

Secrecy during the Communist period—not only in the case of the police—separated the unimportant or average civilian from official police business and thus determined "official" and "unofficial" territorial boundaries in Hungarian society. There were two exceptions: the history of the political police (or secret police)[2] and the revolution of 1956. The most researched topics in Hungary are the history of the political police and the revolution of 1956. Currently, however, the work of historians has become difficult because documents that were inaccessible under Communism but accessible subsequently have been reclassified in the past few years and have thus become inaccessible again. A second, more important issue for the purposes of this chapter, is that the use of secret police is only a small part of the ways in which police use political power nondemocratically. The larger police organization has a wider and deeper influence on citizens' living conditions than the secret police, and it can use its power for oppression, if it chooses to use it for that purpose. Actually, the everyday contact between the police and the citizens is suitable to the goal of stabilizing the society by "subjecting" the citizens to the current government. Thus, unfortunately, the characteristics that made it possible for the police to carry out this function under Communism have become the nature of the contemporary police.

Before 1990, anyone who had graduated from elementary school and military service could be a police officer. Demanding a college

**Table 7.1**    Number of Crimes Committed by Police Officers in Hungary in the 1980s

|  | 1985 | 1986 | 1987 | 1988 | 1989 |
|---|---|---|---|---|---|
| Cause Serious Bodily Harm | 32 | 28 | 43 | 29 | 27 |
| Cause a Traffic Accident | 39 | 32 | 44 | 50 | 60 |
| Driving Under the Influence of Alcohol (Offense and Crime) | 163 | 160 | 174 | 119 | 122 |
| Misuse of Authority | 137 | 99 | 216 | 66 | 74 |
| Forceful Interrogation | 33 | 10 | 18 | 23 | 24 |
| Total | 404 | 329 | 495 | 287 | 307 |

SOURCE: Gáspár (1993, p. 145).

level education as a prerequisite for service was not introduced until 1971; prior to this, all the police officer needed was a "broad back and weak mind"—this type of police officer was sought under Communism because a minimally educated police officer would easily adapt to a system that served oppressive power instead of its citizens; whereas, intelligent and educated police officers would be able to think and decide independently and possibly cross the political will of those in power.

Secrecy, as official policy, made the difference between insignificant cases and significant ones, particularly in administrative and political power. An impenetrable dividing line developed between the police and other parts of society. In this environment of secrecy and power, corruption became one of the most effective ways to cross the line.

The paramilitary structure of the police developed during the most difficult dictatorship in the Rákosi era. However, this sort of police style became so comfortable for many police officers, especially ranking officers, that they insist on maintaining this mode. Moreover, a military-like structure provides the possibility for line officers to continue their autocratic hold over citizens and for the police leadership to do the same over their subordinates.

In 1988, as Communism was beginning to wane, a book was written by György Moldova about the police that provides several interesting facts about police corruption. According to Moldova, the total number of corruption cases in the 1980s was 300 to 400, and the total number of offenders was 700 to 800 (Gáspár, 1993). However, it is difficult to single out all the corruption-related cases. For example, misuse of authority actually is the same as trading in influence and is, therefore, corruption. While corruption seems to be widespread in the society at large, there are only 100 to 200 cases of police corruption officially recorded in any given year.

It seems that the nature of the police misconduct officially recorded changed in the 1980s: During the 1970s most of the cases investigated by prosecutors were categorized as cases of brutality, but in the 1980s corruption took the lead position (Moldova, 1988, p. 574). According to the official statistics from the 1980s (see Table 7.1), "misuse of authority" was indeed more frequent than "forceful interrogation." It is very likely that the increase in the number of corruption cases derives from the changes in economic policy and economic structure. In the 1980s it became possible in Hungary to found private firms, state companies tried to make a profit. In addition to these structural changes, the economic situation in general was bad in spite of these efforts. Limited opportunities and reduced state financial assistance increased competition. Relatively open business possibilities conflicted with the planned economy and legal regulations. A third component of increasing corruption was the falling standard of living, which stimulated people to find new sources of income.

However, fewer police officers were sentenced to prison, as the regime protected them even in extreme cases. Police officers under sentence were considered suitable for duty and, while they were in prison, they were paid half of their salaries. The reasoning for such an unusual approach was that police officers were considered agents of power, and they were thus thought to require different treatment than that given to ordinary citizens.

## DATA AND METHODS

The following study draws first on data from an international survey of police integrity and then on data from two other surveys of the Hungarian police designed by the author to investigate integrity.

The international survey of police integrity interviewed 610 sworn officers from four municipal police departments and two police departments from Budapest, the capital of Hungary. The sample included departments of five medium-sized towns from different regions of Hungary and two districts of Budapest. The sample also included police officers who were studying in the Police College evening course.

Most of the respondents performed either public order duties (i.e., street patrol) or were in the investigative units (40.9% and 42.9%, respectively). In terms of their rank, they were mostly noncommissioned officers or enlisted officers (33.7% and 49.7%, respectively); only 16.1% occupied supervisory

positions. The respondents in the sample were experienced: their average length of service was 8.92 years (only 30.8% of the respondents had 5 years of experience or less). Finally, the respondents were employed at either medium-sized police agencies (46.1%) or small police agencies (34.3%).

The second survey examined the police subculture, working conditions, and the extent of corruption (Krémer & Szakács, 2000). It was conducted in 1999. In that survey, respondents were asked to estimate the frequency of corruption in their department. We wanted to know what they think about how organized corruption is in the Hungarian police force. The questionnaire contained 72 questions and 232 variables. The most important thing about the questionnaire was that it enabled connections to be made about police subculture and corruption in order to ascertain what connections exist between them.

The sampling unit was 994 sworn officers from four county towns' police departments and from nine police departments in Budapest. Most of the surveyed police officers had been police officers for at least 6 years (69.6%) and one out of three served in a supervisory capacity (35.0%). The majority worked either in patrol (45.7%) or in investigation (30.9%).

The topic of the third survey was police officers' attitudes to different police roles, to the war on crime, order maintenance, and community-based policing (Krémer, 2001). This questionnaire contained 26 questions and 66 variables about the attitudes and values of police role models. We wondered what the respondents thought about the paramilitary structure of the police and its chain of command, and what their opinions were about police-community relations.

The third sample was composed of 243 sworn officers from two county towns' police departments and from two police departments in Budapest (Krémer & Molnár, 2000). This sample contained a slightly larger percentage of less experienced police officers (40.0% had 5 years of experience or less). The majority performed either patrol duties (32.5%) or investigative duties (45.8%). Only one out of five respondents was a supervisor (19.0%).

## EFFECTS OF THE TRANSITION FROM COMMUNISM ON POLICE INTEGRITY

At the end of the 1980s, Hungary, just like other Central European countries, started to experience extensive political, economic, and social changes. The transition process has been characterized by radical changes in property relations, privatization of industries, rearrangement of social classes, increased poverty, and greater economic uncertainty generally. The system of political institutions has changed dramatically since the onset of this transition: The one-party system has been replaced by a multi-party system, the Parliament has gained a new democratic role, and citizens are no longer perceived as subjects.

These changes have affected the police as well: The stable position of the police in the Communist system has been shattered. The role of the police has become unclear, many officers have retired, and the rank-to-file ratio has changed. Nonetheless, despite the dramatic sociopolitical events of the last decade, the police organization and police behavior have remained virtually unchanged. Given this, the question arises as to whether it is possible for a democratic political system to coexist with an undemocratic police force and, if so, what the results of such an arrangement are.

The answer is of course yes, an undemocratically organized police force can coexist with democracy, but the society is forced to suffer its aftermath. One of the possible negative consequences of this situation is corruption. The police suffer low prestige and the lack of citizens' trust.

While it is a rational expectation that democratically elected politicians should seek to reform an undemocratic police force, the real situation is far more complicated. The reform of the police hinges on more factors than consistency in organization and democracy. Viewing the last decade of politics in Hungary, it is easy to believe that those in power have no clear conception about the role of the police in a democratic society, let alone how to achieve it. It seems as if the politicians focus on only one fact: the problem of the increasing criminality and its solution through a narrow range of methods.

It is very likely that if formal organizational structures are not able to provide stability, informal structures will have considerable importance in the life of the police. This factor plays a significant role in whether police officers will be able or unable to control corruption.

In the period from 1989 to 1999, the number of uniformed police officers has increased from approximately 20,000 to more than 26,000. These police officers are poorly equipped, have few if any modern tools, suffer from bad working conditions, and increasingly see their prestige decline and watch their salaries remain at the national average.

### The Tolerance of Corruption by the Citizens and the Police

One of the hopes of the past decade's period of transition was to achieve a reduction in corruption—although, curiously, corruption meant citizens "trusted" functioning systems, because it was only through corruption that organizations were rendered workable! Notwithstanding this belief, a recent survey by Vásárhelyi (1998) showed that the public mistrusts the official system. The respondents in the study, which was drawn

**Table 7.2**    Corruption Index of Institutions, According to Citizens

| Institutions | |
|---|---|
| ÁPV Rt. (State Privatization Company Inc.) | 72 |
| Political Party | 55 |
| Banks | 54 |
| Local Authorities | 52 |
| **Police** | **51** |
| Tax Authority | 47 |
| Government | 46 |
| Press (Newspapers) | 46 |
| Ministries | 44 |
| Electronic Media | 43 |
| Parliament | 41 |
| Courts of Law | 39 |
| Trade Unions | 33 |
| Army | 31 |
| Church | 25 |

SOURCE: Vásárhelyi (1998, p. 180).

Note: The scale used here extends from 0 to 100, with an institution characterized as having the least corruption at 0, and an institution characterized as having absolute corruption at 100 on the scale.

**Table 7.3**    According to Police Officers, "What Will People Do, if One of Their Fellows Commits a Corrupt Act?"

| N = 977 | *Percentage* |
|---|---|
| Agree | 1.9% |
| Take Notice and Do Nothing | 38.6% |
| Condemn, But Do Not Break Contact | 39.6% |
| Break Contact, But Do Not Report | 8.2% |
| Report to the Police | 11.7% |
| | 100% |

from a sample of the general population, believe that all the democratic institutions are to some extent corrupt (see Table 7.2).

If people believe that corruption is both a widespread and an accepted solution to the problem of making society work, it increases the possibility that police officers will be corrupt, because they do not expect to be rejected by the citizens when they propose a corrupt transaction, nor do they fear that their fellow police officers will report them (see Table 7.3). Table 7.3 gives strong evidence of police officers' belief that very few citizens will oppose corruption. Of the police officers surveyed, almost half (40.5%) believe that citizens will do nothing about corruption, because they accept corruption as an existing phenomenon. Another 40% think that citizens will not do anything about it in spite of the fact that they condemn corruption. Only 20% of the police who responded are of the opinion that citizens want to do

something to eliminate corruption. And 80% of police officers feel that citizens either support or expect corruption.

According to the opinion of the police officers surveyed, citizens are passive in their acceptance of corruption (i.e., they believe that the boundaries of civil corruption give a wide range for others to behave in a corrupt way). According to the police officers surveyed, citizens passively accept corruption and thus contribute to the flourishing of an environment that is tolerant of corruption. In fact, very few police officers expect citizens to report corrupt behavior to the appropriate authorities.

## Rising Crime Rates and Political Answers

In addition to rapid socioeconomic changes, the Hungarian people have had to confront rising crime rates (see Table 7.4). The increase in crime has accelerated so quickly that citizens have lost their sense of personal security. This has resulted from the instability caused by the introduction of democratic values into a previously authoritarian system that was unprepared for such changes. Subsequently, "a special interpretation of criminality has formed. Plenty of people think

**Table 7.4**     Total Number of Criminal Cases in Hungary

| *1989* | *1991* | *1993* | *1995* | *1997* |
|--------|--------|--------|--------|--------|
| 225,397 | 440,370 | 401,935 | 502,036 | 514,403 |

SOURCE: Póczik (1999, p. 30).

democracy has never been successful in controlling crime" (Finszter, 2000, p. 71).

As a result, a (misguided) nostalgia has developed for the former appearance of security. To wit, a desire for "order" has become more important than democratic values. In this context, the law has been relegated to the background. Consequently, the illegal behavior by police officers is more likely to be tolerated by the public. In fact, after 1990, the "politicians' main goal was to protect totalitarian paramilitary structure of the police" (Finszter, 2000, p. 72), in order for the police to be more capable of controlling crime. This endeavor resulted in a half-success: the paramilitary structure of the police was protected, but the crime rate did not decrease.

The problems of the paramilitary structure of the police and its functioning are closely connected to corruption. First, because "militarism is frequently an element of a deeply antidemocratic state strategy" (Szikinger, 1998, p. 106) and, second, because in that structure values become confused—ethics and law are pushed to the background and command is put foremost. In contrast to the usual practices and regulations in Europe and America, in Hungary, "a police officer must not refuse his [or her] supervisor's command, even if it violates the law" (Act XXXIV of 1994, Section 12). Thus obedience and discipline are more important than professional knowledge, let alone ethics. In fact, the law explicitly states that a "police officer must not refuse his [or her] supervisor's law-violating command"—the only exception to which is if a command forces an officer to commit a crime (Act XXXIV of 1994, Section 12).

The politician's insistence on maintaining a strong and military-like police force has only increased the danger of a police state, as István Szikinger has noted (Szikinger, 1996). Legal regulation, he argued, contains elements in Hungary that are familiar in a police state but unfamiliar in a constitutional state. He pointed out that "law enforcement legislation has refused the requirements of a constitutional state, nevertheless it isn't a well thought-out plan, it is very hazardous" (Szikinger, 1996, p. 53). One could interpret this as a probable consequence of confused conceptions of policing, but it is also possible that it will become an actual policy. As of this writing, the Constitutional Court has not heard a case concerning application of a Police Act for 6 years.

It is worth noting that there is a significant difference between the opinions of the politicians and the opinions of police officers. In a small survey, we asked police officers their opinion about the military-like structure of the police. The overwhelming majority of the responders answered "no" to the questions "Do police need to work in a military way?" (87.1%) and "Do the police need to organize in a military way?" (87.9%). Supervisors and line officers think similarly about this problem (see Table 7.5).

### The Frequency of Corruption as Estimated by Police Officers

Although an estimate of the number of corrupt acts committed inside the police force is difficult to get, and the results that follow asking for such an estimate are always

**Table 7.5**     According to Police Officers, "Do Police Need to Work in a Military Way?" and "Do Police Need to Organize in a Military Way?"

| | Need to Work | | Need to Organize | |
| --- | --- | --- | --- | --- |
| N = 243 | Line Officers | Supervisors | Line Officers | Supervisors |
| Yes | 13.3% | 12.3% | 11.1% | 12.4% |
| No | 86.7% | 87.7% | 88.9% | 87.6% |
| | 100% | 100% | 100% | 100% |

SOURCE: Krémer and Molnár (2000, p. 83).

unreliable, we still chose to ask what police officers think about how often their colleagues commit a corrupt act.

Based on the results shown in Table 7.6, we have every reason to assume that corruption is widespread and takes a variety of forms in the Hungarian police force; close to 80% of the surveyed police officers reported that classic cases of external corruption occur very frequently or at least sometimes. However, some forms of police corruption seem to be more prevalent than others. In particular, the data indicate that a classic corruption case (e.g., a police officer receiving money or other advantages for doing something) seems to occur much more frequently than do other forms of external corruption (e.g., a police officer engaging in a corrupt act for the benefit of his or her relatives or fellow workers) (see Table 7.6).

By contrast, official data on prosecuted cases (see Table 7.7) suggest that the police are only moderately corrupt. The number of officially recorded cases of police corruption in a given year is between 500 and 1,000, resulting in the prosecutions of 3.7% of the overall number of sworn police officers.

Table 7.8 shows police officers' perceptions of the nature of police corruption. The results indicate that police corruption is not perceived as a highly organized group activity; the respondents, both line officers and supervisors, report most frequently that police corruption is primarily committed by individual police officers. These data indicate that police officers are distrustful of both their fellow officers and the police organization. These data also indicate that corruption occurs frequently but is not highly organized.

## Measuring Tolerance of the Corruption Committed by the Police

To obtain empirical evidence about the extent of support for corruption among the police, we used the police integrity questionnaire developed by Klockars and Kutnjak Ivković (Kutnjak Ivkovich & Klockars, 1996). The hypothetical cases described in the questionnaire range from the acceptance of a free cup of coffee to stealing money from a found wallet (see Exhibit 1.1 in Chapter 1 of this volume). The wording of one of the cases needed to be changed in order to adjust the questionnaire to the legal regulations in Hungary. Case 9 thus reads as follows: "One of the pubs in the police officer's beat serves alcohol to minors. Instead of reporting the violation, the police officer agrees to accept a couple of free drinks from the owner."

The police officers' evaluations of the seriousness of the misconduct in the cases range substantially, from the misconduct perceived least serious (Case 1 - Off-Duty Security System Business) to that perceived most serious (Case 5 - Crime Scene Theft of Watch). It comes as no surprise that Case 1 is evaluated as the least serious case in the group; after all, that is the

**Table 7.6**    Frequency of Police Corruption in Hungary, According to Police Officers (*N* = 980)

| Types of Corruption | Never | Sometimes | Very Frequently | Total |
|---|---|---|---|---|
| Police Officer Receives Money or Other Advantages for Doing Something | 20.2% | 65.4% | 14.5% | 100% |
| Shopping* | 47.7% | 47.5% | 4.8% | 100% |
| Police Officer Manipulates Evidences on Behalf of His or Her Relatives | 36.3% | 55.1% | 8.6% | 100% |
| Police Officer Manipulates Evidences on Behalf of His or Her Fellow Workers | 37.7% | 55.8% | 6.5% | 100% |
| Police Officer Manipulates Evidence to Obey an Order | 52.6% | 42.9% | 4.5% | 100% |
| Police Officer Bears False Witness on Behalf of His or Her Relatives | 31.4% | 60.1% | 8.5% | 100% |
| Police Officer Bears False Witness on Behalf of Fellow Workers | 31.3% | 53.8% | 14.9% | 100% |
| Police Officer Bears False Witness on Behalf of a Criminal | 59.6% | 35.9% | 4.5% | 100% |
| Police Officer Uses Illicit Means to Serve Organizational Expectations | 22.1% | 67.8% | 10.2% | 100% |
| Police Officer Uses Illicit Means to Conform to Police Community | 31.5% | 60.1% | 8.4% | 100% |
| Police Officer Uses Illicit Means to Reach the Top of the Ladder | 22.5% | 58.1% | 19.4% | 100% |

*Shopping is, for instance, when police officers at the site of a burglary take a valuable but report that the criminals stole it.

SOURCE: A part of this table was previously published in Krémer (2001, p. 255).

only case for which there is no explicit prohibition of such behavior in the Hungarian set of legal rules and regulations. Rather, whether off-duty employment is illegal is contingent on the supervisor's decision in a particular case.

Police officers did not regard the use of excessive force on a car thief (Case 10) as serious misconduct and thought that no discipline was appropriate, although the majority clearly stated that such behavior violates official rules

**Table 7.7** Number of Cases of Police Corruption Prosecuted in Hungary

|  | 1991 | 1992 | 1993 | 1994 | 1995 | 1996 | 1997 | 1998 | 1999 |
|---|---|---|---|---|---|---|---|---|---|
| Bribery in Official Sphere | 185 | 336 | 212 | 480 | 296 | 604 | 380 | 477 | 458 |
| Bribery in Business Sphere | 136 | 127 | 198 | 143 | 138 | 120 | 270 | 187 | 106 |
| Trading in Influence | 23 | 319 | 54 | 173 | 75 | 243 | 215 | 239 | 46 |
| Total | 344 | 782 | 464 | 796 | 509 | 967 | 865 | 903 | 610 |

SOURCE: Common Statistics of Public Prosecutor's Office and Police (1999).

**Table 7.8** According to Police Officers, "How Organized Is Police Corruption?" ($N = 960$)

| It Is True Corruption If It Is Committed . . . | | Absolutely Not True | 2 | 3 | 4 | Absolutely True | Total |
|---|---|---|---|---|---|---|---|
| Alone | Line Officers | 16.7% | 13.9% | 34.4% | 16.3% | 18.8% | 100% |
|  | Supervisors | 9.5% | 11.9% | 29.8% | 23.8% | 25.0% | 100% |
| In Small Groups | Line Officers | 20.2% | 19.6% | 36.4% | 12.8% | 11.1% | 100% |
|  | Supervisors | 10.7% | 34.5% | 31.0% | 13.1% | 10.7% | 100% |
| By Most Police Officers, But Independent of Each Other | Line Officers | 36.7% | 19.6% | 28.3% | 8.1% | 7.4% | 100% |
|  | Supervisors | 48.2% | 16.9% | 20.5% | 8.4% | 6.0% | 100% |
| In an Organized Way in a Certain Department of Police | Line Officers | 35.5% | 20.1% | 23.7% | 10.2% | 10.5% | 100% |
|  | Supervisors | 38.6% | 21.7% | 18.1% | 9.6% | 12.0% | 100% |
| By the Entire Police Force in an Organized Way | Line Officers | 70.5% | 9.4% | 14.3% | 3.2% | 2.7% | 100% |
|  | Supervisors | 86.6% | 8.5% | 3.7% | 1.2% | — | 100% |

SOURCE: Krémer (2001, p. 267).

and the administration would issue a serious written reprimand if it was reported (see Table 7.9). Similarly, the police officers did not perceive the cover-up of a fellow police officer's DUI accident as serious misconduct and, accordingly, they thought that police officers should not be punished for such behavior, despite their recognition that it violates official rules and that the administration would mete out a serious written reprimand in such cases.

The surveyed police officers distinguished between the occasional acceptance of gifts and gratuities (Case 4 - Holiday Gifts From Merchants) and the acceptance of such gifts and gratuities on a regular basis (Case 2 - Free Meals, Discounts on Beat). Interestingly, while they perceived the occasional acceptance of gifts to be less serious than the routine acceptance of gifts (a difference of 1.22 on a 5-point scale), they thought that police officers should not be disciplined in either case (see Table 7.9). In other words, it seems that even the more serious case—the routine acceptance of gifts—did not enter into the zone that, according to the respondents, deserves correction of behavior in a form of a punishment.

One of the few cases evaluated to be in the middle of the seriousness scale is a case that involves regular kickbacks from the autobody shop for referrals of customers to the shop (Case 6 - Auto Repair Shop 5% Kickback). Although it is an instance of a classical and serious corruption arrangement on a long-term basis, the respondents thought that a serious written reprimand should be the appropriate punishment (see Table 7.9).

While the respondents thought the supervisors' abuse of office by exchanging holiday release time for a car tune-up (Case 7) is an example of a case of intermediate seriousness, their reactions to the discipline questions indicate that they did not expect that the administration would regard the case as serious at all. In fact, the respondents expected no discipline to follow such misconduct and thought that no discipline was an adequate resolution to such a case.

Of the four cases that the respondents evaluated to be the most serious, two involved opportunistic theft (Case 5 - Crime Scene Theft of Watch; Case 11 - Theft From Found Wallet) and one involved a serious bribery case (Case 3 - Bribe From Speeding Motorist), the latter being estimated to be one of the most frequent forms of police corruption in Hungary (see Fric & Walek, 2001, p. 43). The fourth case in the group of the most serious cases is Case 9, which was changed in the Hungarian version of the questionnaire to encompass the acceptance of a bribe in the form of several free drinks in exchange for overlooking the violation of serving drinks to minors in a pub. Disciplinary answers revealed that this case was not evaluated to be as serious as the other three cases in this group: Unlike the other three cases, for which dismissal was the respondents' punishment of choice, only a serious written reprimand was perceived as both the appropriate and the expected punishment in this case.

Unlike the responses regarding the seriousness of the misconduct, which ranged widely on a 5-point scale, the responses about the appropriate and expected discipline for the misconduct were concentrated on only three options (of the six we provided in the questionnaire). While the respondents picked dismissal as the modal discipline for three of the most serious cases, only two other cases deserved a serious written reprimand (Case 6 and Case 9). In the remaining six cases, the modal response favored no discipline (see Table 7.9).

The modal answers for the discipline the respondents thought was appropriate and the modal answers for the discipline they expected the administration to mete out did not overlap in all 11 cases. Rather, in the three less serious cases (Case 2 - Free Meals, Discounts on Beat; Case 8 - Cover-Up of Police DUI Accident; Case 10 - Excessive Force on Car Thief), they think that the administration would mete out punishment they evaluated to be too severe (i.e., a serious written reprimand rather than the respondents' choice of no discipline) (see Table 7.9).

The third measure used in the questionnaire focuses on the respondents' willingness to report misconduct. It can be applied to assess the extent of the code of silence. Indeed, the police culture among the surveyed police officers seems to be tolerant of most of the behaviors described in the questionnaire. In only the three most serious cases are the means for their

**Table 7.9**  Mean Scores and Rank Order of Police Officers' Views of Cases, in Three Dimensions ($N = 609$)

| Case Number and Description | Seriousness | | | | Discipline | | | | | | Willingness to Report | | | |
| --- | --- | --- | --- | --- | --- | --- | --- | --- | --- | --- | --- | --- | --- | --- |
| | Own View | | Most Officers | | Should Receive | | | Would Receive | | | Own View | | Most Officers | |
| | $\bar{x}$ | Rank | $\bar{x}$ | Rank | $\bar{x}$ | Rank | Mode | $\bar{x}$ | Rank | Mode | $\bar{x}$ | Rank | $\bar{x}$ | Rank |
| Case 1 - Off-Duty Security System Business | 1.81 | 1 | 1.67 | 1 | 1.35 | 1 | None | 1.96 | 2 | None | 1.32 | 1 | 1.83 | 2.5 |
| Case 2 - Free Meals and Discounts on Beat | 3.37 | 5 | 2.65 | 5 | 2.15 | 4 | None | 2.87 | 4 | Serious Written Reprimand | 1.96 | 4 | 2.21 | 4 |
| Case 3 - Bribe From Speeding Motorist | 4.79 | 10 | 3.97 | 9 | 5.17 | 10 | Dismissal | 5.54 | 10 | Dismissal | 3.27 | 10 | 3.10 | 10 |
| Case 4 - Holiday Gifts From Merchants | 2.15 | 2 | 1.95 | 2 | 1.46 | 2 | None | 1.94 | 1 | None | 1.54 | 2 | 1.81 | 1 |
| Case 5 - Crime Scene Theft of Watch | 4.84 | 11 | 4.26 | 11 | 5.49 | 11 | Dismissal | 5.74 | 11 | Dismissal | 3.76 | 11 | 3.47 | 11 |
| Case 6 - 5% Kickback From Auto Repair Shop | 3.76 | 6 | 3.21 | 6 | 3.26 | 8 | Serious Written Reprimand | 3.78 | 8 | Serious Written Reprimand | 2.70 | 7 | 2.77 | 8 |
| Case 7 - Supervisor Grants Holiday in Exchange for Car Tune-Up | 3.79 | 7 | 3.32 | 7 | 2.49 | 6 | None | 2.38 | 3 | None | 2.19 | 6 | 2.35 | 6 |
| Case 8 - Cover-Up of Police DUI Accident | 2.78 | 3 | 2.53 | 4 | 2.48 | 5 | None | 3.32 | 6 | Serious Written Reprimand | 2.07 | 5 | 2.24 | 5 |
| Case 9 - Free Drinks to Ignore Juvenile Drinking | 4.70 | 9 | 3.98 | 10 | 3.25 | 7 | Serious Written Reprimand | 3.38 | 7 | Serious Written Reprimand | 3.00 | 9 | 2.82 | 9 |
| Case 10 - Excessive Force on Car Thief | 2.89 | 4 | 2.45 | 3 | 2.11 | 3 | None | 2.98 | 5 | Serious Written Reprimand | 1.88 | 3 | 1.83 | 2.5 |
| Case 11 - Theft From Found Wallet | 4.20 | 8 | 3.52 | 8 | 3.54 | 9 | Dismissal | 3.89 | 9 | Dismissal | 2.76 | 8 | 2.65 | 7 |

own willingness to report at the midpoint of the scale or slightly above it. In fact, even for these three most serious cases, the percentage of the respondents who think that they would not report the misconduct is between 20% and 40%, while this percentage is above 60% for the majority of the other cases. In some cases, such as Case 1 (Off-Duty Security System Business), Case 2 (Free Meals, Discounts on Beat), Case 4 (Holiday Gifts From Merchants), and Case 10 (Excessive Force on Car Thief), the percentage of police officers who think that they would not report a fellow police officer who engaged in such behavior is above 70%, and on occasions reaches even 90% (Case 1).

## CONCLUSION

The police in Hungary are faced with problems similar to those experienced by the police in other Eastern European countries. Undergoing large-scale political and economic change has affected the police as well as the citizens they serve: The stable position the police occupied during the Communist regime has been shattered, while, at the same time, the police organization and police behavior remained relatively stable. Research studies indicate that the police are perceived to be among the most corrupt institutions in Hungarian society (Vasarhelyi, 1998). Police officers suffer low prestige and lack the citizens' trust. The perception of widespread corruption among police officers has fueled the further spread of corruption: Police officers do not expect to be rejected and reported when they propose a corrupt transaction to citizens, nor do they fear that their fellow police officers would report them.

In the empirical part of this study, we examined the level of tolerance of corrupt behavior in the police culture of a sample of Hungarian police officers. Indeed, the results suggest that the surveyed police officers know the official rules quite well (with the exception of Case 1 and Case 4, most of the police officers responded by definitely agreeing that the behavior described in the questionnaire constitutes a violation of the official rules) and that they believe some of the cases in the questionnaire are very serious forms of rule-violating behavior. Yet, the respondents perceive that the Ministry of the Interior and the police administrators do not take most of the official rules prohibiting such behavior as seriously as they should: With the exception of the three most serious cases (Case 3, Case 5, and Case 9), the official discipline expected for the misconduct by the largest percentage of police officers is either a serious written reprimand (in five cases) or no discipline at all (in three cases).

In addition, although most of the behaviors described in the questionnaire are examples of rule-violating behavior, police officers in all except the three most serious cases seem to be quite willing to tolerate such behavior; the mean answers to the question about their willingness to report such behavior in eight cases were all below the midpoint of the scale and in the direction of nonreporting. Even with regard to the three most serious cases (Case 3, Case 5, and Case 11), the cases that the respondents themselves classify as serious misconduct, label as a violation of official rules, and think that dismissal would be both the appropriate and the expected discipline for, a substantial minority of police officers think that they would not be willing to report such misconduct.

The results of this research clearly support the general perceptions identified by the citizen opinion polls; police officers in the sample illustrate the existence of a police culture largely tolerant of police corruption. A successful transition toward a democratic police force that is intolerant of corruption would require more serious efforts in the enforcement of the official rules, changing the norms of police culture, and increasing the level of intolerance toward corruption both among the police and among the citizens.

## NOTES

1. See Act XXXIV of 1994, Section 3 (Police Act, Organizational Structure).
2. During the Stalinist period, the political police were called ÁVH (State Security Police), and in the Kádárist period, they were known as Department III/3 of the Ministry of the Interior.

## REFERENCES

Finszter, G. (2000, January). Rendőrségek a XXI. században, (Police in the 21st century). *Belügyi Szemle,* pp. 64-75.

Frič, P., & Walek, C. (2001). *Crossing the thin blue line: An international annual review of anti-corruption strategies in the police.* Prague: Transparency International ČR.

Gáspár, A. (1993). A társadalmi változások és a rendőrök által elkövetett bűncselekmények alakulása (Transition and police crime). In V. József & K. Géza (Eds.), *Társadalmi változások, bűnözés és rendőrség. Nemzetközi konferencia.* Budapest: BM.

Kránitz, M. (1986). *A korrupció* (Corruption). Budapest: BM Könyvkiadó,

Krémer, F. (2001a). National Reports: Hungary. In T. Vander Beken, B. De Ruyver, & N. Siron (Eds.), *The organization of the fight against corruption in the member states and candidate countries of the EU* (pp. 223-233). Antwerpen/Apeldoorn: Maklu.

Krémer, F. (2001b). *Rivális világok. A szabályos és a kiszámíthatatlan* (Rival worlds: Regular and unpredictable). Unpublished manuscript.

Krémer, F., & Molnár, E. (2000, March/April). Modernizálható-e a magyar rendőrség? A rendőrök véleménye (Is it possible to modernize the Hungarian police? Opinions of police officers). *Magyar Rendészet,* pp. 82-103.

Krémer, F., & Szakács, G. (2000, May/June). A magyar rendőrök élet- és munkakörülményeiről (About living and working conditions of Hungarian police officers). *Magyar Rendészet,* pp. 60-86.

Kutnjak Ivkovich, S., & Klockars, C. B. (1996, March). *Police perceptions of disciplinary fairness and the formation of the code of silence.* Paper presented at annual meeting of the Academy of Criminal Justice Sciences, Las Vegas, Nevada.

Lengyel, L. (1998). Esszé a politikai korrupcióról (Essay on political corruption). In *Írások a korrupcióról* (pp. 105-124). Budapest: Helikon–Korridor .

Moldova, G. (1988). *Bűn az élet: Riport a rendőrökről* (Life is crime. Report on the police). Budapest: Magvető.

Póczik, S. (1999, September). Külföldi bűnelkövetők Magyarországon a kriminálstatisztika tülrében (1989-1997) (Foreign criminals in Hungary 1989-1997). *Belügyi Szemle,* pp. 28-44.

Szikinger, I. (1996, October). A rendőrállam építőkövei (Building material of police state). *Társadalmi Szemle,* pp. 52-60.

Szikinger, I. (1998). Rendőrség a demokratikus jogállamban (Police in a democratic constitutional state). *Sík,* p. 181.

Vásárhelyi, M. (1998). Rejtőzködés, önigazolás, hárítás és egymásra mutogatás (Hiding, self-justification, shifting responsibility). In *Írások a korrupcióról* (pp. 136-209). Budapest: Helikon–Korridor.

# CHAPTER 8

# Police Integrity in Japan

## DAVID T. JOHNSON

*In sum, if generality of agreement among people in a country is the mark of truth, then Japanese police behavior is astonishingly good. The incidence of misconduct is slight and the faults trivial by American standards. Though a cynical American may always wonder if enough is known about the conduct of individual officers— whether by himself or by insiders—he must begin to consider the possibility that police conduct need not inevitably, recurrently, require substantial improvement.*

— Police scholar David H. Bayley (1991, p. 4)

*Actually, corruption is chronic in Japanese police organizations.*

— Former Hiroshima Assistant Police
Inspector Bunro Akagi (2000, p. 51)

*Consider the word "lawless." The dictionary defines it as "where law does not apply." I think that the police are Japan's most lawless group.*

— *Asahi* newspaper journalist
Hiromitsu Ochiai (1998, p. 128)

Which is it? Is Japanese police behavior "astonishingly good," or is corruption so "chronic" that police are Japan's "most lawless group"?

This chapter explores data on both sides of the divide. Although the evidence is thin in many respects, it is substantial enough to support a few central conclusions. First, the results of the integrity survey suggest that compared to their American counterparts, Japanese police may have a strong normative inclination to resist temptations to abuse the authority of their occupation. At the same time, when one compares the most serious deviance that has been revealed in Japan's police scandals to the corollary deviance in, say, Los Angeles, Philadelphia, New Orleans, or New York, the Japanese misconduct does indeed seem "slight" and the faults relatively "trivial" (Johnson, in press).

I argue, however, that police in Japan have less integrity than surveys and scandals suggest. There are good reasons to question the validity of the survey answers, at least in this case, and there are even better reasons to resist making inferences about the true incidence and seriousness of Japanese misconduct from the wrongdoing that has actually been exposed. Scandal is, among other things, misconduct revealed or alleged, and there is some "dark figure" of police deviance that is not now known and may not be knowable (Markovits & Silverstein, 1988). Moreover, if police misconduct seems less serious in Japan than in America, the roots of the difference lie less in disparate levels of integrity than in contrasting contexts of policing. In particular, there are three crucial features of the policing environment that differ in the two places (Johnson, in press). First, America's diversity and division (racial, linguistic, and economic) greatly increase the challenge of policing democratically (Sherman, 2001). Japanese police engage in less misconduct than American police in part because the society they regulate is far less diverse and divided. Second, it is well known that "wars" on drugs, gangs, and crime dehumanize the "enemy," undermine respect for law, and thereby generate some of the worst forms of police misconduct (Chevigny, 1995; Domanick, 1994; Dotson, 2000; Maple, 1999; McNamara, 1999; Skolnick & Fyfe, 1993). Unlike their American counterparts, Japanese police (and the political culture they inhabit) rarely wage "wars." One result is less "collateral damage." Third, so-called victimless crimes (such as gambling, prostitution, and drug addiction) foster much police misconduct, in large part because many people believe that such acts should not be criminalized. Indeed, the most important proximate cause of police corruption is the nature of the criminal law (Walker, 1992). In Japan, most "pursuits of pleasure" (i.e., vice) are policed through regulation rather than prohibition and through harm reduction rather than moral crusade. Herein lies another

source of the perception that Japanese police have high integrity (Bayley, 1991).

The rest of this chapter examines the propriety of that perception. Section one summarizes the results of the integrity survey. Section two presents three reasons for skepticism that police integrity in Japan is as good as the survey seems to suggest. Section three tells a tale of two scandals in order to show that there is a large gap between the high-integrity survey answers and the reality of police behavior in Japan. Section four argues that the mechanisms for exposing misconduct are so weak in Japan that police behavior may well be worse than it appears. Section five presents three problems of police misconduct that have been overlooked and ignored by previous writers: the widespread embezzlement of money from police slush funds, the corruption that occurs because of police control over Japan's massive pinball industry, and police tolerance of organized crime. The concluding section argues that significant police reform is unlikely to occur anytime soon.

## THE INTEGRITY SURVEY

In January of 2001, I administered a police integrity survey to 182 Japanese officers from six prefectures in northern Japan. The survey was conducted in Japanese and through the assistance of a Japanese police executive who distributed and collected the questionnaires.

Exhibit 8.1 presents an English translation of the twelve case scenarios that constitute the core of the survey. The first eight scenarios were borrowed from the first American survey, and the last four scenarios were taken from the second American survey.[1] Only Case 16 (False Report of Drug Possession on Dealer) had to be altered to suit the Japanese context. Since arrests for heroin are rare in Japan (only 100 or so per year), the dealer in this scenario is said to possess methamphetamine instead.

Case 1.   A police officer stops a motorist for speeding. The officer agrees to accept a personal gift of half the amount of the fine in exchange for not issuing a citation. (Bribe From Speeding Motorist)

Case 2.   A police officer is widely liked in the community, and on holidays local merchants and restaurant and bar owners show their appreciation for his attention by giving him gifts of food and liquor. (Holiday Gifts From Merchants)

Case 3.   A police officer has a private arrangement with a local auto body shop to refer the owners of cars damaged in accidents to the shop. In exchange for each referral, he receives a payment of 5% of the repair bill from the shop owner. (5% Kickback From Auto Repair Shop)

Case 4.   A police officer, who happens to be a very good auto mechanic, is scheduled to work during coming holidays. A supervisor offers to give him these days off, if he agrees to tune-up his supervisor's personal car. Evaluate the supervisor's behavior. (Supervisor Grants Holiday in Exchange for Car Tune-Up)

Case 5.   At 2 A.M. a police officer, who is on duty, is driving his patrol car on a deserted road. He sees a vehicle that has been driven off the road and is stuck in a ditch. He approaches the vehicle and observes that the driver is not hurt but is obviously intoxicated. He also finds that the driver is a police officer. Instead of reporting this accident and offense he transports the driver to his home. (Cover-Up of Police DUI Accident)

Case 6.   A police officer finds a bar on his beat that is still serving drinks a half hour past its legal closing time. Instead of reporting this violation, the police officer agrees to accept a couple of free drinks from the owner. (Free Drinks to Ignore Late Bar Closing)

Case 7.   Two police officers on foot patrol surprise a man who is attempting to break into an automobile. The man flees. They chase him for about 200 meters before apprehending him by tackling him and wrestling him to the ground. After he is under control, both officers punch him a couple of times in the stomach as punishment for fleeing and resisting. (Excessive Force on Car Thief)

Case 8.   A police officer finds a wallet in a parking lot. It contains the amount of money equivalent to a full day's pay for that officer. He reports the wallet as lost property but keeps the money for himself. (Theft From Found Wallet)

Case 9.   A police officer is aware that there is a felony warrant for a long-time friend of his. Although he sees his friend frequently over a period of more than a week and warns his friend of its existence, he does not arrest him. (Failure to Arrest Friend With Felony Warrant)

Case 10.  In responding with her male partner to a fight in a bar, a young, female officer receives a black eye from one of the male combatants. The man is arrested and handcuffed, and as he is led into the cells, the male member of the team punches him very hard in the kidney area saying, "Hurts, doesn't it?" (Officer Strikes Prisoner Who Hurt Partner)

Case 11.  A police officer stops a motorist for speeding. As the officer approaches the vehicle, the driver yells, "What the hell are you stopping me for?" The officer replies, "Because today is 'Arrest an Asshole (*baka na yatsu*) Day.'" (Verbal Abuse of Motorist)

Case 12.  A police officer arrests two drug dealers involved in a street fight. One has a large quantity of methamphetamine (*kakuseizai*) on his person. In order to charge them both with serious offenses, the officer falsely reports that the methamphetamine was found on both men. (False Report of Drug Possession on Dealer)

**Exhibit 8.1**   Case Scenarios From Questionnaire Distributed to Japanese Police

The case assessment options in the Japanese survey are identical to those in the American survey (see Exhibit 1.2 in Chapter 1 of this volume), except that for the two questions about the discipline that offenders should and would receive, the options do not include "demotion in rank" as a possible answer (because it rarely occurs). In its place, the Japanese survey uses "reduction in pay" as an answer category. Thus, for the two questions about discipline, the answer categories differ: In the American survey they are

**Table 8.1**     Characteristics of the
                  Japanese Sample

| | |
|---|---|
| Sample size | 182 |
| Sample date | January 2001 |
| Mean length of service | 12 years |
| Mean length of service in current post | 1.5 years |
| Percentage in supervisory post | 30% |
| Number of police who said they did not give their honest opinion | 2 (1.1%) |
| Number of police who said most police would not give their honest opinion | 19 (10.4%) |

*Rank*
| | |
|---|---|
| Officer (*junsa*) | 4 (2.2%) |
| Senior Officer (*junsacho*) | 85 (46.7%) |
| Sergeant (*junsabucho*) | 83 (45.6%) |
| Assistant Inspector (*keibuho*) | 3 (1.6%) |
| Inspector (*keibu*) | 2 (1.1%) |
| Superintendent (*keishi*) | 2 (1.1%) |
| Senior Superintendent (*keishisei*) | 1 (0.5%) |
| Did Not Answer | 2 (1.1%) |

*Assignment*
| | |
|---|---|
| Community (*chiiki*) | 28 (15.4%) |
| Detection/Investigation (*keiji*) | 59 (32.4%) |
| Crime prevention (*seikatsu anzen*) | 23 (12.6%) |
| Security (*keibi*) | 35 (19.2%) |
| Administration (*keimu*) | 10 (5.5%) |
| Other | 25 (13.7%) |
| Did not answer | 2 (1.1%) |

*Agency*
| | |
|---|---|
| Large (201-500) | 25 (13.7%) |
| Medium (76-200) | 51 (28.0%) |
| Small (26-75) | 41 (22.5%) |
| Very small (25 or less) | 1 (0.5%) |
| Headquarters (*keisatsu hombu*) | 59 (32.4%) |
| Did not answer | 4 (2.7%) |

the degree to which Japanese police are more inclined to discipline wrongdoers than are their American counterparts.

Table 8.1 lists several salient characteristics of the Japanese police sample. Comparison with the American samples shows that:

- Japanese police respondents were, on average, about 2 years more experienced than American police respondents (12 years vs. 10.3 years of experience).
- Japanese police were more likely to work in a supervisory post (30% vs. 19.8%).[2]
- Japanese police were less likely to be engaged in patrol or traffic assignments (28% vs. 63.1%).
- Japanese police were less likely to work in large or very large police agencies (13.7% vs. 79.6%).
- Japanese police were concentrated at the senior officer (46.7%) and sergeant (45.6%) ranks.

Tables 8.2 and 8.3 compare Japanese and American responses across three dimensions of police integrity: perceptions of misconduct's *seriousness,* judgments and predictions about the appropriate *discipline* for it, and estimates of officers' *willingness to report* it. There are significant similarities and striking differences across all three dimensions.

Consider the affinities first. For the most part, police in the United States and Japan agree about how to rank order the seriousness of the misconduct depicted in the scenarios. In both countries, Case 1 (Bribe From Speeding Motorist), Case 8 (Theft From Found Wallet), and Case 12 (False Report of Drug Possession on Dealer) are ranked first, second, and third in seriousness; in only three of twelve scenarios do the rank orders of misconduct's seriousness differ by more than one place; and the largest difference in rank (for Case 5 - Cover-Up of Police DUI Accident) is only three places (8th most serious in Japan vs. 11th most serious in America). Police in the United States and

"period of suspension without pay" and "demotion in rank," while in the Japanese survey they are "reduction in pay" and "period of suspension without pay." Because these two categories are less severe in the Japanese survey, comparisons will overstate

**Table 8.2**    Comparison of Japanese and American Officers' Estimates of the Seriousness of the Misconduct in the Cases

| Case Number and Description | Japanese Score | Japanese Rank | American Score | American Rank |
|---|---|---|---|---|
| Case 1 - Bribe From Speeding Motorist | 4.98 | 1 | 4.92 | 1 |
| Case 8 - Theft From Found Wallet | 4.98 | 2 | 4.85 | 2 |
| Case 12 - False Report of Drug Possession on Dealer* | 4.97 | 3 | 4.62 | 3 |
| Case 3 - 5% Kickback From Auto Repair Shop | 4.87 | 4 | 4.50 | 6 |
| Case 6 - Free Drinks to Ignore Late Bar Closing | 4.80 | 5 | 4.54 | 4 |
| Case 9 - Failure to Arrest Friend With Felony Warrant* | 4.79 | 6 | 4.52 | 5 |
| Case 10 - Officer Strikes Prisoner Who Hurt Partner* | 4.74 | 7 | 4.13 | 8 |
| Case 5 - Cover-Up of Police DUI Accident | 4.69 | 8 | 3.03 | 11 |
| Case 4 - Supervisor Grants Holiday in Exchange for Car Tune-Up | 4.57 | 9 | 4.18 | 7 |
| Case 7 - Excessive Force on Car Thief | 4.35 | 10 | 4.05 | 9 |
| Case 11 - Verbal Abuse of Motorist* | 4.33 | 11 | 3.60 | 10 |
| Case 2 - Holiday Gifts From Merchants | 3.53 | 12 | 2.84 | 12 |

Note: Japanese scores are an average of the answers of 182 respondents, while American scores are an average of the answers of 3,235 respondents from 30 different agencies. However, since aggregate American data were not available for the four case scenarios marked with an asterisk, the figures for these cases are an average of the answers of 324 respondents from the Charleston, South Carolina, police department. Charleston received the highest total integrity rank score of the 30 agencies surveyed by Klockars, Kutnjak Ivkovich, Haberfeld, and Uydess (2000).

Japan also agree that Case 2 (Holiday Gifts From Merchants) is the least serious kind of misconduct.

Similarly, in both the United States and Japan, the more seriously police regard the misconduct, the more likely they are to believe that discipline should and would be imposed and the more willing they are to report the wrongdoing. Moreover, in both countries the punishment that respondents think should be imposed is about the same as the punishment they think would be imposed. The largest difference in the Japanese survey concerns Case 4 (Supervisor Grants Holiday in Exchange for Car Tune-Up), and at 0.31 it is three times larger than any other difference. This finding suggests that Japanese police believe the usual punishment for supervisors who ask subordinates to perform personal services is too lenient.[3]

The largest difference in the American survey between estimates of the discipline that misconduct should receive and would receive concerns Case 5 (Cover-Up of Police DUI Accident) and is -0.40, indicating that American police believe that the discipline for drunk driving is too severe. Overall, police in the United States are more likely than Japanese police to think that the usual discipline (what the misconduct would receive) is more severe than it should be.[4]

Compared to these similarities in reported integrity, the cross-national differences seem striking.[5] First, police in Japan regard *every* kind of misconduct *more seriously* than American police do. The smallest differences occur for the most serious misconduct (Case 1 - Bribe From Speeding Motorist and Case 8 - Theft From Found Wallet), while the largest differences exist for the least serious deviance. Indeed, the average difference for the six scenarios seen as least serious in Japan is more than three times greater than the average difference in perceived seriousness for the six scenarios seen as most serious. Thus, police in Japan seem to perceive more seriousness across the whole range of misconduct, but especially at the lower end of the seriousness spectrum. If one employs the rule of thumb that has been used to analyze other integrity surveys—that a difference in score of 0.5 points or more denotes a "real" difference in agency attitudes—then in the Japan-U.S. comparison, even the *average difference* for all twelve scenarios borders on significance (0.48), and it exceeds significance for officers' estimates of others' beliefs and behavior (0.61). By the same standard, Japanese police regard four of the twelve scenarios as significantly more serious in their estimates of their own beliefs and behavior (Case 2 - Holiday Gifts From Merchants, Case 5 - Cover-Up of Police DUI Accident, Case 10 - Officer Strikes Prisoner Who Hurt Partner, and Case 11 - Verbal Abuse of Motorist) and seven of the twelve scenarios

as significantly more serious in their estimates of others' beliefs and behavior (the four above plus Case 3 - 5% Kickback From Auto Repair Shop, Case 7 - Excessive Force on Car Thief, and Case 12 - False Report of Drug Possession on Dealer). In fact, when Japanese police are compared to police in Charleston, South Carolina—the department with the top "total integrity score" of all 30 American agencies surveyed—11 out of 12 of their estimates of their own beliefs and behavior and all 12 of their estimates of others' beliefs and behavior are more serious, and they are significantly more serious for four of the scenarios (Case 5 - Cover-Up of Police DUI Accident, Case 10 - Officer Strikes Prisoner Who Hurt Partner, Case 11 - Verbal Abuse of Motorist, and Case 12 - False Report of Drug Possession on Dealer, see Table 8.4).

Second, police in Japan say they are *more willing to report every kind of misconduct* than are Americans. Indeed, for their estimates of their own willingness to report misconduct, the average Japan-U.S. difference is significant (0.50), as are three of the individual scenarios (Case 2 - Holiday Gifts From Merchants, Case 5 - Cover-Up of Police DUI Accident, and Case 10 - Officer Strikes Prisoner Who Hurt Partner). For their estimates of others' willingness to report misconduct, the average cross-national difference is even more significant (0.55), as is the difference for five individual scenarios (the three just listed, plus Case 8 - Theft From Found Wallet and Case 12 - False Report of Drug Possession on Dealer). For their estimates of both their own and others' willingness to report misconduct, the largest difference occurs for Case 5 (Cover-Up of Police DUI Accident), with Japanese police expressing vastly more willingness to break the code of silence than do their American counterparts. This orientation is part of a larger cultural pattern, for Japan is "exceedingly strict" on drunk driving, no matter who the driver is, and Japanese standards for defining drunkenness are "the most stringent in the world" (Bayley, 1991, p. 100). Compared to police in Charleston, Japanese police are more willing to report misconduct in seven of the twelve scenarios, and three of the differences are significant (for Case 5 - Cover-Up of Police DUI Accident, Case 10 - Officer Strikes Prisoner Who Hurt Partner, and Case 12 - False Report of Drug Possession on Dealer).

Third, the discipline dimension of integrity is more difficult to compare because (as described above) the answer categories in the Japanese and American surveys differ in ways that exaggerate the propensity of Japanese police to discipline. Nonetheless, even when this problem of comparability is taken into account, police in Japan say that more discipline should be imposed and would be imposed for most case scenarios. For example, Japanese police say that significantly more punishment should be imposed for four types of misconduct—Case 1 - Bribe From Speeding Motorist, Case 5 - Cover-Up of Police DUI Accident, Case 8 - Theft From Found Wallet, and Case 10 - Officer Strikes Prisoner Who Hurt Partner—and they believe that significantly more punishment actually would be imposed for the first three of those types. With regard to both the discipline misconduct should receive and the discipline it would receive, the average differences between Japanese and American officers' estimates for all twelve scenarios are large but not significant (0.44 and 0.29, respectively).

Finally, the police surveyed in Japan and Charleston seem about equally inclined to discipline wrongdoers. With regard to the discipline misconduct should receive, the integrity scores of officers from Japan are significantly higher for three scenarios (Case 5 - Cover-Up of Police DUI Accident, Case 10 - Officer Strikes Prisoner Who Hurt Partner, and Case 12 - False Report of Drug Possession on Dealer), while the scores of officers from Charleston are higher for two (Case 2 - Holiday Gifts From Merchants and

Case 4 - Supervisor Grants Holiday in Exchange for Car Tune-Up). As for the discipline misconduct would receive, the scores of officers from Charleston are higher for four scenarios (the same two just noted, plus Case 6 - Free Drinks to Ignore Late Bar Closing and Case 11 - Verbal Abuse of Motorist), and there are no scenarios for which the scores of the officers from Japan are higher. Thus, as measured by this survey, Japanese police have somewhat more disciplinary integrity than average American police but a little less than police in high-integrity Charleston.

In sum, Japanese police report that they have substantially higher integrity than average American officers and somewhat higher integrity than police from even the highest integrity American agency. Compared to police in Charleston, for example, police in Japan have higher integrity scores for 48 of the 72 cells in Table 8.3, and 15 of those differences can be deemed substantively "significant" (greater than 0.5 points). By contrast, police in Charleston have higher integrity scores for only 24 of the 72 cells, and just 6 of those disparities are substantively significant (all for the discipline that misconduct should and would receive). Similarly, Japanese police say that they regard every kind of misconduct more seriously than do American police (see Table 8.3), and they appear more willing to report all kinds of misconduct. Finally, Japanese officers believe that almost all of the deviance depicted in the scenarios violates police policy (see Table 8.2). The only notable exception is the misconduct in Case 2 (Holiday Gifts From Merchants), and even there most Japanese officers believe that accepting food, alcohol, or other gratuities breaks a departmental rule.

If these survey findings can be trusted, then Japanese police have extraordinarily high integrity. Furthermore, if it is true that scholars should focus less on low-integrity agencies and more on "what agencies of high integrity do in order to create and maintain a

**Table 8.3** Police Integrity in Japan and the USA

| CASE SCENARIO | Seriousness | | | | Discipline | | | | Willingness to Report | | | |
|---|---|---|---|---|---|---|---|---|---|---|---|---|
| | Japan | | USA | | Japan | | USA | | Japan | | USA | |
| | Own | Other | Own | Other | Should | Would | Should | Would | Own | Other | Own | Other |
| 1. Traffic Bribe | 4.98 | 4.93 | 4.92 | 4.81 | 5.81 | 5.82 | 4.92 | 4.86 | 4.36 | 4.15 | 4.19 | 3.92 |
| 2. Holiday Gifts | 3.53 | 3.42 | 2.84 | 2.64 | 2.65 | 2.75 | 2.53 | 2.82 | 3.03 | 2.93 | 2.36 | 2.28 |
| 3. Car Kickback | 4.87 | 4.79 | 4.50 | 4.26 | 4.91 | 4.81 | 4.40 | 4.46 | 4.20 | 4.03 | 3.95 | 3.71 |
| 4. Supervisor's Tune-up | 4.57 | 4.34 | 4.18 | 3.96 | 3.36 | 3.05 | 4.59 | 3.43 | 3.80 | 3.50 | 3.45 | 3.29 |
| 5. Police Drunk-Driving | 4.69 | 4.68 | 3.03 | 2.86 | 4.73 | 4.74 | 2.81 | 3.21 | 4.09 | 3.96 | 2.34 | 2.28 |
| 6. Bar Hours | 4.80 | 4.64 | 4.54 | 4.28 | 4.32 | 4.21 | 4.02 | 4.08 | 3.99 | 3.83 | 3.73 | 3.47 |
| 7. Chase and Punch | 4.35 | 4.26 | 4.05 | 3.70 | 3.91 | 4.01 | 3.76 | 4.00 | 3.59 | 3.51 | 3.39 | 3.07 |
| 8. Steal Wallet Money | 4.98 | 4.97 | 4.85 | 4.69 | 5.85 | 5.82 | 5.09 | 5.03 | 4.69 | 4.59 | 4.23 | 3.96 |
| 9. Friend Warrant | 4.79 | 4.76 | 4.52 | 4.45 | 4.59 | 4.66 | 4.62 | 4.64 | 4.40 | 4.28 | 4.09 | 3.98 |
| 10. Prisoner Hit | 4.74 | 4.73 | 4.13 | 3.88 | 4.60 | 4.61 | 3.93 | 4.17 | 4.18 | 4.13 | 3.50 | 3.38 |
| 11. Verbal Abuse | 4.33 | 4.22 | 3.60 | 3.45 | 2.80 | 2.70 | 3.13 | 3.40 | 3.40 | 3.30 | 2.97 | 2.88 |
| 12. False Drug | 4.97 | 4.96 | 4.62 | 4.45 | 5.49 | 5.48 | 4.99 | 5.04 | 4.71 | 4.54 | 4.22 | 3.95 |

SOURCES: Author's survey of 182 Japanese policers (January 2001); Klockars, Kutnjak Ivkovich, Harver, and Haberfeld (2000) survey of 3235 American officers in 30 police agencies; Klockars, Haberfeld, Kutnjak Ivkovich, and Uydess (2001) survey of 324 officers in the Charleston, South Carolina, Police Department.

Note: Charleston data are in italics.

**Table 8.4** Police Integrity in Japan and Charleston, South Carolina

| CASE SCENARIO | Seriousness | | | | Discipline | | | | Willingness to Report | | | |
|---|---|---|---|---|---|---|---|---|---|---|---|---|
| | Japan | | Charleston | | Japan | | Charleston | | Japan | | Charleston | |
| | Own | Other | Own | Other | Should | Would | Should | Would | Own | Other | Own | Other |
| 1. Traffic Bribe | 4.98 | 4.93 | 4.96 | 4.91 | 5.81 | 5.82 | 5.41 | 5.61 | 4.36 | 4.15 | 4.46 | 4.43 |
| 2. Holiday Gifts | 3.53 | 3.42 | 3.57 | 3.41 | 2.65 | 2.75 | 3.50 | 4.05 | 3.03 | 2.93 | 3.26 | 3.26 |
| 3. Car Kickback | 4.87 | 4.79 | 4.60 | 4.54 | 4.91 | 4.81 | 4.95 | 5.15 | 4.20 | 4.03 | 4.26 | 4.21 |
| 4. Supervisor's Tune-up | 4.57 | 4.34 | 4.20 | 4.08 | 3.36 | 3.05 | 4.01 | 4.13 | 3.80 | 3.50 | 3.70 | 3.58 |
| 5. Police Drunk-Driving | 4.69 | 4.68 | 3.59 | 3.44 | 4.73 | 4.74 | 3.71 | 4.28 | 4.09 | 3.96 | 3.06 | 3.04 |
| 6. Bar Hours | 4.80 | 4.64 | 4.59 | 4.40 | 4.32 | 4.21 | 4.69 | 4.87 | 3.99 | 3.83 | 4.13 | 3.98 |
| 7. Chase and Punch | 4.35 | 4.26 | 4.15 | 3.84 | 3.91 | 4.01 | 4.18 | 4.48 | 3.59 | 3.51 | 3.72 | 3.49 |
| 8. Steal Wallet Money | 4.98 | 4.97 | 4.90 | 4.83 | 5.85 | 5.82 | 5.59 | 5.68 | 4.69 | 4.59 | 4.56 | 4.49 |
| 9. Friend Warrant | 4.79 | 4.76 | 4.52 | 4.45 | 4.59 | 4.66 | 4.62 | 4.64 | 4.40 | 4.28 | 4.09 | 3.98 |
| 10. Prisoner Hit | 4.74 | 4.73 | 4.13 | 3.88 | 4.60 | 4.61 | 3.93 | 4.17 | 4.18 | 4.13 | 3.50 | 3.38 |
| 11. Verbal Abuse | 4.33 | 4.22 | 3.60 | 3.45 | 2.80 | 2.70 | 3.13 | 3.40 | 3.40 | 3.30 | 2.97 | 2.88 |
| 12. False Drug | 4.97 | 4.96 | 4.62 | 4.45 | 5.49 | 5.48 | 4.99 | 5.04 | 4.71 | 4.54 | 4.22 | 3.95 |

SOURCES: Author's survey of 182 Japanese police officers (January 2001); Klockars, Kutnjak Ivkovich, Harver, and Haberfeld (2000) survey of 324 officers in the "high integrity" Charleston, South Carolina, Police Department.

police culture intolerant of corruption" (Klockars, Kutnjak Ivkovich, Haberfeld, & Uydess, 2000, p. 26), then Japanese police must be reckoned a singularly instructive example (Bayley, 1991). But the opening "if" in this paragraph is decisive. The next section shows that there are good reasons to question whether the survey accurately measures police integrity in Japan.

## REASONS FOR SKEPTICISM

There are at least three reasons for skepticism about the survey results. First, the Japanese norm of separating formal from actual reality may have encouraged respondents to engage in a significant amount of socially sanctioned deceit. Second, the survey was administered in a way that may have undermined its validity. Third, the survey elicited answers from a prominent police whistle-blower that are inconsistent with his published views about the seriousness of police misconduct and the strength of Japan's blue wall of silence.

### The Management of Reality

All cultures distinguish between principal and practice, between the way things are supposed to be and the way they actually are. Japan stands out amidst this ubiquitous experience because the distinction is vast, and because it seldom seems to bother people (Yamada, 1997). Indeed,

> The difference of degree [of distinction] between Japan and the West is great enough to constitute a difference in kind. Not only are things in Japan almost never what they seem: a gap between formal and substantial reality has been institutionalized, because it is essential to the way power is exercised. (van Wolferen, 1989, p. 227)

There is, of course, cultural variation in "the degree to which subjects believe that

their interview replies should mirror their actual behavior" (Nelken, 2000, p. 39), and Japanese culture frequently forgives an irregular reflection. In fact, a variety of "double codes" manifest the Japanese norm of discouraging forthright communication (Sugimoto, 1997, p. 26). The most relevant contrasts *tatemae*—formal truth, facade, and pretense—and *honne*—real feelings, observed reality, and the truth you know or sense. Although the *tatemae-honne* distinction is legitimized in many spheres of Japanese life, it is especially salient among government officials (Miyamoto, 1994, p. 175). The dichotomy is often referred to, and "it is usually considered an ethically neutral if not positive aspect of Japanese society" (van Wolferen, 1989, p. 235). As a result, people in Japan can feign honesty without fear of being chided for deceit. Officials who cannot or will not juggle *tatemae* and *honne* are considered "immature," and many are punished for their "foolish frankness" (Hendry, 1995, p. 45; Miyamoto, 1994, p. 194). In this way, the double code of *tatemae-honne* sanctions deceit in situations where candor is inconvenient. It is one main mechanism for "managing reality" (van Wolferen, 1989, p. 227).[6]

For decades, Western philosophers and scholars have premised their discussions of mental life on the cardinal assumption that the same basic processes underlie all human thought, whether in the 48 prefectures of Japan or in the 13,000 police forces of America. Recent research in social psychology "is turning this long-held view of mental functioning upside down" (Goode, 2000). Studies comparing Americans to East Asians show that people who grow up in different cultures do not just think about different things; they think differently. In particular, Japanese subjects show more tolerance for "contradiction" than do Americans, a penchant that may confound attempts to compare cross-national survey results (Nisbett, 2003; Peng & Nisbett, 1999).

**Table 8.5**    Japanese Officers' Views About Whether the Misconduct is a Violation of
Official Policy

| Case Number and Description | Score | Rank |
|---|---|---|
| Case 1 - Bribe From Speeding Motorist | 5.00 | 1 |
| Case 8 - Theft From Found Wallet | 4.98 | 2 |
| Case 12 - False Report of Drug Possession on Dealer | 4.95 | 3 |
| Case 3 - 5% Kickback From Auto Repair Shop | 4.84 | 4 |
| Case 10 - Officer Strikes Prisoner Who Hurt Partner | 4.84 | 5 |
| Case 6 - Free Drinks to Ignore Late Bar Closing | 4.73 | 6 |
| Case 9 - Failure to Arrest Friend With Felony Warrant | 4.73 | 7 |
| Case 5 - Cover-Up of Police DUI Accident | 4.70 | 8 |
| Case 4 - Supervisor Grants Holiday in Exchange for Car Tune-Up | 4.35 | 9 |
| Case 7 - Excessive Force on Car Thief | 4.32 | 10 |
| Case 11 - Verbal Abuse of Motorist | 4.01 | 11 |
| Case 2 - Holiday Gifts From Merchants | 3.63 | 12 |

Note: 5 = Definitely a violation of official policy; 1 = Definitely not a violation of official policy.

## The Administration of the Questionnaire

If the tilt to *tatemae* tends to bias Japanese answers toward the appearance of integrity, then the way in which the survey was administered probably deepened the lean. As mentioned above, I could not have administered the questionnaire without the assistance of a senior police executive whom I shall call Mr. Ono. In fact, it is more accurate to say that he administered the survey himself, after several rounds of consultation with me about the content of the scenarios and the aptness of the answer categories. During those consultations, Ono often told me that the survey was likely to elicit more "approved answers" (*tatemae*) than truthful ones (*honne*).[7] As the officer in charge of Internal Affairs for the six prefectures in his region, Ono directed training courses for police. When the survey was administered in January of 2001, police in Japan were being so buffeted by a wave of scandals that one major theme of those courses was the need to improve police integrity. It was to police in six such classes that Ono distributed the questionnaire.[8] All

completed the survey in class after a lecture. The finished forms were then mailed to me.

Thus, the survey was administered in a context that encouraged conformity to official police norms and in a manner that may have undermined the conditions of anonymity and voluntariness that are known to nourish candor. The 100% response rate for the Japanese survey is nearly double the 54% rate for all American agencies and for the Charleston department featured in Table 8.3. Some of the Japanese respondents probably participated grudgingly, fearfully, or both. The congruence in answers between supervisors and rank-and-file police officers gives further cause for pause. Previous descriptions of Japan's police culture suggest that there are real and significant differences between the attitudes of patrol police and detectives on the one hand and their supervisors on the other (Akagi, 2000; Kuroki, 2000a; Miyazawa, 1992).

Police in both Japan and the United States were asked two questions at the end of the surveys about the validity of their responses. The first was "Do you think most police officers would give their honest opinion in filling out this questionnaire?" and the second was "Did you?" In response to the first question, 89.6% of Japanese police said that most officers would answer honestly, compared to 84.4% of American police. In reply to the second, 98.9% of Japanese police said that they themselves had answered honestly, compared to 97.8% of American police. Hence, police in Japan were unlikely to say that their answers were invalid. Some may infer that this finding suggests there is little reason to distrust the Japanese survey results; I think otherwise. For one thing, the cultural penchant for managing reality may apply to the honesty questions too (as several Japanese journalists told me). More important, many Japanese believe there is no tension between the "socially sanctioned deceit" of *tatemae* and the assertion that *tatemae* answers are honest. As described above, cultures differ in the degree to which they insist that survey answers mirror actual behavior, and Japan's *honne-tatemae* dichotomy is usually considered an "ethically neutral" or even "positive" feature of Japanese society (van Wolferen, 1989, p. 235).

The final flaw in the administration of the Japanese survey is the absence of case scenarios depicting the most common and serious forms of police misconduct (such as the creation and use of "slush funds," which is discussed below). The scenarios were not tailored to Japan for two reasons: to preserve the possibility of cross-national comparison, and because Mr. Ono forbade deviations from the American scenarios that might reveal deviance in the Japanese police.

## Serpico's Survey

The third reason to question the integrity of the answers is that the survey evoked replies from a whistle-blower that are inconsistent with his published views about the seriousness of police misconduct and the strength of the police code of silence. The whistle-blower is Kuroki Akio (2000a), Japan's closest

counterpart to Frank Serpico, the New York cop who pierced the "blue curtain" of silence that for years had protected the NYPD's culture of corruption (Maas, 1973). In February of 1999, Kuroki resigned from the Tokyo Metropolitan Police Department where he had received 23 commendations over 23 years of service. He then began writing at a rate that even James Michener might envy. Within 18 months, Kuroki wrote four books exposing "how corruption has ruined the force."[9] His most trenchant criticisms were directed at three features of the police organization:

- a training system that is designed to "brainwash" police into unthinking conformity to organizational norms, especially the code of silence;
- a system of discipline whose true purpose is not to purge the system of problems but to defend it against criticism; and
- a network of meticulously detailed "bylaws" that enables managers to oust any police who do not conform to expectations (Kuroki, 2000b).

In January of 2001 I interviewed Kuroki for 2 hours, at the end of which I gave him a questionnaire and asked him to complete and return it to me at his convenience. His answers arrived about 2 weeks later, complete with comments in the margins about ambiguities in some scenarios and the reasons for his replies.

It is widely agreed that Kuroki was a cop of unusually high integrity (Hirao, 2000). If so, then it is difficult to explain why his answers to several questions fall far below the survey means. For example, Kuroki's own willingness to report misconduct averaged just 3.25, far below the sample average of 4.04. The disjuncture between his answers and the sample averages suggests that either Kuroki is not the exemplar of integrity that he is widely believed to be, or else the survey failed to accurately measure the integrity environment in Japan.[10] Based on my conversations with Kuroki (and journalists who know him) and my reading of his books and other works about policing in Japan, I believe the problem lies more with the survey's integrity—at least as it was designed and administered in this instance—than with Kuroki's.[11]

## THE SURVEY-SCANDAL GAP

There is room for disagreement about how to interpret the survey results. Although it would be inappropriate to disregard them entirely, it would be equally unwise to construct an account of police integrity in Japan based on this single pillar. What can be concluded is that the survey does not measure the amount or extent of police *corruption,* it attempts to assess the police *culture of integrity*—nothing more and nothing less. Significantly, there is a large gap between what the survey suggests about Japan's culture of integrity and the evidence of police misconduct gleaned from other sources. In particular, from 1999 through 2001, police in Japan were buffeted by a wave of scandals that pose serious challenges to the view that Japanese police behavior is "astonishingly good" and police misconduct "minimal" (Ames, 1981, p. 203; Bayley, 1991, p. 4; Parker, 2001, p. 237).[12] This section recounts two such scandals; if space permitted, dozens more could be described.

### *The Kanagawa Cover-Up*

Consider first the scandal that broke in Kanagawa prefecture, home to Yokohama, Japan's third largest city. It has been called "the most serious" police scandal ever uncovered in Japan and "the worst disgrace in the history of Japanese police" (Ochiai, 2000, p. 50; Tsuchimoto, 2000, p. 42).

The original offense was committed by Yoshihisa Sakayori, a 37-year-old assistant inspector with the Kanagawa Police Department (KPD). On December 12, 1996, Sakayori

phoned a police colleague to report, in a babbling, incoherent voice, that he was "being followed by somebody." The officer who took the call suspected Sakayori was experiencing a drug-induced hallucination and instructed him to come to police headquarters. When Sakayori arrived 2 hours later with his lover, he declared that he had injected methamphetamine earlier in the day, and he rolled up his sleeve to reveal the mark on his arm. He was interrogated the next day by the KPD's Inspection Department (Japan's counterpart to Internal Affairs), to whom he admitted using stimulant drugs on several previous occasions.

Sakayori's drug use was a crime in Japan, where even first-time stimulant users are routinely indicted. In this case, however, the stimulant offense stimulated a massive cover-up. Following his confession, Sakayori was confined in a hotel room near KPD headquarters where police regularly collected urine samples from him and had them tested at their forensic lab. The scientists were told only that the samples were from "an unknown suspect." Each specimen tested positive for methamphetamine. The test results were passed from the inspection department to various police executives, including KPD Chief Watanabe Motoo, who instructed everyone to keep silent about the results. It was later revealed that in 1991 the KPD had produced an in-house manual about how to cover-up a scandal (Kuroki, 2000a, p. 98). The manual was distributed to some 200 high-ranking officers, and its policies have been adopted "in all [Japanese] police organizations" (Yokoyama, 2001, p. 197). Watanabe further instructed investigators to pressure Sakayori to resign on the grounds that he had engaged in an extramarital affair. Sakayori complied. His urine samples finally tested negative 8 days after he turned himself in. Only then was he handed over to the KPD's drug control section, which proceeded to conduct its own drug tests. Finding no objective evidence of drug use by their colleague, they dropped the case.

The cover-up was revealed in the fall of 1999, when officers implicated in other misconduct (shoplifting, prostitution, police hazing) exposed it. In the end, nine KPD police had their cases sent to the prosecutors office, five of whom were indicted and convicted, including ex-chief Watanabe. All received suspended terms of imprisonment, a punishment that Japan's newspaper of record deemed "incomprehensibly" lenient ("Tensei Jingo," 2000).[13]

The Kanagawa case triggered a wave of scandals that drew unprecedented criticism of the Japanese police.[14] In a public opinion poll, 60% of Japanese adults said that their trust in police has declined, and fully 45% said they do not trust the police at all.[15] As one elderly man put it, "Today the police are a shame and an embarrassment for all of Japan" (Sims, 2000).[16]

More important, public distrust has harmed police performance. The most obvious indicator is Japan's clearance rate, which plummeted from 40% in 1997 to 20% in 2001—a 50% decline (Masui, 2002). Some of the decline is explained by the scandal wave, which induced lower levels of public confidence in and cooperation with the police (Nakada, Shinya, & Nagasawa, 2001). But the plunging clearance rate is also partly artifactual, for scandals have focused so much scrutiny on police that they can no longer "cook the clearance rate books" (lie about their performance) as they routinely did in the past (Akagi, 2000; Kuroki, 2000a).[17] Since certainty of punishment influences potential offenders more than severity does, the spike in the percentage of unsolved crimes has likely reduced the deterrent effect of Japanese criminal justice (Johnson, 2002, p. 191). If so, then the clearance rate drop helps explain why "Japan has experienced an unprecedented crime wave in recent years" ("Crooked Cops Lorded Over Fukuoka Sex Shops," 2001). Moreover, the government's recent efforts to impose stiffer punishments on a wide variety

of offenders may be in part an effort to recover some of the "lost deterrence." Through its impact on the clearance rate, police corruption thus affects the level of crime in Japanese society and the content of Japanese criminal justice.

### The Chiba Rape Case

The Kanagawa cover-up reflects a powerful penchant to conceal wrongdoing. Indeed, the most striking revelation in the wave of scandals is how often and how thoroughly the cover-ups occur. The reality of silence contradicts the survey finding that Japanese police are unwilling to tolerate misconduct in silence. The gap between survey and scandal is gaping.

Consider another, less publicized scandal. On September 5, 1995, a 28-year-old woman called "K" went to one of Japan's ubiquitous "love hotels" with a Chiba police sergeant named Nishino. The event was unexceptional until Nishino left the room, whereupon a hotel maid discovered K lying unconscious on the bed. She called the police and K was arrested for possession and use of methamphetamine. As is customary in Japan, K was interrogated for several days about how she acquired the drugs and how often she used them. In this case, however, police had little interest in exploring K's connections to Sergeant Nishino. Instead, they pressured her to remain mum about her lover and, just as in the Kanagawa case, quietly accepted Nishino's "resignation" (with pension) for having engaged in "an affair."

In November of 1995, one day before she was to be transferred from her police cell to an official detention facility, K was raped by officer Tsukade Sakaichi, one of the jail guards. After the rape, Tsukade gave K juice, candy, and cigarettes (all considered contraband in Japanese jails) and said to her, "This is a secret, okay?" The next day, K described the rape to a police interrogator named Miyauchi. He told K that Tsukade had been warned about fondling female inmates, but he pressured K to sign a "written oath" (*seiyakusho*) that she would not file a criminal complaint and would "keep the rape to herself." After prolonged resistance, K eventually relented and wrote and signed the oath. It was addressed to "The Chief of Police in East Funabashi" (the head of the precinct in which she was detained). In a familiar pattern, police had the rapist resign, with pension, and then helped him find employment in a private security firm that was friendly to the police.

In June of 1999, when K returned home from prison, she telephoned police in East Funabashi in order to make three demands: she wanted Tsukade to apologize; she wanted her oath destroyed; and she wanted Miyauchi, the former chief of criminal investigation, to apologize for forcing her to sign the oath. The Deputy Chief of police arranged to meet K at a family restaurant along with Tsukade and the officer who had supervised many of her interrogations. Tsukade apologized perfunctorily, whereupon the Deputy Chief gave K an envelope containing 300,000 yen (about US$2,500). She was urged to accept the hush money and pressured to sign a receipt addressed to an anonymous "Dear Sir." The receipt stated that "this resolves everything."

In February of 2000, Deputy Chief Kobayashi telephoned K after learning that she had discussed the rape and cover-up with Terasawa Yu, a freelance reporter. K tape-recorded the phone conversation. In it, Kobayashi reminded her of the hush money and receipt, urged her to refuse further calls from Terasawa, and tried to convince her that the money she was given had come from Tsukade the rapist, not from Internal Affairs as he had originally said. Whatever the source of the money (and there is evidence that Tsukade could not afford to pay such a sum), it is clear that the Chiba police organization participated directly in the payment of the hush money (Terasawa, 2000a, p. 28). If the money was paid by Chiba police, then it almost certainly came from the kind of slush

fund (*uragane*) that is manufactured and abused by police throughout Japan (as the penultimate section of this chapter shows).

But the worst is still to tell, for the cover-up was orchestrated by executives in the National Police Agency. In fact, a cover-up "conference" was held in 1995 involving the two most elite officers in Chiba, Chief Endo and Division Chief Fukushima; Kunimatsu Takaji, the head (*Keisatsucho Chokan*) of *all* Japanese police; Sekiguchi Yuko, his successor; and other elite police. They agreed that news of K's rape case should be kept "in house," that Tsukade should not be arrested or investigated, and that he should be "taken care of" after his retirement so as to minimize the likelihood of damaging leaks (Terasawa, 2000b, p. 6).[18] It is instructive that while K was in prison, the Chief of Chiba (Endo) became headmaster (*kocho*) of the National Police College, and the Chief of East Funabashi (Sugiura) became headmaster of the Chiba Police Academy. Watanabe Motoo, the chief who directed the Kanagawa cover-up, also became headmaster of the National Police College.

In these ways, the elite police who enforced the code of silence were rewarded with promotions that enabled them to inculcate in new recruits the sanctity of the silence norm (Terasawa, 2000b, p. 6). Ex-officer Kuroki Akio (2000b, p. 218) is right: Japan's celebrated training system is designed to "brainwash" police into conformity with the code of silence. This lesson is a major legacy of Japan's wave of scandals (Ochiai, 2000, p. 54; Tsuchimoto, 2000, p. 49).

## WORSE THAN IT APPEARS?

While the scandal wave counsels caution in interpreting the survey results, there are other reasons to believe that Japanese police conduct is worse than it appears. Since much scandal is corruption revealed, the scope and seriousness of a scandal depends in part on the effectiveness of the mechanisms for revealing misconduct. In Japan, these mechanisms are so few and so weak that "police have nothing to fear as an institution" (Ochiai, 2000, p. 56).

First, consider the police's own internal controls. Research shows that proactive methods such as undercover integrity stings are especially effective inhibitors of misconduct. Lawrence Sherman (1998), for example, notes that the "how" of control matters more than the "who":

> Public demands for control of police misconduct have focused largely on whether police or civilians do the controlling. Yet empirical evidence suggests that method matters more than structure. Repeated studies have shown virtually no difference in the outcomes of internal investigations conducted by police and civilian oversight agencies. Yet the few examples of changes in misconduct control from reactive to proactive investigations have shown an enormous difference. (p. 450)

Police in Japan seldom use proactive methods of control. Without such techniques, they are unlikely to uncover and unravel scandals of the scope that undercover stings have revealed in the United States (Daley, 1978; Maas, 1973; McAlary, 1987; Sherman, 1978, p. 168).[18] Thus, if "the incidence of [Japanese] misconduct [appears] slight and the faults trivial by American standards" (Bayley, 1991, p. 4), it is partly because Japan's methods for exposing misconduct are deficient. To restrict certain investigative techniques is to countenance the kinds of misconduct those methods are meant to control (Heymann, 1985). It is therefore notable that Japanese law forbids plea bargaining and grants of immunity, strategies that are routinely used in America to break through the blue wall of silence (Johnson, 2002). To cite one example among many, the Rampart misconduct in the Los Angeles Police Department—involving perjury, brutality, and the framing of innocent citizens—would never

have been exposed if prosecutors had been unable to cut a deal with Raphael Perez, the main police informant (Cannon, 2000).

External controls on Japanese police are even more deficient. In addition to their inability to plea bargain, Japanese prosecutors are notoriously *amai* (lenient) toward police wrongdoers, in large part because they depend on police for the information they need to charge and try cases (Miyazawa, 1989). More specifically, prosecutors seldom investigate credible allegations that the police embezzle money, perhaps because prosecutors themselves commit similar crimes (Johnson, 2001). As for judges, Japanese police perceive "no significant threat in judicial control" of their behavior (Miyazawa, 1992, p. 225). Of course, judges everywhere have limited capacity to control police because the opportunities to do so occur indirectly and after the fact, but judicial decisions that are unfavorable to the police are exceptionally rare in Japan. One result is that judicial scrutiny functions mainly to legitimate police behavior, not to restrain it.

Similarly, for more than 50 years Japan's Board of Audit has conducted spot inspections of all of the nation's prefectural police headquarters. Despite clear evidence of systemic embezzlement, the Board has exposed no cases of spurious accounting. Where police are involved, "this watchdog trembles" (Ochiai, 2000, p. 55). Politicians dissemble, too, often because they fear that if they attempt to disclose police misconduct, their own corruption will be exposed (Ochiai, 2000, p. 56). As one veteran journalist told me in an interview, "everyone fears the police but the police fear no one." The National Public Safety Commission and prefectural public safety commissions were established after World War II to ensure that police operate independently of political pressure, but these organizations, composed of citizens appointed by governors and the prime minister, are largely "useless" watchdogs (Ochiai, 2000, p. 57). Their members tend to be elderly, conservative men from the community—business owners, doctors, and the like—who have neither police experience nor expertise and who, more importantly, have no staff or office with which to conduct investigations. The safety commissions are, de facto, run and controlled by the police.[19]

Finally, these weak formal controls are little supplemented by journalistic, scholarly, or other outside scrutiny. If the question is who controls Japanese police, then "the answer is simply that the police are totally autonomous in a formal organizational sense; they control themselves and are ultimately responsible only to the head of the National Police Agency" (Ames, 1981, p. 219).[20] One analyst has observed that this makes Japan a very "strange land":

> If a prominent sociologist from the West (not someone like David Bayley, who wrote *Forces of Order: Policing Modern Japan*) came here to research the Japanese police, that scholar undoubtedly would conclude that this country is "a strange land." First he would run into the police wall of secrecy, and he would be unable to investigate actual police practices and conditions. Next he would be informed that there is no investigative reporting about the police by newspaper or other mainstream journalists, and that there are very few free-lance journalists who follow police issues. Then he would learn that in Japanese colleges and universities there are no courses about the police (as there are in the West) and no scholars who seriously study them. In the end, our friend the sociologist would discover that citizens and taxpayers (who have entrusted their safety to the police) have an extremely weak consciousness to try to check the police. Such a scholar, I think, would be seized by this question: Is Japan really a democratic country? (Kobayashi, 1998, p. vi)

## A TRINITY OF TROUBLE

Japanese police engage in serious misconduct that has been overlooked and ignored by previous writers. This penultimate section summarizes three of the worst areas of abuse: the systematic creation and expenditure of slush funds (*uragane*), the corruption caused by police control over Japan's huge pinball industry (*pachinko*), and the illicit connections between police and organized crime (the *yakuza*).

## Uragane: *Why Officer Friendly Is a Tax Thief*

In 1984, Matsuhashi Tadamitsu, a former executive officer in the National Police Agency, published a 400-page mea culpa with a title taken from the 51st Psalm: *My Sin is Ever Before Me*. The book meticulously details how police agencies throughout Japan embezzle money from their budgets in order to create slush funds to cover under-the-table payments to senior police officials, to pay for gifts and entertainment for police and their friends and supporters, and to buy silence from people such as the woman who was raped in the Chiba jail. Since the book's publication, Matsuhashi's revelations have been confirmed by numerous sources. In 1996, for example, Ochiai Hiromitsu, a journalist for Japan's newspaper of record, obtained accounting records from the Aichi Prefectural Police that document more than 10 years of slush fund abuses. The register shows that every division in the bureau of general affairs diverted and pooled money, and that almost all the cash was spent by supervising officers. According to one police informant, "about 1 billion yen [US$8,333,000] in travel expenses is being stashed as a slush fund each year" (Ochiai, 2000, p. 53). Since Aichi is just one of Japan's 47 prefectures, police nationwide probably embezzle hundreds of millions of dollars every year (Matsuhashi, 1984; Terasawa, 1998).[21]

The crimes of embezzlement have been acknowledged by many police whistle-blowers (Akagi, 2000; Kuroki, 2000a; Ouchi, 2002). In 1996, for example, an association of anonymous officers known as "The Police Group for Justice" sent a letter to several journalists lamenting the crimes and urging reporters to expose them:

> The police are supposed to control lawlessness and injustice. It is therefore unforgivable that they turn citizens' hard-earned tax money into their own private allowances to use however they want. In this prefecture alone [where the city of Nagoya is located], police invest almost one billion yen [over US$8 million] in "travel expenses" each year. It is inexcusable that they have become numbed by the perception that if everyone does it then there is nothing to fear. (quoted in Ochiai, 1998, p. 148)

The evidence of embezzlement is overwhelming and the criminal mechanisms clear. Terasawa Yu (1998), editor of *Officer Friendly Is a Tax Thief*, explains how police generate *uragane* ("back money") by cooking the books through illegal accounting:

> "The police are creating slush funds systematically. They concoct money from business trips never taken, they skim funds they pretend to have paid to fictitious informers and sources, and so on. But stopping this practice is impossible. After all, there are no police to control the police." When I was covering the police beat ten years ago, how many times did I hear words like these from Old Boy police and from officers still on the job? I must have heard it from 30 different people. Every time I did, I resolved that one day I would expose it. The chance came in 1996 [and led to publication of this book]. (p. 2)

More recently, Akira Ouchi (2002), who retired from the police force after 18 years in its employ, published an expose titled *I Was In Charge of Slush Funds at the Tokyo Metropolitan Police Department*. His book verifies many of the revelations made by Matsuhashi, Kuroki, and other police whistle-blowers, yet it does so in more detail than any previous account. The book's biggest revelation

is its disclosure of a form of fraud that was unknown to many police: the embezzlement of "travel expenses" (*ryohi*) from the Tokyo riot police (*kidotai*)—the same officers who have been called "the epitome of police subculture" in Japan and "the chief postwar repository of the ideals of patriotism and absolute loyalty of the prewar police and army" (Ames, 1981, pp. 129, 154). So thorough was this deception that even many riot police were unaware that the law gives each of them the right to receive travel expenses ranging from $179 to $444 per month. When Ouchi began exposing the scam in weekly magazines prior to publication of his book, the riot police's "patriotism and loyalty" were overwhelmed by their anger about being betrayed. Shortly before the book appeared in print, the National Police Agency announced a "revision of regulations" ostensibly designed to eliminate this kind of fraud. It remains to be seen how Tokyo police will use the $10 million a year in riot police travel funds that they have been embezzling heretofore. Ouchi calls the illogic of the police responses to his expose "utterly self-serving," but he insists that he does not intend to criticize individual officers. In his view, "the creation of slush funds is the result of an organized system, and all officers who have been dragged into it are, in one sense, victims" (Ouchi, 2002, p. 3). For Ouchi, as for other critics, one key cause of these ongoing frauds is an arrogant "authority consciousness" (*okami ishiki*) that makes many police unable to distinguish between public interest and private wealth (Ochiai, 2000; Otani, 2000; Ouchi, 2002, p. 170; Terasawa, 1998). The slush fund facts raise at least two questions. First, how has police embezzlement persisted for decades without the offenders being called to account? And second, why has it escaped the notice of previous researchers? Police embezzlement persists because, first of all, other agencies that could blow the whistle engage in similar crimes. Bureaucratic embezzlement is endemic in Japan. In recent years, massive slush funds have been uncovered in the Ministry of

Foreign Affairs, the Ministry of Finance, the Prosecutors Office, and several other agencies (Johnson, 2001). These illicit funds are not concocted by a few "bad apples," as the exposed agencies routinely allege, they are the intended result of organizational policies. There appears to be a quid pro quo arrangement between the police and these other agencies. If you overlook our wrongdoing, the "this for that" goes, we will overlook yours. Embezzlement also persists because external controls on police behavior are weak and ineffective in Japan (as explained above) and because, most obviously, police executives have little incentive to prevent a practice that primarily benefits themselves.

As for the second question, embezzlement has gone unnoticed in academia because there are few Japanese scholars who study the police (Kobayashi, 2000) and because the Western scholars who do either cannot read the Japanese sources that document slush fund abuses (Bayley, 1991; Parker, 2001) or else conducted their studies before reliable documentary evidence appeared (Ames, 1981). It is notable that students of Japanese police who speak and read their language have been far more critical of the police than have scholars who must rely on translators and interpreters (Miyazawa, 1992; Murayama, 1990; Ochiai, 2000; Sato, 1999; Terasawa, 1998; Tsuchimoto, 2000).

## Pachinko: *Why Police Like Pinball*

*Pachinko*, or vertical pinball, poses another challenge to the view that police in Japan have exceptionally high integrity. The game first emerged in the 1920s but was prohibited during the war as an "unpatriotic amusement." It became popular again after Japan surrendered, when military plane manufacturers in Nagoya sought new uses for surplus ball bearings. Soon thereafter it became the country's top leisure pastime. Today, some 28 million people—a quarter of the population—play at least once a year, spending an average of $700 per person per year (Sibbitt, 1997).[23] The most active players are middle-aged, white-collar, urban males (Manzenreiter, 1998).

The game itself is simple. Players purchase a supply of small metal balls that they propel with flippers and dials through a pinball-like maze in an upright machine. As the balls bounce through the maze, they either fall into the gutter at the bottom of the machine or else hit jackpots that generate more balls. Each ball costs about 3 cents (4 yen). At game's end they can be traded in for prizes (cigarettes, soap, coffee, and the like) at exchange counters inside the *pachinko* parlor. The prizes, in turn, can be traded for cash at nearby "independent" shops (*kokansho*) at the exchange rate of about 2 cents per ball of merchandise value (Sibbitt, 1997). Many of these brokerages are controlled by organized crime (Manzenreiter, 1998). In the early 1990s, Tokyo police estimated that *yakuza*-controlled exchange business generated by the capital's 1,500 *pachinko* parlors yielded the *yakuza* about $500 million per year (Hill, 2000, p. 179).

The *pachinko* industry is huge, accounting for fully 4% of Japan's gross national product. Annual revenues from the game exceed the worldwide sales of Japan's automobile industry. Profits are high, too, since the "system" sells balls for about 37.5% more than it pays out in prizes. The industry has placed two people, Nakajima Kenkichi and Busujima Kunio, in the Forbes index of billionaires. In 2001, 12 of the top 100 people on Japan's "rich list" were *pachinko* businessmen. There are over 17,000 parlors and 4.7 million machines in the country, 60% to 75% of which are owned by ethnic Koreans. Japan's National Tax Administration Agency deemed *pachinko* owners "the nation's worst tax evaders" for 12 consecutive years, a pattern that helps explain why those owners make vast "contributions" to many members of Parliament (Sibbitt, 1997). In 1989, the Diet held rancorous hearings about those contributions, although the core concern seemed to be the industry's ties to North Korea (Manzenreiter, 1998).

Police have "enormous leverage" over *pachinko* parlors because owners need their permission to operate (Hasegawa, 1996; Holley, 1997), and they have narrowly construed the relevant gambling statutes in order to enhance their control over the industry. Gambling is illegal in Japan but, according to the police, *pachinko* is not gambling because the prizes exchanged inside the parlors are goods, not currency, and because the game does not rely on chance alone (Manzenreiter, 1998). The industry's vast wealth, the police's expansive power over the business, and the widespread involvement of the yakuza in running and protecting the market constitute "a systemic formula for police corruption and *conflicts* of interest" (Sibbitt, 1997, p. 577; see also Hill, 2000, p. 180).[23] Damage to police integrity can be difficult to discern, but several of Japan's most serious scandals were bred by this industry. In the biggest police scandal of the 1980s, for example, at least 135 officers in Osaka and Hyogo received regular payoffs from *pachinko* parlor owners in return for tip-offs about upcoming investigations (Kaplan & Dubro, 1986, p. 159). Less than 10 years later, another major *pachinko* scandal struck the same region (Terasawa, 1994, p. 243). As a source of police corruption, the *pachinko* business may be Japan's closest counterpart to the American drug trade, for it is here that police encounter both extensive opportunity and ample reward ("Aete Iu: Pachinko Wa Iho Da," 1996).[24]

Beginning in the mid-sixties, the police in some parts of Japan put pressure on the *pachinko* industry to sever its links with organized crime. In some regions (especially Kansai), their efforts may have had some

success. Even in Kobe and Osaka, however, cutting *yakuza* ties resulted in shifting control of the exchange trade (and opportunities for corruption) to "public welfare businesses" that are run by retired police executives (Hill, 2000, p. 178; see also "Aete Iu: Pachinko Wa Iho Da," 1996; Terasawa, 1994). And in Tokyo and Hokuriku (the northern part of Japan), police have left the *yakuza*-controlled exchange businesses largely untouched, perhaps in part to ensure that the gangsters do not indulge in more malevolent forms of mischief. In the end, *pachinko* remains "a highly attractive target" for *yakuza* criminality and a major source of corruption for police throughout the country ("Gangster Rams Truck Into Pachinko Parlor," 2003; Hill, 2000, p.180; "Pachinko Gyosei o Kangaeru," 1994).

### The Yakuza: *Why Police Prefer Organized Crime*

Police scandals in the United States have chronically involved the regulation of vice and relationships with the gangs that organize the "industries" of prostitution, pornography, gambling, and drugs (Lardner & Reppetto, 2000). In this respect, Japan is like and unlike America. Similar pleasures are pursued in both countries, but drinking, gambling, and the sex trade are policed differently in Japan than they are in America, through regulation rather than prohibition and through harm reduction instead of moral crusade (Bayley, 1991, p. 98).[25] The result is fewer opportunities to engage in misconduct; smaller incentives for doing so; and less, and less serious, vice-induced corruption.

Nevertheless, a peculiar relationship does exist between Japan's police and its estimated 43,500 full-time gangsters (Parker, 2001, p. 232). It is, "in a Western sense, a much more far-reaching, more institutionalized form of corruption" than one sees in the United States (Kaplan & Dubro, 1986, p. 161). The most remarkable aspect of their relations may be "the *yakuza*'s function as a kind of alternative police force" (p. 163). Police have periodically cracked down on the *yakuza* (and with increased intensity over the last decade), but most police remain sympathetic to the conservative views held by gangsters, and many seem to welcome the ways in which gangsters help control some *unorganized* crime (Ames, 1981; Milhaupt & West, 2000; Stark, 1981). As one study of the *yakuza* observed,

> The one thing that terrifies Japanese police is unorganized crime. That's why there's so little street crime here. Gangsters control the turf, and they provide the security. If some hoods come around the neighborhood and start making trouble, chances are the *yakuza* will reach them first. Japanese police prefer the existence of organized crime to its absence. (Kaplan & Dubro, 1986, p. 163)

Many *yakuza* like the resulting arrangement. One has said that if politicians and police want crime reduced,

> Fine. The *yakuza* will make sure the streets are safe, but you'd better pay us. You want a right-wing sound truck silenced so you can maintain your phony public image? Okay, we'll take care of it, but pay us. We keep the crime rate low; we make sure people don't sue companies; we keep scandals from becoming public. We're just the servants of the rich people. . . . In many ways, we're the grease in the machine, but, of course, we're the monkey wrench as well. (Seymour, 1996, p. 191)

*Yakuza* grease does not come free. Police pay for theirs with the currency they control—discretion: to regulate *pachinko* (Terasawa, 1994), sanction sex shops

("Crooked Cops Lorded Over Fukuoka Sex Shops," 2001), tolerate gambling (Bayley, 1991), and overlook extortion (Szymkowiak, 2001). To show their appreciation for such indulgences, *yakuza* vice-operators frequently give "substantial gifts" to their police protectors (Mizoguchi, 1993, p. 225; see also Kaplan & Dubro, 1986, p. 162), a form of payoff known as *mekoboshiryo*, or "connivance tariff" (Kobayashi, 2000, p.79). This may help explain why police regarded receiving holiday gifts (Case 2) as the least serious misconduct (by far) of the misconduct in the cases in the Japanese integrity survey.

A new anti-organized-crime law came into force in 1992, and some analysts believe that it has curtailed corrupt ties between the *yakuza* and police by giving the latter an array of administrative levers to control gangster behavior (Hill, 2000, p.480). If traditional ties have been cut back, they have not diminished nearly as much as in New York City, where the once "comfortable modus vivendi" between police and the mafia was destroyed by "major innovations and 'institution building' in organized-crime control," resulting in "the successful purging of Cosa Nostra groups from New York City's core economy" (Jacobs, 1999, pp. 3, 223). Whatever the successes of the *Botaiho* (as Japan's new law is called), a major reduction in *yakuza*-police corruption does not seem to be one of them. In July of 2002, for example, the former head of one branch of the *Yamaguchi-gumi*—Japan's largest gang—told me that police in Kobe continue to be corruptly influenced by mobster gifts, cash, and cooperation. There has been "no change" in relations since 1992, he averred, "the police are as corrupt as they have ever been." Similarly, Mizoguchi Atsushi (1993), one of Japan's most knowledgeable students of organized crime, told me that illicit quid-pro-quos between police and the *yakuza* remain "widespread," and Kuroki Akio, a retired officer whose job was to monitor right-wing groups (*uyoku*) and the criminal gangs with which they affiliate, states that the police

> are very close to the right-wingers and their mentality. If the right-wingers break the law [by flouting nuisance laws with their sound trucks or by extorting pays-offs from businesses while bombarding them with martial music], they are supposed to be arrested, but many police feel that would spoil the relationship. (French, 2002)

An executive officer in the National Police Agency concurs, for he told me that the *Botaiho* has done little to alter the pattern of "co-existence and co-prosperity" (*kyoson kyoei*) that has long characterized police-*yakuza* relations (Kubo, 1987, p. 65; Whiting, 1999).

Finally, it is important to recognize that police complicity in *yakuza* racketeering brings benefits besides bribes. As mentioned earlier, some organized criminals perform unorganized-crime control functions, and the "gentle" approach that police tend to adopt toward *yakuza* leaders helps restrain turf wars and other intergang violence by bringing "organizational stability" to the underworld (Ramseyer & Nakazato, 1999, p. 182). One must also realize that relations between the *yakuza* and the police have changed over time, depending on the sociolegal context, and that neither the gangs nor the police is a monolithic organization (Hill, 2000, p. 458). Still, after these qualifications have been made and the real complexities have been acknowledged, one core fact is clear: Police in Japan are linked to organized crime in ways that encourage corruption and undermine equal enforcement of the laws.

## CONCLUSION

The evidence about police integrity is mixed. Some—from previous studies and the survey—suggests that Japanese police have an unusually strong normative inclination to resist temptations to abuse their authority. Other data—from scandals, slush funds, *pachinko*, organized crime, and, above all, the striking police propensity to cover up corruption, often from the top-down—implies the opposite, that corruption is so "chronic" that police may well be one of Japan's "most lawless groups" (Akagi, 2000, p. 51; Ochiai, 1998, p. 128). My assessment of the evidence is that the critical inferences come closer to the truth, though it has to be said that the evidence all around is thinner than it should be. Japan's police establishment is so "keenly suspicious of academic scholars" (Bayley, 1991, p. 76) that it is impossible to make conclusions as confidently as can be made about integrity among police in most American agencies. I join other scholars in urging Japanese police to open their agencies to more outside scrutiny (Bayley, 1994b). If two hallmarks of democratic policing are transparency and accountability (Marx, 2001), then the near absence of those qualities among police Japanese renders them conspicuously undemocratic (Abe, 2001).

The scandal wave that began in 1999 has generated movements for increased openness and accountability that police have recalcitrantly resisted (Johnson, 2001). For example, when Japan's national Freedom of Information Act took effect in April of 2001, disclosure of how taxpayers' money is spent became the rule for all government agencies. Unfortunately, the police remain, in crucial respects, "beyond the scope" of the new law's purview.[26] Even in Miyagi prefecture, where the citizens' ombudsman fought valiantly for increased openness, the government capitulated to almost all police demands for sustained secrecy (Kurayama, 2000). Until such loopholes are filled, Japanese police have little incentive to stop stealing taxes (Terasawa, 1998).

Police corruption is a double problem in Japan: It reinforces a culture of secrecy and deceit that is itself the breeding ground for other abuses of authority, and it prevents police from properly enforcing laws against other wrongdoers. This chapter illustrates only a few facets of each problem. It describes some of the ways in which Japanese police misuse their authority, but it ignores several serious forms of misconduct, including brutality on the street (Mikami & Hiroshi, 1996), deception in the interrogation room (Miyazawa, 1992), and perjury at trial (Yamaguchi, 1999). This chapter also says little about the effects of police corruption on the quality and equality of law enforcement in Japan. The effects, needless to say, are not salutary (Fox, 1999; Johnson, 2001; Takai, 2001). Scandals have eroded public trust and thereby undermined the capacity of the police to solve crimes and maintain order. At the same time, the highly *organized* nature of police embezzlement inhibits their ability to pursue allegations of corruption in other organizations.

The problem of police corruption in Japan is a matter not of a few rotten apples but of a failed organization. The challenge, therefore, is how to fix the organization. Japanese police must confront the problem of corruption more resolutely than they have heretofore. In the words of one former officer, if they do not "excise the rotten pus of corruption and recover the confidence and trust of the people, their 'rebirth' is but a distant dream" (Akagi, 2000, p. 51). Since scandal can be a powerful "agent of change"

(Sherman, 1978, p. xv), the wave of scandals could provide an occasion for police to reform themselves so that they come to merit the reputation for rectitude they have hitherto enjoyed but not deserved (Kobayashi, 1998, p. v).

I am pessimistic. Police reform requires three conditions that are absent in Japan and unlikely to emerge anytime soon: the creation of a new "dominant coalition" to control the organization; the removal of the "environmental influences" that encourage corruption; and the institution of "premonitory" control policies that attempt to prevent corruption or to detect it as it occurs (Sherman, 1978, p. 247). Japan's scandal wave has not occasioned a new leadership coalition. Instead, the elites who direct cover-ups are routinely promoted to positions of increased power. As long as the National Police Agency monopolizes executive positions, "leadership change cannot be expected to produce radically different approaches" (Miyazawa, 1989, p. 22). Similarly, the environmental influences that encourage *uragane*, *pachinko*, and *yakuza* abuses are so deeply embedded that they will not change without concerted effort. Significantly, the recommendations for "reform of the justice system" (*shiho kaikaku*) say almost nothing about police problems or the circumstances that maintain them (Sato, 2002). Most fundamentally, police in Japan seem more interested in buttressing their code of silence and defending their system against criticism[26] than in proactively preventing or detecting the kinds of misconduct described in this chapter (Kuroki, 2000, p. 218). Under these conditions, significant reform seems unlikely.[27] If Japanese police want corruption to spread, all they need to do is nothing.

## NOTES

1. The original draft of this survey had seventeen scenarios: all eleven cases from the first American survey, and the 6 new ones that Klockars, Kutnjak Ivkovich, Haberfeld, and Uydess (2000) added to their second questionnaire. A Japanese police executive cut five of the seventeen scenarios, ostensibly out of concern that the original version would take too long to administer.

2. The distribution of police across ranks varies from country to country, and Japan has a higher percentage of police supervisors than Australia, Britain, Canada, and the United States (Bayley, 1994, p. 61).

3. Interviews with rank-and-file officers reinforce this finding, as do the tell-all accounts of former officers (Akagi, 2000; Kuroki, 2000a).

4. The gap between estimates of the discipline misconduct should receive and the discipline it would receive may be especially large in Los Angeles, where 93% of police union members who responded to a poll said they had "no confidence" in LAPD Chief Bernard C. Parks, who at the time of the poll was seeking a second 5-year term. The officers' major grievance was that Parks's disciplinary system was so harsh and arbitrary that it devastated their morale (Leovy, 2002).

5. One reader of a draft of this chapter suggested that Japan's higher integrity scores may be in part an artifact of the fact that a larger proportion of respondents were supervisors in the Japanese survey (30%) than in the American survey (20%). That supposition is unsupported by data from the Japanese survey. American police agencies do have two distinct cultures—"that of the workers, who continually search for space within its authoritarian system, and that of the managers, who seek to achieve organizational objectives through command-and-control objectives" (Bayley, 1994a, p. 66). In some American agencies (like the LAPD), these two police cultures "are often at war" (Chemerinsky, 2000, p. 65). What is more, the integrity survey that was administered in 30 American agencies revealed that supervisors tend to rate the misconduct's seriousness, the appropriate discipline for it, and (especially) their willingness to report it higher than do rank-and-file officers. In the data from the Japanese survey, however, there was only one statistically significant line-versus-supervisor difference in "mean answer" (for Case 2 - Holiday Gifts From Merchants, with supervisors more willing to report the misconduct in the case than were rank-and-file officers). Moreover, out of the 84 core questions (7 questions for each of the twelve scenarios), none of the line-supervisor differences comes close to the threshold of "substantive significance" (0.5) used in similar studies of police integrity, in only 4 questions do the line-supervisor differences exceed half of that threshold (0.25), and in two thirds of the questions the line-supervisor difference is less than 0.1. Since line-supervisor differences in reported integrity seem less salient in Japanese police departments than in American ones, this chapter reports the *aggregate* Japanese survey results.

6. Americans also distinguish between rhetoric and reality, but there is a difference of degree. In general, when rhetoric (*tatemae*) is compared cross-nationally, one often finds "huge differences," but when reality (*honne*) is compared, one is more apt to find "striking similarities" (Reed, 1993, p. 112).

7. It is notable that three veteran journalists who examined the survey said the same thing.

8. Thus, the survey results reflect the views of a sample of Japanese police from those six prefectures, not all Japanese police. This raises the question as to whether generalizations can be made from the survey about *all* Japanese police. Perhaps. Environments of integrity vary dramatically among American police agencies, but as one scholar has noted, policies and practices are so standardized in Japan that "it is proper to refer to the *Japanese* police" (Bayley, 1991, p. xi).

9. Since Kuroki came out against misconduct, other whistle-blowing police also have emerged (Akagi, 2000; Kurusu, 2000; Ouchi, 2002). For the classic whistle-blower's account, see Matsuhashi (1984).

10. One can imagine a third possibility: that Kuroki has suffered from his reputation as a snitch and now compensates for it. But this seems unlikely, not least because Kuroki has reaped great financial and reputational benefits from his books and interviews.

11. There is no significant difference between Kuroki's assessment of others' willingness to report misconduct (which averaged 4.08 for the twelve scenarios) and the Japanese sample average (3.90). Both are significantly higher than the American average of 3.35.

12. According to the Associated Press, between September 1999 and March 2000, there were 166 cases of police misconduct in Japan in which 113 police employees were arrested or had their files sent to prosecutors for investigation. In addition, 434 police officers (including managers) received administrative punishments such as dismissal from the job or cuts in pay. Ex-officer Kuroki Akio (2000b, pp. 205, 219) believes these numbers represent just the tip of an iceberg of police misconduct, and ex-sergeant Akagi Bunro (2000) contends that the police crimes revealed in the wave of scandal "did not just begin now. . . . They simply were exposed now" (p. 225).

13. This description of the Kanagawa scandal relies on Kuroki (2000a), Sato (1999), and articles from Japanese newspapers.

14. After the Kanagawa case, the next most loudly lamented scandal occurred in Niigata prefecture, 160 miles north of Tokyo, where two senior police officials were forced to resign over a series of blunders involving the case of a 19-year-old woman who escaped the man who had kidnapped and held her captive for 9 years. Ironically, on the night the woman escaped, Yoshiaki Nakada, head of the National Police Agency's Kanto Regional Police Bureau, was in Niigata, ostensibly to inspect local police operations so as to restore public trust in the wake of the Kanagawa scandal. In actuality, Nakada was partying at a local resort with Koji Kobayashi, the chief of police in Niigata. When these police executives were informed of the victim's escape, they conspired to release a false news report that credited Niigata police with finding the woman. (She in fact was freed by health care workers who had been drawn to her captor's house by his erratic behavior.) The police lie was exposed and Nakada and Kobayashi were forced to resign—with pensions. The public was outraged. "Police departments across Japan were inundated with telephone calls and e-mail messages from people expressing anger over what they considered lenient treatment of the officials" (Sims, 2000). For accounts of other cases in the same wave of scandals, see Akagi (2000), Kobayashi (2000), Kuroki (2000a, 2000b), Ochiai (2000), Otani (2000), Sato (1999), Terasawa (1998), and Tsuchimoto (2000).

15. In the United States, by contrast, only 15% of city residents said they were dissatisfied with local police, and even among black citizens only 24% expressed discontent ("Local Police Ratings Vary By Race," 1999).

16. Previous scholarship (Ames, 1981; Bayley, 1991; Parker, 2001) has wrongly concluded that Japanese police enjoy wider support from the public they

serve than do police in the United States. In fact, the best available evidence shows that Japanese have significantly lower confidence in police than do Americans. More generally, countries with a history of fascist governments (such as Germany, Italy, and Spain) tend to have lower confidence in the police than do Americans (Cao, Stack, & Sun, 1998).

17. In October of 2000, 5 years after he raped K, Tsukade was convicted of "abuse of official authority" and sentenced to 2 years and 6 months in prison (Terasawa, 2000b, p. 5). But for the victim's determination and a journalist's diligence, there would have been no trial.

18. The New York Police Department conducts some 700 integrity stings a year, and Boston police use similar methods to ferret out misconduct (Fyfe, 2001).

19. Police commissioners are well paid, with each member of the national commission receiving an annual salary of US$222,000 (Ochiai, 2000, p. 57). The national commission meets just once a week, on Thursday afternoons, and its deliberations are, for the most part, "empty rituals" (Kubo, 2001, p. 147). In the wake of the wave of scandals described above, the Police Law was amended, purportedly to enable commissioners to exercise greater supervision over the police. The changes are largely cosmetic and are unlikely to stimulate significant reform ("Revised Police Law," 2001). More ambitious reform was avoided at least partly because conservative politicians (such as Shizuka Kamei, an ex-police officer and a leading member of the ruling Liberal Democratic Party) said the police should control themselves because "policing the police would be bizarre" (Iitake, 2000).

20. Ames (1981, p. 226) also argues that the *informal mechanisms* of public opinion and an "unfettered and aggressive press" account for the "remarkably retrained" way in which Japanese police use their power, but he overstates the importance of both mechanisms. Japan's press is more a lapdog than a watchdog, especially vis-à-vis the police (Freeman, 2000, pp. 109, 113), and the Japanese public has few channels through which its opinions can affect police behavior (Miyazawa, 1992, p. 227; Ochiai, 2000). More fundamentally, Ames exaggerates how "restrained" Japanese police are.

21. Police embezzlement has also plagued some American agencies. In Newark, for instance, slush fund abuses have been chronic for decades (Kocieniewski & Sullivan, 1995). Unlike their Japanese counterparts, however, some Newark embezzlers have been criminally charged. Most notably, ex-police director William R. Celester was sentenced to 30 months in federal prison for fraud and embezzlement (Petersen, 1996).

22. To improve the industry's image, the Japan Gaming Enterprise Association has begun sending "*pachinko* mobiles" to homes for the elderly. The infirm are not charged to play (Sibbitt, 1997).

23. It has been estimated that the *yakuza* extort an average of about US$1,600 per month from each *pachinko* parlor, ostensibly to protect the shops from criminal racketeers. According to the National Police Agency, this makes *pachinko* one of the largest sources of *yakuza* income (Sibbitt, 1997).

24. In his insightful account of the ways in which "the pursuit of pleasure" is policed in Japan, David Bayley (1991, p.107) argues that "once in while the police crack down [on *pachinko*], but by and large they consider it too insignificant to bother about." In my view, Japanese police seldom "crack down" on *pachinko* precisely because the existing system's benefits are *too significant* for police to do without.

25. There is one notable exception to the Japanese rule of regulation and harm reduction: illicit drugs, of which methamphetamine is the most commonly used. Drug prohibition in Japan is strict, and enforcement of drug laws is

unrelenting. Nonetheless, the use of illegal drugs is much less common in Japan than it is in the United States, in part because few residents of Japan live in the circumstances of concentrated disadvantage that breed the most serious drug abuse problems (Bayley, 1991, p. 117; Massing, 1999). One result is that police in Japan have fewer opportunities to be corrupted by the drug trade.

26. The most comprehensive discussions of police reform in Japan are Shinohara (2001), a collection of essays by scholars, journalists, and lawyers, and *Keisatsu Gyosei no Aratanaru Tenkai Henshu Iinkai* (2001), an edited volume with several chapters authored by police.

---

## REFERENCES

Abe, Y. (2001). Keisatsu fuhai no boshisaku: Keisatsu sasshin kaigi no kinkyu teigen to Kokka Koan Iinkai no keisatsu kaikaku yoko o chushin toshite (Prevention policy for police corruption . . . ). In S. Hajime, *Keisatsu ombuzuman* (Police Ombudsman) (pp. 39-76). Tokyo: Shinsansha.

Aete iu: Pachinko wa iho da (Dare to say it: Pachinko is illegal). (1996, September 2). *AERA (Asahi Shimbun Weekly)*.

Akagi, B. (2000). *Akagi keibuho, Hiroshima Kenkei o kiru* (Sergeant Akagi exposes the Hiroshima Prefectural Police Department). Tokyo: Daisan Shokan.

Ames, W. L. (1981). *Police and community in Japan.* Berkeley: University of California Press.

Bayley, D. H. (1991). *Forces of order: Policing modern Japan.* Berkeley: University of California Press.

Bayley, D. H. (1994a). *Police for the future.* New York: Oxford University Press.

Bayley, D. H. (1994b). Review essay rejoinder [to Patricia Steinhoff's review of Bayley's (1991) Forces of Order]. *Law & Society Review*, 963-964.

Cannon, L. (2000, October 1). One bad cop. *New York Times Magazine*.

Cao, L., Stack, S., & Sun, Y. (1998). Public attitudes toward the police: A comparative study between Japan and America. *Journal of Criminal Justice*, 26(4), 279-289.

Chemerinsky, E., with P. Hoffman, L. Levenson, R. S. Paz, C. Rice, & C. Sobel. (2000). An independent analysis of the Los Angeles Police Department's Board of Inquiry Report on the Rampart Scandal. Los Angeles: Los Angeles Police Department Police Protective League.

Chevigny, P. (1995). *Edge of the knife: Police violence in the Americas.* New York: The New Press.

Crooked cops lorded over Fukuoka sex shops. (2001, December 15). *Mainichi Daily News*. Retrieved from http://www.mainichi.co.jp/english/news/opinion.html.

Daley, R. (1978). *Prince of the city: The true story of a cop who knew too much.* New York: Berkeley.

Domanick, J. (1994). *To protect and to serve: The LAPD's century of war in the city of dreams.* New York: Simon & Schuster.

Dotson, D. D. (2000, February 27). Culture of war. *Los Angeles Times*.

Fox, M. H. (1999). *The Yasuda arrest: Criminal and political considerations.* Cardiff, CA: Japan Policy Research Institute.

Freeman, L. A. (2000). *Closing the shop: Information cartels and Japan's mass media.* Princeton, NJ: Princeton University Press.

French, H. W. (2002, July 21). Behind blaring Tokyo vans, a whisper of conspiracy. *The New York Times*.

Fyfe, J. (2001, November 7). *Changes in patterns of career-ending misconduct*. Paper presented at the annual meetings of the American Society of Criminology, Atlanta, GA.

Gangster rams truck into pachinko parlor over courtesy call. (2003, May 1). *Mainichi Daily News*. Retrieved from http://www. mainichi.co.jp/english/news/opinion.html.

Goode, E. (2000, August 8). How culture molds habits of thought. *New York Times*.

Hasegawa, H. (1996, September 2). *Aete iu: Pachinko wa iho da* (If anything, pachinko is illegal). *AERA*, pp. 15-17.

Hendry, J. (1995). *Understanding Japanese society* (2nd ed.). London and New York: Routledge.

Heymann, P. B. (1985, Summer). Understanding criminal investigation. *Harvard Journal on Legislation, 22*, 314-334.

Hill, P. B. E. (2000). *Botaiho: Japanese organised crime under the Boryokudan Countermeasures Law*. Unpublished doctoral dissertation, Scottish Centre for Japanese Studies, University of Stirling.

Hirao, A. (2000, December 3). Deeply rotten at the corps. *Asahi Evening News*.

Holley, D. (1997, January 20). Pains and profits of a pachinko passion. *Daily Yomiuri*.

Iitake, K. (2000, March 17). Accord made on police reforms. *Asahi News*. Retrieved from http://www.asahi.com/english/asahi/0317/asahi031706.html.

Jacobs, J. B., with C. Friel & R. Radick. (1999). *Gotham unbound: How New York City was liberated from the grip of organized crime*. New York: New York University Press.

Johnson, D. T. (2001, April). *Bureaucratic corruption in Japan*. JPRI Working Paper No. 76. Cardiff, CA: Japan Policy Research Institute.

Johnson, D. T. (2002). *The Japanese way of justice: Prosecuting crime in Japan*. New York: Oxford University Press.

Johnson, D. T. (in press). Police misconduct in the United States and Japan. In S. Einstein & M. Amir (Eds.), *Corruption, policing, security and democracy*. Huntsville, TX: Office of International Criminal Justice.

Kaplan, D. E., & Dubro, A. (1986). *Yakuza: The explosive account of Japan's criminal underworld*. Reading, MA: Addison-Wesley.

Keisatsu no Aratanaru Tenkai Henshu Iinkai (The Editorial Committee for New Police Developments). (2001). In *Keisatsu Gyosei no Aratanaru Shintenkai* (New developments in police administration). Tokyo: Tokyo Horei Shuppan.

Klockars, C. B., Kutnjak Ivkovich, S. Harver, W. E., & Haberfeld, M. R. (2001). A minimum requirement for police corruption. In R. A. Silverman, B. Cohen, & T. P. Thornberry (Eds.), *Crime and justice at the millennium: Essays by and in honor of Marvin E. Wolfgang* (pp. 185-208). New York: Kluwer.

Klockars, C. B., Kutnjak Ivkovich, S., Harver, W. E., & Haberfeld, M. R. (2000, May). *The measurement of police integrity*. National Institute of Justice Research in Brief (NCJ 181465). Washington, DC: National Institute of Justice.

Kobayashi, M. (1998). *Nihon keisatsu no genzai* (Contemporary Japanese Police). Tokyo: Iwanami Shoten.

Kobayashi, M. (2000). *Nihon keisatsu: Fuhai no kozo* (Japan's police: The structure of corruption). Tokyo: Chikuma Shobo.

Kocieniewski, D., & Sullivan, J. (1995, December 23). Newark police troubles: Out of control at the top. *New York Times*.

Kubo, H. (1987). *Nihon no keisatsu: Keishicho vs. Osaka Fukei* (The police of Japan: The Tokyo Metropolitan Police Department vs. The Osaka Prefectural Police). Tokyo: Kodansha.

Kubo, H. (2001). *Do sureba "keisatsu" wa shimin no mono ni naru no ka* (What should be done to make "police" more responsive to citizens?). Tokyo: Shogakukan.

Kurayama, T. (2000, December 7). *Keisatsu no joho kokai o meguru Miyagi no ugoki* (Developments in Miyagi related to the disclosure of information by the police). Paper presented at The Symposium on Police in Japan, Japan Federation of Bar Associations, Tokyo.

Kuroki, A. (2000a). *Keisatsu fuhai: Keishicho keisatsukan no kokuhatsu* (Police corruption: A Tokyo police officer's charge). Tokyo: Kodansha.

Kuroki, A. (2000b). *Keisatsu wa naze daraku shita no ka* (Why have the police become corrupt?). Tokyo: Kusashisha.

Kurusu, S. (2000). *Fushoku seru keisatsu: Keishicho moto keishisei no kokuhaku* (Corrupt police: The confessions of a former Tokyo senior superintendent). Tokyo: Shakai Hihyosha.

Kutnjak Ivković, S., Klockars, C. B., Cajner-Mraović, I., & Ivanušec, D. (2002). *Controlling police corruption: The Croatian perspective. Police Practice and Research*, 3(1), 55-72.

Lardner, J., & Reppetto, T. (2000). *NYPD: A city and its police*. New York: Henry Holt.

Leovy, J. (2002, February 3). A new way of policing the LAPD. *Los Angeles Times*.

Local police ratings vary by race. (1999, June 3). *New York Times*.

Maas, P. (1973). *Serpico: The classic true story of the cop who couldn't be bought*. New York: Harper & Row.

Manzenreiter, W. (1998). *Pachinko monogatari: Soziokulturelle exploration der Japanischen glucksspielindustrie* (The *Pachinko* story: A socio-cultural exploration of the Japanese gambling industry). Munich: Iudicium Verlag GmbH.

Maple, J., with C. Mitchell. (1999). *The crime fighter: How you can make your community crime-free*. New York: Broadway.

Markovits, A. S., & Silverstein, M. (Eds.). (1988). *The politics of scandal: Power and process in liberal democracies*. London: Holmes & Meier.

Marx, G. (2001). Police and democracy. In M. Amir & S. Einstein (Eds.), *Policing, security & democracy: Theory and practice*. Huntsville, TX: The Office of International Criminal Justice.

Massing, M. (1999). *The fix*. Berkeley: University of California Press.

Masui, S. (2002, January 17). Back to basics to beat crime. *Daily Yomiuri*.

Matsuhashi, T. (1984). *Wagatsumi wa wagamae ni ari: Kitai sareru shinkeisatsucho chokan e no tegami* (My sin is ever before me: A letter to the new chief of the National Police Agency). Tokyo: Shakai Shisosha (reissued in 1994, with commentary by Watanabe Osamu).

McAlary, M. (1987). *Buddy boys: When good cops turn bad*. New York: Charter.

McNamara, J. D. (1999). How to police the police. *Hoover Digest*, 4, 1-6.

Mikami, T., & Hiroshi, M. (1996). *Sabakareru keisatsu: Hanshin fan boko keikan to fushinpan jiken* (Police on trial: The case of police violence against Hanshin baseball fans and the analogical institution of prosecution). Tokyo: Nihon Hyoronsha.

Milhaupt, C. J., & West, M. D. (2000). The dark side of private ordering: An institutional and empirical analysis of organized crime. *University of Chicago Law Review*, 67 (Winter), 41-98.

Miyamoto, M. (1994). *Straitjacket society: An insider's irreverant view of bureaucratic Japan*. Tokyo: Kodansha International.

Miyazawa, S. (1989). Scandal and hard reform: Implications of a wiretapping case to the control of organizational police crimes in Japan. *Kobe University Law Review, 23*, 13-27.

Miyazawa, S. (1992). *Policing in Japan: A study on making crime* (F. G. Bennett, Jr., with J. O. Haley, Trans.). Albany: State University of New York Press.

Mizoguchi, A. (1993). *Gendai yakuza no chishiki* (Knowledge of today's yakuza). Tokyo: JICC.

Murayama, M. (1990). *Keira keisatsu no kenkyu* (Research on police patrol). Tokyo: Seibundo.

Nakada, K., Shinya, H., & Nagasawa, C. (2001, January 31). Shijo saiaku: "Hanzai kenkyoritsu 24.2%" ga imi suru mono (The worst in history: What does the "24.2% clearance rate" mean?). *Spa*, pp. 20-23.

Nelken, D. (Ed.). (2000). *Contrasting criminal justice: Getting from here to there*. Burlington, VT: Ashgate.

Nisbett, R. E., Peng, K., Choi, I., & Norenzayan, A. (2001). Culture and systems of thought: Holistic vs. analytic cognitions. *Psychological Review*.

Nisbett, R. E. (2003). *The geography of thought: How Asians and Westerners think differently . . . and why*. New York: The Free Press.

Ochiai, H. (1998). "Ura chobo" "naibu kokuhatsu" "taisaku manyuaru" no santen setto de semero (Using the trio of "back books," "whistleblowers," and "countermeasure manuals" to attack the police). In Y. Terasawa (Ed.), *Omawari san wa zeikin dorobo* (Officer Friendly is a tax thief) (pp. 128-161). Tokyo: Mediaworks.

Ochiai, H. (2000, April-June). Corruption: Who polices the police? *Japan Quarterly*, 50-57.

Otani, A. (2000). *Nihon keisatsu no shotai: Jiken no inpei, sosa misu, fushoji wa naze okoru?* (The true colors of Japan's police: Why do cover-ups, investigative mistakes, and scandals occur?). Tokyo: Nihon Bungeisha.

Ouchi, A. (2002). *Keishicho uragane tanto* (I was in charge of slush funds at the Tokyo Metropolitan Police Department). Tokyo: Kodansha.

Pachinko gyosei o kangaeru (Thinking about the administration of pachinko). (1994). *Amyuzumento Nyusu*, pp. 16-19.

Parker, L. C., Jr. (2001). *The Japanese police system today: A comparative study*. Armonk, N.Y. and London: M. E. Sharpe.

Peng, K., & Nisbett, R. E. (1999). Culture, dialecticism, and reasoning about contradiction. *American Psychologist, 54*, 741-754.

Petersen, M. (1996, December 3). Newark's ex-police director sentenced: 2 ½-year term for theft is longer than recommended by law. *New York Times*.

Ramseyer, J. M., & Nakazato, M. (1999). *Japanese law: An economic approach*. Chicago: The University of Chicago Press.

Reed, S. R. (1993). *Making common sense of Japan*. Pittsburgh and London: University of Pittsburgh Press.

Revised Police Law. (2001, February 22). *Mainichi Daily News*. Retrieved from http://www.mainichi.co.jp/english/news/opinion.html.

Sato, I. (2002). Judicial reform in Japan in the 1990s: Increase of the legal profession, reinforcement of judicial functions and expansion of the rule of law." *Social Science Japan Journal, 5*(1), 71-83.

Sato, M. (1999). *Fushoji zokushutsu keisatsu ni tsugu* (On the series of police scandals). Tokyo: Shogakkan.

Seymour, C. (1996). *Yakuza diary: Doing time in the Japanese underworld*. New York: Atlantic Monthly Press.

Sherman, L. W. (1978). *Scandal and reform: Controlling police corruption.* Berkeley: University of California Press.

Sherman, L. W. (1998). American policing. In M. Tonry (Ed.), *The handbook of crime & punishment* (pp. 429-456). New York: Oxford University Press.

Sherman, L. W. (2001). Consent of the governed: Police, democracy, and diversity. In M. Amir & S. Einstein (Eds.), *Policing, security & democracy: Theory and practice.* Huntsville, TX: Office of International Criminal Justice.

Shinohara, H. (2001). *Keisatsu ombuzuman* (Police ombudsman). Tokyo: Shinsansha.

Sibbitt, E. C. (1997). Regulating gambling in the shadow of the law: Form and substance in the regulation of Japan's pachinko industry. *Harvard International Law Journal, 38*(Spring), 568-586.

Sims, C. (2000, March 7). Misdeeds by once-honored police dismay the Japanese. *New York Times.*

Skolnick, J. H., & Fyfe, J. J. (1993). *Above the law: Police and the excessive use of force.* New York: The Free Press.

Stark, H. (1981). The *yakuza*: Japanese crime incorporated. Unpublished doctoral dissertation, Department of Anthropology, University of Michigan.

Sugimoto, Y. (1997). *An introduction to Japanese society.* Cambridge, UK: Cambridge University Press.

Szymkowiak, K. (2001). *Sokaiya: Extortion, protection, and the Japanese corporation.* Armonk, NY and London: M.E. Sharpe.

Takai, Y. (2001). Keiji shiho shisetemu to keisatsu fushoji (The criminal justice system and police corruption). In *Shinohara hajime, Keisatsu ombuzuman* (Police ombudsman) (pp. 198-208). Tokyo: Shinsansha.

Tensei jingo (Vox populi, vox dei). (2000, June 1). *Asahi Shimbun.*

Terasawa, Y. (1994). Kunimatsu Takaji Keisatsucho Chokan ni pachinko giwaku (Police Chief Kunimatsu Takaji's pachinko scandal). In *Keisatsucho deiri kinshi* (Forbidden to enter the National Police Agency) (pp. 243-268). Tokyo: Fushin Shobo.

Terasawa, Y. (1998). *Omawarisan wa zeikin dorobo* (Officer Friendly is a tax thief). Tokyo: Mediaworks.

Terasawa, Y. (2000a, April 13). Chiba Kenkei ga inpei suru ryuchijonai reipu (The jail rape concealed by the Chiba Prefectural Police Department). *Shukan Hoseki,* pp. 26-29.

Terasawa, Y. (2000b, October 31). Dai 150 kai kokkai shugiin chiho gyosei iinkai giroku, dai 3 go (Testimony to the 150th Parliamentary House of Representatives Committee on Regional Administration), Tokyo.

Tsuchimoto, T. (2000, April-June). Corruption: Light and shadow in Japan's police system. *Japan Quarterly,* 41-49.

Walker, S. (1992). *The police in America: An introduction.* New York: McGraw-Hill.

Whiting, R. (1999). *Tokyo underworld: The fast times and hard life of an American gangster in Japan.* New York: Pantheon.

Wolferen, K. van (1989). *The enigma of Japanese power: People and politics in a stateless nation.* New York: Alfred A. Knopf.

Yamada, H. (1997). *Different games, different rules: Why Americans and Japanese misunderstand each other.* New York: Oxford University Press.

Yamaguchi, H. (1999). *Shiho fuzai: Yuzai, muzai wa doko de kimaru no ka* (Corrupt justice: Where are convictions and acquittals decided?). Tokyo: PHP Kenkyusho.

Yokoyama, M. (2001). Analysis of Japanese police from the viewpoint of democracy. In M. Amir and S. Einstein (Eds.), *Policing, security & democracy: Theory and practice* (pp. 187-209). Huntsville, TX: Office of International Criminal Justice.

# CHAPTER 9

# Integrity Perceptions and Investigations in The Netherlands

MAURICE PUNCH

L.W.J.C. HUBERTS

M.E.D. LAMBOO

## INTRODUCTION

A central question in police corruption and integrity research is whether perceptions and opinions of police officers reflect the actual extent and characteristics of the phenomenon. In this chapter, we will use data for The Netherlands on integrity perceptions and integrity investigations to reflect on certain aspects of that question.

First, we present a number of characteristics of the police in The Netherlands (one of the smaller Western European countries, with 16 million inhabitants). Next, we describe the methodology of the research on police integrity in The Netherlands that is used in this chapter. The results of the research are presented in the paragraphs that follow. The integrity-measuring instrument developed by Klockars and Kutnjak Ivkovich and their colleagues (Klockars, Kutnjak Ivkovich, Harver, & Haberfeld, 1997; Kutnjak Ivkovich & Klockars, 1996) was used to collect information about police officers' perceptions of the integrity of police officers. The views of Dutch police officers

AUTHORS' NOTE: This chapter is a revision and extension of a paper presented at the annual meeting of the American Society of Criminology in 2000. The research drawn on here is part of a National Institute of Justice funded project on police integrity under the leadership of Professor Carl Klockars of the University of Delaware, with the participation, in various roles and at different stages of the project, of Bill Geller, Maki Haberfeld, Sanja Kutnjak Ivković, William Harver, and Aaron Uydess. We would like to thank Carl Klockars and the members of his team mentioned above for their support in various ways with our project of conducting and analyzing the Dutch part of the survey and for sharing their collective publications. For assistance in gaining access to the sample for the Dutch survey, we are thankful for the support of Chief Commissioner P. Tieleman, then responsible for the area of integrity on the Council of Chief Commissioners of the Dutch Police, and Dr. A. van den Berg, both of Police Force of South Holland South.

on the seriousness of the misconduct in the case scenarios and their willingness to report it are described. After that, we present the results of research on the actual number of investigations on integrity violations in the Dutch police. That research enables us to reflect on the relationship between the officers' perceptions of police officers and the investigations on integrity violations within the Dutch police.

We conclude that the measurement instrument appears to be an important instrument for research and policy, but that for a country like The Netherlands the incorporation of other scenarios also seems necessary. Police integrity is a complex, multidimensional phenomenon and the police forces of different countries are confronted with different types of integrity violations. Nevertheless, the instrument has proven to be useful in adding insights about the awareness and alertness of the police. This type of research on police integrity can contribute to the development of more effective strategies to safeguard integrity and to curb integrity violations such as corruption, fraud, waste, discrimination, and leaking information.

## POLICE AND POLICE INTEGRITY IN THE NETHERLANDS

The Dutch police force employed 41,400 people full time in 1998. It is divided into 25 regional police forces and a central force (with the size of the forces ranging from 550 to 5500 personnel). The regional structure was the result of a major institutional reform in 1992 (Punch, van der Vijver, & van Dijk, 1998). As a consequence, the Dutch police are highly centralized compared to the police in the United States. Most of the decisions regarding recruitment, training, salaries, uniforms, and equipment are made nationally, and all officers are civil servants

who are subject to the same regulations as other civil servants and who enjoy a very high security of tenure. Within that national framework, the 25 police forces are operationally autonomous, with resulting differences in policies and culture.

The Netherlands, unlike the United States, does not have a record of corruption, either in public life in general (Huberts, 1995) or in the police in particular (with corruption seen primarily as the abuse of office for private gain) (Newburn, 1999; Sherman, 1974). There were a number of police corruption scandals in the 1970s in Amsterdam, and there was a national commotion about illegal police investigation techniques in the 1990s (Punch, 1985, 1997). Nevertheless, the goal of integrity has reached the political agenda and now plays a role in *every* Dutch police force. In fact, we can determine precisely when the subject was launched in the public arena. The late Ms. Ien Dales, then Minister of Home Affairs, brought up the matter in a speech in 1992. She was responding to a number of cases of corruption in local government, particularly related to tendering for contracts by firms and pay-offs to local politicians, and to the fear that organized crime was becoming powerful enough to infiltrate local and even central government—and perhaps also the police (there was something of a "moral panic" about organized crime at the time). Following the speech, the Ministry and many other agencies developed integrity policies. Also, every police force in the country was required to take initiatives to implement integrity policies based on a proclamation from the Ministry of Home Affairs (Ministerie van Binnenlandse Zaken, 1995). For example, every officer in the country was meant to receive a copy of the integrity statute, a sort of code of conduct, developed and distributed by the Council of Chief Commissioners in 1997.

A major scandal contributed to the increased importance of the integrity issue. It involved a parliamentary commission of inquiry into police methods of tackling organized crime (which was conducted from 1994 to 1996). The commission's focus was on specialized detective units (known as Interregional Detective Squads or IRTs), but the inquiry brought out not only dubious methods in police investigations within one particular IRT but also considerable conflicts between police chiefs, between police forces, between forces and the prosecution service, and between the police and other agencies. Although no major corruption was exposed, and there were only two criminal prosecutions for perjury, the impact was considerable in revealing an organization that was poorly coordinated and controlled and that had adopted devious and illegal methods of investigating organized criminals (Fijnaut, Bovenkerk, Bruinsma, & van de Bunt, 1998; Punch, 1997). The inquiry resulted in a new law regulating investigative methods. It also hastened the demand both for internal investigation units (equivalent to Internal Affairs in the United States) and for each force to address the issue of integrity.

To summarize, since 1992 the Dutch police forces are paying more attention to integrity and ethics (which does not mean there is uniformity in policy and approach) as a result of more general changes in public administration, initiatives by central government, and questions about police integrity following the discovery of illegal investigative methods through a parliamentary inquiry. The policies include, for example, the establishment of internal investigation units in all forces, new conflict of interest rules (on gifts and secondary functions), a national code of conduct, ethics and integrity as a more integrated part of education and training, and integrity as part of the required audits on the quality of police organizations.

## RESEARCH METHODOLOGY

In this chapter we present data about integrity perceptions and integrity investigations. The data about *police perceptions* in The Netherlands were gathered by Punch, in the framework of the international comparative study by Klockars and colleagues (1997). The questionnaire used was a translation of the questionnaire used elsewhere. It is comprised of 11 scenarios or cases (see Exhibit 1.1 in Chapter 1 of this volume), and each scenario includes questions as to what the officers think regarding the seriousness of the offense, the appropriate discipline for it, and their willingness to report it.

Three Dutch police forces were selected for research on the basis of advice and personal contacts and on the expectation that they might be willing to participate; also, an attempt was made to spread the selection around the country in an effort to get a regional balance in the responses to the questionnaires. All the participants were guaranteed anonymity and are, therefore, not named.

The questionnaire was sent out in early to mid-1999. The rules for distribution were as follows: only sworn police officers and not civilians were to be involved, and the distribution of the questionnaires, which was done by the forces themselves, should be to as broad a population as possible with regard to branch, age, rank, gender, and so on. Three police forces were surveyed; one with between 2,000 and 2,500 officers and two with about 1,000 officers (the average size of the Dutch forces is 1,600 officers). The response rates were 69.2%, 44.6%, and 46.2%, respectively (342, 223, and 230 questionnaires were returned).

There was a predominance of constables first-class, brigadiers, and inspectors and there were relatively small numbers of ordinary constables and senior officers among the respondents. Roughly 60% of those surveyed belonged to the uniform

**Table 9.1**     Dutch Officers' Views of the Seriousness of the Misconduct in the 11 Scenarios

| Case Number and Description | Rank* | Average | SD |
|---|---|---|---|
| Case 5 - Crime Scene Theft of Watch | 11 | 5.00 | 0.05 |
| Case 3 - Bribe From Speeding Motorist | 10 | 4.98 | 0.17 |
| Case 11-Theft From Found Wallet | 9 | 4.87 | 0.49 |
| Case 7 - Supervisor Grants Holiday in Exchange for Car Tune-Up | 8 | 4.67 | 0.59 |
| Case 9 - Free Drinks to Ignore Late Bar Closing | 7 | 4.57 | 0.62 |
| Case 10 - Excessive Force on Car Thief | 6 | 4.56 | 0.69 |
| Case 6 - 5% Kickback From Auto Repair Shop | 5 | 4.37 | 0.86 |
| Case 2 - Free Meals and Discounts on Beat | 4 | 4.28 | 0.80 |
| Case 4 - Holiday Gifts From Merchants | 3 | 4.11 | 0.87 |
| Case 8 - Cover-Up of Police DUI Accident | 2 | 3.83 | 1.03 |
| Case 1 - Off-Duty Security System Business | 1 | 2.53 | 1.32 |

Note: * From most serious (11) to least serious (1).

branch in all three forces, 4% to 5% worked in administrative positions or in the control room, and the remainder, about 35%, were in general detective functions and specialized units. Most of the respondents worked in units of 25 to 75 people or 76 to 200 people.

The data about the integrity investigations conducted in the forces were collected by a well-known national news and current affairs program, *Nova*, and by researchers at the Free University Amsterdam. The television program asked the police forces to give information about all investigations on integrity violations, including the disciplinary or criminal sanctions they resulted in. This request was accompanied by a reference to a law on the transparency of governance (equivalent to a freedom of information act); transparency is the rule, secrecy is only acceptable when openness would damage major state interests or would be very harmful for the privacy of the people involved. The authority and reputation of the program, and the threat of negative exposure (for non-cooperation) on national television, stimulated the forces to cooperate. All the police forces presented data.

The quality of the data differed significantly, in part due to how advanced their information gathering processes were. The results of this research by journalists were first used in a television news program and later analyzed by researchers at the Center for Police Science of the Free University. The disciplinary and penal investigations were coded in 12 categories, which offered a first overview of the types of integrity investigations and the resulting sanctions (Van der Steeg, Lamboo, & Nieuwendijk, 2000).

## POLICE OFFICERS' PERCEPTIONS OF INTEGRITY

How do the Dutch police think about integrity and integrity violations? What are the results for The Netherlands of the utilization of the integrity-measuring instrument developed by Klockars and colleagues (1997)? Table 9.1 gives a general indication of the responses from Dutch officers from three different regional police forces on the seriousness of transgressions of integrity. The scenarios are placed in relation to their ranking.

On the issue of the seriousness of the presented cases, there was almost complete agreement across all three forces. This seems to reflect a strong consensus among Dutch police officers as to what they consider serious. The respondents also felt that others would think similarly.

Case 5 (Crime Scene Theft of Watch) is considered the most serious and is accorded a rank order of 11. On a scale from 1 to 5, the average score for this case is 5.00, which means that virtually everyone found the offense quite serious. Case 1 (Off-Duty Security System Business) is held to be the least serious and scored on average 2.53 (rank 1), which indicates that on the scale from not serious to very serious it scored in the middle. The standard deviation (SD) is also important. This indicates how large the spread of answers was—the less the spread the more the respondents agreed with one another. The third column in the table shows that the answers to Case 1 are the most diverse ($SD = 1.32$). It also shows there is a clear relationship between seriousness and diversity: About the most serious cases, there is almost complete unanimity ($SDs = 0.05$ and $0.17$).

Almost all the scenarios have an average of more than 4. This means that almost all the cases score on average as serious to quite serious. Only Case 1 and Case 8 score lower. A police officer's running his or her own business clearly receives the most "tolerance" (with a score of 2.53)—presumably because it is not considered against formal rules. Also, bringing a colleague home who is under the influence and has landed in a ditch with his car is treated fairly leniently (with a score of 3.38) compared to the other cases.

The top three rows in the table contain Cases 3, 5, and 11, with an average score of 4.75. Many respondents clearly consider these serious offenses. The three scenarios have in common that they relate to a combination of abuse of duty and direct personal profit (theft of watch, theft from wallet, bribe from speeding motorist). These two elements are also to be found in Case 9 (Free Drinks to Ignore Late Bar Closing), but this case appears to relate to a more acceptable form of gaining advantage—a type of relatively passive and limited "private profit." The same sort of reasoning seems to be at work in the officers' responses to Case 6 (5% Kickback From Auto Repair Shop), which is surprising given that a kickback is really a form of bribe. The judgment of the respondents is also mild when the profit is not directly related to a specific act for a particular individual by the officer—the free meals and holiday gifts can be found in the lower middle range.

## The Relationship Between Officers' Perceptions of the Seriousness of Misconduct and Their Willingness to Report It

To what extent does judging behavior negatively also lead to reporting that behavior? In Table 9.2 we can see that Dutch police officers are not prepared to report every matter that they consider quite serious. The first column shows the officers' perceptions of the seriousness of the misconduct; the second column shows their willingness to report it. The officers' willingness to report the misconduct is lowest for Case 1 (Off-Duty Security System Business), with an average of 2.25 and Case 8 (Cover-Up of Police DUI Accident), with an average of 3.12. Police employees are also not very willing to report about free meals and holiday gifts (with an average that is less than 3.5).

There are a number of cases where the respondents clearly show that they would be less quick to report what they consider less serious offenses. The third column in Table 9.2 shows the differences between the averages for the measures of the perceived seriousness of misconduct and the officers' willingness to report it. We focus on the cases with the highest discrepancy (with as a somewhat arbitrary criterion), a difference between the measures of "seriousness" and "would report" of more than 0.5). Six cases

**Table 9.2**    Dutch Officers' Views of the Seriousness of the Misconduct and Their Willingness to Report It

| Case Number and Description | Seriousness Average* | Reporting Average | Difference |
|---|---|---|---|
| Case 5 - Crime Scene Theft of Watch | 5.00 | 4.87 | 0.13 |
| Case 3 - Bribe From Speeding Motorist | 4.98 | 4.67 | 0.31 |
| Case 11 - Theft From Found Wallet | 4.87 | 4.49 | 0.38 |
| Case 7 - Supervisor Grants Holiday in Exchange for Car Tune-Up | 4.67 | 4.13 | 0.54 |
| Case 9 - Free Drinks to Ignore Late Bar Closing | 4.57 | 3.78 | 0.79 |
| Case 10 - Excessive Force on Car Thief | 4.56 | 3.79 | 0.77 |
| Case 6 - 5% Kickback From Auto Repair Shop | 4.37 | 3.93 | 0.44 |
| Case 2 - Free Meals and Discounts on Beat | 4.28 | 3.42 | 0.86 |
| Case 4 - Holiday Gifts From Merchants | 4.11 | 3.49 | 0.62 |
| Case 8 - Cover-Up of Police DUI Accident | 3.83 | 3.12 | 0.71 |
| Case 1 - Off-Duty Security System Business | 2.53 | 2.25 | 0.28 |

Note: * From most serious to least serious.

are characterized by this discrepancy. On the one hand, there are the two dilemmas where loyalty to colleagues and mutual dependence play a role: protecting colleagues using excessive force (where the difference between the measures "seriousness" and "would report" is 0.77) and protecting a drunken colleague stuck in a ditch (where the difference between the measures is 0.71). On the other hand, there are three cases that in police circles are widely seen as fairly passive and innocent forms of what was once was called "grass-eating": accepting free meals (where the difference between the measures is 0.86), presents on holidays (where the difference is 0.62), and free drinks to ignore a late bar closing (where the difference is 0.79). The sixth case concerns the supervisor giving days off in exchange for the tune-up of his personal car (where the difference between the measures is 0.54).

## AN INTERNATIONAL PERSPECTIVE

As this book shows, the research in The Netherlands was part of a large international project that allows us the unique chance to compare countries (see also Haberfeld, Klockars, Kutnjak Ivkovich, & Pagon, 2000). Is the Dutch police officer more or less critical of misconduct and more or less prepared to speak out about that misconduct than others? Table 9.3 shows data for the United States, Slovenia, Croatia, Poland, and The Netherlands.

A first conclusion we can draw from this data concerns the ranking by Dutch officers compared to the rankings by officers in the other countries. There seems to be considerable agreement. It is the cases involving forms of theft and corruption that are generally the most condemned; the cases involving a kickback from the garage, misuse of office by the supervisor, and excessive violence belong to the middle categories; and the cases involving an officer's running his own company, accepting free meals, accepting presents at holiday time, and helping a drunken colleague are treated the most leniently. Apparently, there is a near universal perception across the countries as to norms and values with regard to defining in a common fashion what undermines police integrity.

A second important finding from the data is that there are significant differences in the

**Table 9.3**  Differences Between Five Countries: Officers' Views of the Seriousness of the Misconduct in 11 Cases

| Case Number and Description | The Netherlands | United States | Slovenia | Croatia | Poland |
|---|---|---|---|---|---|
| | | | *Average and Rank* | | |
| Case 1 - Off-Duty Security | 2.53 | 1.46 | 2.73 | 2.57 | 2.29 |
| System Business | 1 | 1 | 3 | 2 | 1 |
| Case 2 - Free Meals and | 4.28 | 2.60 | 2.80 | 3.01 | 3.70 |
| Discounts on Beat | 4 | 2 | 4 | 4 | 5 |
| Case 3 - Bribe From | 4.98 | 4.92 | 4.78 | 4.47 | 4.79 |
| Speeding Motorist | 10 | 10 | 10 | 9 | 10 |
| Case 4 - Holiday Gifts | 4.11 | 2.84 | 1.99 | 2.13 | 3.21 |
| From Merchants | 3 | 3 | 1 | 1 | 3 |
| Case 5 - Crime Scene | 5.00 | 4.95 | 4.87 | 4.72 | 4.80 |
| Theft of Watch | 11 | 11 | 11 | 11 | 11 |
| Case 6 - 5% Kickback | 4.37 | 4.50 | 4.32 | 3.86 | 4.02 |
| From Auto Repair Shop | 5 | 7 | 8 | 7 | 6 |
| Case 7 - Supervisor Grants | 4.67 | 4.18 | 4.15 | 4.09 | 4.18 |
| Holiday in Exchange for Car Tune-Up | 8 | 6 | 7 | 8 | 7 |
| Case 8 - Cover-Up of | 3.83 | 3.03 | 2.37 | 2.79 | 3.02 |
| Police DUI Accident | 2 | 4 | 2 | 3 | 2 |
| Case 9 - Free Drinks to | 4.57 | 4.54 | 3.81 | 3.85 | 4.77 |
| Ignore Late Bar Closing | 7 | 8 | 6 | 6 | 9 |
| Case 10 - Excessive Force | 4.56 | 4.05 | 3.01 | 3.03 | 3.46 |
| on Car Thief | 6 | 5 | 5 | 5 | 4 |
| Case 11 - Theft From | 4.87 | 4.85 | 4.70 | 4.55 | 4.48 |
| Found Wallet | 9 | 9 | 9 | 10 | 8 |

comparative strength of opinion on condemning misconduct. The scores clearly differ. The Dutch officers tend to be somewhat more critical than their counterparts abroad. If we focus, for instance, on the differences between the United States and The Netherlands—on the grounds that Eastern Europe represents, in some respects, a less readily comparable policing situation—then the one exception is the kickback from the garage owner (for recommending clients for repairs to their cars). Such kickbacks play a more prominent role in the United States than they do in The Netherlands when integrity issues are debated. This probably is related to the degree to which a genuine problem exists (or has been uncovered—for it is rarely heard of in The Netherlands, which does not necessarily mean it does not happen).

In the rankings, then, the American respondents considered this offense more serious than the Dutch officers did.

All the other forms of misconduct attract a more critical evaluation from the Dutch officers than they do from the American officers. With regard to five offenses there are scarcely differences—these are the serious cases that are widely condemned—but with regard to the five cases relating to the minor offenses there is quite some variation.

It seems that with regard to integrity, the Dutch officers are somewhat more stringent than their American colleagues are. Their judgement is particularly critical with regard to the minor "perks" that in many countries are associated with the standard, informal benefits of being a police officer. The free meal and holiday presents are not offenses that the average American respondent sees as morally reprehensible. The opinion on this within the Dutch police is quite different; these are seen as serious or very serious, and Table 9.3 displays a difference in evaluation of 1.68 and 1.27.

It is not possible to uncover from the data why such a variance exists. Possibly one explanation is that there has been a considerable commotion about the minor forms of conflict of interest and unacceptable forms of involvement as a result of cases in The Netherlands in the 1970s and 1980s (Geerts & Van Laere, 1984; Punch, 1985). These even added a new word to the police vocabulary—the verb *naggen* from *norm afwijkend gedrag* (or *n.a.g.*), which is equivalent to the terms *bumming* in America and *mumping* in Britain (which are something like cadging or sponging but generally mean day-to-day compensations and perks) (see Manning, 1977, pp. 151-155, in which bumming and mumping are defined as soliciting gifts and discounts in a low-key fashion, and there is more on "fiddles, skiving, perks, mumps, gimmicks, and gifts"). Although we do not know exactly what caused the changes, research shows that the practices that existed in The Netherlands in the past have slowly disappeared (Huberts, Naeye, Busato, Zweden, & Berger, 2002). Before 1990, accepting such benefits was often rationalized as part of the job, now this behavior is now strongly condemned by officers.

Whatever the explanation, it is clear that Dutch police officers appear to be quite strong in their opinions on these offenses, that these opinions are stronger than they were in the past and that this justifies some optimism about the possibility of making police culture and practice more alert to norms of integrity.

Having another job alongside police work (Case 1) is seen as less serious by the American sample than by the Dutch sample and the samples in the other countries. This is in line with the fact that having a second job, formally or informally, is widely accepted in many American police departments. In The Netherlands, there are regulations limiting the secondary job possibilities of police officers. The variation with regard to the misbehavior of a supervisor (Case 7) is fairly small. It is noticeable that the Dutch and American samples display a limited difference on the violence against a suspect case (Case 10), in comparison to the perceptions of the seriousness of this case in the three Eastern European countries.

### Solidarity

To a certain extent, the solidarity with colleagues appears to be less pronounced in The Netherlands than it is in the United States and elsewhere, given that it is less taken for granted that a drunken colleague will be brought home (having been found under the influence in a car that has landed up in a ditch). A more general measure as to whether or not the collegial solidarity is greater than the norm of integrity can be gleaned by looking at the respondents' willingness to report colleagues when they engage in misconduct. We observe that Dutch officers consider the scenarios to be more serious than their American counterparts do. It appears that Dutch officers are also more likely than Americans to report their colleagues for misconduct. That holds true for most of the offenses in the scenarios—except for the one in which an officer accepts free drinks to turn a blind eye to a late bar closing and the one in which the officer has a deal involving a kickback from a garage.

These differences in officers' willingness to report the cases are directly related to their perceptions of the seriousness of the cases. Given that Dutch respondents perceive the scenarios to be more serious than others do, then it also follows that they are more likely to report them.

If we examine the differences between the two countries in the averages for the measures of the perceived seriousness of each offense and the officers' willingness to report it, we see comparable differences. In the American sample, the difference between the measures of seriousness and willingness to report is 0.58, and in the Dutch sample the difference is 0.53.

## INTEGRITY INVESTIGATIONS

Police forces possess information about the cases of police deviance that have been investigated, especially if they resulted in disciplinary or criminal sanctions (which might have been dealt with informally and/or have not been recorded). As was mentioned before, this information has been collected and analyzed by both journalists and researchers. All police forces cooperated and presented data (Van der Steeg, Lamboo, & Nieuwendijk, 2000). Table 9.4 summarizes the results. The 26 police forces (25 regional forces and a national force) reported a total of 1,707 investigations for the years 1997 to 1999. Of these, 344 investigations resulted in the dismissal or conditional/probational dismissal of officers.

In practice, it proved difficult to construct a usable typology of misbehavior and deviance because the information given on integrity investigations was often unclear and because the police forces use different concepts and categories. For example, whether an investigation on "leaking information" concerned the involvement of a journalist or a criminal was seldom clear, and the same applied for the question of whether private gain was involved (corruption).

The integrity investigations involved 11 categories of offense. Many investigations concern the use or abuse of violence by police officers (286 investigations, 17% of all investigations), theft and fraud (crimes against property; 14%), and leaking information (11%). Police corruption appears to be very scarce. It does not appear as a separate category in this research, although it is clear that private gain was relevant in a limited number of cases of leaking information, contacts with criminals, and activities and jobs outside the police force.

Given the variable quality of this data, it is important to add that these figures have to be interpreted with caution. The standard investigative procedures on the different forms of deviance differ widely. In The Netherlands these procedures are mandatory for the use of violence, which means that many cases will be the subject of investigation (including less serious cases). For other integrity violations, it might be that only the more serious offenses become the subject of official disciplinary or criminal investigations.

### Dismissals

The total number of conditional and immediate dismissals in the 3-year period was 344 (see the third column in Table 9.4). This means that yearly about 0.3% of the 41,400 employees of the Dutch police forces are punished with dismissal or conditional dismissal for integrity violations (it also means that 1.4% of the force are investigated). When the number of dismissals is a criterion for the importance of the different types of deviance, the top three are fraud and theft, misbehavior in the officer's private time, and alcohol and drug abuse (51, 37, and 32 dismissals). A better idea of the seriousness of deviance in the perception of the police authorities might be inferred from the sanctions that are applied. Table 9.5 shows how often an investigation results in a (conditional) dismissal.

Investigations on the use of violence seldom result in a dismissal (only 7% of investigations have such serious consequences). This can be explained, as mentioned before, by the procedure that all uses of violence have to be investigated. The data on dismissals suggest that the Dutch police seem to be rather harsh on officers who are

**Table 9.4**     Integrity Investigations Within the Dutch Police From 1997 to 1999

| Behavior: Integrity Violation | Investigations | | (Conditional) Dismissals | |
|---|---|---|---|---|
| | *n* | *%* | *n* | *%* |
| (Excessive) Violence | 286 | 17% | 20 | 6% |
| Fraud and Theft | 247 | 14% | 51 | 15% |
| Leaking Information | 182 | 11% | 31 | 9% |
| Waste and Neglect | 151 | 9% | 29 | 8% |
| Discourteous Treatment of Citizens | 136 | 8% | 29 | 8% |
| Other Misbehavior in Office | 135 | 8% | 14 | 4% |
| Private Misbehavior | 145 | 8% | 37 | 11% |
| Contacts With Criminals | 92 | 5% | 19 | 6% |
| Discourteous Treatment of Colleagues | 70 | 4% | 25 | 7% |
| Alcohol and Drug Offenses | 68 | 4% | 32 | 9% |
| Secondary Activities/Jobs | 31 | 2% | 7 | 2% |
| Others, Unclear | 164 | 10% | 50 | 15% |
| Total | 1707 | 100% | 344 | 100% |

investigated for alcohol or drug abuse (47% of such investigations result in dismissals), for misbehavior toward colleagues (36% result in dismissals), and for not being able or willing to behave appropriately in their private time (26% result in dismissals). Unacceptable treatment of colleagues more often leads to dismissal than the same type of behavior against citizens. In the last section, we will compare these data on integrity violations with the data on the integrity perceptions of police officers.

## AN ANALYSIS OF INTEGRITY PERCEPTIONS AND INVESTIGATIONS

To compare the data on the measures of misconduct's seriousness and officers' willingness to report it with the data on investigations is not that easy. Nevertheless, an analysis of both types of data enables us to say something about a number of issues. What is the relationship between the content of the cases being investigated and the officers' perceptions of their seriousness? What

can be said about the extent of the problem: Which cases that are seen as serious are scarce and which are more common? What can be said about the importance of the "wall of silence" for police integrity investigations? And what implications for integrity policies might be derived from the analysis?

### The Content of the Police Integrity Problem

What exactly is the content of the police integrity problem? *Integrity,* in our view, denotes the quality of acting in accordance (in "togetherness") with the relevant moral values and norms (and rules). A number of *integrity violations* or forms of misconduct can be distinguished. Recently we developed a typology with the following 10 categories of integrity violations: (1) corruption, including bribing, nepotism, cronyism, and patronage; (2) fraud and theft; (3) conflict of (private and public) interest (e.g., through assets or gifts); (4) conflict of interest through jobs and activities; (5) improper use of violence; (6) other improper methods of policing (improper means for what are often noble

**Table 9.5**    Integrity Investigations and Sanctions Within the Dutch Police

| Behavior: Integrity Violation | Investigations n | (Conditional) Dismissals n | Percentage Dismissals % |
|---|---|---|---|
| (Excessive) Violence | 286 | 20 | 7% |
| Fraud and Theft | 247 | 51 | 21% |
| Leaking Information | 182 | 31 | 17% |
| Waste and Neglect | 151 | 29 | 19% |
| Discourteous Treatment of Citizens | 136 | 29 | 21% |
| Other Misbehavior in Office | 135 | 14 | 10% |
| Private Misbehavior | 145 | 37 | 26% |
| Contacts With Criminals | 92 | 19 | 21% |
| Discourteous Treatment of Colleagues | 70 | 25 | 36% |
| Alcohol and Drug Offenses | 68 | 32 | 47% |
| Secondary Activities/Jobs | 31 | 7 | 23% |
| Others, Unclear | 164 | 50 | 30% |
| Total | 1707 | 344 | 20% |

causes) (Crank & Caldero, 2000); (7) abuse and manipulation of information; (8) discrimination and sexual harassment (i.e., indecent treatment of colleagues or citizens); (9) the waste and abuse of resources; (10) private time misconduct.

In the cases used in the perception of integrity research, much attention is paid to forms of corruption and fraud (Cases 3, 5, 6, 7, 9, and 11 involve the abuse of office for private gain) and cases with possible conflict of interest (through gifts, as in Cases 2 and 4), while there is one case on the improper use of violence (Case 10) and one on possible conflict of interest through jobs (Case 1). Case 8, the cover-up for a colleague, might be seen as an example of improper methods of policing.

The data indicate that the violations that are considered most serious are only a small minority of the violations actually being investigated. Eleven categories of integrity violation were distinguished, and many investigations concern the use or abuse of violence by police officers, theft and fraud (crimes against property), leaking information, waste and neglect, treatment of citizens, and private time misbehavior. Many of these are absent in the integrity-measurement instrument on

police perception. Our knowledge and insight could benefit if the remarkable international endeavor could be continued on the basis of an extended instrument.

## The Extent of the Problem

Perception research shows that participating Dutch police officers consider both fraud and corruption (as bribery) very serious and because of that they are very much willing to report both types of integrity violation. The research on investigations shows that police corruption investigations are scarce (not manifest enough to make it a separate category), while fraud and theft are much more frequent. Conflict of interest is considered somewhat less serious and officers are less willing to report it than fraud (Cases 2, 4, and 1). The number of actual investigations on these subjects is limited, as is the number of investigations of situations like that in Case 8, in which an officer helps his drunken colleague. The use of excessive force by officers is more often the subject of investigation, although there is a considerable difference between the officers' perception of the seriousness of such misconduct and their willingness to report it.

**Table 9.6** Typology of Cases Based on Officers' Expressed Willingness to Report Misconduct and Actual Investigations

| | Number of Investigations: Low | Number of Investigations: High |
|---|---|---|
| Willingness to Report: Relatively low | Conflict of Interest: Gifts, Jobs Helping a Drunken Colleague | Excessive Force By a Fellow Officer |
| Willingness to Report: Relatively high | Bribery | Internal Fraud, Theft |

The possible relationship between the officers' expressed willingness to report misconduct and the actual number of investigations is summarized in Table 9.6. The simple typology might be useful for policy development.

Policies to curb conflict of interest and excessive violence might benefit from strategies to increase officers' willingness to report. For the struggle against internal fraud, however, this would not help because the willingness is already high. Extra initiatives against a serious offense such as bribery may well prove ineffective because the table shows that bribery is probably scarce (officers are willing to report it, but the number of investigations is low).

### The Wall of Silence

One of the most cited characteristics of police culture is the solidarity evidenced in "the code" or the " blue curtain" (Crank, 1998; Skolnick, 2000), which is the informal prohibition in the occupational culture of policing against reporting the misconduct of fellow police officers. The reported data showed that there is a difference between the officers' perception of the seriousness of an offense and their willingness to report it. This seems to prove the existence of a wall of silence that may compromise officers' willingness to behave with integrity. However, there is still reason to be optimistic. First, the differences are not as large as the metaphor of the wall of silence, or curtain of secrecy, might suggest. A majority of Dutch officers claim to be willing to report even the minor violations. Second, the "height" of the wall varies quite a lot in relation to the type of deviance involved. Bribery, theft, and fraud will be reported; at least, that is what almost every officer tells us. The wall seems more relevant for less serious cases of, for example, conflict of interest.

The research on integrity investigations shows at the same time that many violations belong to the category of less serious offenses (waste and neglect, discourteous treatment of citizens or colleagues, alcohol and drug offenses). This illustrates that in The Netherlands attention is being paid to a broad spectrum of integrity violations. Unfortunately, we do not know which part of those investigations resulted from an internal complaint or report. Further research should focus on that aspect because it would clarify whether Dutch police officers actually report colleagues when their misconduct is seen as serious.

At the same time, it is evident that it is all but easy for officers to report a colleague. This inevitably leads to an underestimation of the integrity problem, in particular concerning the extent of the violations that are considered less serious.

## POLICY LESSONS: SOME REASONS FOR OPTIMISM

When police management wishes to improve its insight into the content and extent of the integrity situation, a number of measures can be taken. First, it seems worthwhile to use an integrity-measurement instrument to get an idea about the attitudes in the police force and officers' willingness to participate in policies. The available Klockars and colleagues (1997) instrument has been helpful, but an extension seems worthwhile. For a country like The Netherlands, the incorporation of other scenarios seems necessary. The reason simply is that police integrity is a complex, multidimensional phenomenon and the police forces of different countries are confronted with different types of integrity violation.

Second, and more structurally, it would be wise to aim policies at increasing officers' willingness to report—and to direct such initiatives at specific categories of integrity violation. To be able to choose these cases, specific integrity policies have to be formulated (aimed at what is considered most important). This has to be combined with knowledge about the state of the art (data on officers' perceptions of the seriousness of the various forms of misconduct, on their willingness to report misconduct, and on actual investigations) (see also Table 9.6).

There is some reason for optimism about the potential effectiveness of such policies.

The international comparative research shows that Dutch police officers are significantly more critical of several types of integrity violation as well as more willing to report them. Police officers' perceptions have definitely changed since 1990 (Huberts et al., 2000). Officers' awareness has increased, which contradicts the pessimistic belief held by many that police culture is permanent and unchangeable. Although police management claims that this has been the result of their policies, the precise causality of the relationship remains a theme for further research.

## A RESEARCH AGENDA

Policy as well as theory development could profit from a combination of research on police officers' perceptions, investigations, and actual cases of integrity violation. More specifically, it would be helpful if information about investigations would also reveal more systematically the source of the investigation (what is actually reported by police officers) and perception research would cover more of the broader spectrum of the integrity problem. In addition, a more dynamic approach would be appropriate: If we could establish which changes take place in officers' perceptions and reporting patterns, and what causes those changes, then a breakthrough in knowledge as well as policy could be achieved.

## REFERENCES

Crank, J. (1998). *Understanding police culture*. Cincinnati, OH: Anderson.

Crank, J. P., & Caldero, M. A. (2000). *Police ethics. The corruption of noble cause*. Cincinnati, OH: Anderson.

Fijnaut, C., Bovenkerk, F., Bruinsma, G., & Bunt, H. van de (1998). *Organized crime in The Netherlands*. The Hague/London/Boston: Kluwer Law International.

Geerts R. W. M., & Van Laere, E. M. P. (1984). *Wetshandhaver of wetsontduiker* (To uphold or to break the law). The Hague: Ministry of the Interior.

Haberfeld, M., Klockars, C. B., Kutnjak Ivkovich, S., & Pagon, M. (2000). Police officer perceptions of the disciplinary consequences of police corruption in Croatia, Poland, Slovenia, and the United States. *Journal of Police Practice and Research, 1*(1), 34-51.

Huberts, L. W. J. C. (1995). Public corruption and fraud in The Netherlands: Research and results. *Crime, Law & Social Change, 22*, 307-321.

Huberts, L. W. J. C., Naeye, J., Busato, V., Zweden, C. van, & Berger, B. (2002). *Politiemoraal* (Police ethics). Zeist, The Netherlands: Kerckebosch.

Huberts, L. W. J. C., Punch, M., & Lamboo, M. E. D. (2000, November). *Police integrity in comparative perspective: The Netherlands*. Paper presented at the annual meeting of the American Society of Criminology, San Francisco.

Klockars, C. B., Kutnjak Ivkovich, S., Harver, W. E., & Haberfeld, M. (1997). *The measurement of police integrity: Executive summary*. A report to National Institute of Justice, Washington, DC.

Kutnjak Ivkovich, S., & Klockars C. B. (1996, March). *Police perceptions of disciplinary fairness and the formation of the code of silence*. Paper presented at the annual meeting of the Academy of Criminal Justice Sciences, Las Vegas, Nevada.

Manning, P. K. (1977). *Police work*. Cambridge: MIT Press.

Ministerie van Binnenlandse Zaken (Ministry of Home Affairs). (1995, March 17). *Politie en integriteit* (Police and integrity). Letter to the Second Chamber of Parliament, The Hague.

Newburn, T. (1999). *Understanding and preventing police corruption: Lessons from the literature*. Police Research Series, Paper 110. London: Home Office Policing and Reducing Crime Unit.

Punch, M. (1985). *Conduct unbecoming: The social construction of police deviance and control*. London: Tavistock.

Punch, M. (1997). The Dutch criminal justice system: A crisis of identity. *Security Journal, 9*, 177-184.

Punch, M. (2000). Police corruption and its prevention. *European Journal on Criminal Policy and Research, 8*, 301-324.

Punch, M., Vijver, K. van der, & Dijk, N. van (1998). *Searching for a future. Reappraising the functioning of the police*. Dordrecht, The Netherlands: The Dutch Foundation for Society, Safety and Police.

Sherman, L. W. (Ed.). (1974). *Police corruption. A sociological perspective*. New York: Doubleday.

Skolnick, J. H. (2000, March 27-April 10). Code blue. Prosecuting police brutality requires penetrating the blue wall of silence. *The American Prospect*, pp. 49-53.

Van der Steeg, M., Lamboo, T., & Nieuwendijk, A. (2000). Als zich een integriteitsschending voordoet (When there is a violation of integrity). *het Tijdschrift voor de Politie, 62*(9), 23-30.

# CHAPTER 10

# Police Misconduct
## The Pakistani Paradigm

Zubair Nawaz Chattha

Sanja Kutnjak Ivković

## INTRODUCTION

Police are generally responsible for regulating the law of the land, with the additional aim of accomplishing this with the slightest possible commotion in the society at large. However, the police in Pakistan—one of the Third World countries in which the police still adhere to the British colonial tradition of serving the government rather than the people—are alleged to be the single largest source of corruption and abuse of official authority in the country ("Probe Into Police Corruption," 2000). Police behavior in Pakistan has evolved in the context of a complex set of socioeconomic and political circumstances, which have culminated with the present crisis of "police misconduct."

The police force in Pakistan is under the control of the Home Ministry. The Chief Minister of a province has the duty to maintain the law and order in the province. The police station is the focal unit of the police organization. The number of police stations in any district varies from many, like the 74 stations in the Lahore district,[1] to few, like the 9 stations in the Hafizabad district.[2] A police station, headed by an inspector or a subinspector with a team of constables, head constables, assistant subinspectors, and subinspectors, is responsible, among other duties, for the recording, detection, and investigation of criminal cases. The staff of any police station patrols the area by foot and automobile patrol. Since police work in Pakistan is not based on specialization, every police officer performs almost all tasks: patrol, detection of crime, investigation of crime, and prosecution.

The police force consists of a three-tier cadre system. The lowest tier is composed of the constabulary, which is comprised of constables and head constables. The middle-ranking cadre is at the inspector level, which starts from the position of Assistant Subinspector and goes up to the rank of Inspector. The head of the force is the "gazetted officer" cadre, which consists of all the higher ranks, ranging from the Assistant

Superintendent to the Inspector General of the Police. The gazetted officers include two types of officers: federal officers (direct entrants) and provincial officers (promoted officers who come from the ranks). The Inspector General of the Police is the departmental head of the Provincial Police Force, which is divided into Divisions[3] and Districts.[4] Punjab, the most densely populated province, has a police force of around 100,000.

## TYPES OF POLICE MISCONDUCT IN PAKISTAN

### The Use of Excessive Force

Next to the military, the police are the only entity authorized to use force in fulfilling their obligations of law enforcement in Pakistani society. Officers are expected to use only the minimum force required to accomplish their task (Sections 46 and 50, The Pakistan Criminal Procedure Code of 1898). Since there has been little research on law enforcement in Pakistan, we use the classification of police brutality developed by Barker. While summarizing citizens' complaints against the police, Barker noted the following six categories of police brutality (cited in Kornblum, 1976):

1. profane and abusive language

2. commands to move or get home

3. field stops and searches

4. threats

5. prodding with a nightstick or approaching with a pistol

6. the actual use of physical force

From the Pakistani perspective, the first five categories are neither considered serious nor reported to the higher authorities, as it is expected that the police will abuse and harass the citizens. The personal experience of one of the authors (Zubair Nawaz Chattha) bears out what is common knowledge in Pakistan—that the police use abusive language with the public. When the police ask people to leave any scene, they use polo sticks to violently push people away from the place. When field stops and searches are conducted, the most common police practice in Pakistan is to use roadblocks to stop people and search their vehicles. The police kick and push people with sticks, point weapons at them, and openly threaten those who disobey their commands. In this context, the use of excessive force is only potentially questionable if it falls within the last type of complaint—the actual use of physical force. There are three broad types of situations involving police use of excessive force: (1) torture and/or rape in police custody; (2) the use of excessive force to cause death; and (3) unlawful search, seizure, and arrest.

### Torture and/or Rape in Police Custody

It is customary that any interrogation of the accused by the police be supplemented by physical torture to extract a confession (Mohammad, 2001). The police use torture because they lack professional competence to elicit confessions through intelligent interrogation. The brutality of the torture often results in the death of the victims ("Muttahida Man Dies," 1999). The police are also blamed for torturing people so that they will change their political views (Rodley, 1996) or relinquish their property or other valuable claims to other, more influential individuals.

The police stations are equipped with horrible tools to beat and torture those who are apprehended. Some notorious police officers also maintain private torture cells (Human Rights Commission of Pakistan, 1999, p. 99); the media and bailiffs of higher courts have often discovered such places. In the areas with higher crime rates, this trend has been somewhat ignored and thus tacitly tolerated by the police administrators and governments.

Although the courts have the power under the Evidence Act to exclude any part of a confession believed to have been extracted through torture (Section 37 of The Evidence Act of 1984), they do not apply this rule and thereby implicitly encourage the police to torture the accused. The authorities' tacit approval of such police misconduct is mostly due to the paucity of resources to improve the fight against crime.

Another deplorable type of police torture in Pakistan is the custodial rape of accused women or the female relatives of absconding criminals (Ghosh, 1993). Numerous studies conducted by human rights organizations have described this brutal crime by police officials, but little attention has been given by the authorities to punishing the culprits or reducing such incidents (Human Rights Commission of Pakistan, 1999, p. 219). It is understood that if an individual accused of some serious criminal case is absconding, that person's movable property and close relatives will be brought to the police station in hope that doing so will compel the accused to appear. Rape occurs most frequently in these situations, and the police authorities (U.S. Department of State, 1999a) give little attention to these crimes because they would rather not acknowledge a rape than prosecute it.

### The Use of Excessive Force to Cause Death

The use of excessive force by the police in Pakistan has its own characteristics, developed through the years of policing based on the British colonial tradition. For example, an attempt to arrest a suspect can turn into a shoot-to-kill scene if the suspect attempts to escape. This history of willingness to use deadly force is essentially derived from 18th-century English common law (Brenner & Kravitz, 1979, p. 20). At that time in England, many minor offenses, like attempting to escape, carried capital punishment, so the use of brutal force was condoned because the felon was to face death anyway.

A prominent example of the "trigger happy" attitudes of the officers in the Pakistani police force took place in 1996. Mir Murtaza Bhutto, the brother of former Prime Minister Benazir Bhutto, was killed in Karachi after the police stopped his party for a search of the vehicles in his convoy. The police suspected that a few of Bhutto's bodyguards were absconders who possessed illegal weapons. The search operation triggered a police encounter, which resulted in the death of all eight people traveling with Bhutto. This tragedy came at the end of a 2-year period during which the police of Karachi engaged in a continuous antiterrorist fight against elements of a local militant ethnic group, resulting in hundreds of police deaths. The police tried to crush the wave of terrorism through the use of excessive force, which in no small part contributed to the "trigger happy" attitudes.

Between January and June of 1998, 265 people were killed in 182 police encounters reported in Punjab, most of which are alleged to be fake and staged (U.S. Department of State, 1999b). The high rate of crime motivated an ill-equipped police force to resort to the easiest way to get rid of criminals—by shooting them—rather than undergo the arduous task of prosecuting them (U.S. Department of State, 1999b). In one case, four of the top ten wanted criminals were arrested in Karachi on July 18, 1998, and were taken to Lahore. The newspapers carried stories and photographs of their arrest; 3 days later, they were killed in a so-called police encounter (U.S. Department of State, 1999b). Interestingly, no police officers were injured in the exchange of fire. The case was officially closed with the finding of a justified use of deadly force in an encounter between the police and the group of suspects.

### Unlawful Search, Seizure, and Arrest

The obsolete laws of Pakistan allow the police to arrest anyone named by the complainant in the F.I.R. (First Information Report)[5] without the need to obtain a warrant from the courts.[6] The "probable cause" test is not imposed on police officers, so in almost all cases it is left to their discretion to arrest or refuse to arrest the accused (Khan, 2000). The practice is such, however, that the police are generally under pressure to arrest anyone the complainant mentioned in the F.I.R.

The Pakistani equivalent of the Fourth Amendment requirements of the U.S. Constitution is virtually science fiction for the Pakistani police, who have the lawful authority to break into any residence when a cognizable offense is supposed to have been committed by the occupants (Sections 47 and 48 of The Pakistan Criminal Procedure Code of 1898). Because of this broad procedural power, it is very rare that warrants are used when the police want to conduct a search. Another type of search operation is conducted by the police on the roadsides, where automobile passengers are asked to step out of their vehicles and are physically searched. These types of search operations are aimed at deterring criminals—at the cost of annoyance to the majority of the population.

### Corruption

Corruption in the Pakistani police, as well as in the society at large,[7] is endemic. The pervasive and epidemic corruption in the police was pointed out as early as 1902 to 1903 in the Fraser Commission Report (Chaudhry, 1997):

> The forms of this corruption are very numerous. It manifests itself in every stage of the work of the police station. The police officer may levy a fee or receive a present for every duty he performs. The complainant has often to pay a fee for having his complaint recorded. He is to give the investigating officer a present to secure his prompt and earnest attention to the case. More money is extorted as the investigation proceeds. When the officer goes down to the spot to make his investigation, he is a burden not only to the complainant, but to his witnesses. (p. 70)

The police enjoy wide discretion, which encourages kickbacks, payoffs, and shakedowns. Police corruption in Pakistan is similar in nature to the police corruption in the West, but with the addition of the role of the middleman, who is popularly called the "tout." The tout is an individual who looks after the expenditures of police officers and entertains them to gain their confidence, which he utilizes in dealing with the victims or the accused in criminal cases to negotiate the amount of the bribe. The payments are generally made through a tout—someone who has established a reputation of dealing with the police officers and the criminals at the same time, and it is customary that the tout keeps a certain percentage. It is believed that, with their contacts on both sides, these middlemen are in the most effective position for changing the direction of police activities. For example, they can gather police support for some illegal businesses and can even affect the results of investigations.

The Western police literature classifies police corruption into eight different types (Roebuck & Barker, 1974), which include corruption of authority, kickbacks, theft from arrestees or victims, shakedowns, protection of illegal activities, fixes, direct criminal activity, and internal payoffs. For expository convenience, the same classification will be used with Pakistani examples to illustrate the nature of police corruption in Pakistan. An additional type of police corruption particular to Pakistan is the involvement of the police in civil matters.

In Pakistan, "corruption of authority" exists in a variety of forms. Police—the symbol of authority—are entertained with gifts and free merchandise. Police officers enjoy free meals, drinks, and other treats from citizens who want to prove that they are connected with those who have authority. The leadership of the police considers this to be a system of informal rewards, provided that the officers receiving such gifts are acceptable to the department and that the corruptors belong to the respectable class of citizens. The number of officers who receive kickbacks is limited, as such arrangements involve only the few senior officers assigned by police headquarters to make bulk purchases for the police, like the cloth for the uniforms, weapons, and communications equipment.

Theft from arrestees or crime victims is an act in which police officers indulge in quite often, as the victims are generally unaware of it and criminals stand reluctant to report such losses. Police officers in Pakistan have also been found using recovered stolen vehicles for their private use. It is an accepted practice within Pakistan's police departments that police officers, who are poorly paid and receive no reimbursement for the costs incurred during investigations, take the property of arrestees to cover their expenses or as a fee for their services.

The police in Pakistan are also inclined to shake down drunk drivers, absconders, and others who want to avoid the legitimate legal process. Such shakedowns primarily target offenders who commit victimless crimes such as drinking liquor,[8] dating,[9] and smoking marijuana. Although fake cases are sometimes registered on the instructions of the government, which uses such tactics to put pressure on its political opponents, the shakedown is largely used by the police officers for personal monetary gain.

The most lucrative form of corruption for the police in Pakistan is "protection of illegal activities." Money is mostly demanded from organized crime figures. Drug peddling, prostitution, and running gambling dens are all activities that could hardly exist without the active support of the area police station (Ghayur, 1994). Similarly, the traffic police can obtain substantial financial gains by ignoring the violations of buses and wagons plying on the commercial routes. Although there are few recorded examples, police officers have also been found committing serious crimes, such as robberies, with the purpose of achieving material gain for themselves. However, such involvement in direct criminal activity by police officers does not induce a strong level of support from other officers and is not tolerated to the same extent by supervisors in police departments as are other forms of corruption.[10]

Finally, the police station activities are greased with money provided by those who require legitimate police services (Khan, 2000). A victim has to provide bribes to have a criminal case registered with the police and to have an investigation initiated. This bribery begins the victim's endless journey to satisfy the ever-increasing demands made by the police officers. The victim has to take the police officers to the scene of the crime, feed them, and provide them with the stationery on which to write up the crime report. Police officers also make money in the process of deciding the outcome of criminal investigations. Such corruption is carried out through the popular touts, who make these activities their livelihood.

Whenever a murder is committed and the immediate or extended family of the victim have some suspicion regarding the murderer, it is customary for the police to urge them to add as many names as they want to the list of potential suspects. Since murders in Pakistan are mostly committed because of family feuds, the option of adding more names to the list of potential suspects is readily accepted by the victim's relatives. Ultimately, those people who claim to be innocent are dropped from the list after they pay off the police. In addition, internal payoffs also seem to be rampant.[11] Since the police do not work in shifts and should be available at all times, police officers absent themselves from their duty by paying a bribe to the officer in charge of the police station. Even police officials have to pay a bribe—to acquire the travel allowance that is included in their salary package.

Finally, a popular type of police corruption in Pakistan, which is not included in the Western classification of police corruption, is the use of nuisance to coerce people into deciding or abandoning their claims in civil litigation. The police may step into civil disputes over property or money either through their influence or by paying bribes. Citizens are generally discontented and consider this involvement by police high-handedness, which is sanctioned neither by the Constitution of Pakistan nor by other laws.

## *Unprofessional Conduct*

Genuine criminal cases are padded with fake evidence, mostly resulting in the failure of prosecution in the court of law (Amnesty International, 1996). The police, as a tool of exploitation of the government, make citizens subjects of these corrupt activities. This encourages the officers to misbehave with the public, who are in turn unable to respect the police. The general public loses faith in the custodians of law when they become aware of the extent of the professional incompetence of the police.

## THE CAUSES OF THE CURRENT STATE OF AFFAIRS

The causes of police misconduct in Pakistani society are deeply embedded in the country's socioeconomic and political structure. To begin with, the society is highly tolerant of corruption in general, as indicated by the overall evaluation of Pakistan by Transparency International. In the 2001 Corruption Perceptions Index, Pakistan was ranked 79th of the 91 countries included in the index (Transparency International, 2002).

A police officer is expected to possess a high degree of intelligence and the interpersonal skills required to exercise discretion in enforcing the law. However, the education level required of the constables, who (together with head constables) comprise 89% of the police force (Chaudhry, 1997, p. 101), is matriculation[12] or even less. Such educational requirements have created a situation in which the majority of the police force have a low level of education. The education of a typical constable cannot support the demands of the job; the constable is therefore someone who is trained to serve as a mechanical functionary obeying the orders of those more senior rather than an officer using personal judgment to solve policing issues. Unable to perform the police task in accordance with professional standards, constables tend to behave in a crude manner and to generate hostility in the citizens in the process. Furthermore, the illiterate police force cannot gain the respect and trust of the citizens because they lack the interpersonal skills to win the citizens' confidence.

The consequences of the constables' lack of higher education extend further and have a major impact on the police—to the point of potentially crippling the efficiency of the whole force. Because of their lack of appropriate education, constables have been excluded from the cardinal police functions of investigation and prosecution, thus straining the quality of policing due to the overburdening of other ranks.

Direct recruitment into the police in Pakistan takes place in the ranks of constable, assistant subinspector, and assistant superintendent (Nadeem, 1989, p. 108). The remaining 11% of the police force consists of inspectors, who have an F.A.[13] level of education, and superintendents, who are mostly college graduates. Only the higher ranks of officers are selected through a competitive examination; all the other ranks are recruited departmentally, but generally those positions are filled through political recommendations or explicit bribery. Both police officers' importance as members of the governmental apparatus and their influence as a result of their estimated illegal income make policing such an attractive profession that people are ready to pay any price to get their dear ones a position with the police force. Politicians attach such importance to police service that even the members of the National Assembly get their close relatives (such as their sons and brothers) inducted into police service as Deputy Superintendents of Police—by direct notifications of the Prime Minister and without any exam or procedure.[14]

The police officers who join the force by paying bribes or based on their political connections regard policing as a business in which their very first task is to recover the basic cost or repay the favor incurred through their recruitment. Such officers are less likely to be law-abiding and more likely to disregard the probability of possible punishment for rule-violating behavior, as they perceive their induction itself as evidence of the success that can be achieved through corruption and the use of other illegal means. A comparison of the offending rate of such police officers with the rate of those inducted by merit potentially could provide support for the hypothesis that officers recruited on the basis of their capability are less prone to violate the discipline of their institution than are those recruited for other reasons. Unfortunately, such data are not available. In their absence, we rely on personal experience of one of the authors (Zubair Nawaz Chattha), which suggests unequivocally that police officers with dubious backgrounds are more likely to be involved in all forms of police misconduct.

Indeed, the past two decades have seen a trend of political inductions in which the basic standards of recruitment were ignored and candidates were inducted by relaxing all rules. The Inspector General of Police in Punjab noted in 1996 that in the previous 5 years an estimated 25,000 police officers had been recruited by way of quotas allotted to politicians—without checking the officers' character or competence for police work (Amnesty International, 1997).

A proposal to insulate police authorities from the negative interference of politicians in internal departmental matters (such as recruitment, training, posting, promotion, and discipline) has been discussed in connection with the upcoming reform package. The government has faced severe opposition from the interest groups in the Civil Service. Nevertheless, according to the new Police Act, police chiefs are given independence to work within the framework of law without any external governmental and political pressures.

The situation with the merit-based recruitment and selection could indeed be changing in the view of recent reforms. One of the authors (Zubair Nawaz Chattha) participated in recruitment tasks in 2001. His experience was that it was possible to independently recruit 500 constables based on the results of official testing, without the interference from the politicians. Furthermore, the military government is now trying to verify the integrity of prospective officers through different intelligence agencies.

In the police system of Pakistan, training is the most deficient area, partly because it is precisely those officers who are sidelined because of their incompetence who are assigned to train others (Nadeem, 1989, p. 124). The candidates who join the police are welcomed into the most depressing environment imaginable: training institutions that lack basic facilities, including water and electricity. The training is outdated and consists of no more than a few drills and lessons based on orally transmitted police culture, and the teaching faculty successfully spread a feeling of pessimism to convince the trainees of the futility of any training in the police. The instructors are mostly busy teaching the recruits how to successfully violate the code of ethics and thus become notorious and successful cops. However, the numerous problems with police training in Pakistan have not gone unnoticed. The training and the problems associated with it were analyzed by a U.K.-sponsored program. Consequently, in 1995 the Central Planning and Training Unit (located within the National Police Academy) designed a new syllabus for police instruction.

Training institutions form the first stage in shaping the police subculture, where standards

**Table 10.1**    Outcomes of Disciplinary Proceedings and Criminal Cases Initiated Against Police Officers From 1996 to 2001

|  | *1996* | *1997* | *1998* | *1999* | *2000* | *2001* |
|---|---|---|---|---|---|---|
| Minor Punishments | | | | | | |
| Reduction in Pay and Other Fines | 841 | 6,532 | 8,047 | 8,171 | 9,013 | 8,161 |
| Dismissal | 388 | 461 | 327 | 477 | 346 | 391 |
| Total Discipline | 1,229 | 6,993 | 8,374 | 8,648 | 9,359 | 8,552 |

SOURCE: Office of the City Police Chief, Lahore.

of occupational socialization are inculcated to form the popularly known "thana culture."[15] Thana culture, traditionally accepted as corrupt, cruel, and incompetent (Chaudhry, 1997, pp. 54-80), has gained notoriety during the more than 50 years of Pakistan's independence from British colonial rule. Police recruits learn through the stories and experiences of their seniors the concept of a "thanedar"[16] (the officer who is in charge of a police station and registers and investigates cases). The product of the training process is a graduate ready to be assimilated into thana culture; that is, a police officer who is unskilled as to how to employ critical thinking and problem-solving techniques in police work and who is prepared to use brutal force.[17]

It is expected that most members of the police force are involved in some type of police misconduct and are thus participating in the code of silence. The stubborn and secretive attitude of police officers stops any outside effort to reform the police or affect police misconduct. While the corrupt practices of the police may be deplorable to the citizens, they accept them because of the convenience of escaping penalization. Consequently, thana culture has become a deviance of common interest involving the police and the citizens.

The criminal justice system, struggling with its own credibility as a successful enforcer of laws and prosecutor of offenders, also provides a reason for police deviance. Police officers, motivated with the realization that the criminal justice system is not capable of punishing criminals and, at the same time, committed to the fighting crime as their primary task, are ready

to punish the criminals themselves (even to the extent of killing them). Thus, it is no exaggeration to state that the "Dirty Harry" phenomenon (Klockars, 1980) thrives in Pakistan.

The latest extrajudicial killings in Pakistan mostly involved organized crime leaders, who have historically been successful in evading the criminal justice system (U.S. Department of State, 1998) and legitimate punishment. This practice of police killing criminals also receives tacit support from those in power, who believe the judicial process to be too expensive and lengthy. Such extrajudicial killings have terminated a few career criminals, but they have also probably resulted in the deaths of many first-time offenders. The police chiefs have been hostage to the wishes of higher authorities to use fake police encounters and terminate hardened criminals whom the criminal justice system could neither convict nor process in a reasonable period of time with reasonable expenses.

Yet another important cause of police misconduct is the failure of both the internal and external accountability processes. Disciplinary records for the City Police of Lahore (see Table 10.1) indicate that disciplinary proceedings were initiated in approximately 8,000 to 9,000 cases each year from 1997 to 2001. Statistically speaking, this amounts to the initiation of a individual cases against one half of the officers in the police force. While it may appear at first glance that the initiation of so many internal processes portrays an impressive account of internal police accountability, the reality, as depicted by the Human Rights Watch and media accounts, is much

**Table 10.2**     Corruption-Related Court Cases From 1996 to 2001

|                               | *1996* | *1997* | *1998* | *1999* | *2000* | *2001* |
|-------------------------------|--------|--------|--------|--------|--------|--------|
| Initiated                     |        |        |        |        |        |        |
| Sentenced  (% initiated)      |        |        |        |        |        |        |
| Prison Sentence (% sentenced) | 7%     | 3%     | 3%     | 1%     | n/a    | n/a    |

SOURCE: Office of the Director General of Anti-Corruption Department of Punjab.

closer to the notion that most of the police officers engage in police misconduct most of the time. Despite the difficulties in obtaining the overall number of court cases (the records are not kept at a central location), the available data indicate that court cases were initiated against very few police officers indeed (see Table 10.2).

Despite the existence of a system of internal[18] and external checks on paper, these have actually been reduced to a minimal, ineffective level. The police leadership, which is often not well developed because of the strength of the police culture, lacks the vision necessary to guide the force toward transformation into a civilized police force intended to serve the people rather than to oppress them.

Furthermore, the police leadership succumbs to undue political interference; as discussed earlier, the decision-making process of the police department is influenced by the politicians, who pursue the police administrators in order to obtain the police postings for new candidates and secure transfers of their favorite police officers to specific assignments (Amnesty International, 1997).[19] The police officers use this outside influence to escape any attempt at effective internal accountability within the department, while the hands of those police administrators willing to address police misconduct are effectively tied.

Every Pakistani government in the past has used the police to suppress opposition parties and thus to achieve their short-term political goals. Consequently, even if they were willing to do so, politicians are left with no moral courage to discipline police officers who are involved in misconduct. Thus, external accountability of police administrators to the elected representatives of the Pakistani government is not only highly ineffective but also extremely problematic.

Obsolete laws are one of the major causes of the degeneration of the police system in Pakistan. The laws were designed by the British colonial rulers to maintain their empire, with little concern for the rights and welfare of the local population. The Police Act of 1861, still applicable in Pakistan, was designed along the lines of the Irish Constabulary Act. At the time, the imperatives for the Irish laws were to suppress the society, with draconian authority entrusted to the law enforcement agencies (Chaudhry, 1997, p. 42). Although in theory colonial rule ended over 50 years ago, today the police in Pakistan still practice law enforcement in a manner similar to that practiced before 1947. Changing times have not convinced local governments to pass laws that would provide the citizens with their rights and effectively shield them from police misconduct. According to the Freedom in the World 1999-2000 survey, the overall level of political rights and civil liberties in Pakistan is rather low, and the country is considered "not free" (*Freedom in the World*, 2000). Even when there are laws that provide citizens with a certain degree of protection from police abuse (such as Section 37 of the Evidence Act, which prohibits the inclusion of confessions obtained through torture), they are rarely applied by the courts.

The frustration and hopelessness of a criminal justice system unable to convict police officers engaging in serious police misconduct is evident from the rulings of different High

Courts in Pakistan on petitions regarding police misconduct ("High Court Asks Police to Be Fearful of God," 2000). For example, a serious incident took place in Sargodha, in which the offenders, who were police officers, were sentenced by the Anti-Terrorist Court[20] judge on charges of faulty investigation and prosecution. These judicial orders to arrest the convicted police officers were defied by the police officers on the spot; rather, the judge was kept hostage for a short while (Human Rights Commission of Pakistan, 1999, p. 55).

Similarly, the press play a minor role in the control of police misconduct because any impact the press may have in affecting public opinion has been neutralized by the overall state censorship of the press. Any news potentially portraying the police in a negative light is generally suppressed by the government. Indeed, Pakistan's score of 26 on the 2002 Freedom House survey (Sussman & Karlekar, 2002) indicates that, compared to other countries, the "degree of political influence over the content of news media" in Pakistan is rather high.

In sum, the utterly ineffective process of accountability does not deter police officers from repeatedly violating the ethical standards of policing and legal rules. The reports of various human rights groups over the past few years suggest that police officers accused of serious police misconduct (even killing people) have escaped unharmed from the accountability process of both the criminal justice system and the internal accountability system.

Since weak departmental supervision also encourages police misconduct, the ineffective supervision in the Pakistani police is another problem. Although the nature of the police job in Pakistan affects the ability of those in charge to provide effective supervision, supervisors in the Pakistani police are at an additional disadvantage: They do not perceive that it is within the realm of their responsibility to regulate the behavior of their subordinates in accordance with the official rules and procedures, and they do not have a guide or manual to follow that has clear statements outlining their duties as supervisors. The consequences of relaxed supervision are clearly visible. For example, many police officers spend long hours on patrol and none of them are asked to write down the details of their patroling activity. Similarly, no analysis is performed of the failures of the police supervisors and administrators to change the conduct of the police officers they supervise. The recent move by the government to collect the names of the most corrupt governmental officials, including police officers—and to force them to end their governmental careers—should be taken as a positive sign. However, rather than officially prosecuting these officials and firing them, the government has decided to force them into early retirement (thus providing them with a pension and full benefits).

Finally, the extent of police misconduct in Pakistan is also related to the lack of resources to provide a suitable salary package and good working conditions for police officers. Like other third world police agencies, the Pakistani police are victims of several types of deprivations, including the lack of stationery, fuel, services of car mechanics, and travel funds, to list but a few of the basic limitations. The allocation of inadequate amounts of money for essential tasks encourages corruption and other types of police misconduct, as it also provides the most frequent justification for corruption and abuse of police authority. Thus, the government's stance in providing scarce resources in fact abets corrupt behavior and the weakening of the internal system of control.

The funds and supplies allocated to the police by the government are unrealistic—for example, there are liters of fuel available but nominal amounts for car repair, which leaves police officers with no choice but to ask the local community to cover their car-related expenses and other costs. However, citizens interacting with the police are mostly victims of crimes, and the police officers' demands for transportation to conduct raids and/or visit the crime scene could well be taken by the victims as a rude gesture, if the victims can afford to cover these costs at all. Therefore, the paucity of funds in policing is bound to compromise the integrity of police officers. Consequently, because of the lack of basic resources to honorably detect, investigate, and prosecute criminal cases, the integrity of the police is relegated.

Low salaries and lack of health care and fulfillment of their basic needs keep police officers depressed and disturbed. The police officers posted in police stations are expected to be on duty or available in case of emergency around the clock. Thus, Pakistani police officers have no formal leave system and suffer from the long ("No Death in Custody," 1999), practically never-ending hours they spend on the job, which leaves them frustrated and prone to use excessive force and abusive language in their interactions with citizens. The officers' level of stress, related to their long hours and low salary, is further exacerbated by the strain of miserable living conditions: Police officers are housed either in the old government quarters or in small houses in the slums.

## EMPIRICAL MEASUREMENT OF OFFICERS' TOLERANCE OF CORRUPTION

The media reports, accounts by international human rights groups, and the Transparency International findings all suggest the existence of a Pakistani police culture that is tolerant of various forms of police misconduct. We took a step forward and sought to measure the extent of this tolerance using a questionnaire that was originally developed by Klockars and Kutnjak Ivkovich (1996) as part of a larger cross-cultural study of police integrity.

The questionnaire, which provides descriptions of 11 hypothetical scenarios, measures the integrity level of the police by examining officers' perceptions of the seriousness of the misconduct in the scenarios, their level of support for disciplinary consequences for the misconduct,[21] and their expressed willingness to report it. The aim of the questionnaire has been to provide descriptions of the scenarios that are

feasible in modern, industrialized societies. While the questionnaire was originally designed with the cross-cultural application in mind (e.g., the stimulus is expressed in relative terms rather than with an absolute monetary value in a particular currency), some scenarios needed to be adjusted to fit the Pakistani circumstances.

In particular, the behavior described in Case 1—a police officer running an off-duty security system business—would be quite unusual in Pakistan. Instead, we substituted for it a police officer running an agency that provides private security guards. Similarly, parties involved in traffic accidents are mostly left to sort things out by themselves. Thus, police officers in Pakistan would not have the opportunity to have a kickback arrangement with an auto repair shop (Case 6). Instead, we used similar behavior that is more realistic given the Pakistani circumstances: "A police officer has a private arrangement with a lawyer to refer persons requiring legal assistance to the lawyer. In exchange for each referral, he receives a payment of 5% of the legal bill from the lawyer."

The misconduct described in Case 7 rests on the assumption that the subordinate reaps the benefits in exchange for providing certain extraordinary services to the supervisor. The original case—the supervisor giving the officer days off during upcoming holidays in exchange for the officer's tuning up his car—is not applicable in Pakistan. Rather, we used what is a more prevalent practice in Pakistan: the use of subordinates for domestic jobs. Finally, Case 9 relies on the proposition that police officers are in charge of checking the bars' closing times. However, since there are no bars in Pakistan, we adjusted the scenario as follows: "A police officer allows a roadside café/tea shop to operate after the legal closing time at 12:00 A.M. He also overlooks the public display of movies on the video, which is not allowed without a valid license. In return, he takes free food and drinks from the owner."

The questionnaires, translated into Urdu, were distributed to police officers in the Lahore City Police. The completed questionnaires were returned by 499 police officers from 16 police stations. With a population of 6.3 million, Lahore is the second largest city in Pakistan and the provincial capital of Pakistan's largest province, Punjab. The city has 76 police stations, out of which one is a "women's police station" dedicated to the prevention and control of crime against women. The police force consists of approximately 16,000 men and 200 women. The majority of the force is composed of line officers (14,000), while approximately one eighth are supervisors (in ranks from Assistant Subinspector to Inspector).

## The Results of the Survey

### The Misconduct as Violations of Rules

Although all the behaviors in the questionnaire constitute violations of official rules, ranging from violations of the penal code to service ordinances (see Table 10.3), only a small percentage of the surveyed police officers report that this is the case. In particular, with the exception of Case 1 (Private Security Service Business), less than 20% of the respondents classify the behavior described in the remaining 10 cases as violations of official rules.

There are several possible reasons, which are not necessarily mutually exclusive, why such a small percentage of police officers report that the described behaviors constitute violations of official rules. First, because of their rather limited education and inadequate training, police officers simply do not have a sufficient level of knowledge of the *official* legal rules. Second, police officers may be replying to a different question than the one we actually asked. While we asked the respondents whether these behaviors violate the *official* rules in their agency, the police officers could have had in mind the *unofficial* rules in the agency. In the agencies in which there is a large discrepancy between the official and unofficial rules (i.e., the rules actually enforced in the agencies), the unofficial rules have a particularly strong tendency to completely overpower the official rules.

### The Seriousness of the Misconduct

When asked to evaluate the seriousness of the misconduct described in the questionnaire, the respondents tended to evaluate most of the misconduct as rather serious, despite the fact that a very small percentage of the respondents actually consider these behaviors to be violations of official agency rules and criminal laws. With the exception of Case 1 (Private Security Service Business), which is consistently evaluated among the least serious cases in the cross-cultural analyses, the surveyed Pakistani police officers as a group estimate that every other case is rather serious: the means for the remaining 10 cases are all above 4.00 on our 5-point scale (see Table 10.4).

There are several explanations for such an extraordinary evaluation of the seriousness of the misconduct in the scenarios. First, it is possible that these outstanding evaluations of seriousness, comparable in their magnitude to those expressed by the Finnish police officers (see Table 6.1 in Chapter 6 of this volume), are part of an overall set of attitudes intolerant of police misconduct held by the surveyed Pakistani police officers. Although possible, this explanation does not seem very likely.

To begin with, Pakistani society, according to the accounts by international organizations,[22] seems to be highly tolerant of corruption, including police corruption. Tolerance of corruption implies that the official rules prohibiting corruption, if they exist at all, are not enforced and that corrupt behavior by government officials (including police officers) is unofficially connived. Such a state of affairs, in which nepotism is a routine part of life, is highly incompatible with a high level of police integrity—the ability to resist any and all temptations of one's office (Klockars, Kutnjak Ivkovich, Harver, & Haberfeld, 1997), including for-gain temptations.

**Table 10.3**    Rule-Violating Aspects of the Behavior Described in the Survey

| Case Number and Description | Is the Behavior in the Case a Violation of Official Rules, and if so, What Rules? | Percentage of Respondents Who Declared Behavior as Rule-Violating |
|---|---|---|
| Case 1 - Private Security Service Business | Yes: Police Act; Section:10, 29 | 27.6% |
| Case 2 - Free Meals and Discounts on Beat | Yes: Police Rules 14:26; Penal Code | 13.6% |
| Case 3 - Bribe From Speeding Motorist | Yes: Anti-Corruption Act | 8.2% |
| Case 4 - Holiday Gifts From Merchants | Yes: Police Rules | 10.0% |
| Case 5 - Crime Scene Theft of Watch | Yes: Penal Code | 9.1% |
| Case 6 - 5% Kickback From Lawyer | Yes: Police Act | 10.9% |
| Case 7 - Supervisor Grants Holiday in Exchange for Domestic Work | Yes: Removal From Service Ordinance | 10.9% |
| Case 8 - Cover-Up of Police DUI Accident | Yes: Penal Code | 12.4% |
| Case 9 - Free Drinks to Ignore Late Café Closing | Yes: Anti-Corruption Act | 9.4% |
| Case 10 - Excessive Force on Car Thief | Yes: Penal Code | 16.7% |
| Case 11 - Theft From Found Wallet | Yes: Penal Code | 9.7% |

Furthermore, assuming that there are no obvious biases in the sample and that the police officers' answers represent a valid description of the level of police integrity in their agencies, the considerable homogeneity of the answers to the questions about rule violation suggest not confusion (indicating, for example, ambiguous rules or uncertainty about the particular set of rules actually enforced) but a clear message (see Table 10.3): The surveyed Pakistani police officers do not recognize these behaviors as violations of official rules. Since official rules do exist and prohibit every behavior described in the questionnaire (see Table 10.3), it is

clear that there is an absence of a strong message that would convey a sincere and serious effort to enforce these official rules. The lack of enforcement, or the perception thereof, creates new, unofficial rules that not only tolerate corruption but also ultimately trump the official rules prohibiting it. Thus, the small percentage of police officers who actually said that a described scenario constitutes rule-violating behavior may have been considering the official, unenforced rules.

Thus, a more realistic explanation for the officers' saying that the misconduct in all the scenarios is very serious could be that the police officers, unaccustomed to participation

**Table 10.4** Police Officer's Views of the Seriousness of the Misconduct, the Discipline It Should and Would Receive, and Officers' Willingness to Report It.

| Case Number and Description | Seriousness | | | | Discipline | | | | | | Willingness to Report | | | |
|---|---|---|---|---|---|---|---|---|---|---|---|---|---|---|
| | Own View | | Most Officers | | Should Receive | | | Would Receive | | | Own View | | Most Officers | |
| | $\bar{x}$ | Rank | $\bar{x}$ | Rank | $\bar{x}$ | Rank | Mode | $\bar{x}$ | Rank | Mode | $\bar{x}$ | Rank | $\bar{x}$ | Rank |
| Case 1 - Private Security System Business | 3.44 | 1 | 3.70 | 1 | 2.59 | 1 | Reduction in Pay | 2.60 | 1 | Reduction in Pay | 2.68 | 11 | 2.78 | 11 |
| Case 2 - Free Meals and Discounts on Beat | 4.29 | 3 | 4.19 | 3 | 2.89 | 3 | Reduction in Pay | 2.80 | 3 | Reduction in Pay | 2.12 | 9 | 2.41 | 9 |
| Case 3 - Bribe From Speeding Motorist | 4.81 | 11 | 4.64 | 11 | 3.32 | 9 | Reduction in Pay | 3.28 | 9 | Reduction in Pay | 1.68 | 4 | 2.13 | 4.5 |
| Case 4 - Holiday Gifts From Merchants | 4.43 | 4 | 4.26 | 4 | 2.98 | 4 | Reduction in Pay | 2.91 | 4 | Reduction in Pay | 1.94 | 8 | 2.35 | 8 |
| Case 5 - Crime Scene Theft of Watch | 4.76 | 9 | 4.58 | 10 | 3.68 | 11 | Reduction in Pay | 3.60 | 11 | Reduction in Pay | 1.57 | 1 | 1.98 | 1 |
| Case 6 - 5% Kickback From Lawyer | 4.55 | 5 | 4.33 | 5 | 3.06 | 6 | Reduction in Pay | 3.01 | 6 | Reduction in Pay | 1.76 | 6 | 2.13 | 4.5 |
| Case 7 - Supervisor Grants Holiday in Exchange for Domestic Work | 4.66 | 7 | 4.38 | 7 | 3.00 | 5 | Reduction in Pay | 2.95 | 5 | Reduction in Pay | 1.85 | 7 | 2.31 | 7 |
| Case 8 - Cover-Up of Police DUI Accident | 4.57 | 6 | 4.35 | 6 | 3.30 | 8 | Reduction in Pay | 3.18 | 8 | Reduction in Pay | 1.68 | 4 | 2.15 | 6 |
| Case 9 - Free Drinks to Ignore Late Bar Closing | 4.74 | 8 | 4.44 | 8 | 3.12 | 7 | Reduction in Pay | 3.06 | 7 | Reduction in Pay | 1.68 | 4 | 2.10 | 6 |
| Case 10 - Excessive Force on Car Thief | 4.10 | 2 | 3.89 | 2 | 2.75 | 2 | Reduction in Pay | 2.66 | 2 | Reduction in Pay | 1.68 | 4 | 2.10 | 3 |
| Case 11 - Theft From Found Wallet | 4.79 | 10 | 4.48 | 9 | 3.61 | 10 | Reduction in Pay | 3.50 | 10 | Reduction in Pay | 1.64 | 2 | 2.06 | 2 |

in scientific studies, are trying to provide answers that they think their immediate supervisors and any police administrators checking or learning about their answers would like to hear. Because it is crucial for Pakistani officers to adhere to the strategy of remaining on good terms with influential supervisors in a society characterized by nepotism, the incentives to cheat when filling out the questionnaire are undoubtedly stronger in Pakistan than they are in a merit-based democratic society (in which the supervisors or administrators may change the environment in the agency in reaction to the aggregate answers provided in the survey). This is especially the case when supervisors, in addition to learning about the aggregate results of the survey, know officers' individual answers and are perceived as at best to be willing only occasionally to breach the guarantees of respondents' anonymity and the confidentiality of their answers. Indeed, an unusually high percentage of the respondents (26.7%) did not provide an answer to the question of whether they answered truthfully, and an additional 9.7% explicitly said that they had lied. However, even if they wanted to cheat on the questionnaire to make it more appealing to the potential answer-checkers, not all the questions are equally easy to cheat on. Furthermore, the consequences of respondents' trying to inflate the answers to fit the presumed expectations are not the same for all the questions, and the difficulty of subsequently checking the questions for accuracy varies across questions. Unlike the questions about the discipline the misconduct should and would receive and the officers' willingness to report the misconduct, the two questions about the misconduct's seriousness have the least far-reaching consequences attached to them (i.e., no direct behavioral implications) and could be more easily defended as the respondents' personal opinions rather than as

(in)accurate descriptions of what goes on in the agency (which supervisors are or should be well aware of). In sum, if the respondents did try to cheat on the questionnaire by inflating their answers to fit whatever the supervisors may have wanted to hear, the two questions about the seriousness of the misconduct would have been the best candidates for such deception. This may explain the respondents' evaluations of all the cases except Case 1 (Private Security Service Business) as very serious.

### The Appropriate and Expected Discipline for the Misconduct

The officers' responses about the appropriate and expected discipline for the misconduct do not reflect the actual level of police integrity in Pakistan and can be perceived as hitting the "middle ground" between lenient and severe discipline. On one hand, although the majority of police officers did classify the misconduct in the scenarios as not rule violating (and thus not requiring punishment), the respondents did not think no discipline either the appropriate or expected punishment for the misconduct (see Table 10.4). On the other hand, while the officers say that almost all of the described forms of misconduct are quite serious (and thus deserving of severe punishment), they did not pick dismissal as either the appropriate or expected discipline for the misconduct (see Table 10.4). Thus, probably under the influence of the impact their answers may have on the actual disciplinary environment via potential changes, the type of both appropriate and expected punishment most frequently selected by the respondents for every case in the questionnaire, regardless of whether it is an acceptance of free drinks and meals or a theft of money from a found wallet, is a reduction in pay, a disciplinary option in the middle of the disciplinary scale.

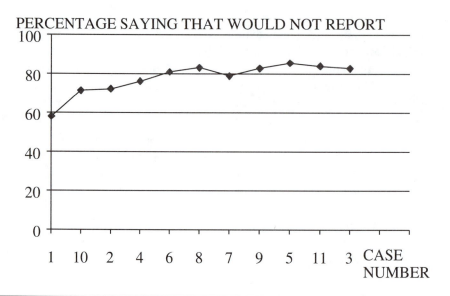

**Figure 10.1**    Percentage of Police Officers Who Say That They Would Not Report the Misconduct, by Case

While such a choice may seem strange at first glance, it actually makes perfect sense once real disciplinary cases are included in the equation: The respondents' choice of the most frequent discipline resembles the most frequent discipline meted out in actual disciplinary cases (see Table 10.1).

*Officers' Willingness to Report the Misconduct*

The answers to the two questions about the officers' willingness to report the misconduct of their colleagues seem to provide the answer to the dilemma regarding what the true extent of police integrity is in Pakistan: Virtually every behavior described in the questionnaire is protected by the code of silence, indicating that the unofficial rules allow corrupt behavior not only to exist but to flourish. In particular, the strong majority of the surveyed police officers (at least 6 out of 10) say that they would not report the misconduct in *any* case in the questionnaire (see Figure 10.1). The percentage of the respondents who would not be willing to

report the misconduct of their colleagues actually reaches 80% or more in the majority of the cases (6 out of 11) (see Figure 10.1).

## CONCLUSION

The daily newspapers in Pakistan abound with stories of police misconduct. These are mostly reports of torture in police stations, with the purpose of getting the alleged criminals to confess to some undetected crime, or stories about fake police encounters to eliminate "undesired" elements of society (Human Rights Commission of Pakistan, 2000, p. 82). The phenomenon of unlawful search, seizure, and arrests seems to be widespread in Pakistan. The raucous police attitude is becoming a norm in Pakistani society, in which the people are increasingly frightened of their own police. Corruption is endemic and pervasive, and it is even unusual for a crime report to be filed before the concerned police officer has been bribed. A police officer, entrusted with the sensitive job of law enforcement, is often involved in registering fake criminal cases and extorting money for overlooking serious criminal cases.

These lapses in professional competence have rendered police officers silent spectators to or participants in the outrageous activities of criminal elements in Pakistani society. The results of our empirical research conducted in one of the Pakistani provinces indicate that the police officers seem to be willing to tolerate police misconduct in silence; the overwhelming majority of our respondents say that they would not report fellow police officers who engage in police corruption.

Police misconduct is brewing in the context of numerous administrative and institutional misadventures that have persisted for a long period of time. The haphazard recruitment process is followed by obsolete training strategies, both of which produce a typical police officer whose behavior further worsens the conduct of the police. Indeed, the recruitment process is far from ideal and has many problems: The standard recruitment procedure is often circumvented in response to the recommendations of influential people in the government. Subsequently, the recruitment procedure is followed by a training period based on an outdated program (the training manual is based on the Police Rules of 1934). The lack of serious determination

by the administration to deal with police misconduct contributes to this bleak situation.

The paucity of resources available to the police is another major area of concern in analyzing the causes of police misconduct. This situation is common in most of the third world law enforcement agencies, which are generally neither efficient nor public-friendly. In Pakistan, the unrealistic allocation of funds in policing makes it less morally deplorable for the police officers to indulge in corrupt practices ("Probe Into Police Corruption," 2000).

The successive governments have been unable to muster the political will to reform the administrative structure of the police departments in Pakistan. The original police laws and rules are almost a century old and require a complete overhaul to provide for the appropriate internal organizational accountability. In the absence of an established political process, an external political check of the Pakistani police is also missing. The judiciary, which is unable to exert its authority due to the fragile political process in domestic affairs, also contributes to the lack of viable external accountability of the police. This apathy has created deterioration in police behavior, which is one of the major causes of the present high levels of police misconduct in Pakistan.

## NOTES

1. Lahore is the provincial capital of Pakistan's most populous province, Punjab.

2. Hafizabad is a district of the central part of Punjab. It is mostly rural and was recently made into a district.

3. A "Division" is an administrative unit of government in Pakistan, which is fairly large and is composed of several districts.

4. A "District" is the administrative unit of a province, which is composed of cities, towns, and villages. It is a large area of 3,000 square kilometers or more.

5. F.I.R. (First Information Report), which can be found in Section 154 of The Pakistan Criminal Procedure Code of 1898, is used to initiate an investigation into a crime. All the criminal proceedings are initiated after the recording of an F.I.R., so its importance cannot be overemphasized. Anyone whose name is mentioned by the complainant in his or her application is accused and can be apprehended by the police without a warrant having been issued by the courts.

6. Under Section 54 of The Pakistan Criminal Procedure Code of 1898, any person involved in a cognizable offense can be arrested without a warrant.

7. Pakistan is ranked 79th of the 91 countries included in the *2001 Corruption Perceptions Index* designed by Transparency International (Transparency International, 2002).

8. Drinking liquor is punishable in Pakistan, per the Prohibition Enforcement of Hadd Order IV of 1979.

9. Although dating is not a crime, it is nevertheless socially embarrassing for the couple.

10. In April of 2000, one of the authors (Zubair Nawaz Chattha) registered a criminal case against a police officer of the Allama Iqbal police station who jumped into a house and robbed the owner of money at gunpoint.

11. As part of an assignment in police headquarters, one of the authors (Zubair Nawaz Chattha) interviewed police officers about their working conditions and related problems. The complaint of internal payoffs, related to the leave system, was repeated by almost all the people interviewed. As a consequence, the police in that particular area designed a procedure whereby all the police officers have a scheduled leave every month (the schedule is announced on the first day of every month).

12. Matriculation is equivalent to 10 years of education in Pakistan.

13. An F.A. is equivalent to 12 years of education in Pakistan.

14. In 1995, two Members of National Assembly of Pakistan got their close relatives inducted into the police by a direct notification of Prime Minister Benazir Bhutto. The Prime Minister used the powers of Chief Executive to relax all the rules and proceed with the induction. These officers completed their training with one of the authors in Islamabad.

15. *Thana* is the word used for "police station" in the local Punjabi language. The term "thana culture" was repeatedly used by the former Chief Minister of Punjab, Shahaz Sharif, to both signify the deteriorated police culture and promise to reform it.

16. *Thanedar* is a Punjabi term used to depict someone who is notorious, discourteous, cruel, and powerful.

17. A case study could be the behavior of police officers trained at the Elite School of Training in Lahore. One of the authors (Zubair Nawaz Chattha) has personally encountered situations in which police officers from traditional training institutes and from the Elite School, who are performing the same duty side by side, demonstrate different levels of integrity. For example, a traditional officer would accept drinks even from criminals in custody or their relatives, but the Elite-trained officer typically would firmly refuse any such offers.

18. The anticorruption department in each province has the responsibility for conducting the inquiry into, investigating, and prosecuting all corruption cases initiated on the basis of complaints in provincial departments.

19. The Inspector General of Police in Punjab noted in 1996 that in the previous 5 years an estimated 25,000 police officers had been recruited by way of quotas allotted to politicians (Amnesty International, 1997).

20. The Anti-Terrorist Act of 1998 established special courts that are empowered to hear serious and heinous cases regarding events that are causing terror in Pakistani society. The judges are provided with special allowances and are given police protection. A judge of the Anti-Terrorist Court holds a status equivalent to that of a Judge of the High Court (the Apex Court of a Province).

21. The disciplinary options used in the questionnaires distributed in Pakistan were as follows: 1. none; 2. censure; 3. stoppage of yearly increments; 4. reduction in pay; 5. reduction in rank; and 6. dismissal.

22. See the Transparency International Corruption Perceptions Index, which is available at http://www.transparency.org/cpi/2001/cpi2001.htm#cpi.

## REFERENCES

Amnesty International. (1996). *Pakistan—The death penalty.* Retrieved from http://www.web.amnesty.org/ai.nsf/index/ASA330101996.

Amnesty International. (1997). *Pakistan: A time to take human rights seriously.* Country Report 1997. Retrieved from http://www.web.amnesty.org/ai.nsf/index/ASA330121997.

Brenner, R. N., & Kravitz, M. (1979). *A community concern: Police use of deadly force.*

Chaudhry, M. A. K. (1997). *Policing in Pakistan.* New York: Vanguard.

*The Evidence Act of 1984.*

Freedom in the World 1999-2000. (2000). Retrieved from http://www.freedom-house. org/ratings/index.htm.

Ghayur, B. A. (1994). Jurm Jail aur Police, 250–275.

Ghosh, S. K. (1993). Torture and Rape in Police Custody, 29-33.

High Court Asks Police to Be Fearful of God. (2000, December 9). *Jang* (National Urdu Newspaper of Pakistan)

Human Rights Commission of Pakistan. (1999). *State of Human Rights in 1998.* Pakistan: Author.

Human Rights Commission of Pakistan. (2000). *State of Human Rights in 1999.* Pakistan: Author.

Khan, A. A. (2000). *The defense journal.*

Klockars, C. B. (1980). The Dirty Harry. *The Annals, 452,* 33-47.

Klockars, C. B., Kutnjak Ivkovich, S., Harver, W. E., & Haberfeld, M. R. (1997). *The measurement of police integrity.* Final Report Submitted to the National Institute of Justice, Washington, DC.

Kornblum, A. K. (1976). *The moral hazards.* Lexington, MA: Lexington Books.

Kutnjak Ivkovich, S., & Klockars, C. B. (1996, March). *Police perceptions of disciplinary fairness and the formation of the code of silence.* Paper presented at the annual meeting of the Academy of Criminal Justice Sciences, Las Vegas, Nevada.

Mohammad, F. (2001). *Torture, murder, confession and hegemony: A case study of Pakistan.* Retrieved from http://www.ftss.ilstu.edu/injustice/issue2/1confess.html#_ftnref3visited 2001.

Muttahida man dies in mysterious circumstances. (1999, January 29). *DAWN/The News International, Karachi.*

Nadeem, A. H. (1989). *The Punjab police in a comparative perspective.*

No death in custody from now. (1999, December 15). *Dawn/The News International, Karachi.*

The Pakistan Criminal Procedure Code of 1898.

Probe Into Police Corruption Ordered. (2000, July 27). *The Jang.* Retrieved from http://www.jang.com.pk/thenews/ju12000-daily/27-7-2000/metro/k10.htm.

Rodley, N. S. (1996). *Question of the human rights of all the persons subjected to any form of detention or imprisonment, in particular: torture and other cruel, inhuman or degrading punishment.* New York: United Nations Commission on Human Rights.

Roebuck, J. B., & Barker, T. (1974). A typology of police corruption. *Social Problems, 21,* 423.

Sussman, L. R., & Karlekar, K. D. (2002). *The Annual Survey of Press Freedom 2002.* New York: Freedom House. Retrieved from http://www.freedom-house.org/research/pressurvey.htm.

Transparency International (2002). *2001 Corruption Perceptions Index.* Available at http://www.transparency.org/cpi/2001/cpi2001.htm#cpi.

U.S. Department of State. (1998). *Country Reports on Human Rights Practices.* Retrieved from http://www.state.gov/www/global/human_rights/1998_hrp_report/pakistan.html.

U.S. Department of State. (1999a). *Country Reports on Human Rights Practices.* Retrieved from http://www.state.gov/www/global/human_rights/1998_hrp_report/pakistan.html.

U.S. Department of State. (1999b). *Pakistan Country Report.* Human Rights Practices for 1998. Washington, DC: Author.

CHAPTER 11

# The Heritage of Police Misconduct
## The Case of the Polish Police

Maria R. Haberfeld

## INTRODUCTION

Police officers' acceptance of material gains and other abuses of the rights of their office is a phenomenon as old as the documented history of police forces around the world. It is safe to assume that police misconduct is present in any and every force around the world. What differs from place to place, however, is the level or degree of such behaviors and the contextual history and response or reaction to this phenomenon. This chapter looks at a police force that has undergone a major transformation during the last decade, from a communist to a democratic form of law enforcement. The transformation, no matter how dramatic on paper, has yielded very little actual difference—police performance in Poland is no closer to the desired goal of effective and professional policing than it was a decade ago. The police force appears to be locked into its less-than-favorable image, a label that has followed its traditions through the last 200 years, during the times of partitions, the Communist regime and, finally, the transformation period.

Allegations of police officers' misconduct, lack of effectiveness, and involvement in full-fledged corruption—even going so far as cooperation with organized crime groups—are part of the daily struggle in the transformation process.

External and internal circumstances and pressures contribute to and continue to halt the process of changing the police in Poland into a democratic and professional police force. These processes are described and analyzed in this chapter through the historical developments in Poland over the last two centuries and contrasted with some empirical data, gathered by the author and others, including events portrayed by the media and the findings made public by the police organization itself. The results of a survey distributed to 2,000 sworn officers in 1997 are presented here. These data represent the first and (to this date) only data available to use in discussing the perceptions of integrity of Polish police officers in the post-Communist era. This paucity of data is unfortunate. My ongoing research on the transformation process of the Polish police has led me to conclude that it is imperative that thorough research be conducted to follow up the findings from the 1997 survey, as the focus group discussions during the years 1999 to 2001 portrayed a slightly different picture of police integrity.

The main goal of this chapter is to present misconduct from an unusual perspective, one that views it not necessarily as an aberration but, rather, as a normative inclination in the context of a particular society at a particular time. This normative inclination differs from the one that excludes misconduct, which can be observed in police forces around the world, by being a clear extension of a long history in Poland during which what we think of as misconduct was actually perceived as acceptable conduct.

## AN OVERVIEW OF HISTORICAL DEVELOPMENTS IN POLAND DURING THE LAST TWO CENTURIES

In order to understand the phenomenon of corruption within the Polish police in the proper context, one has to look at the history of the country, going as far back as the 18th century. The nature of policing in any country is directly related to its history, and no analysis can be adequately performed without an appreciation of the social, economic, demographic, and political factors that have shaped a given state.

In the case of Poland, it is not only the more recent history that should be analyzed but also the developments during the last 200 years that have clearly contributed, in varying degrees, to the subculture and the conduct of its police force. Since 1772, Poland has been an independent and sovereign country only for 33 years, from 1918 to 1939 and from the end of 1989 until today. For about 200 years Poland was occupied by various countries and enjoyed freedom and independence only for about 30 years. Historically,

these 200 years can be divided into a number of periods. The so-called First Partition (1772), during the 18th century, was when the Kingdom of Poland was surrounded by three empires and was forced, without fighting, to give up parts of its territory. The Second Partition, which took place at the end of the 18th century (1792 to 1793), was when Prussia obtained 58,000 square kilometers and Russia 250,000 square kilometers from Poland. This was followed by the Third Partition of the Kingdom of Poland, which took place in 1793, when all the rest of its territory and population fell under foreign rule of Prussia, Russia, and Austria (Gieysztor, 1968).

Thus, with few exceptions (e.g., during Napoleon's rule from 1807 to 1812), for almost 150 years the population of Poland was under the foreign rule of the three empires. Those states, by and large, ruled through imposing severe economic sanctions and the repression of Polish nationalism. It is, therefore, understandable that the police force that represented the occupying states was bitterly hated by the Poles for almost 150 years of its existence. Any type of cooperation with the occupying force was almost always rejected by the majority of patriotic Poles. On the other hand, any type of subversive behavior against the occupying forces, including of course the police force, was always received with the great support and admiration of the public.

The second significant period in the development of the attitudes of the police and toward the police took place during WWII. This period (from September 1, 1939, to May 8, 1945) included the Nazi occupation, as well as the Soviet occupation from 1939 through 1941. The police force was divided between two territories. Part of Poland was annexed to the Third Reich. This part was subject to the operations of the German police. The other part, about one third of the former Poland, was under German occupation and subject to the German administrative order. Under this order, the police force (called "the dark blue police") essentially consisted of the former Polish police under the jurisdiction of the German police. It was in charge of law and order in the occupied territories. For the Poles, who fought bravely against the occupying forces, it was quite a shock to see, on a daily basis, their former police force (wearing the same dark blue uniforms, but without the Polish national symbol) protecting and serving the occupying forces. Not only were the police protecting and serving the occupying forces, they were doing so with zeal, frequently "hunting" Polish underground fighters and Polish Jews and delivering them to the Germans, at whose hands they faced certain death. There were, of course, exceptions to the rule, such as when police officers cooperated with the underground fighters, but these were few and far between. It is no wonder that this period is marked by an extremely grim view of the police officer, one that did not contribute to a positive relationship between the police and the public. In the territories occupied by the Soviets, almost all the Polish police officers were imprisoned and sent to the infamous death camp in Katyn, where they were all executed, together with Polish army officers who were taken by the Soviets as prisoners of war.

In the territories that were annexed to the Soviet Union, in 1939 to 1941, the Soviet militia took charge of law enforcement, supplemented by some local supporters, none of them of Polish decent. This militia cooperated closely with the NKVD (the Soviet political police) in an attempt to get rid of Polish underground organizations, and it helped send people to exile in Siberia. During 1939 to 1945, based on an order from the exiled Polish government, located in London, a unit called the Safety Corps was established in the part of Poland occupied by the Nazis. It was supposed to provide some sort of a baseline for the Polish police, in case Poland got freed from the occupation. However, Poland was freed by the Red Army, which did not recognize the legitimacy of this unit and imprisoned all its known members (Korbonski, 1990).

The third significant period—and probably the period of greatest integrity—of the Polish police was during the Communist reign. This period, which lasted for almost 45 years, from July of 1944 to June of 1989, was relatively long and defined Poland as a country that was partially sovereign, partially independent, and mostly under the omnipresent control of the Soviet Union. Over the years, the socioeconomic and political environments varied. However, there was one constant: the police-community relationships were always antagonistic, regardless of the particular situation.

During all those years, the majority of the Polish citizens were opposed to the so-called socialist system of government of the nation. It really was a communist regime, despite some important differences between the one instituted in the Soviet Union and the one practiced in Poland. The basis of the conflict was that the majority of the population was in some type of indirect or direct opposition to the governing system, and the police were a tool of the government. This conflict was of a rather permanent nature. Of course, the Polish police, or rather the Polish militia, at least in theory, was supposed to act in the interest of the community. In its official and formal function, this law enforcement organ did not differ much from its democratic counterparts. It was supposed to provide safety and security by fighting crime and preserving order. In practice, however, for the average citizen the militiaman was just another symbol of the hated political system (Grabowski, 2000).

The governing body, fully aware of the antigovernment sentiment, amassed quite an impressive internal security system to fight the "enemy within" and, in essence, to protect its power. One of the pillars of this system was the political police, also known as the Security Bureau. At the height of its strength, it was composed of over 50,000 officers. In addition, the Bureau also had two military formations, and together with these formations the number of security and military officers totaled over 100,000 (Jaworski, 1984). The second pillar of the "people's government" was the Citizens Militia (MO) or criminal police. Similar to the Security Bureau, it was structured and deployed around the country. Its numbers varied from 50,000 at its inception to 100,000 in later years. (Compare this with pre-WWII Poland, with more or less the same population, which had about 35,000 police officers, including the political police.)

All the ranks within the militia, from the commanding officer of a station on up, were part of the Communist party. This system was put in place to secure all the ranking positions within the police for people who were approved by the Communist party. The Chief of the Police was an appointee of the highest organ within the party, the PolitBureau, or the Political Bureau. In other words, it was subject to the heads of the Communist party, who decided on the nominations and promotions. The professional qualifications of the ranking militia officers were of secondary importance, as their careers within the militia primarily depended on the degree of their loyalty and submissiveness to the party and on their having the "right" personal background (Sadykiewicz, 1989).

Since everything, or almost everything, during those times belonged to the government (including factories, shops, means of communications, transportations, and so on), the government, or rather the Communist party, was in charge of all the decision-making processes, from establishing the price of parsley to the distribution of steel. It was considered to be quite patriotic to act against this governing body.

One of these patriotic activities included plain theft of government property, from stealing light bulbs to car parts. What encouraged and contributed greatly to these illicit behaviors was a very low standard of living and permanent shortage of the most basis products available for sale. Over the years, this quite prevalent theft of products from various plants and factories caused tremendous losses to the country's economy. To counter these losses, new legislation was introduced in the 1950s, and the penalties for theft of government property reached unprecedented heights. For example, theft of a bicycle from a private person was sanctioned with a fine and, usually, a suspended prison sentence of up to 6 months; the same crime committed against a government-owned bicycle carried 5 years of mandatory imprisonment (The Polish Penal Code, 1957).

Of course, given that the first line of defense against theft was the militia, which arrested the culprits, the popularity of law enforcement deteriorated even further. The decade from 1989 to 1999 was marked with many far-reaching changes. Poland became an independent country, with full membership in NATO, while aggressively applying for membership in the European Union. The church regained its powerful stance and many post-Communist, democratically oriented parties emerged.

A new constitution, introduced in 1997, validated all the changes that had been instituted after 1989. Among them were the following:

Separation of power of the legislative, administrative, and judicial branches of government

Democratic elections to the Parliament and the self-governing bodies

Political pluralism

Freedom of speech

Freedom of political affiliation

Freedom to unionize

Democratization of uniformed services, including security, police, and armed forces

The political system and individual freedoms in today's Poland do not differ from those in any of the established democracies in Western Europe. However, this statement has its functional and dysfunctional sides. The rise in crime in contemporary Poland offers myriad temptations for the newly transformed, understaffed, and underpaid police, a theme that will be briefly discussed following a description of the Polish police and the structural and political environment in which they operate.

## THE POLISH NATIONAL POLICE

The Polish police force is a national force, comprised of about 100,000 sworn officers. Since 1990, the Polish Police Service has been undergoing an intensive process of staff changes. During the period from 1990 to 1996, 46% of the staff was replaced. A need for the effective, fast, and methodologically sound training of the new police staff became paramount to the force's successful transformation from the Communist militia (of until 1989) to a newly established police force (of 1990 on) based on democratic principles of government (Haberfeld, 1997).

Since January of 1999, the Polish Police Service has been operating under a new structure, reflecting the responsibilities and hierarchical relations provided for under the relevant statutes passed by the Sejm (the Polish Parliament). The Polish Police Service is composed of three main types of forces: criminal, preventive, and organizational (logistics and technical support). Under the General Headquarters of Police there are 16 district headquarters (Voivodeship), 1 metropolitan police headquarters, 263 county headquarters (Powiat), 65 municipal headquarters, and 1,793 police stations, the numbers of which change as

some are liquidated or consolidated from time to time (Haberfeld & Walancik, 1999).

On January 1, 1999, the Polish Police Service, facing growing criticism of its performance, introduced a new organizational structure, which differed significantly from the one introduced at its inception in 1990. The new force was to be divided into 16 Voivodeships or province commands, 329 district commands, and 2,000 police stations. This new structure was supposed to reflect the administrative division of the local government, but it was primarily introduced to bring police officers closer to the public. More police officers were to be deployed to the districts and the police stations, and more police officers were to be allocated to work on the streets.

According to the Chief, General Jan Michna, the new goal of the force was "to become a tool in the hands of the public." Commanding officers, for both provinces and districts, were to be elected through a contest. Local politicians would have their input into the nomination, both at the province and district levels, through a joint decision-making process with the Chief of Police. A revolutionary concept was introduced in the budget area. Until then, the budget allocated for the police had come from the central government directly to headquarters, and through headquarters was allocated to specific forces throughout the country. Beginning in 2000, the general headquarters was to be allocated a budget sufficient for its operations only.

The Voivodeships were to receive their funding from the heads of the Voivodeships (the Voivodeships were to receive adequate amounts secured for the operations of the police units, based on the assessment received from the Chief of Police; this money was to come from the state budget). The district commands were to get the money from heads of the districts in the form of "goal donations." The money was to be under the public's control, since both Voivodeship and district commands would be accountable for budget allocations to the heads of the respective areas. The self-governing councils were vested with a significant input into police planning and operations (Haberfeld & Walancik, 1999). In 2000 through 2001, the implementation of these concepts met with varying degrees of success, and it became quite clear that the pressure exercised on the police by local governing bodies did not contribute to effective policing or to the elimination of integrity-related problems (Haberfeld, 2001b). But in order to put the problems, which the police force in Poland faces daily, into the right context, a look at the crime situation in Poland is necessary.

## CRIME IN CONTEMPORARY POLAND

A comparison of the level of crime in Poland prior to 1989 to the situation after the transformation to the new, democratic form of government reveals a number of very significant changes in the pattern of criminal behavior. To begin with, certain types of behavior were either decriminalized or, to the contrary, actually gained the label of deviance. Some categories of illicit behavior decreased significantly, and others almost disappeared. Some newly labeled criminal activities that were previously practically unknown emerged as a new category, presenting a serious threat to the security of the country.

Recent data show an almost catastrophic rise in crime. In 1999, 1,121,000 crimes were recorded, in comparison to 1989; this is a rise of almost 105%. The law enforcement agencies have been able to solve about 45% of the cases. What will, therefore, present the biggest danger to the Polish society in the near future? According to media reports:

- Drug trafficking, especially cocaine coming from South America Expansion of organized crime groups, specifically Asian and Russian

- Concentration of organized crime groups in smaller cities and border areas, which will evolve into control over local social and economic life
- Cross-fertilization of traditional criminal activities and white collar crime
- In "traditional" crime activities an increase in burglaries, car theft, bank robberies, etc. (Jachowicz, 2000)

Crimes that are burdensome mostly for the average citizen are steadily increasing. Those crimes involve robbery, burglary, drugs, car theft, and the like, and they are increasing in a rather alarming manner, placing a tremendous and unprecedented burden on local law enforcement. Economic crime is blooming as well. With the onset of the new government system at the beginning of the 1990s, the variety of economic crime was not so spectacular and included primarily bank-related fraud, tax evasion, and the corruption of government employees. With time, increasing sophistication in this area has become noticeable. Nowadays, the crime catalogue is supplemented with new types and categories of crime, which include, among others, fraudulent use of credit cards, computer crime, and falsification of documents related primarily to stock and bonds.

The police force, in a continuous mode of being understaffed and underpaid, does not have the tools to counter this crime avalanche effectively. What follows is their unsurprising involvement in various forms of misconduct, as part of the historically normative and presently reinforced modes of adaptation to unfavorable socioeconomic and political circumstances.

## THE PROBLEM OF THE PERCEPTION OF CORRUPTION AS NORMATIVE BEHAVIOR

According to the World Bank Report, Poland is one of the more corrupt countries in the world. It is estimated that corruption, in its various forms, is steadily on the rise in many of its government institutions ("Polska Przesiaknieta Korupcja," 2000). In the eyes of the public, corruption is an established phenomenon and an integral part of daily life. Of the surveyed population, 71% feel that the phenomenon of corruption has intensified under the new, coalition-based government. Some of the most corrupt areas are the licensing units of the government. Those units, responsible for issuing thousands of documents necessary to run businesses and other enterprises, are alleged to be more criminogenic than any other entity (Kaleta, 2000). One of the areas related to police organization are the self-governing bodies; a form of a decentralized governmental structure. These local governments, which control almost all the facets of public life, are extremely corrupt and presumed to be even more corrupt than the centralized government agencies.

Kaleta, a well-known economist, views the effectiveness of the police force as one of the major tools in the fight against corruption (Kaleta, 2000). However, allegations of corruption are also directed at law enforcement. Most frequently, the traffic police and local police headquarters are cited as the main culprits. Until quite recently, one form of misconduct was almost legal: the public's sponsorship of local police departments. Because the budget situation of the police force is less than adequate, instances of donating equipment, free renovations of police quarters, and other "benefits" became the norm rather than the exception. Some of the departments involved included large city departments like Poznan, Warsaw, and Gdansk. In some instances, almost the entire police staff was dismissed, like the one in the city of Poznan, following accusations of their having taken part in the corruptive practices outlined above and received the generous donations.

The public is under the impression that the police are a highly corrupt institution. In a recent survey conducted by the Center for Research of Public Opinion, respondents rate the Polish police as the second most corrupt government institution (Domagala, 2000). One of the more frequent and ongoing debates related to the corrupt practices of the police involves the credibility of crime statistics. Andrzej Siemiaszko (2000), director of a Warsaw research institute, Delivery of Justice, claims that the Polish police are unaware of about three quarters of the crimes that are actually committed, including over 80% of pickpocketing, 60% of battery, 50% of car thefts, and 45% of burglaries, a fact that is in itself not necessarily surprising, as in the United States it is estimated that less than 50% of all crimes committed are not reported to the police (Wroblewski & Hess, 2003). Consumer crime is an even less represented phenomenon in Polish crime statistics—since only about 1% of the victims complain about the violations, the dark figures of crime in that area approach 100%. Siemiaszko does not dispute the crime statistics presented by the police; his claim is related to police officers' source of knowledge. Their chief source of information is the victim, and the picture painted by the police portrays just a fraction of the actual crime. According to his research, the main reason for the low number of complaints to the police is the public's lack of faith in the effectiveness of the police.

While conducting my research in Poland, I talked to a number of crime victims who were very adamant in their unwillingness to report crime. They, too, cited lack of police effectiveness as the main reason for their decision not to complain. On the other hand, some ranking police officers strongly denied the conclusions reached by Siemiaszko, and it was quite obvious that his findings were challenged by the police organization. Although, in general terms, one should not equate lack of police effectiveness with corruption, in the case of the Polish police there seems to be a correlation between the two, at least from the perspective of the public. The lack of effectiveness is perceived as a direct outcome of some type of involvement with the criminal element and/or the lack of desire to challenge the offenders (Haberfeld, 2001b).

There is an additional interesting phenomenon that contributes to a doubtful view of the official statistics. This phenomenon, called "complaints received but not accepted," is quite ubiquitous. Sometimes a victim will express the desire to sign a complaint, but the police will persuade him or her not to do so. This is especially common in cases where there is no direct knowledge of the suspect and the chances for clearing the case are minimal to nonexistent. Since the effectiveness of a given police station is measured, primarily, by the number of crimes committed and cleared, it is rather obvious what motivation lies behind the police's discouragement of such complaints. Cases of falsification of crime statistics are not a new or recent trend. One of the most infamous cases took place in the city of Debica, where police officers used to convince victims not to report crimes because the chances of finding the perpetrators were minimal. Informal instructions existed explaining which crimes should not be reported and in what circumstances. Officers who opposed this illicit subculture were ostracized and punished in other ways. As a result, between 1992 and 1996, about 1,000 crimes went unrecorded in Debica and Debica's police department was the best in its district as far as crime clearance was concern. This procedure was finally discovered by some external sources and 10 officers were indicted (Siemiaszko, 2000). Similar situations can be found in many other police stations in Poland. In 1998, the Internal Affairs Bureau of the Polish Police audited 335 police stations across Poland and found some type of manipulation of the crime statistics in 65 of the stations under review (Domagala, 2000).

Daszkiewicz (2000) analyzed crime clearance rates in Poland from 1990 to 1997. He has stated that crime clearance was about 40% in 1990 and about 54.4% in 1996, but that it declined again in 1997 to 53.5%. Therefore, about 50% of the crimes were not solved and/or cleared and the perpetrators remained at large. Nonetheless, it is still doubtful that those figures are representative of the true numbers, given the preoccupation with the manipulation of crime statistics and the ill-defined laws that do not criminalize certain offenses, which would otherwise be included in the annual crime report. How, therefore, can police misconduct be addressed in Poland? The following section addresses a number of control mechanisms available to the citizens and the police.

## FORMS OF EXTERNAL AND INTERNAL CONTROL OVER THE POLISH POLICE

To enable me to fully embrace the extent to which various forms of external and internal control over the Polish police are needed, I was told the following joke by a participant in one of the focus groups I conducted during a recent visit to Poland (Haberfeld, 2001b):

*Two traffic patrol officers are trying to come up with an idea for a birthday gift for one of their colleagues. Let's buy him a Mercedes Benz, says one. He already has one, replies the other. Well, then let's buy him a villa by the sea. Already has one, comes the response. OK then, let's leave him on patrol by himself during the forthcoming weekend. Oh, no! protests the other. He doesn't deserve such a huge gift.*

The truth is that the traffic police are the police officers most frequently faced with

**Table 11.1** Misconduct in the Polish Police From 1993 to 2000

| | 1993 | 1994 | 1995 | 1996 | 1997 | 1998 | 1999 | 2000 |
|---|---|---|---|---|---|---|---|---|
| Number of Violations or Crimes | 6,027 | 5,945 | 6,397 | 6,661 | 7,045 | 4828 | 3,915 | 5,255 |
| Number of Officers Punished | 4,850 | 4753 | 4,661 | 4,891 | 4,757 | 2547 | 2,244 | 2,838 |
| Number of Officers Dismissed From the Force | 493 | 408 | 259 | 336 | 288 | 172 | 197 | 295 |

SOURCE: Retrieved April 2, 2001, from www.kgp.gov.pl.

accusations of corrupt behavior, since until very recently the traffic officer played the triple role of prosecutor, judge, and collection agent. The officer, based on his or her own discretion, decided what type of traffic violation had been committed, decided on the amount of the fine, and collected the fine, in cash, as checks and credit cards were not considered an acceptable form of payment. This situation presented a wide range of opportunities for misconduct, especially since it allowed the officer to drop the formal charges and receive a bribe instead. During one of my visits to Poland (in 2000), I was told by a number of people who participated in my focus groups that if a person stopped by the police did not offer to pay a bribe and was willing to get the ticket and pay the fine, the officer offered, on his own initiative, a simple alternative: pay half of the fine and leave without the ticket (Haberfeld, 2000).

However, new legislation and technology have come to the rescue recently. Cameras have been installed in a number of police cars, and entire shifts have been recorded on tape and the tapes kept as possible evidence in allegations of misconduct. Also, a new law has been introduced to replace the on-the-spot collection of fines; since 2001, the fines have been paid by check or credit card, as it is done in the United States (see www.trybuna.com.pl for August 2, 2001). It remains to be seen whether the Polish police can afford to mount electronic cameras in each of their patrol cars and whether the new legislation will significantly eliminate the

acute problem of police corruption. Meanwhile, the budget for the police does not reflect any of the major changes required to allow for such expensive equipment, and police officers' salaries remain extremely low and their temptation extremely great.

Police misconduct, however, is not found just within the traffic police. As already discussed, it appears to be especially prevalent with regard to citizens' complaints. The official statistics on police misconduct are released by police headquarters (see www.kgp.gov.pl for April 21, 2001, p. 11), but the interpretation of the data is highly problematic due to the way the data are presented (see Table 11.1).

This table was compiled by the Central Bureau of Investigations, known by its Polish acronym as the CBS, a unit of the central police headquarters that was established on January 1, 1998, and is modeled after the American Federal Bureau of Investigation (FBI). The CBS is mandated to investigate the most serious types of crimes, including various forms of corruption. The CBS is directly accountable to one of the deputy chiefs of the police. It is fully independent and is not accountable to any local and regional police headquarters of self-governing bodies. In addition, this unit was reinforced by a new milestone in the war against corruption when a new type of unit was established (within the structure of the Warsaw headquarters), also in January of 1998, as the equivalent of the Internal Affairs Bureau in the United States. These newly created units can be found not only at the central headquarters but also at the regional headquarters. The units are accountable to the Deputy Chief at the central headquarters.

During 2001 and 2002, those units did not produce any official data about police misconduct; therefore Table 11.1 is the only source of information for possible interpretation of the degree of misconduct present within the Polish police force. However, as already mentioned, these data are problematic in and of themselves. First, the table does not differentiate between different types of misconduct. Second, it does not provide any specific information about what kind of discipline the officers received for the misconduct. The word *punished* is too vague for interpretation. There is no information about the types of sanctions imposed, which of course correlates with the fact that we don't have any information about the type and/or seriousness of the violations. Also, the total number of sanctions added to the number of dismissals from the force do not match the number of violations; therefore, we do not know how many officers were involved in the cases. In addition, the overall number of violations, varying by year from almost 4,000 to slightly above 7,000 for a police force of over 100,000 officers, appears to be quite low and does not reflect recent research findings (Haberfeld, 2000, 2001a, b). In any event, at least there is a perceptual satisfaction that represents a limited but nevertheless important step in creating an environment of integrity. Finally, one can complain against any police misconduct to a higher office within the police structure—for example, one may complain to the central headquarters about someone in regional headquarters.

This overview of the internal mechanisms of control of the police cannot be complete without mentioning the powerful self-governing bodies. These bodies by law have so much input into police work that they qualify as an internal rather than external

mechanisms of control. Unfortunately, on the local level it is a well-known "secret" that these self-governing bodies represent the most corrupt forms of government. The situation varies by jurisdiction and locality, but overall it can be said that despite the ability of the self-governing bodies to serve as controllers of corruption, they are corrupters rather than guardians of integrity.

There are two mechanisms of external control. First, there is the office of the Ombudsman, known by the Polish acronym as the RPO, which was established in the early 1980s during the last years of the Communist regime. The RPO is a position elected by the Sejm (the Polish parliament) and is accountable only to the Sejm. It does not have any enforcement or control powers and acts only on behalf of an institution or an individual that approaches its office. It is the duty of the Ombudsman to present all the findings from the investigation to all the legislative, judicial, and enforcement bodies. Within the structure of the RPO's office there is a special unit dedicated to the investigation of complaints against the uniformed services, which include the police forces. The other mechanism of control is the office of Attorney General and its local offices. By law, the office of Attorney General has the authority to investigate complaints against the police (Haberfeld, 2001b).

There is yet another form of external control that is informal but not less powerful than the more formal control mechanisms. It is the fourth mechanism of control (after the self-governing bodies, the police, and the office of the Ombudsman), and it is represented by the Polish media. The influence of the media is extremely powerful, especially the influence of daily and weekly newspapers such as the *Rzeczpospolita, Gazeta Wyborcz, Wprost, Nie,* and *Polityka.*

The press have unveiled many instances of police corruption, including cooperation with organized crime groups in three major cities—Poznan, Lodz, and Gdansk. As a result of these discoveries, many high-ranking police officers have been dismissed from the force and structural changes have been made. In Poznan, the entire commanding structure of the local force was replaced and dismissed. Therefore, quite frequently victims of police misconduct, instead of complaining to the police or the Ombudsman or the Attorney General's office, go directly to the press, hoping (for good reason) that their grievances will be addressed in a much more effective way (Walancik & Haberfeld, 2001).

Given this overview of the situation in Poland, it is especially interesting to contrast the aforementioned depiction of issues related to police integrity with actual empirical data. The validity of the instrument used in this survey can be further analyzed by comparing the statistical results with those of other environments and with testimonial evidence.

## POLICE INTEGRITY IN POLAND?

We surveyed this force in 1997, distributing 2,000 questionnaires in six major districts and collecting the data within a week as part of a larger study. To our great surprise we encountered a tremendous degree of cooperation, despite the fact that this was the first national study of the newly restructured force (Klockars, Kutnjak Ivkovich, Harver, & Haberfeld, 1997). To my knowledge it is the only survey of its type formally distributed to the Polish Police by an external research group. The force is surveyed internally from time to time by some ambitious and integrity-oriented commanding officers; however, no official statistics are available as to the findings of such surveys. The only officially available data are the statistics on police misconduct published by the Polish police headquarters, the validity of which was discussed in the preceding section. Therefore, the data presented here represent the only empirical evidence available for the analysis of the level of integrity of the Polish police.

The survey instrument, used previously in the United States and Croatia by Klockars and colleagues (1997) (see Exhibit 1.1 in Chapter 1 of this volume), was slightly modified to fit the reality of life in Poland. For example, the scenario about a bar open after legal closing hours had to be modified to one about serving alcohol to minors, since in Poland the closing hours for a bar are not clearly defined. The discipline options were modified slightly as well, based on the discipline sanctions prevalent in the Polish police; however, those modifications were strictly technical and, overall, did not differ from the American sample in their degree of significance.

### The Polish Police Officer Sample

As part of the attempt to make the police force responsive to new and changing social conditions, and to eliminate former collaborators with the Security Bureau from the new democratic force, during the first months of its transformation many commissioned and warrant police officers were dismissed from the force. These dismissals included the highest ranking generals, the Chief of Police and his deputies, and chiefs of police in major cities. Approximately 50% of the commissioned officers and 30% of the warrant officers were eventually dismissed. This drastic action may have eliminated a number of old-fashioned, Communist militiamen, but it also eliminated some professional police officers, which necessitated dramatic promotions of younger and less experienced police officers (Haberfeld, 1997, p. 646).

We secured the approval of police headquarters in Warsaw to distribute a sample of 2,000 questionnaires, which would constitute a representative and stratified sample of this national force. A liaison officer from headquarters provided suggestions regarding which districts we might wish to survey. Eventually, 23 police agencies from 6 police districts throughout the country were selected for the sample and 1,477 questionnaires were collected.

Most of the Polish police officers had been police officers for at least 5 years (74%), while only one third (37%) had been police officers for at least 10 years. A somewhat smaller percentage of Polish police officers reported working in the same police station for at least 5 years (53%). The majority of the officers either performed patrol functions (37%) or were on call (27%). The majority (63%) were employed in small police agencies (with 25 to 74 officers) or medium-sized police agencies (with 75 to 200 officers). Very few of the Polish police officers in our survey performed supervisory functions (12%) (Haberfeld, Klockars, Kutnjak Ivkovich, & Pagon, 2000).

It is important to acknowledge the fact that the sample consisted of both newly hired officers (hired after the transformation) and officers who had served during the times of the Communist militia. Therefore, the research population represents a blend of the old and the new system and, basically, at least on the face of it, should represent two distinctively different schools of thought, or police subcultures. Yet we did not find any distinct differences between the officers based on the length of their service, which in itself presents an interesting finding worthy of future research. The data presented in Table 11.2 summarize the respondents' perceptions of the misconduct in the scenarios— its seriousness, the appropriate discipline for it, and their own and others' willingness to report it. Table 11.2 presents the results from the entire national sample.

The respondents rate the theft of a watch from a crime scene (Case 5) as the most serious offense, followed by a bribe from a speeding motorist (Case 3) and serving drinks to minors (Case 9). The offenses the respondents perceive as the least serious include running an off-duty security system business (Case 1), followed by the cover-up of a police DUI accident (Case 8) and holiday gifts from merchants (Case 4). The discipline the respondents think should and would follow discovery of the misconduct appears to be quite consistent with the perceived seriousness of the violation, with dismissal being the mode for Cases 3 and 5 and with a written reprimand the mode for Case 9. The respondents' own and estimate of others' willingness to report the misconduct match the seriousness they attribute to the misconduct and the discipline they think appropriate for it; that is, the more serious the officers perceive the violation to be, the harsher the discipline they chose for it and the more likely they say they would be to report it. It is interesting that with regard to the case perceived most serious (Case 5), for the measures of seriousness, discipline, and willingness to report, the ranking is exactly the same, with slight deviations in Cases 3 and 9. Regarding Case 3, their own view is that the offense is more serious than they perceive others would think it is, while regarding Case 9 their own view is that it is less serious than they perceive others would think it is (but the appropriate discipline that they chose for this case was more lenient than the one they thought would be actually received). Therefore, it appears that there is some type of consensus regarding the perceptions of integrity that Polish police officers have of themselves and of the others on the force.

On the other end of the spectrum, with the least serious offenses, the differences are much more noticeable; this might be explained by a lack of clearly defined or written procedures in a given police district. If this is the case, then clearly defined and disseminated rules and regulations and/or standard operating procedures could remedy the differences in perceptions or attitudes. Although these findings do not appear to be

**Table 11.2** Police Officers' Views About the Seriousness of Misconduct, the Discipline It Should and Would Receive, and Officers' Willingness to Report It

| Case Number and Description | Seriousness Own View $\bar{x}$ | Own View Rank | Most Officers $\bar{x}$ | Most Officers Rank | Violation $\bar{x}$ | Should Receive $\bar{x}$ | Should Rank | Should Mode | Would Receive $\bar{x}$ | Would Rank | Would Mode | Willingness Own View $\bar{x}$ | Own View Rank | Most Officers $\bar{x}$ | Most Officers Rank |
|---|---|---|---|---|---|---|---|---|---|---|---|---|---|---|---|
| Case 1 - Off-Duty Security System Business | 2.29 | 1 | 2.27 | 1 | 3.84 | 1.81 | 1 | 1 | 3.46 | 4 | 3 | 1.64 | 1 | 2.29 | 2 |
| Case 2 - Free Meals and Discounts on Beat | 3.70 | 5 | 3.27 | 5 | 4.14 | 2.65 | 5 | 2 | 3.48 | 5 | 6 | 2.19 | 5 | 2.47 | 6 |
| Case 3 - Bribe From Speeding Motorist | 4.79 | 10 | 4.38 | 9 | 4.84 | 4.74 | 10 | 6 | 5.26 | 10 | 6 | 2.95 | 9.5 | 2.95 | 9.5 |
| Case 4 - Holiday Gifts From Merchants | 3.21 | 3 | 2.91 | 3 | 3.86 | 2.40 | 4 | 1 | 3.27 | 3 | 3 | 2.11 | 2 | 2.40 | 4 |
| Case 5 - Crime Scene Theft of Watch | 4.80 | 11 | 4.52 | 11 | 4.85 | 4.91 | 11 | 6 | 5.31 | 11 | 6 | 3.25 | 11 | 3.22 | 11 |
| Case 6 - 5% Kickback From Auto Repair Shop | 4.02 | 6 | 3.70 | 6 | 4.32 | 3.44 | 7 | 3 | 4.04 | 9 | 6 | 2.65 | 7 | 2.80 | 7.5 |
| Case 7 - Supervisor Grants Holiday in Exchange for Car Tune-Up | 4.18 | 7 | 3.87 | 7 | 3.54 | 2.26 | 2 | 1 | 2.20 | 1 | 1 | 2.23 | 6 | 2.42 | 5 |
| Case 8 - Cover-Up of Police DUI Accident | 3.02 | 2 | 2.81 | 2 | 4.14 | 2.82 | 6 | 3 | 3.87 | 6 | 6 | 2.12 | 3 | 2.31 | 3 |
| Case 9 - Free Drinks to Ignore Bar's Serving Minors | 4.77 | 9 | 4.42 | 10 | 4.68 | 3.57 | 9 | 3 | 3.92 | 7 | 3 | 2.95 | 9.5 | 2.95 | 9.5 |
| Case 10 - Excessive Force on Car Thief | 3.46 | 4 | 3.21 | 4 | 3.93 | 2.39 | 3 | 2 | 3.18 | 2 | 3 | 2.19 | 4 | 2.25 | 1 |
| Case 11 - Theft From Found Wallet | 4.48 | 8 | 4.15 | 8 | 4.55 | 3.52 | 8 | 3 | 4.00 | 8 | 6 | 2.75 | 8 | 2.80 | 7.5 |

the most significant feature of the data, they are still noteworthy, especially given the fact that the sample is comprised of officers who served under the Communist regime as well as officers hired after the transformation.

However, the main significance of this data set, at least from the purely statistical standpoint, can be found in the overall picture of a strong code of silence present within the force. Based on the preceding descriptive review of the phenomenon of corruption within the Polish Police force, which culminates with an emerging picture of a force highly tolerant of various forms of misconduct, one would tend to predict that the empirical data will tend to support the historical trends. The statistical analysis, on the surface, indicates that the broad picture emerging from the data is that, while the police officers perceive these cases to be relatively serious, with the exception of two cases, they think that the appropriate discipline should be rather mild (a written reprimand at best) and are quite unwilling to report the misconduct of their colleagues (in only one case, the most serious one, is the mean value above the midpoint). Their perceptions reflect an extremely punitive attitude, when dismissal is expected in 6 cases, but those attitudes might have something to do with the formalized and recorded nature of the offense.

Table 11.3 contains the percentage of police officers who say that they and other police officers would not report a fellow police officer who engaged in various types of police corruption. The cases are listed from the case reported to be the least serious (Case 1 - Off-Duty Security System Business) to the one they regarded as the most serious (Case 5 - Crime Scene Theft of Watch). The respondents' willingness to report the offenses is related to their perceptions of the seriousness of each case: the less serious they perceive the case to be, the more likely they were to say that they would not report it.

The results indicate that the code of silence—measured as the percentage of the respondents who say that they would not report the offense—is indeed quite strong in the respondents. In fact, the overwhelming majority of respondents (close to two thirds or more) say that they would not report a colleague for the majority of the offenses in the cases in the questionnaire (6 out of 11). In the remaining 5 cases, which constitute the most severe violations of criminal law and abuses of authority (ranging from the acceptance of a bribe from a speeding motorist to the theft of a watch from a crime scene), a substantial minority of police officers say that they would not report the offense of their fellow officer.

## CONCLUSION

It is important to mention that the most serious accusations of corruption against the Polish police were directed against the traffic police and their accepting or demanding bribes from motorists. Given the fact that this case was identified as the second most serious offense by the police officers, it is interesting to speculate about the discrepancies between what is objectively identified as a serious violation but subjectively practiced as a normative behavior. Since police officers in post-Communist Poland suffer from the same problem their predecessors in the service of the militia suffered from (specifically, being severely underpaid), it appears that the tradition of corrupt behavior will continue to flourish, even though its orientation might be different. During Communist times and earlier in the historical development of the Polish nation, the police force appears to have been corrupt either through many attempts of the more-than-willing citizens or on their own initiative. Nowadays, the public is not eager to participate in the game in which police are the "corrupt tool of the corrupted government,"

**Table 11.3** Officers' Views of Their Own and Others' Willingness to Report Misconduct

| *Case Number and Description* | *Percentage Saying They Would Not Report Misconduct* | *Percentage Saying Other Police Officers Would Not Report Misconduct* |
|---|---|---|
| Case 1 - Off-Duty Security System Business | 80.7% | 57.5% |
| Case 8 - Cover-Up of Police DUI Accident | 64.5% | 56.0% |
| Case 4 - Holiday Gifts From Merchants | 65.3% | 51.9% |
| Case 10 - Excessive Force on Car Thief | 62.5% | 59.0% |
| Case 2 - Free Meals and Discounts on Beat | 63.8% | 50.0% |
| Case 6 - 5% Kickback From Auto Repair Shop | 49.7% | 39.3% |
| Case 7 - Supervisor Grants Holiday in Exchange for Car Tune-Up | 61.4% | 52.3% |
| Case 11 - Theft From Found Wallet | 46.7% | 39.8% |
| Case 9 - Free Drinks to Ignore Bar's Serving Minors | 40.9% | 34.9% |
| Case 3 - Bribe From Speeding Motorist | 40.3% | 33.5% |
| Case 5 - Crime Scene Theft of Watch | 34.4% | 28.2% |

but the police appear to want to continue to play the game—not necessarily through conviction so much as through the sheer necessity to survive. Nothing seems to validate the above conclusion more than a sentence written by one of the respondents to the survey: "People, you don't understand! I have to feed my family!"

What are the prospects for the future? If one assumes that there is enough testimonial and empirical evidence to justify the claim that there is a corrupt police force in Poland (albeit with the knowledge that the strong code of silence might be slightly weakening), the following conclusions can be offered.

Corruption in the Polish police can be traced to three distinct factors: historical roots, an ineffective economic system, and a less-than-perfect legal system that is still in transition. From the historical perspective, a corrupt police force, or a force with officers who participate in corrupt activities, seems to be an extension of a deeply rooted tradition, or almost normative behavior. However, this tradition is being uprooted through a number of control mechanisms, both external and internal, that are being put in place by the police force itself and the citizens they police. Therefore, it appears that there is some hope for the future.

From the economic standpoint, however, there is less reason for optimism. The salaries of police officers are not being upgraded, nor are there any prospects for significant changes in the future. To the contrary, the newly appointed Chief of Police has stated that the problem with police conduct or misconduct is not related to the amount of money an officer earns. This, at least in theory, might be a valid point, but not when 30% of police officers' families live below the poverty line. As there is no hope for the immediate improvement of police officers' economic situation, there is little prospect of changing officers' behavior that is connected with their economic survival.

Finally, the legal system is in transition and undergoes periods of improvement and periods of regression with respect to opportunities for corruption. Through recent legislation, police officers have once again been given too much discretion in estimating traffic violation fines, and the new legislation targets the corrupted and the corrupter in same exact manner by imposing the same punishment for both. Hence, the experiments in legislation do not offer the much-desired response and solution to the corruption problems.

In sum, when two out of three causation factors do not appear to point to a different direction for the future, the prospects look quite dim. What appears to be police misconduct from a perceptual (empirically measured) standpoint translates, and will continue to translate, into police conduct (from historical and testimonial evidence) on the streets and highways of the country.

## REFERENCES

Daszkiewicz, K. (2000, May 6). O statystyce wykrywalnosci przestepstw (Criminal statistics). *Rzeczpospolita,* p. C3-9. (Polish daily newspaper)

Domagala, J. (2000, March 3). *Przestepstwa ktorych nie ma* (Crimes that do not exist). *Reczpospolita,* p. A1.

Gieysztor, A. (1968). *History of Poland.* Warsaw: Polish Scientific Publishers.

Grabowski, S. (2000). *Historia Policji w Polsce.* (History of the Polish police). Szczytno, Poland: Higher Police Academy.

Haberfeld, M. R. (1997). The police are not the public and the public are not the police: Transformation from Militia to Police. *Journal of Police Studies, 4*(20).

Haberfeld, M. R. (2000). Field notes from focus groups meetings in January and May, 2001, Warsaw, Gdansk, and Krakow.

Haberfeld, M. R. (2001a, June). *Police misconduct and control in Poland.* Paper presented at the Global Forum II in The Hague, The Netherlands.

Haberfeld, M. R. (2001b, July). Field notes from focus groups meetings in Krakow and Warsaw.

Haberfeld, M. R., Klockars, C. B., Kuntjak-Ivkovich, S., & Pagon, M. (2000). Police officer perceptions of the disciplinary consequences of police corruption in Croatia, Poland, Slovenia, and the United States. *Police Practice and Research, 1*(1).

Haberfeld, M. R., & Walancik, P. (November, 1999). *To become a tool in the hands of the public: Restructuring the Polish police force.* Paper presented at the annual meeting of the American Society of Criminology, Toronto.

Jachowicz, J. (2000, January 9). Raport z rozbitych gangow (Report about broken gangs). *Gazeta Wyborcza,* p. 2. (Polish daily newspaper)

Jachowicz, J. (2000, April 25). Raport na zlo I przemoc (Report about evil and force). *Gazeta Wyborcza,* p. 4.

Jachowicz, J. (2000, May 15). Zawodowiec (The professional). *Gazeta Wyborcz,* p. 17.

Jaworski, M. (1984). *Korpus bezpieczenstwa wewnetrznego w latach 1945-1965.* (Internal Security Corps during the years 1945-1965). Warsaw. Ministry of Public Defense.

Kaleta, J. (2000a, May 11). We draw in corruption. *Trybuna*, p. 11. (Polish daily newspaper)

Kaleta, J. (2000b, June 1). *About corruption—again. Gazeta Wyborcza*, p. 3.

Klockars, C. B., Kutnjak Ivkovich, S., Harver, W. E., & Haberfeld, M. R. (1997). *The measurement of police integrity.* Final report submitted to the National Institute of Justice (NIJ Grant No. 95-IJ-CX-0058), Washington, DC.

Korbonski, S. (1990). *Polskie panstwo podziemne* (The Polish underground state) (5th ed.) Warsaw: Ksiazka I Wiedza.

Podlaski, J. (2000, March 8). Statystyka policyjna. (Police statistics). *Rzeczpospolita*, p. A3.

The Polish Penal Code. (1957). Ministry of Justice, Warsaw.

Polska przesiaknieta korupcja (Poland soaking in corruption). (2000, March 22). *Rzeczpospolita*, p. B3.

Sadykiewicz, M.(1989). *The nomenklatura system in Poland.* Vienna, VA: Orion Research.

Siedlecka, E. (2000, August 1). Against corruption. *Gazeta Wyborcza*, p. 4.

Siemiaszko, A. (2000, March 3). Policja nie chce wiedziec (The police don't want to know). *Magazyn Rzeczpospolitej*, p. 8. (Polish daily newspaper, magazine edition)

Siemiaszko, A. (2000, May 15). Przestepczosc, (Criminality). Retrieved from www.gazeta.pl, p. 1.

Walancik, P., & Haberfeld, M. R. (2001, November). *The role of the media as a paradigm for police integrity in Poland.* Paper presented at the annual meeting of the American Society of Criminology in Atlanta, GA.

Wroblewski, H. M., & Hess, K. M. (2003). *Introduction to law enforcement and criminal justice* (7th ed.). Belmont, CA: Wadsworth/Thomson Learning.

# CHAPTER 12

# Police Integrity in Slovenia

MILAN PAGON

BRANKO LOBNIKAR

## INTRODUCTION

The concept of integrity is believed to have a central role in policing as a profession (see Delattre, 1996; Pagon, Kutnjak Ivkovich, & Klockars, 1998; Vicchio, 1997). It is also believed that the lack of integrity results in a whole spectrum of deviant behaviors usually labeled as "police corruption." While this might be the case, we should not simply equate integrity and lack of corruption. As Vicchio (1997) points out, "in departments where corruption appears to be low and where citizen complaints are minimal, we assume that our officers on the job are people of integrity. Sometimes this is a faulty assumption, particularly if the motivation to do the right thing comes from fear of punishment" Therefore, we cannot measure police integrity by simply measuring the existence and frequency of the corrupt police behaviors.

Delattre (1996) defines integrity as "the settled disposition, the resolve and determination, the established habit of doing right where there is no one to make you do it but

yourself" (p. 325). He believes that integrity is "irreplaceable as the foundation of good friendship, good marriages, good parenthood, good sportsmanship, good citizenship, and good public service" (p. 325).

Vicchio (1997) defines a person of integrity as someone who has a reasonably coherent and relatively stable set of core moral values and virtues, to which he or she is freely and genuinely committed, which are reflected in his or her actions and speech. So, the person's words and actions should be of a piece.

Becker (1998) subscribes to the objectivist view of integrity, namely, that integrity is loyalty, in action, to rational principles (general truths) and values; "that is, integrity is the principle of being principled, practicing what one preaches regardless of emotional or social pressure, and not allowing any irrational consideration to overwhelm one's rational convictions" (p. 158).

Integrity in policing, then, means that the police officer genuinely accepts the values and moral standards of policing and possesses the virtues of his or her profession, and that the officer consistently acts, out of his or her own will, in accordance with those values, standards, and virtues, even in the face of external pressures (Pagon, 2000). In this chapter, we describe an approach to measuring police integrity in Slovenia.

While the research (Haberfeld, Klockars, Kutnjak Ivkovich, & Pagon, 2000) demonstrates that there are some unified contours of police integrity among different countries, there are also some country-specific differences. Therefore, to understand a phenomenon of police integrity in a particular police force, one has to understand the broader context and societal forces at work in that particular environment. To that end, this chapter first describes some basic facts about the Republic of Slovenia, followed by some crime statistics and a general description of the Slovenian Police. It then discusses recent developments regarding police integrity in Slovenia and presents current research findings in that area. The chapter concludes with a discussion of the future of police integrity in Slovenia.

## THE REPUBLIC OF SLOVENIA[1]

Slovenia is a small Central European country, situated on 20,273 square kilometers. It has a population of 1,965,986, of which 87.9% are Slovenes. The official language is Slovene.

Slovenia was part of the former Socialist Federal Republic of Yugoslavia from its beginning in 1945. However, after the death of President Josip Broz Tito in 1980, the economic and political situation became very strained. In 1988 and 1989, the first political opposition parties emerged, which in the 1989 May Declaration demanded a sovereign state for the Slovene nation. In April of 1990, the first democratic elections in Slovenia took place and were won by DEMOS, the united opposition movement. In the same year, more than 88% of the electorate voted for a

sovereign and independent Slovenia. The declaration of independence followed on June 25, 1991. The next day, the newly formed state was attacked by the Yugoslav Army. After a 10-day war, a truce was called, and in October of 1991 the last soldiers of the Yugoslav Army left Slovenia. The European Union recognized Slovenia in the middle of January of 1992, and the United Nations accepted it as a member in May of 1992. In February of 1999, Slovenia's association agreement with the European Union (EU) came into effect and Slovenia also applied for full membership in the EU.

Slovenia's constitutional order is parliamentary democracy. The head of the state is president of the republic, popularly elected every 5 years, for a maximum of two 5-year terms. The legislative authority is the national assembly, which has 90 deputies. The government consists of the Prime Minister and other ministers, who are responsible to the National Assembly.

Slovenia is among the most successful of the countries in transition from socialism to a market economy. The greatest number of the more than 144,000 registered companies in Slovenia are engaged in trade and commerce, followed by industry, services, real estate, construction, transportation, and communications. More than 90% of companies are classified as small business enterprises. In 1999, GDP per capita was US$10,078, while the standardized rate of unemployment (ILO) was 7.5. As a result of the relatively small Slovenian market, the economy is oriented toward export. Slovenia's main foreign trading partners are Germany, Italy, Croatia, France, and Austria.

### Crime in Slovenia[2]

The sharp increase in the number of criminal offenses handled by the Slovenian police continues. From 1997, when the police handled 37,000 criminal offenses, to

2000, their number has nearly doubled to over 67,000 offenses. This statistical growth is a reflection of a deteriorated security situation and, even more, of a changed (more precise) way of dealing with and recording minor crimes, which simultaneously are the most frequent and have the highest impact on statistical indexes of crime.

The work of the police has been particularly marked by (1) a growing number of mass smuggling of illegal refugees, (2) better organization and ruthlessness of perpetrators of serious crimes, and (3) a growth of secondary crime (i.e., criminal offenses committed by addicts who commit crimes to obtain money for illegal drugs).

The number of property crimes and crimes related to the abuse of illegal drugs have shown a particularly sharp increase. In spite of the unfavorable security situation, the police have successfully coped with the most dangerous forms of crime and succeeded in detecting and preventing several serious forms of organized criminal activity, such as extortion and murders of business-people, mass smuggling of illegal migrants, international trafficking of illegal drugs, and the corruption of state officials. In 2000, the overall crime clearance rate was 46.9%.

## THE SLOVENIAN POLICE[3]

Once it had gained independence from the former Yugoslavia, the new Slovenian state reorganized its political and economical system and started to reorganize its public services, including the police force. The Slovenian Police is now an independent part of the Ministry of the Interior of the Republic of Slovenia. The police perform their tasks at three levels: the state, the regional, and the local level. The Slovenian Police organization is composed of the General Police Directorate, regional Police Directorates, and police stations. The police headquarters are in Ljubljana.

All together, there were 6,882 police officers and 716 detectives employed by the Slovenian Police in 2001, which is a ratio of 274 police officers and 36 detectives per 100,000 inhabitants. The officers' average age was 31 years; their average length of service was 13.5 years. The vast majority (70%) had a high school-level education, while some 20% had education above the high school level (i.e., associate, bachelor's, master's, or doctoral degrees).

Similar to many Eastern, Central, and Western European police organizations, the Slovenian Police was (and still is to some extent) characterized by a bureaucratic, centralized, and paramilitary organization and philosophy (Pagon, 1998). Police officers within such an organization are likely to be rewarded for producing desirable statistics and reinforced for exhibiting obedience and conformity, while the paramilitary organizational structure encourages an authoritarian leadership approach. Police work is mainly repressive and reactive in nature, characterized by its orientation to the past, because the majority of the things the police are dealing with have already happened. The police officers, reinforced by their commanders and the media, perceive themselves as "crime fighters," as the "thin blue line" between the rule of law and general disorder, constantly at war with criminals, liberals, and enemies of other sorts. This kind of police organization and philosophy has been linked to the misuse of police discretion and reinforcement of police subculture (characterized by cynicism, insularity, secrecy, defensiveness, etc.) on the one hand and to public dissatisfaction with the police on the other (Pagon, 1998).

This has led police scholars and some police practitioners in Slovenia to seek a different approach to policing. According to the Western experience, community policing (including problem-solving policing) seems to be the answer. Trojanowicz and Bucqueroux (1994) argue that community policing is a philosophy and organizational strategy that promotes cooperation between people and their police officers. In community policing, the police and community work together to identify, prioritize, and solve contemporary problems such as crime, drugs, fear of crime, social and ecological disorder, and overall neighborhood decay. Community policing is characterized by organizational decentralization, and the police function is legitimized by community support as well as by the traditional sources of law, the political structure, and professionalism (Hahn, 1998). Under community policing, individual police officers are valued for, and evaluated on, communication skills (sensitivity to cultural diversity, problem solving, mediation, negotiation, etc.), and a host of other skills that have not appeared in police evaluation previously (Hahn, 1998).

The Slovenian Police is in a transition from the old to the new approach to policing. Every transition process has its problems, and so does this one. It would be far too optimistic to conclude that the police in Slovenia have fully embraced the philosophy and practice of community policing. Furthermore, some recent developments regarding police integrity show that there is room for improvement in this regard.

## RECENT DEVELOPMENTS REGARDING POLICE INTEGRITY IN SLOVENIA

The hardest blow to the Slovenian Police's confidence came recently in the form of the European Commission's Report on Slovenia's progression as a candidate country (Commission of the European Communities, 2001). Based largely on the judgments made by some other governmental and nongovernmental organizations, the Commission accused the Slovenian Police of being brutal and violent in some cases. The report specifically mentioned two problem areas, namely, the use of excessive force against individuals in police custody and police brutality toward Romas (i.e., Gypsies). These accusations coincide with the accusations made by Amnesty International, the UN Committee against torture, the European Court for Protection of Human Rights, the Slovenian Ombudsman, and the Open Society. The accusations all have common themes: excessive use of force, improper treatment, unnecessary display of powers, and threats (Mekina, 2001).

Although the police denied these accusations, the media devoted a lot of attention to the European Commission's Report. In this context, the media reported several recent incidents of alleged police misconduct and police-related problems. Here are a few cases that are typical of those included in such reports (Praprotnik, 2001):

- Seven police officers from one of the police stations consumed alcoholic beverages at the station. One or more of them fired 14 shots from their duty firearms. The desk officer failed to report the incident to his superiors. After the superiors learned about the incident and started to investigate it, the involved officers protested by putting their firearms in a trash dumpster. As they left the police station, they proceeded to a local bar, where they consumed alcohol again, made a lot of noise, and refused to pay the bill.
- Three police employees, who were in charge of destroying confiscated weapons in a police warehouse, were caught selling those weapons on the black market instead of destroying them.
- A police officer was indicted for soliciting and accepting bribes from foreign citizens while stopping them for traffic violations.

Also, the media reported cases in which citizens who were involved in police procedures and afterwards filed a complaint about the police, were not satisfied with the way those complaints were handled by the police. Some even implied that the police organization is

**Table 12.1**     Citizen Complaints Against the Police in Slovenia From 1997 to 2000

|             | *1997* | *1998* | *1999* | *2000* |
|-------------|--------|--------|--------|--------|
| Complaints  | 1,363  | 1,672  | 1,853  | 1,552  |
| Index       | 100    | 123    | 136    | 114    |
| Processed   | 1,285  | 1,575  | 1,760  | 1,496  |
| Sustained   | 213    | 245    | 214    | 201    |
| Percentage  | 16.6%  | 15.5%  | 12.2%  | 13.4%  |

SOURCE: Pagon and Lobnikar (2001).

unduly protecting its corrupt officers (Praprotnik, 2001).

So, let us take a brief look at the citizen complaints against the police in Slovenia, as shown in Pagon and Lobnikar (2001). In 2000, the police received a total of 1,552 complaints, 1,240 of which were submitted in writing, 258 in person, 29 by phone, 7 through the Office of the Ombudsman, 5 anonymously, 3 over television, and 10 in some other way. Table 12.1 shows a 4-year comparison of citizen complaints against the police.

As can be seen from Table 12.1, the number of complaints was relatively stable over the 4 years. Roughly 5% of all the complaints were dismissed immediately, while around 95% were processed. The ratio of sustained complaints is slowly decreasing. The police statistics for 1999 show that there were 285.7 complaints per 1,000 police officers; there was 1 complaint against every 582nd repressive police measure and 1 sustained complaint against every 4,783rd repressive police measure. These data are quite favorable, showing that very few police repressive measures result in complaints against the police. Table 12.2 shows the outcomes of the sustained complaints against the police.

As can be seen from Table 12.2, a warning was by far the most common outcome of complaints against the police, followed by a report to a district attorney and counseling. While in 5% to 15% of sustained complaints the police officers become subject to a disciplinary case, very few officers end up in court because of a citizen complaint against them.

Also interesting are the data on disciplinary cases (resulting from various causes, not only from public complaints). Pagon and Lobnikar (2001) report that there were 158 disciplinary cases in the Slovenian Police in 2000. Of those, 32.1% were stopped due to a statute of limitations, lack of evidence, or a not-guilty decision. And 23% of all disciplinary decisions were appealed. On the average, it took 39 days from the violation to the initiation of the disciplinary process, and 64 days from the initiation to the decision in the disciplinary process.

However, as we pointed out earlier, one could not draw conclusions about the current state of police integrity solely on anecdotal evidence or simply on statistics about disciplinary cases. To address this question, we conducted two studies that approached the question of police integrity in Slovenia in a more or less indirect way.

## STUDYING POLICE INTEGRITY IN SLOVENIA: STUDY 1

The first study presented here (Pagon, Kutnjak Ivkovich, & Lobnikar, 2000) examines attitudes and behavioral intentions regarding corrupt police behaviors, while the second one (Pagon, Duffy, Ganster, & Lobnikar, 1998) explores personal and interpersonal determinants of police deviance. In this study, we understand integrity as the congruence between a person's moral beliefs and his or her actions, along the lines of Vicchio's (1997)

**Table 12.2**    Outcomes of the Processed Complaints Against the Police in Slovenia From
1997 to 2000

|  | *1997* | *1998* | *1999* | *2000* |
|---|---|---|---|---|
| *Outcomes* | | | | |
| Warning | 249 | 262 | 195 | 170 |
| Misdemeanor cases | 4 | 2 | 2 | 1 |
| Felony cases | 4 | 5 | 1 | 2 |
| Cases reported to DA | 14 | 34 | 19 | 79 |
| Disciplinary cases | 32 | 20 | 10 | 15 |
| Apology | 12 | 3 | 3 | 0 |
| Counseling | 1 | 84 | 23 | 38 |
| Total | 316 | 410 | 254 | 305 |

SOURCE: Pagon and Lobnikar (2001).

Note: The total number of outcomes is greater than the number of sustained complaints because there were multiple
outcomes in some cases (e.g., simultaneously a felony case and a disciplinary case).

position that "first, a person of integrity has a reasonably coherent and relatively stable set of core moral virtues. And second, the person's act and speech tend to reflect those principles." To assess someone's integrity, we should, therefore, first measure that person's set of moral beliefs and then compare it to that person's words and actions. An individual with a high level of integrity will act on his or her beliefs in a nonopportunistic manner, meaning that this individual will do what he or she believes to be morally right, regardless of other people's opinions and regardless of the consequences. The present study aims at measuring police integrity from the described perspective. In doing so, it does not enter the realm of operational reality, namely, it is not concerned with the actual behavior of the subjects. Instead, it measures their perceptions and intentions and tries to infer their level of integrity from them.

Our approach was to measure attitudes, perceptions, and behavioral intentions related to various behaviors that come under the umbrella of police corruption. We understand police corruption in a broader sense than just behaviors that result in personal gain for the offender. Like Whisenand and Ferguson (1996), we believe that police

corruption includes legalistic, professional, and ethical misconduct.

Also, we believe that there are no exact guidelines for assessing someone's moral standards or beliefs. Therefore, in addition to analyzing the data for a particular group (i.e., the police), we used the "assessment by comparison" approach. We assessed the level of moral standards of our group by comparing it to the level of moral standards of other groups. The details of our approach are described in the next section.

## The Method

### The Sample

Data were obtained from 767 police officers, 160 police cadets, and 254 University of Ljubljana and University of Maribor students in Slovenia.

Of the 767 police officers, 71 (9.2%) were currently students at the College of Police and Security Studies. Of the other 696 police officers, 36.1% worked in a small police department (with less than 25 officers), 53.8% worked in a medium-sized police department (with 25 to 75 police officers), and 10.1% worked in a larger police department (with more than 75 police officers).

Also, 34% had less than 6 years of service, 40% had between 6 and 15 years of service, and 26% had more than 15 years of service. And 3.5% of them were trainees, 81.9% held various ranks within the category of police officer (from Junior Policeman to Independent Policeman), while 14.6% held various inspector ranks. 4.7% were dispatchers, 22.1% were traffic officers, 11.2% were crime investigation officers, 22.6% were public order officers, 7.7% were border control officers, 9.0% were community policing officers, 9.1% were police station administrators, 3.5% were shift commanders, and 10.1% held some other kind of assignment.

Of the 160 police cadets, 132 (82.5%) were students in their third year of the Police High School, while 28 (17.5%) were new recruits currently in training at the Police Training Center.

Of the 254 students, 39 (15.3%) were (nonpolice) students at the College of Police and Security Studies, 93 (36.6%) were students at the Faculty of Organisational Sciences, 59 (23.2%) were students at the Faculty of Social Sciences, and 63 (24.8%) were students at the Faculty of Arts. Also, 30.8 % were first-year students, 46.2% were second-year students, 16.2% were third-year students, and 6.7% were fourth-year students.

### The Measures and Procedure

We employed the survey instrument that has been used previously to measure police integrity in the United States, Croatia, and Poland (Klockars, Kutnjak-Ivkovich, Harver, & Haberfeld, 1997; Kutnjak Ivkovich & Klockars, 1996). The questionnaire was modified to reflect the structure of disciplinary actions in the Slovenian Police.

The questionnaire presented 11 brief scenarios describing a range of corrupt behaviors. Respondents were asked several questions about each of these scenarios that measured the following perceptions and intentions: own perception of the seriousness of corruption, belief about other officers' perception of its seriousness, appropriate discipline for the corruption, expected discipline for it, willingness to report the corruption, and belief about other police officers' willingness to report it. In addition, we collected some demographic data about the respondents and their departments. The details of scenarios and the measures are presented in Exhibit 1.1 in Chapter 1 of this volume.

All the data were collected in group administrations supervised by a research assistant during working hours at the police stations, the Police High School, and the Police Training Center. Data from the students were collected in group administrations supervised by a research assistant during various classes at the University of Ljubljana and the University of Maribor (College of Police and Security Studies, Faculty of Organizational Sciences, Faculty of Social Sciences, Faculty of Arts). Confidentiality and anonymity were guaranteed and all participation was voluntary.

### The Results and Discussion

Table 12.3 lists the descriptive statistics for the Slovenian police sample. We begin our analysis by comparing the mean scores for the officers' own perceptions of the seriousness of corruption and their beliefs about other officers' perceptions of the seriousness of corruption. Although the observed differences suggest that police officers in our sample perceive themselves as more morally responsible than are other police officers (in nine out of eleven cases, the differences in the means were statistically significant, indicating the respondents' beliefs that other officers would perceive cases of police corruption less seriously), none of the differences is of substantive importance (they are considerably lower than .5). The degree of seriousness aside, the rank order of the seriousness of cases is practically identical in both instances. Therefore, we

**Table 12.3**  Police Officers' Views About the Seriousness of Misconduct, the Discipline It Should and Would Receive, and Officers' Willingness to Report It

| Case Number and Description | Seriousness | | | | Discipline | | | | | | Willingness to Report | | | |
| --- | --- | --- | --- | --- | --- | --- | --- | --- | --- | --- | --- | --- | --- | --- |
| | Own | | Others | | Should Receive | | | Would Receive | | | Own | | Others | |
| | Mean | Rank | Mean | Rank | Mean | Rank | Mode | Mean | Rank | Mode | Mean | Rank | Mean | Rank |
| 1 - Off-Duty Security System Business | 2.72 | 3 | 2.71 | 4 | 2.37 | 4 | 1 | 3.55*† | 7 | 5 | 1.95 | 3 | 2.53*† | 5 |
| 2 - Free Meals and Discounts on Beat | 2.83 | 4 | 2.52* | 3 | 2.16 | 3 | 1 | 2.56* | 3 | 2 | 2.15 | 4 | 2.27 | 4 |
| 3 - Bribe From Speeding Motorist | 4.78 | 10 | 4.57* | 10 | 5.12 | 10 | 6 | 5.12 | 10 | 5 | 4.01 | 9 | 3.81* | 9 |
| 4 - Holiday Gifts From Merchants | 2.00 | 1 | 1.94 | 1 | 1.58 | 1 | 1 | 1.87* | 1 | 1 | 1.66 | 1 | 1.80* | 1 |
| 5 - Crime Scene Theft of Watch | 4.87 | 11 | 4.80* | 11 | 5.57 | 11 | 6 | 5.53 | 11 | 6 | 4.48 | 11 | 4.32* | 11 |
| 6 - 5% Kickback Auto Repair Shop | 4.33 | 8 | 4.10* | 8 | 4.41 | 8 | 5 | 4.60* | 8 | 5 | 3.74 | 8 | 3.65 | 8 |
| 7 - Supervisor Grants Holiday in Exchange for Car Tune-Up | 4.16 | 7 | 4.07* | 7 | 3.15 | 7 | 3 | 2.49*† | 2 | 1 | 3.15 | 7 | 3.09 | 7 |
| 8 - Cover-Up of Police DUI Accident | 2.41 | 2 | 2.27* | 2 | 2.10 | 2 | 1 | 2.76*† | 4 | 3 | 1.85 | 2 | 1.97* | 2 |
| 9 - Free Drinks to Ignore Late Bar Closing | 3.84 | 6 | 3.52* | 6 | 2.89 | 6 | 2 | 3.01* | 5 | 3 | 2.85 | 6 | 2.79 | 6 |
| 10 - Excessive Force on Car Thief | 3.03 | 5 | 2.72* | 5 | 2.45 | 5 | 2 | 3.13*† | 6 | 3 | 2.20 | 5 | 2.13 | 3 |
| 11 - Theft From Found Wallet | 4.71 | 9 | 4.56* | 9 | 4.87 | 9 | 5 | 4.98* | 9 | 5 | 4.09 | 10 | 3.94* | 10 |

*p < .001

†a substantive difference (> .5)

can conclude that there are no substantive differences in the police officers' perceptions of the seriousness of corruption and their beliefs about other officers' perceptions.

A comparison of the mean scores for the measures "appropriate discipline" and "expected discipline" shows that in eight out of eleven cases, the differences were statistically significant. Only four of those differences were of a substantive importance (following the .5 rule), so we can neglect the others. Therefore, there are three cases where police officers believe that the actual discipline for the corruption would be more serious than it should be (Case 1 - Off-Duty Security System Business, Case 8 - Cover-Up of Police DUI Accident, and Case 10 - Excessive Force on Car Thief). In one case, they believe that corrupt supervisors (Case 7 - Supervisor Grants Holiday in Exchange for Car Tune-Up) would get away with less serious discipline than they would deserve, while in all other cases they more or less believe that offenders would actually receive the appropriate discipline.

If we compare the mode answers instead of the means, we can identify three cases where the difference in modes is greater than 1. The first one is the already described case of the corrupt supervisor. The second case is Case 1 (Off-Duty Security System Business), where the discrepancy is the largest. While the respondents most frequently answer that the corruption merits no discipline, they most frequently answer that the discipline they expect to be imposed is a suspension. This reflects the current situation in Slovenia, where the police are unhappy with their pay and their standard of living, so they believe they should be given the opportunity to make some extra income by working off duty, while at the same time realizing that the existent laws do not allow for such a solution. The third case is Case 8 (Cover-Up of Police DUI Accident), where the respondents most frequently answer that the corruption merits no discipline, while they most frequently answer that

the discipline they expect to be imposed is a written warning. This reflects the standard of internal solidarity that will be discussed later.

A comparison of the mean scores for the measures "willingness to report" and "beliefs about other police officers' willingness to report" suggests a slight tendency of the respondents to perceive themselves as having more discriminating judgment than other police officers do. In what they perceive to be less serious cases, they believe they would report offenders less often than other officers do. In what they perceive to be cases of intermediate seriousness, they don't perceive their willingness to report corruption as any different from that of other police officers. In what they perceive to be the most serious cases, they believe they would report offenders more often than other officers would. The differences, however, are not of a substantive importance. Only the difference for Case 1 (Off-Duty Security System Business) is greater than .5.

Tables 12.4 and 12.5 show comparisons of the measures "own perceptions of the seriousness of corruption" and "willingness to report" of the police, police cadets, and students in Slovenia. Since in this chapter we are particularly interested in comparisons between the police and other groups, we will disregard comparisons between cadets and students. As can be seen from the tables, the measures of police perceptions about seriousness of corruption and their willingness to report it are significantly higher than the measures of police cadets, students, or both. The notable exceptions are Case 8 (Cover-Up of Police DUI Accident) and Case 10 (Excessive Force on Car Thief), where the police are significantly lower than the students in their perceptions of the seriousness of the corruption and their willingness to report it . A possible explanation for this finding might be the police subculture that fosters the "us versus them" mentality, internal solidarity, and police cynicism, which in turn generate acceptance of using excessive force on perpetrators,

**Table 12.4** A Between-Group Comparison of Officers' Perceptions of the Seriousness of the Corruption

| Case Number and Description | Average | Police 1 | Cadets 2 | Students 3 | Stat. Sign. Differences (α = .5) | | |
|---|---|---|---|---|---|---|---|
| | | | | | 1-2 | 1-3 | 2-3 |
| Case 5 - Crime Scene Theft of Watch | 4.73 | 4.87 | 4.59 | 4.38 | x | x | x |
| Case 3 - Bribe From Speeding Motorist | 4.60 | 4.78 | 4.36 | 4.19 | x | x | |
| Case 11 - Theft From Found Wallet | 4.52 | 4.71 | 4.19 | 4.18 | x | x | |
| Case 6 - 5% Kickback From Auto Repair Shop | 4.11 | 4.33 | 3.78 | 3.68 | x | x | |
| Case 7 - Supervisor Grants Holiday in Exchange for Car Tune-Up | 3.92 | 4.16 | 3.56 | 3.44 | x | x | |
| Case 9 - Free Drinks to Ignore Late Bar Closing | 3.70 | 3.84 | 3.39 | 3.47 | x | x | |
| Case 10 - Excessive Force on Car Thief | 3.25 | 3.03 | 2.90 | 4.12 | | x | x |
| Case 1 - Off-Duty Security System Business | 2.82 | 2.72 | 3.07 | 2.93 | x | | |
| Case 8 - Cover-Up of Police DUI Accident | 2.75 | 2.41 | 2.92 | 3.70 | x | x | x |
| Case 2 - Free Meals and Discounts on Beat | 2.74 | 2.83 | 2.08 | 2.92 | x | | x |
| Case 4 - Holiday Gifts From Merchants | 2.00 | 2.00 | 1.88 | 2.08 | | | |

as well as a sense of entitlement to certain privileges as police officers.

Next, we wanted to assess the police integrity according to the approach described earlier. We believe that an officer's making a decision about his or her own perceptions of the seriousness of corruption is a moral judgment and—as such—an indirect measure of the set of moral principles guiding such judgment. An officer's willingness to report corruption reflects a behavioral intention that is a precursor of action. To the extent that a person's willingness to report corruption is a consequence of his or her perception of its seriousness, the person demonstrates integrity, which is congruence between his or her moral beliefs and his or her propensity for action. If the willingness to report corruption is influenced more by other exogenous variables (such as other people's beliefs and actions, fairness of discipline, rank, assignment) than by the person's own perception of the seriousness of corruption, the person does not demonstrate integrity.

Rather than examining the described relationship separately for each case, we used an aggregate measure (a sum of all 11 cases) of the measures of "own perceptions of the seriousness of corruption" (OSALL), "beliefs about other officers' perception of the seriousness of corruption" (MSALL), "appropriate discipline" (ADALL), "expected discipline"

**Table 12.5** A Between-Group Comparison of the Officers' Willingness to Report Corruption

| Case Number and Description | Average | Police 1 | Cadets 2 | Students 3 | Stat. Sign. Differences ($\alpha = .5$) | | |
|---|---|---|---|---|---|---|---|
| | | | | | 1-2 | 1-3 | 2-3 |
| Case 5 - Crime Scene Theft of Watch | 4.37 | 4.48 | 3.89 | 4.37 | x | | x |
| Case 11 - Theft From Found Wallet | 3.96 | 4.09 | 3.32 | 3.98 | x | | x |
| Case 3 - Bribe From Speeding Motorist | 3.82 | 4.01 | 3.30 | 3.60 | x | x | |
| Case 6 - 5% Kickback From Auto Repair Shop | 3.51 | 3.74 | 3.01 | 3.11 | x | x | |
| Case 7 - Supervisor Grants Holiday in Exchange for Car Tune-Up | 2.99 | 3.15 | 2.78 | 2.65 | x | x | |
| Case 9 - Free Drinks to Ignore Late Bar Closing | 2.73 | 2.85 | 2.25 | 2.69 | x | | x |
| Case 10 - Excessive Force on Car Thief | 2.51 | 2.20 | 1.80 | 3.91 | x | x | x |
| Case 8 - Cover-Up of Police DUI Accident | 2.10 | 1.86 | 1.90 | 2.98 | | x | x |
| Case 2 - Free Meals and Discounts on Beat | 2.02 | 2.15 | 1.38 | 2.01 | x | | x |
| Case 1 - Off-Duty Security System Business | 1.86 | 1.95 | 1.77 | 1.64 | | x | |
| Case 4 - Holiday Gifts From Merchants | 1.54 | 1.66 | 1.26 | 1.37 | x | x | |

(EDALL), "willingness to report" (ORALL), and "beliefs about other police officers' willingness to report" (MRALL). We also calculated scores for the perceived fairness of discipline (a sum of differences between "appropriate discipline" and "expected discipline" for all cases–FAIR).

Table 12.6 shows the results of hierarchical regression for the dependent variable "willingness to report." As can be seen, the officers' own perceptions of the seriousness of corruption were the most significant determinant of their willingness to report corruption, accounting for as much as 43.6% of the variance. The respondents' organizational attributes (assignment, length of service, and rank) and their beliefs about appropriate discipline accounted for 11.4% and 9.4% of the variance, respectively. The influence of their beliefs about other officers' perceptions of the seriousness of corruption and perceptions about the discipline's fairness did not reach statistical significance.

We believe that these results demonstrate a high level of police integrity among police officers in Slovenia. However, since there are no established guidelines as to the amount of variance in the officers' "willingness to report" explained by their "own perceptions of the seriousness of corruption" that would differentiate between low and high integrity, we performed an additional analysis.

**Table 12.6**  Hierarchical Regression for the Dependent Variable ORALL

| Variables Entering Equation | $R^2$ | $\Delta R^2$ | df | F | p |
|---|---|---|---|---|---|
| OSALL | .4365 | .4365 | 1, 558 | 432.276 | .0001 |
| ADALL | .5303 | .0938 | 1, 557 | 111.277 | .0001 |
| MSALL | .5318 | .0015 | 1, 556 | 1.688 | .1944 |
| FAIR | .5322 | .0004 | 1, 555 | 0.515 | .4733 |
| ASSIGN LENGTH RANK | .6459 | .1137 | 3, 552 | 59.107 | .0001 |

Table 12.7 shows the results of stepwise regression. We regressed the variable "willingness to report" on the set of other variables common to the police, cadet, and student samples. As can be seen from the table, only in the police sample were the officers' own perceptions of the seriousness of the corruption the major determinant of their willingness to report it. The police cadets' willingness to report corruption was mainly determined by their beliefs about the "appropriateness of reporting" (i.e., their beliefs about other police officers' willingness to report it), while the students' willingness to report was mainly determined by their beliefs about the appropriate discipline for the corruption. We consider these comparisons to be a further demonstration that the level of integrity is higher in police than in the other two samples.

## Study 1's Conclusion

The present study aimed at measuring police integrity, which is defined as congruence between a person's moral beliefs and his or her words and actions regarding police corruption. Since our results showed that the respondents' own perceptions of the seriousness of corruption were the most significant determinant of their willingness to report it, we concluded that the respondents in the Slovenian police demonstrate a high level of integrity. Comparing these results with the

results obtained from the police cadet and student samples further supports this finding. Police respondents in most instances compared favorably with the other two samples in terms of both their moral standards (i.e., how seriously they perceived instances of police corruption) and their behavioral intentions (i.e., their willingness to report corruption). The notable exceptions were the two cases dealing with covering up a police DUI accident and using excessive force on a car thief, where the police score was significantly lower than the student score on their perceptions of the seriousness of the corruption and their willingness to report it. This problematic finding, in our view, reflects the existing subculture of the police organization.

A practical implication of this study's findings is that efforts to combat police corruption are most likely to be successful if they are directed at changing perceptions and moral beliefs about the seriousness of corruption.

## STUDYING POLICE INTEGRITY IN SLOVENIA: STUDY 2

This study focuses on some personal and interpersonal determinants of deviant work behaviors in police organizations. We do not focus on any particular form of police deviance, such as police corruption, brutality, or abuse of police discretion. Instead, we

**Table 12.7** The Percentage of the Variance in ORALL Explained by OSALL, ADALL, MSALL, EDALL, and MRALL

| Group | OSALL | ADALL | MSALL | EDALL | MRALL | Total |
|---|---|---|---|---|---|---|
| Police | 43.3% | 4.0% | 8.1% | 0.7% | 11.6% | 67.8% |
| Cadets | — | 15.7% | 1.6% | 1.2% | 44.9% | 63.4% |
| Students | 0.7% | 28.6% | — | 2.4% | 9.1% | 40.7% |

understand police deviance as a broad concept, including all counterproductive work behaviors that are either *active* and retaliatory in nature (e.g., stealing things from work, engaging in unethical behaviors for self-interest, falsifying reports), or *passive* (e.g., taking extended breaks, being absent from work without sufficient cause).

The personal variables that we examined were self-efficacy, organizational commitment, well-being, and depression. We hypothesized a significant positive relationship between police deviance and depression and significant negative relationships between police deviance and the other personal variables included in this study.

The interpersonal variables that we examined were supervisor support and undermining and coworker support and undermining. Because the so-called police subculture is known for isolation, secrecy, suspicion, and internal solidarity, we would expect police officers to be susceptible to support and undermining from their supervisors and coworkers to an even larger extent than are workers in many other occupations. We therefore hypothesized a significant negative relationship between police deviance and social support and a significant positive relationship between police deviance and social undermining.

Finally, we wanted to examine whether workplace undermining and support interact to predict police deviance. It has been proposed that socially supportive behaviors from a person who also provides undermining would actually magnify the detrimental effects

of undermining behaviors (Pagel, Erdly, & Becker, 1987). Discrepant behaviors (support *and* undermining) from network members may be very distressing to individuals and may result in feelings of relationship insecurity and feelings of a lack of control and predictability (Major, Zubek, Cooper, Cozzarelli, & Richards, 1997). We therefore hypothesized that when employees receive higher amounts of both undermining and support within the same relationship (supervisor, coworkers), higher levels of police deviance will result.

### The Method

#### The Sample

The data for this study were gathered as a part of a larger study on human resource practices and workplace stress. There were 143 police officers who participated in this study. The majority of the sample was male (93%), with ages ranging from 18 to 55. The respondents' average length of tenure in their current position was about 4 years and average length of time under the current supervisor was 2.5 years.

#### The Measures and Procedure

The following measures were used in the study: "deviance" (deviant work behaviors), "social undermining behaviors," "social support behaviors," "organizational commitment," "depression," "subjective well-being," "job-related self-efficacy," and control variables (age, tenure under current supervisor,

**Table 12.8** Descriptive Statistics and Correlations Between Police Deviance and Other Study Variables

| Variables | Mean | SD | 1. |
|---|---|---|---|
| Deviance | 1.87 | .30 | — |
| Supervisor Undermining | 1.98 | .75 | .33** |
| Supervisor Support | 2.10 | .88 | −.09 |
| Co-worker Undermining | 1.89 | .71 | .24** |
| Co-worker Support | 2.83 | 1.09 | .04 |
| Organizational Commitment | 4.32 | .94 | −.27** |
| Depression | 2.20 | .45 | .22** |
| Well-Being | 4.91 | .95 | −.29** |
| Self-Efficacy | 4.75 | .77 | −.28** |
| Age | 27.85 | 7.45 | −.15* |
| Supervisor Tenure | 2.53 | 1.79 | .03 |
| Position Tenure | 3.77 | 3.25 | −.05 |

$N = 142$

$**p < .01$ $*p < .05$

and tenure in current position). For details regarding these measures, see Pagon and colleagues (1998).

The police stations in which the respondents worked were randomly selected from the list of all possible stations. Members of the research team visited the selected stations on three occasions (for each of the three shifts). The selected officers were gathered in one room, during work time, where the questionnaires were administered. The participants were guaranteed confidentiality and assured that participation was voluntary. The completed questionnaires were collected immediately.

### The Results and Discussion

Table 12.8 shows the correlation coefficients between police deviance and other variables included in this study, along with descriptive statistics. A review of this table reveals the following findings.

First, on average the subjects report moderately low levels of work-related deviance. This is not too surprising, considering that the subjects are police officers who were asked to report their own deviant behaviors.

As we noted earlier, the police subculture is characterized by the elements of secrecy and suspicion. Although they were guaranteed confidentiality, the subjects were asked to write their names on the questionnaires (for the purpose of the follow-up research), which might have had an impact on their answers. If the questionnaire had been anonymous, the levels of reported deviance might have been higher.

Also, the officers reported moderately low levels of support and undermining from their supervisors and coworkers. This pattern is in contrast to much of the work using clinical and college samples where research results indicate higher levels of support and lower levels of undermining (Major et al., 1997). The subjects report receiving significantly more support from their coworkers than from their supervisors ($t = 9.59$, $p < .00$). The undermining from supervisors and coworkers that the subjects report does not significantly differ from this. The subjects report relatively high levels of organizational commitment, well-being, and self-efficacy, and they report only moderate levels of depression.

All correlations between police deviance and personal variables have the predicted direction and significance. Organizational commitment, well-being, and self-efficacy are significantly and negatively correlated with police deviance, while the correlation between depression and police deviance is significant and positive. The results support our hypothesis. In other words, individuals who report higher levels of organizational commitment, well-being, and self-efficacy, and lower levels of depression, also report lower levels of personal deviant work behaviors.

As expected, both supervisor and coworker undermining are significantly and positively correlated with police deviance. The subjects who perceive higher levels of social undermining also report higher levels of personal deviant work behaviors. Surprisingly, neither supervisor nor coworker support is significantly correlated with police deviance. The extent to which the subjects perceive the level of social support did not influence their report of personal deviant work behaviors. Therefore, the results support the hypothesized relationship between police deviance and social undermining. Police officers obviously react with deviant work behaviors when they experience negative social exchanges with their supervisors and coworkers. The predicted beneficial effects of social support in terms of lowering or preventing deviant work behaviors were not found in this study.

Next, we examined the interaction between social undermining and social support in influencing police deviance, to test our hypothesis that when employees receive higher amounts of both undermining and support within the same relationship (e.g., from a supervisor or a coworker), higher levels of police deviance will result. We found strong support for this hypothesis in the supervisor analysis but not in the coworker analysis. The "supervisor undermining–supervisor support" interaction term added an additional 16% of explained variance to the deviance equation. Moreover, the

form of the interaction fit the hypothesized form. In other words, support behaviors from a supervisor who also provided undermining actually had a negative effect in terms of increased police deviance. Our interpretation is that this effect stems from employees receiving conflicting messages about the relationship with the supervisor. If the supervisor is an important source of support, then undermining behaviors can be coded as even more threatening to the employee because they signal a potential loss of support from the supervisor when the employee has come to depend on that support. In essence, a strong provider of support can make the employee more vulnerable to undermining from that provider. These results were not replicated in the coworker analysis. We suggest that results for supervisors and coworkers differ, in part, because of the distinctly different roles they play in the workplace.

Finally, we performed a hierarchical regression analysis for the dependent variable "police deviance." The "social undermining" variables were entered first, followed by the "social support" variables in the second block. Finally, the "individual differences" variables were entered. The results are shown in Table 12.9.

As can be seen from the table, all the variables in the model together explained almost 22% of the variance in police deviance. The social undermining variables explained about 9%. The social support variables did not significantly add to the explained variance, while all the individual difference variables together added an additional 12%.

### Study 2's Conclusion

The goal of this study was to examine some personal and interpersonal determinants of police deviance, which were defined in terms of counterproductive work behaviors that are either active and retaliatory in nature or passive. The results suggest that among the examined variables (supervisor

**Table 12.9**    Hierarchical Regression Results for the Dependent Variable of Police Deviance

| Block | $R^2$ | $\Delta R^2$ | df | F | p |
|---|---|---|---|---|---|
| 1. Social Undermining (Supervisor Undermining, Co-worker Undermining) | .089 | .089 | 2; 135 | 6.579 | .002 |
| 2. Social Support (Supervisor Support, Co-worker Support) | .096 | .007 | 2; 133 | .523 | .594 |
| 3. Individual Differences (Organizational Commitment, Well-Being, Self-Efficacy, Depression) | .217 | .121 | 4; 129 | 4.997 | .001 |

support and undermining, coworker support and undermining, self-efficacy, organizational commitment, well-being, and depression), supervisor undermining is the strongest single predictor of police deviance (as measured in this study). Although there is no main effect for supervisor support, a significant interaction exists among supervisor support and supervisor undermining in predicting deviant work behaviors. Support behaviors from a supervisor who also provided undermining actually had a negative effect on employee deviance. Also, people higher in job-related self-efficacy, organizational commitment, and well-being, and lower in depression, report lower levels of personal deviant work behaviors.

The results emphasize the role of good management and people skills in combating police deviance. Police managers who are consistent in their support, and try to increase their employees' organizational commitment, well-being, and self-efficacy through empowerment and encouragement, are more likely to be successful in their attempts to decrease counterproductive work behaviors in their organization.

## DISCUSSION

Taken together, the presented results show that while police officers in Slovenia exhibit high levels of police integrity and report low levels of work-related deviance, the police organization is still plagued with some problems typical of the paramilitary approach to policing. One problem is the police subculture, which is seriously eroding otherwise high police integrity by leading the officers to believe that (1) it is acceptable to cover-up for fellow officers' wrongdoings, (2) it is acceptable to use excessive force in performing their duties, and (3) corrupt supervisors can get away with less serious discipline than they deserve. Another problem is the style of management in the police organization, which is obviously not immune to negative social interactions (i.e., social undermining). If we want to ensure that we will have police officers of high integrity, we should, therefore, strive to change police subculture so as to improve the quality of police management and leadership.

## CONCLUSION: THE FUTURE OF POLICE INTEGRITY IN SLOVENIA

For all of us in the field of police and security studies, it has become obvious that we are witnessing a paradigm shift. While we cannot expect this shift to result in a uniform approach to policing everywhere in the world, we can assume that all the various approaches will be based on the same set of assumptions about modern policing—community involvement; a proactive approach that emphasizes prevention, professionalism, innovation, and problem solving; and an integrated view of criminal justice (Pagon, 1998). In this process, policing is getting closer to professionalization, a change long advocated by police scholars. As several authors (e.g., Delattre, 1996; Fry & Berkes, 1983; Hahn, 1998; Murphy, 1996; Vicchio, 1997) point out, aspirations by the police to become professionalized either create or at least re-emphasize several requirements, such as a wide latitude of discretion, higher educational requirements, higher standards of professional conduct, and self-regulation.

Corruption, brutality, and other forms of police deviance go against the above-mentioned efforts toward police professionalization and community involvement. The community cannot trust or attribute a professional status to deviant police officers. No wonder, then, that modern police organizations all over the world are fighting police deviance, trying to achieve proper conduct and integrity in their members. However, according to Sykes (1993), a brief history of efforts to enhance police accountability reveals that they relied on rules and punishment.

> Although each of these reform efforts had an impact, the sum total fell short of providing assurances that they were adequate and serious incidents continued. . . . In short, the various rule-based systems of accountability seem insufficient if officers hold different values or there is a subculture which nurture values different from the ideals of democratic policing. (p. 2)

Sykes believes that the answer lies in approaches based on ethics, where accountability rests more on individual responsibility than it does on external controls and threatened punishment.

A proper development of police ethics and integrity is one of the most important steps toward the professionalization of policing, and it is one of the most powerful antidotes to police deviance and neglect of human rights by the police. In the context of discussing ethical behavior in police organization, we should also stress the importance of social relationships within the organization. Organizational actors are embedded within a network of relationships. These ongoing social relationships provide the constraints and opportunities that, in combination with characteristics of individuals, issues, and organizations, may help explain the ethical or unethical behavior in organizations (Brass, Butterfield, & Skaggs, 1998; Pagon et al., 1998). If police officers experience inconsistent behavior from their supervisors, preferential treatment of some officers and/or citizens, and solidarity with and cover-ups for the officers who violate the standards of their profession, they will sooner or later become cynical regarding the value and appropriateness of the ethical conduct in their organization. One cannot expect a cynical police officer to be motivated to adhere to the rules of ethical behavior (Pagon, 1993).

Therefore, to set a climate conducive to ethical behavior and integrity in the Slovenian Police organization, police leaders have to foster the desired character development and moral habits of police officers by educating and training them in police ethics; establish a high moral climate through the appropriate use of goals, means, rewards, and support; facilitate development of strong and dense social networks, extending into the community; prevent cliques and conspiracies; and establish both cognitive-based and affect-based trust among all the organizational members and between the police and the public (Pagon, 2000). As shown in this chapter, our research findings support these conclusions.

In doing what we have outlined above, the managers will not only facilitate ethical behavior in their officers—they will also prevent or at least lessen the strength of the infamous police subculture that is so typical of paramilitary policing. In trying to achieve the above goals, police managers will soon discover that setting an example is of the utmost importance and that ethics apply not only to their police officers' dealings with the community but also to their own dealings with their officers. Police officers' human rights are as important as those of all other citizens (Pagon, 2000).

We agree with Sykes (1993) that the quality of policing in a democratic society relies on the quality of the people doing the work.

This is why we believe that in policing we should strive to achieve a virtue of integrity in all police officers and supervisors, including top management.

The study results presented in this chapter clearly show that Slovenian police officers demonstrate high levels of integrity and low levels of deviant work behaviors. However, there are certain problematic areas that have a negative impact on the police—namely, police subculture and supervisor undermining—and that need to be improved if the Slovenian police is to become a truly democratic police force with a high level of integrity.

## NOTES

1. The source for this information is *Facts About Slovenia*, which is a Government Public Relations and Media Office publication available at http://www.uvi.si/eng.

2. This information is from Svetek (2001).

3. This information is available at http://www.mnz.si/en and http://www.policija.si/en.

## REFERENCES

Becker, T. E. (1998). Integrity in organizations: Beyond honesty and conscientiousness. *Academy of Management Review, 23*(1), 154-161.

Brass, D. J., Butterfield, K. D., & Skaggs, B. C. (1998). Relationships and unethical behavior: A social network perspective. *Academy of Management Review, 23*(1), 14-31.

Delattre, E. J. (1996). *Character and cops: Ethics in policing* (3rd ed.). Washington, DC: AEI.

Fry, L. W., & Berkes, L. J. (1983). The paramilitary police model: An organizational misfit. *Human Organization, 42*(3), 225-234.

Haberfeld, M. R., Klockars, C. B., Kutnjak Ivkovich, S., & Pagon, M. (2000). Police officer perceptions of the disciplinary consequences of police corruption in Croatia, Poland, Slovenia and The United States. *Police Practice and Research, 1*(1), 41-72.

Hahn, P. H. (1998). *Emerging criminal justice: Three pillars for a proactive justice system.* Thousand Oaks, CA: Sage.

Klockars, C. B., Kutnjak Ivkovich, S., Harver, W. E., & Haberfeld, M. R. (1997). *The measurement of police integrity.* Final Report to the National Institute of Justice (NIJ Grant # 95-IJ-CX-0058, The Cross Cultural Study of Police Corruption), Washington, DC.

Kutnjak Ivkovich, S., & Klockars, C. B. (1996). *A cross-cultural comparison of police officers' perceptions of the seriousness of corruption.* A paper presented at the American Society of Criminology Annual Meeting, Chicago.

Major, B., Zubek, J., Cooper, M. L., Cozzarelli, C., & Richards, C. (1997). Mixed messages: Implications of social conflict and social support within close relationships for adjustment to a stressful life event. *Journal of Personality and Social Psychology, 72,* 1349-1363.

Mekina, B. (2001, December 3). Slovenski policist kot Dirty Harry? (The Slovenian Policeman as Dirty Harry?). *Newspaper Večer,* http://www.vecer.com/e/ Prikaz_ clanka/Prikaz_clanka_vecer.asp? id=279256&ImeTabele=Arh2001VEC& vzorec= .

Murphy, P. V. (1996). Foreword. In E. J. Delattre, *Character and cops: Ethics in policing* (3rd ed., pp. xiii-xvi). Washington, DC: AEI.

Pagel, M. D., Erdly, W. E., & Becker, J. (1987). Social networks: We get by with (and in spite of) a little help from our friends. *Journal of Personality and Social Psychology, 53,* 793-804.

Pagon, M. (1993). Policijski cinizem: vzroki, značilnosti in posledice (Police cynicism: Antecedents, characteristics, and consequences). *Revija Policija, 13*(4-5), 389-403.

Pagon, M. (1998). Organizational, managerial, and human resource aspects of policing at the turn of the century. In M. Pagon (Ed.), *Policing in Central and Eastern Europe: Organizational, managerial, and human recourse aspect* (pp. 3-14). Ljubljana: College of Police and Security Studies.

Pagon, M. (2000). Police ethics and integrity. In M. Pagon (Ed.), *Policing in Central and Eastern Europe: Ethics, integrity, and human rights* (pp. 3-14). Ljubljana, Slovenia: College of Police and Security Studies.

Pagon, M., Duffy, M. K., Ganster, D. C., & Lobnikar, B. (1998). Understanding police deviance: Personal and interpersonal determinants. *Security Journal, 11,* 179-184.

Pagon, M., Kutnjak-Ivkovich, S., & Klockars, C. B. (1998, March 10-14). *The measurement of police integrity in Slovenia.* Paper presented at the 35th annual meeting of the Academy of Criminal Justice Sciences, Albuquerque, New Mexico.

Pagon, M., Kutnjak Ivkovich, S., & Lobnikar, B. (2000). Police integrity and attitudes toward police corruption: A comparison between the police and the public. In M. Pagon (Ed.), *Policing in Central and Eastern Europe: Ethics, integrity, and human rights* (pp. 383-396). Ljubljana, Slovenia: College of Police and Security Studies.

Pagon, M., & Lobnikar, B. (2001, April 3-7). *Disciplining the police: Dealing with police misconduct in Slovenia.* Paper presented at the 38th annual meeting of the Academy of Criminal Justice Sciences, Washington, DC.

Praprotnik, R. (2001, December 15). Kdo je mačka in kdo miš?–Slovenska policija v padcu ali vzponu? (Who's a cat and who's a mouse?–Is Slovenian police on the rise or in descent?). *Newspaper Delo–sobotna priloga,* p. 7.

*Regular report on Slovenia's progress towards accession,* SEC(2001) 1755. Brussels: Commission of the European Communities.

Svetek, S. (2001). Kriminaliteta in kriminalistično delo v letu 2000 (Crime and crime investigation activities in 2000). *Revija za kriminalistiko in kriminologijo, 52*(2), 99-108.

Sykes, G. W. (1993). *Why police ethics?* Law Enforcement Ethics Center, Southwestern Law Enforcement Institute. Available from http://web2. airmail.net/slf/oct93/why.html.

Trojanowicz, R., & Bucqueroux, B. (1994). *Community policing: How to get started*. Cincinnati, OH: Anderson.

Vicchio, S. J. (1997, July). Ethics and police integrity. *FBI Law Enforcement Bulletin*. Available from http://www.fbi.gov/leb/july972.htm.

Whisenand, P. M., & Ferguson, R. F. (1996). *The managing of police organizations* (4th ed.). Upper Saddle River, NJ: Prentice Hall.

# CHAPTER 13

# Out of Step

## Integrity and the South African Police Service

GARETH NEWHAM

*Corruption is when a policeman works for himself rather than his country.*

—A South African police officer (2001)

Since the advent of democracy in South Africa during April 1994, the South African Police Service (SAPS) has undergone dramatic reforms. It would not be an exaggeration to say that the SAPS is now unrecognizable from what it was during the dark days of apartheid. However, even as this organization marches into the new millennium with new plans, policies, technology, and training to become a model African police service, it continues to be "out of step" as far as integrity is concerned. Indeed, substantial numbers of South Africans still tend to perceive the police as corrupt or incompetent (Louw & Pelser, 2001). It is true that many negative perceptions are largely held as a result of the role the police played in harshly enforcing the racist laws and brutal policies of the apartheid regime. However, despite a decade of deliberate and ongoing police reform, these perceptions still persist. As we move into a decade of democracy in South Africa, the country's high crime rate, poor police service delivery, and corruption continue to undermine the public's

confidence in the police. Indeed, this situation is a common problem facing most governments and societies undergoing a transition to democracy (Shaw, 2001).

One of the characteristics of a society undergoing a transition to democracy is a relatively rapid pace of change in its institutions. This is certainly the case with the South African Police Service. Indeed, there has been a complete overhaul of the policies and legislation affecting the police, so as to bring the organization and its work into line with the country's liberal democratic rights-based constitution. Having good policing policy on paper is one thing, while effectively implementing it is another. This is one of the biggest challenges facing the South African police as it attempts to reform itself into a professional organization. This reform process is by no means over and there are a number of new policies that are in various stages of development and implementation. However, when it comes to tackling police corruption and building integrity, the SAPS has yet to develop a coherent strategy. This chapter will present a contextual approach to understanding the issue of police integrity in the South African Police Service (SAPS). First, a conceptual framework for analyzing the integrity of a police agency will be offered. This framework will be used to identify some of the key integrity challenges confronting the police reform process following the demise of apartheid. Second, a contemporary overview of the situation facing the SAPS in relation to integrity will be presented. Toward this end, a variety of indicators that can be used to reflect on the nature and extent of corruption in the SAPS will be briefly discussed. Finally, this chapter will provide some insight into what this means for police integrity at a particular present-day police station in South Africa. This insight will be based on a presentation and analysis of the results of a police integrity-measuring instrument that was conducted in a high-crime area at a high-priority, inner-city police station.

## INTEGRITY AND POLICE REFORM IN SOUTH AFRICA

Traditionally, police administrators have blamed incidents of corruption on a small group of deviant police officers, often referred to as "bad apples." This relatively narrow approach resulted in anticorruption strategies that focused primarily on how to improve the quality of the candidates selected into the police and on how to put in place systems to identify and remove individual corrupt officers already employed in the police. This approach has gained much currency and Sherman (1983) has argued that all successful cases of police corruption control have come about due to transformations from "a less authoritarian to more authoritarian administration" (p. 375). While elements of this approach are necessary, they can fail to address other factors

that allow for the emergence and spread of police corruption.

As the limits of "reactive" or rule-tightening approaches to police reform have been recognized, arguments have been made that attention needs to be given to the organizational culture of the police (Chan, 1997; Goldsmith, 1990). Over the past few decades, researchers and analysts have increasingly begun to recognize that there are certain occupational and organizational characteristics of policing that allow police corruption to flourish. While it is very necessary for the police to have strong internal systems of control, such systems are seldom sufficient to adequately handle police corruption as a general phenomenon. Incidents of corruption are usually difficult to identify due to low levels of reporting and, therefore, different strategies need to be considered to minimize the extent of the problem. Increasingly, emphasis has been placed on the importance of promoting an environment in police agencies that supports and promotes police officials' compliance with departmental policies and regulations (Palmer, 1992; Sherman, 1983).

According to Klockars, Kutnjak Ivkovich, Harver, and Haberfeld (2000), contemporary approaches to police corruption are based on the following four particular organizational and occupational dimensions:

> how organizational rules that govern corruption are established, communicated and understood,
>
> the prevention and control mechanisms employed to prevent and control corruption,
>
> the extent to which the "code of silence" dominates the police culture, and
>
> the influence that the social, economic and political environments have on police agencies. (pp. 1-2)

Therefore, it should be possible to develop deeper insight into the integrity challenges confronting a police agency through an investigation of these four dimensions. As Klockars and colleagues (2000) have argued, this approach is amenable to systematic, quantitative research that can interrogate the key organizational and occupational characteristics underpinning integrity in a police agency. Furthermore, this approach also combines the rule-tightening approach with the aspects of police culture that are related to combating and preventing corruption. Klockars and colleagues (2000) define the notion *police integrity* as "the normative inclination amongst police officers to resist the abuse of the powers and privileges of their occupation" (p. 4). Such a definition sets up a vision of a police agency in which there is a strong sense of esprit de corps among the rank-and-file officers, underpinned by an ethos that resists abuses of police power.

The ethos that fostered unity in the South African police force during the apartheid era was the quite the opposite of this. The South African Police force (the SAP, as it was then called) was run by a secret, powerful inner core of individuals called the Security Branch. Senior police members of the Security Branch were closely connected to the head of state through a shadow cabinet called the Security Council. This security structure influenced almost all public policy implemented by the apartheid state. Police power was therefore largely unchecked, which allowed for the brutal oppression of those who openly opposed apartheid. The Truth and Reconciliation Commission (TRC) found that "torture was used systematically by the Security Branch, both as a means of obtaining information and of terrorizing detainees and activists. Torture was not confined to particular police stations, particular regions or particular individual police officers" (1998, p. 187). However, during apartheid the police denied using torture and assassinations, as such activities were clearly at odds with the government's professed Christian beliefs. A "code of silence" therefore formed a significant part of South African police culture during this time.

With the birth of democracy in South Africa, the collusion of police and state power fell away, leaving a confused and disparate police organization. Consequently, by the mid-1990s it has been argued that

> the ideological departure point—in this case grand apartheid—had long receded into the mists of time. It had been replaced by corruption, the imperatives of personal power, and—at the lower ranks—increasingly foggy, but tenacious, notions of what the fight was about. Senior officers were frequently little more than warlords, their jealous guarding of turf made easier both by distant and over-centralised command structures of the police, and by a culture that for decades had produced terror, not safety and security, its primary product. (Laufer, 2001, p. 17)

A primary reason for this state of affairs was the incremental nature of police reform in South Africa. The country achieved its democracy through long and inclusive negotiated political settlement. One of the significant compromises that had a substantial impact on the police was known as the "sunset clause," which guaranteed apartheid-era public servants their jobs for a period of 5 years following the first democratic elections. The first challenge to building a democratic police service entailed the amalgamation of the 10 "homeland"[1] police forces and various subsidiary policing structures[2] with the old SAP into a single national South African Police Service.

The SAPS is a highly centralised organization, and as the only public policing agency in the country it has sought to assume a national persona. The South African Police Service Act of 1995 gives the National Commissioner extensive authority over the size, structure, and priorities of the entire organization. The organization is structured along four tiers, with the National Office being the highest policy and standard setting level, followed by the provincial level, which consists of headquarters in each of the nine provinces. This tier is responsible for implementing and monitoring national policy throughout each province. Below the provincial level are the 42 "Area level" offices throughout the country, with each Area office responsible for overseeing the implementation of policy, financial affairs, and the recorded crime rate of a cluster of roughly 20 police stations. The lowest organizational level consists of the roughly 1,136 individual police stations distributed throughout the country.

Most of the police officers hired during the apartheid era did not join the police for vocational reasons—they joined because they needed a job. For many of the homeland governments, the police were a means of maintaining social order and political power. As a result, thousands of apartheid era police officers were recruited on criteria primarily related to their physical size and health, following which they were given little more than a few weeks of training in marching and weaponry.

As a result of the amalgamation of the various police agencies into one service, the country was saddled with a police organization consisting of 140,000 police officers who spoke different languages and had different rankings and uniforms, different firearms, and different levels of training, dedication, and commitment. Furthermore, approximately one third were functionally illiterate, almost two thirds did not have drivers licenses, and 20,000 possessed criminal records (Mabuza, 2001). There has been no purge of any of the apartheid-era police, and such personnel factors place huge constraints on the ability of the new SAPS to provide adequate policing services to the public. Furthermore, an argument can readily be made that the high proportion (14%) of police officers with criminal records has contributed to the ongoing problems of police corruption and

criminality. In spite of this, current disciplinary regulations only provide for one situation that can result in the automatic dismissal of a police officer—when a police officer receives a jail sentence without an option for a fine following a criminal conviction in a court of law.

The reform program that was adopted by the newly elected democratic government sought to make the South African police more like police in Western liberal democracies. Indeed, the two central principles underpinning the reform program were, first that policing should be constrained by a "rights-based rule of law," and second that policing should have the "support of the people" (Brogden & Shearing, 1993, p. 93). Toward this end, a host of policies and regulations aimed at changing almost every aspect of policing were adopted during the years following the election. The driving philosophy behind policing became "community policing." This was to be promoted through the compulsory establishment of Community Policing Forums to be attached to every police station in the country. The police service was restructured and a new ranking system was introduced. In particular, symbols of the old order were replaced by those of the new, so police officials were issued different uniforms with different insignia and all police vehicles were painted white (as opposed to the yellow used during apartheid). New recruitment criteria and training courses were designed, a different promotion system was implemented, and a performance management system was introduced for the first time.

In relation to accountability, a national, civilian-run Secretariat was established in the Ministry of Safety and Security to monitor the implementation of police policy. Furthermore, an independent civilian-led investigations body called the Independent Complaints Directorate (ICD) was established to investigate all deaths of suspects in police custody or as a result of police action, along with other service delivery and corruption complaints against the police. However, there are a number of structural factors that substantially limit the effectiveness of this body. It only has 250 investigators to oversee the entire police service, and it can only make recommendations, as it has no formal power over the police. Unions were also allowed for the first time and have had a significant impact on the process and direction of organizational reform through a national bargaining forum.[3] Furthermore, much more space was given to independent, civil social research and policy organizations to contribute to the development of police policy and training.

In spite of all of these policy and structural changes, there has been very little "new blood" joining the police since 1994. For the first few years following the establishment of the new police service, a moratorium was placed on the hiring of new police officials. This was to cut down on personnel expenditure so that more of the police budget could be spent on resources. Over the past few years, the size of the SAPS has decreased by approximately 19,000 people to 121,040 employees.[4] While much of the downsizing resulted from "natural" processes of attrition, there was an attempt to promote resignations of police officials through generous voluntary retirement packages. However, one of the unintended consequences of this policy was that many of the more skilled and experienced police managers left the organization because they could use their skills in the more lucrative[5] private sector, particularly in the private security industry.[6] Furthermore, there are relatively few line-officers at the lower ranks due to the low levels of recruitment since 1994.[7] Recently, the national police commissioner has announced that 16,000 new police officials will be recruited, trained, and inducted into the SAPS over the next 3 years.

A major feature of police "transformation" (as the reform process is commonly known in South Africa) has been affirmative action. During apartheid, racism was deeply entrenched in the police force through various policies and regulations.[8] Although the police agency was comprised of 55% black police officials during 1994, the senior ranks were overwhelmingly (95%) white (Rauch, 2000). Since then, racial representation at management level has increasingly become the primary standard against which the transformation of the SAPS is being judged. By 1997, the SAPS formulated its own equity policy, and rigorous affirmative action was pursued. By 2001, 78% of the SAPS personnel were black and 28% were white. However, race has remained a key area of difference and contestation as a result of the continuing overrepresentation of white officers in the management ranks, in which approximately 54% of commissioned officers are white and 46% are black. Rauch (2000) points to the reason for this: "A history of discrimination, which had prevented blacks from accessing senior posts and technical career paths, meant that there were few candidates, other than white SAP incumbents, for most of the senior posts in the new SAPS" (p. 10). Nevertheless, the underrepresentation of black officers in management structures has remained a bone of contention for the unions, who have consistently complained that affirmative action has not been pursued rigorously enough at the management level.

Racial differences, and to a lesser extent ethnic differences, continue to represent one of the biggest obstacles to the development of a shared set of norms and values within the SAPS. While little research has explored the issue of race in the SAPS, the commonly accepted analysis is that white police officials generally feel threatened by affirmative action, while black police officials feel that transformation is not occurring quickly enough and still feel excluded from "certain flows of information" (Kessel, 2001, p. 9). Such dynamics affect the police culture in the SAPS in a number of ways. The disjuncture often found between police managers and line officers is further compounded by the current racial

**Table 13.1**  Number of SAPS Police Officials, by Rank and Race[9]

| Commissioned Officers | Black | White | Total |
|---|---|---|---|
| National Commissioner | 1 | 0 | 1 |
| Deputy National Commissioner | 1 | 2 | 3 |
| Divisional Commissioner | 5 | 6 | 11 |
| Provincial Commissioner | 8 | 0 | 8 |
| Assistant Commissioner | 62 | 51 | 113 |
| Director | 219 | 220 | 439 |
| Senior Superintendent | 372 | 564 | 936 |
| Superintendent | 1,035 | 1,872 | 2,907 |
| Captain | 4,288 | 4,430 | 8,718 |
| **Total** | **5,991** | **7,145** | **13,136** |
| *Noncommissioned Officers* | | | |
| Inspector | 31,874 | 13,641 | 45,515 |
| Sergeant | 28,006 | 5,310 | 33,316 |
| Constable | 5,575 | 518 | 6,093 |
| Students | 2,106 | 271 | 2,377 |
| **Total** | **67,561** | **19,740** | **87,301** |
| *Civilian Staff* | 13,200 | 7,403 | 20,603 |
| **Total** | **86,752** | **34,288** | **121,040** |

imbalances. Furthermore, the code of silence plays itself out along racial lines. Police officials may be more inclined to protect colleagues of the same race, particularly if the internal investigators are of a different race. On the other hand, some police members may feel less inclined to cover up for officers of a different race. The extent to which this occurs will probably be determined by the particular historical and social context of the area where particular police officers are based.

The issue of racial diversity intersects with another key challenge facing the transformation of the SAPS, namely, morale. Kessler (2001) points out that a departmental climate study conducted during 1997 found that only 18% of white police officials and 47% of black police officials saw a prosperous future for themselves in the SAPS.

Another factor behind the low level of morale has to do with the general public's perception of the police. The national Victims of Crime Survey (Statistics South Africa, 1998) revealed that 26% of respondents believed that since the 1994 democratic elections the

effectiveness of the police had improved, 32% believed that it had stayed the same, and a majority of 42% believed that the police had become less effective. In a more recent survey, the situation had changed slightly, with a majority of 46% perceiving no change in the police in the past 5 years, and 30% stating that they think the police have become worse (Louw & Pesler, 2001). While it could be construed as a good sign that the relative proportion of people who think the police are deteriorating is declining, those who think there has been no change are generally stating that they think that the police are as bad as they have always been. However, this same research found significant differences in the perceptions of members of the public who actually made use of police services at certain priority police stations. A clear majority of 77% of respondents stated that they were satisfied with the service they received at police stations (Louw & Pesler, 2001). While this may reflect that the initiatives to improve front-line service over the past few years are beginning to bear fruit, it also may be that those making use of the police had relatively low expectations about engaging with the police and were pleasantly surprised by the service they received.

While part of the dissatisfaction of the average member of the public has to do with the long-standing problems of inadequate levels of service and perceptions of police as corrupt, it also had to do with the rapid increase in the level of crime in the country during the 1990s.[10] Furthermore, police safety has become a key issue during this time, with an average of 228 police officers killed per year.[11]

Certainly, problems relating to racial diversity and morale have had a significant impact on integrity in the SAPS. Police officials generally feel under pressure and unappreciated by the public. This can make it easier for individual officers and groups of police officers to justify using their policing powers for personal gain. Furthermore, the racial differences and tensions (compounded with cultural and language differences) have hindered the development of a positive *esprit de corps* among police officers. This has prevented the establishment of a common set of standards and values that define the accepted norms of integrity throughout the police agency. The code of silence, however, continues to exist, with police officers generally very hesitant to testify against or provide information on their colleagues—in spite of having little in common with them. Apart from these sociopolitical factors, there are significant shortcomings in the formal systems of internal control, particularly the SAPS disciplinary system.

To promote the new liberal democratic philosophy of the SAPS, a process of "demilitarization" was undertaken as part of the police reform program. Apart from changes in the rank structure, uniforms, and training, this required a new disciplinary system based on labor law rather than the military procedures that had been used previously. Many officers have credited demilitarization and the emergence of police unions with a significant decline

in discipline throughout the SAPS since 1994 (Newham, 2000). The new disciplinary system requires many more procedures than the old system did.[12] Furthermore, managers are removed from the disciplinary process, as formal disciplinary hearings are held away from the station at the Area level. An inadequate number of officials available to conduct hearings has led to backlogs and delays of many months, so the system is generally perceived as unwieldy, slow, and ineffective[13] (Newham, 2000). However, the procedures are in the process of being simplified, more officers are being trained, and hearings are going to start taking place at the station level.

The above section has provided a brief historical and sociopolitical context for the current integrity problem facing the SAPS. The next section will examine this problem in more detail, with particular emphasis on police corruption.

## THE INTEGRITY STATUS OF THE SAPS

Whereas it may be almost impossible to ever gauge accurately the amount of corruption taking place in any given police agency, there are certainly indicators that can give some insight into the problem a police agency is facing. Sherman (1983) explains that

> any statement about police corruption by any source—from any newspaper story to interviews with convicted police officers—can open a window to the organization of corruption at that point in time to which the statement refers. Some windows will provide more a complete view than others, but all will offer some information of value. (p. 375)

Since the birth of democracy, there have been significant changes in the society and government in terms of transparency. As a result, the public has started to hear a lot more about police corruption from the media and other sources than ever before. Furthermore, academic and independent researchers have far more access to police statistics and to police officials that was the case during apartheid.

Stories describing police corruption and other forms of criminality often make news headlines and appear regularly in newspaper, television, or radio reports. The following headlines from a variety of the country's biggest mainstream newspapers provide some insight into the kinds of stories that regularly make it into the South African media.

"Gauteng Police Chief Facing Fraud Charges" (*The Star*, November 12, 2000)

"Rotten Heist Cops Still on the Beat—Officer Supplied Armour-Piercing Bullets for Highway Robbery" (*Sunday Times*, March 4, 2001)

"Stiff Sentence for Guilty Officer Urged" (*The Star*, March 30, 2001)

"Prisoner Bribed Cops to Be With Me, Says Girlfriend" (*Sunday Times*, April 8, 2001)

"Give Me R300 and I'll Drop Charges— Police Sergeant Arrested in Sting Involving Woman and Anti-Corruption Unit" (*Saturday Star*, May 12, 2001)

"Jo'burg Cop Linked to Hijacks" (*Sowetan*, May 26, 2001)

"Watchdog Slams Tembisa Police" (*Sowetan*, September 27, 2001)

"Corrupt Cops Bust" (*The Citizen*, October 1, 2001)

While the media can provide a valuable source for gauging police corruption, they are far from reliable in giving an accurate picture of the extent of actual police corruption. With regard to the relatively few cases that do make it into the media, it is not always clear if the allegations reported on are verified. Criminal trials involving police corruption often take longer than a year to finalize and the media generally do not follow

such cases through to their completion. Generally, media reporting on incidents of police corruption in South Africa tends to be ad hoc, sensationalist, and lacking in detail. Nevertheless, the media provide a valuable source of information about some of the types of police corruption and anticorruption activities that are taking place in the country.

To get a sense of what could be learned about police corruption from press stories, Syed and Bruce (1998) collected and analyzed the instances of police corruption reported over a 15-month period from February of 1996 to April of 1997. They identified the occurrence of 16 distinct categories of police corruption out of a typology they had developed of 22 categories of possible police corruption from international literature. This research led Syed and Bruce (1998) to conclude that "the occurrence of reports on so many different types of corrupt activities in the South African press in little over a year may indicate that police corruption in South Africa is fairly extensive as well as being varied in nature" (p. 11).

Opinion surveys provide another source of information on perceptions of the extent of corruption and, thereby, on the broader societal context in which the police work. A recent survey found that out of all government services, the police were perceived to be the most corrupt, with 37.1% of respondents stating that they believe it to be "very likely" or "likely" that they would be expected to offer some material reward or favor in return for services rendered from a police officer (United Nations Office on Drugs and Crime, 2003, p. 96). An earlier, 1996 Johannesburg Victimisation Survey revealed that of the bribery and corruption experiences reported, 53.6% involved members of the South African Police (Naude, 2000). A further survey into police detectives' attitudes was undertaken by University of South Africa (UNISA) professor Ben Smit (1999), who found that a majority of the participants agreed with the statement "Many police officials are corrupt." More recently, a nation-wide representative survey on police service delivery found that of those members of the public who state that policing services have deteriorated, the single largest reason given for this belief (by 29% of the respondents) was that "the police are corrupt" (Louw & Pesler, 2001). Of course, public opinion surveys are based on people's subjective opinions and do not necessarily reflect the actual extent of police or public sector corruption. It could be that public perceptions are colored by the regular messages about police corruption that they pick up in the media. Furthermore, not everyone has the same understanding of the word *corruption*. It is likely that various other problems that people experience with the police that are related to poor discipline or incompetence could be construed as corruption. Nevertheless, the few surveys that touch on the issue of police corruption reveal that it is considered a serious problem by a substantial number of South Africans.

Indeed, official figures on police criminality and corruption are alarming. Approximately 1,500[14] police officials were convicted of criminal offenses in 1999, while 14,600 criminal cases were opened against police members during 2000 (Masuko, 2001). Reckless driving made up the single biggest offense (25% of the cases) of which police officers were convicted in 1999, but convictions were also obtained for assault (15%), aggravated assault (9%), theft (7%), corruption (3%), attempted murder (3%), and murder (1%).

While these criminal cases reflect a serious problem relating to police integrity, official figures released by the SAPS Anti-Corruption Unit (ACU) begin to provide more of a glimpse into the extent of police corruption problems in South Africa. The ACU started operating in 1996 and its key objective is the "effective prevention and investigation of corruption within the SAPS" (South African Police Service, 2000, p. 3). The ACU acts on behalf of the Divisional Commissioner of Detective Services and is coordinated by a national head office that is responsible for setting guidelines and overseeing the provincial units. Up until the end of 2000, there were approximately 250 members of the ACU charged with investigating allegations of corruption committed by police officers around the country. The figures released by the ACU for the period from 1996 to 2001 can be found in Figure 13.1.

Given that police corruption is accepted as an underreported phenomenon, the figures provided by the ACU are astounding. Apart from the sheer numbers of cases reported[16] what is also striking is the extent to which these numbers have increased consistently over the past few years. Whereas 2,300 cases were reported during 1996, this figure had risen by 263% to 6,048 for the year 2000. As can well be imagined, this unit has not been popular within the SAPS and almost half its offices were closed at the end of 2000 with a loss of about 100 personnel. No official explanations were given for this decision but the affect on the work of the unit can be seen in the reduction of reported cases and police members charged and arrested for corruption. At the end of 2002, an official announcement was made that the unit would be closed down as part of a restructuring process of the detective units and that some of its members would continue to investigate police corruption from within the Organised Crime Unit.

What is immediately striking is the discrepancy between the number of cases reported and the number of police officials formerly charged and then finally convicted in a court of law. A key reason for this difference is that the anticorruption legislation presently in place is seriously flawed, as it has a number of loopholes (Hartley, 2001).[17] Under this legislation, successful convictions are extremely difficult to obtain, as it

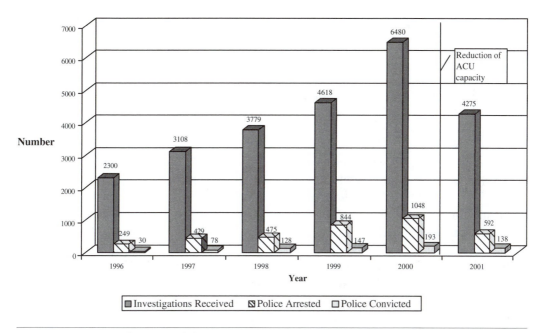

**Figure 13.1**     Annual Figures of the SAPS Anti-Corruption Unit

requires a hugely complicated chain of evidence. Consequently, most convictions obtained by the ACU are for other criminal offenses, such as bribery, extortion, fraud, or theft.[18] Furthermore, because of the large number of cases the ACU receives and its limited human and resource capacity, it is impossible for the ACU to thoroughly investigate each case it receives. A further problem confronting the ACU is that a large number of the informants on which the unit relies prefer to remain anonymous and will not testify in a court of law. Often these individuals are directly implicated and could face charges of corruption themselves if their identities are known,[19] or they fear repercussions if their identities are made known to the police member under investigation.[20] In addition to the substantial amount of time it takes to thoroughly investigate police corruption so as to be able charge a police official, it can take well over a year before the court reaches a verdict on a case.[21]

The large number of cases opened by the ACU is the clearest indication that corruption is widespread throughout the SAPS. A significant number of these cases are defined as "petty" corruption. This refers to cases where a police officer is involved sporadically or routinely in incidents of bribery involving relatively small amounts of money. This appears to be a common form of corruption involving lower ranking police officers. However, internal police investigations have also revealed that corruption is prevalent at all levels of the SAPS. Corrupt behavior at the highest levels of the SAPS is particularly disturbing. The very senior ranking National Head of Organized Crime was arrested and pled guilty a number of fraud charges involving approximately R40,000 (US$3,624), bringing into question the integrity of some of those at the highest levels of the organization.

While this may have been one of the most high-ranking officials to be arrested on criminal charges, there have been a number of other cases of senior officers involved in systematic organized police corruption. A noteworthy incident is the criminal trial of a senior ranking Provincial Head of Organised Crime, who is presently standing trial for taking substantial bribes to protect illegal gambling establishments, drug lords, and members of biker gangs and for falsely claiming reward money for informers who never existed (Kirk, 2001). However, it is to the credit of the SAPS that they investigate and criminally charge such individuals rather than just attempting to cover the incident up.

The stated approach of the SAPS toward corruption is that of "zero tolerance." Senior officers throughout the various levels of the police repeat this message and point to the arrest and conviction of police officials to emphasize it. However, it is apparent that there is no total consensus at a national level as to the extent and nature of the problem. While the previous Minister of Safety and Security, the late Mr. Steve Tshwete, seemed to think he was speaking to "the small minority who are brutal or corrupt,"[22] the National Police Commissioner Jackie Selebi publicly stated that there is "an immense problem with corruption" (Greybe, 2000). Although the anti-corruption statements made by senior officials are intended to signal the political will to fight corruption, they also reflect the lack of a coherent, well-thought-out strategy to tackle the problem. Consequently, the approach to tackling corruption in the SAPS remains largely reactive and rhetorical, although there are signs that a process is under way to develop a specific anti-corruption strategy for the police.

## INTEGRITY MEASUREMENT AT AN INNER-CITY POLICE STATION

This last section of the chapter will reflect on the results of a survey (using the measuring instrument developed by Klockars and colleagues, 2000) that was conducted in a high-crime area at an inner-city police station located in Johannesburg, South Africa's largest city. At the time the survey was conducted, about 250 police officers were based at the station and were responsible for policing approximately 200,000 people.

One of the unique characteristics of the station is that it has one of the highest crime rates in the country, with an average of over 2,000 serious crimes recorded each month. Typically, 19 of these cases are murders, and most of the rates for categories of serious and violent crime (such as armed robbery, aggravated assault, and burglary) are high. This station is one of the 145 in the country that record over 50% of the national crime rate (Lamberti, 2000). All of these police stations have been prioritized in accordance with the latest National Crime Combating Strategy (NCCS). As a result of its priority status, this station receives particular attention in relation to personnel and resources. Indeed, since 1999 its senior management component has been almost entirely replaced and restructured. Although this station and precinct have unique characteristics, the police officials based at the station largely reflect the demographics of the SAPS.

The methodology used for running the survey was to initially consult with key informants as to the clarity of the language and case studies. Although almost all police officers can speak English, only a small minority speak it as their first language. A few very small changes were made to ensure that the cases and questions in the survey were clear and unambiguous for the participants.[23] Otherwise, the content of the cases and the questions asked were presented exactly as in the original measuring instrument. The survey was then piloted among most of the senior management of the station, to obtain their understanding of and support for the research. After factoring in the absence of police officers due to sick leave, vacation

**Table 13.2**  Mean Scores and Rank Order of Inner-City Police Officers' Views of the Seriousness of the Misconduct, the Discipline It Should and Would Receive, and Officers' Willingness To Report It

| Case Number and Description | *Seriousness* Own View | Other Officers' View | *Discipline* Should Receive | | Would Receive | | *Willingness to Report* Own | Other Officers' |
|---|---|---|---|---|---|---|---|---|
| Case 1 - Off-Duty Security Systems Business | 2.82<br>3 | 2.41<br>3 | 2.16 | None | 2.34 | None | 2.29<br>2 | 2.02<br>2 |
| Case 2 - Free Meals and Discounts on Beat | 2.50<br>1 | 2.04<br>1 | 2.13 | None | 2.13 | None | 2.01<br>1 | 1.97<br>1 |
| Case 3 - Bribe From Speeding Motorist | 4.80<br>11 | 4.03<br>11 | 4.03 | Suspension Without Pay | 3.87 | Suspension Without Pay | 3.89<br>9 | 3.02<br>8 |
| Case 4 - Holiday Gifts From Merchants | 2.58<br>2 | 2.19<br>2 | 2.12 | None | 2.20 | None | 2.53<br>3 | 2.11<br>3 |
| Case 5 - Crime Scene Theft of Watch | 4.70<br>10 | 3.89<br>10 | 4.27 | Dismissal | 4.14 | Dismissal | 4.37<br>11 | 3.37<br>11 |
| Case 6 - 5% Kickback From Auto Repair Shop | 3.46<br>4 | 2.95<br>4 | 3.01 | Verbal Warning | 3.08 | Written Warning | 3.28<br>5 | 2.49<br>5 |
| Case 7 - Supervisor Grants Holiday in Exchange for Car Tune-Up | 4.10<br>8 | 3.56<br>8 | 3.16 | Written Warning | 3.15 | Written Warning | 3.41<br>8 | 3.16<br>9 |
| Case 8 - Cover-Up of Police DUI Incident | 3.77<br>5 | 3.23<br>7 | 3.14 | Written Warning | 3.09 | Written Warning | 3.33<br>6 | 2.80<br>7 |
| Case 9 - Free Drinks to Ignore Late Bar Closing | 4.54<br>9 | 3.74<br>9 | 3.56 | Written Warning | 3.46 | Written Warning | 4.11<br>10 | 3.19<br>10 |
| Case 10 - Excessive Use of Force on Car Thief | 3.89<br>6 | 3.16<br>6 | 2.98 | Written Warning | 3.03 | Written Warning | 3.18<br>4 | 2.46<br>4 |
| Case 11 - Theft From Found Wallet | 3.98<br>7 | 2.99<br>5 | 3.23 | Written Warning | 3.27 | Written Warning | 3.33<br>7 | 2.55<br>6 |

**Table 13.3**    Percentage of Officers Who View the Misconduct as a Violation of Official SAPS Policy

| Case Number and Description | n | Not a Violation | Unsure | Definitely a Violation |
|---|---|---|---|---|
| Case 1 - Off-Duty Security Systems Business | 104 | 30.77% | 8.65% | 60.58% |
| Case 2 - Free Meals and Discounts on Beat | 104 | 40.38% | 11.54% | 48.08% |
| Case 3 - Bribe From Speeding Motorist | 104 | 5.77% | 0.00% | 94.23% |
| Case 4 - Holiday Gifts From Merchants | 104 | 36.54% | 11.54% | 50.96% |
| Case 5 - Crime Scene Theft of Watch | 104 | 6.73% | 3.85% | 89.42% |
| Case 6 - 5% Kickback From Auto Repair Shop | 104 | 23.08% | 8.65% | 68.27% |
| Case 7 - Supervisor Grants Holiday in Exchange for Car Tune-Up | 104 | 11.54% | 8.65% | 79.81% |
| Case 8 - Cover-Up of Police DUI Accident | 104 | 10.58% | 11.54% | 75.96% |
| Case 9 - Free Drinks to Ignore Late Bar Closing | 104 | 6.73% | 6.73% | 86.54% |
| Case 10 - Excessive Force on Car Thief | 104 | 10.58% | 9.62% | 79.81% |
| Case 11 - Theft From Found Wallet | 104 | 21.15% | 6.73% | 72.12% |

leave, and suspension, 200 questionnaires were distributed throughout the station. Of this number, 104 were usable, which resulted in a sample size of 42.8% of the police officials based at the station. The characteristics of the sample size are as follows:

- 58% had been police officers for longer than 10 years, with 42% of the sample having served less than 10 years
- 42% of those surveyed held some form of supervisory position
- 52% were uniformed officers and 48% were nonuniformed officers

With regard to the perceived seriousness of the offenses, the 11 case scenarios fall into three categories. These categories include cases that were not considered serious, cases considered to be of intermediate seriousness, and cases considered more serious.

A majority of the respondents did not consider the following cases as serious at all: Case 1 (Off-Duty Security System Business), Case 2 (Free Meals and Discounts on Beat), and Case 4 (Holiday Gifts From Merchants). In answering the question as to whether they

thought their colleagues would consider these serious, from 60% to 70% indicated that they would not. While a majority of the respondents recognized that these cases reflect violations of police policy, as much as 40% of the respondents were unsure or did not recognize a violation taking place (Table 13.3). These findings suggest that such practices are relatively common among the police officers in this station.

Respondents considered the offenses in Case 6 (5% Kickback From Auto Repair Shop), Case 8 (Cover-Up of Police DUI Accident), Case 10 (Excessive Force on Car Thief), and Case 11 (Theft From Found Wallet) to be of an intermediate level of seriousness. Once again, respondents revealed that they think their colleagues would not consider these offenses nearly as serious as they themselves do. This difference was particularly noticeable with regard to Cases 6 and 11, where, respectively, 30% and 21% of respondents indicated that they do not consider these cases serious, while 42% (for both cases) indicated that their colleagues would not consider these cases serious. Surprisingly, regarding both these cases (Case 11 was considered the most serious of the four intermediate cases), over 20% of the respondents indicate that they do not think that there was an official violation of policy at all, whereas in each case 10% indicated that they are not sure whether or not there was a violation. Notably, for Case 11 (Theft From Found Wallet), which would be considered by many a serious offense, as many as one in five respondents appears to be unaware that it involves a violation of the regulations. For these two cases, it could be that substantial numbers of police officers consider kickbacks a legitimate return for a favor and consider finding money in a lost wallet "good luck" for the person who found it.

Case 3 (Bribe From Speeding Motorist), Case 5 (Crime Scene Theft of Watch), Case 7 (Supervisor Grants Holiday in Exchange for Car Tune-Up), and Case 9 (Free Drinks to Ignore Late Bar Closing) were considered by the officers to be the most serious of all the cases. Once again there were substantial differences between respondent's self-reports and how they think their colleagues would respond. While 8% state that they do not think Case 9 is serious, 25% state that their colleagues would not consider it as serious. For the cases generally considered most serious (Cases 3 and 5), 4% state that they do not consider the offenses in either of these cases serious, while 19% (almost one in five) state that their colleagues would not consider the offenses serious. Although a vast majority of respondents recognize that there is a violation of policy in the cases considered most serious, still 5% or more do not.

In relation to discipline, for the three cases considered least serious, the officers generally think that no discipline is appropriate and would be forthcoming if these violations were discovered. The exception is Case 1 where the officers consider a verbal warning appropriate, while the mode response for what would occur was either no discipline or

a written warning. This suggests that some respondents perceive the disciplinary system as too lenient, while others see it as too harsh in this case.

For the cases considered to be of intermediate seriousness, respondents generally think that a written warning is the appropriate discipline for the offenses, and that this is what would happen if such offenses were discovered. For the cases considered most serious, only Cases 3 and 5 are considered to be serious enough to warrant dismissal or suspension without pay. Notably, while Case 3 is considered slightly more serious than Case 5, it is seen as warranting considerably less disciplinary sanction.

Interestingly enough, for all cases there was quite a spread of answers when one looks at the ratio for each answer. Generally, for each case, three forms of discipline would each receive 20% to 30% of the responses. The mode response was rarely above 40%. For example, with regard to the appropriate discipline for the offense in Case 3 (considered the most serious case), 24% think dismissal would be appropriate, 8% think demotion would be appropriate, 32% think suspension without pay would be appropriate, 18% think a written warning would be appropriate, and 13% think a verbal warning would be the appropriate discipline. These findings reveal that there is no shared perception as to the type of disciplinary sanction that should be applied in cases of misconduct.

The mode responses give the overall impression that respondents think that the discipline that would be imposed would be fair, as there was little difference between the discipline respondents think should be meted out and would be meted out. However, the various perceptions as to how the organization would respond to the cases presented reveals that the respondents have no common understanding of how the organization responds to misconduct.

When it comes to the extent of the code of silence, with respect to only five cases did the majority of respondents indicate that they would report the misconduct. Regarding Case 6 (5% Kickback From Auto Repair Shop), 53% indicate they would report it; regarding Case 7 (Supervisor Grants Holiday in Exchange For Car Tune-Up), 50% indicate they would report it; regarding Case 9 (Free Drinks to Ignore Late Bar Closing), 72% indicate they would report it; regarding Case 5 (Crime Scene Theft of Watch), 80% indicate that they would probably report the misconduct. Interestingly enough, for Case 3 (Bribe From Speeding Motorist), which the respondents considered the most serious offense, only 66% of the respondents indicate that they would report the violation. However, when it came to the question about whether respondents think that their colleagues would report violations, only with regard to Case 5 did as many as 50% indicate that they think so. Regarding all the other cases, a clear majority of the respondents indicated that either their colleagues would not report the violations or that they were unsure as to what their colleagues would do.

From these results, a number of conclusions relating to police integrity at this station become clear. First, the respondents generally did not think that most of the cases presented in the survey constituted a serious abuse of police powers. Notably, Case 11 (Theft From Found Wallet) is considered to be of intermediate seriousness and ranked only fourth lowest as misconduct that officers think they would report. This calls into question the ethical standards of these officers generally and where they draw the line on misusing their police powers for personal gain. This strongly suggests that ethical standards are not commonly shared throughout the agency, nor are acceptable ethical standards being adequately communicated and consistently enforced.

Second, there were significant differences between officials' personal responses and what they think their colleagues' responses would be. This was clearly expressed in responses to most of the questions on the survey. The issue was again highlighted in the responses to the last two questions of the survey, regarding whether the respondents answered the questionnaire honestly or not. Whereas 95.2% of the respondents indicate that they gave their honest opinions when answering the survey, only 60.6% of respondents think that their colleagues gave their honest opinions. This discrepancy reveals the relatively low level of trust that the police officers at this station have of each other. Certainly it will be difficult to promote a normative inclination to resist abuses of power when police officers perceive their colleagues to hold different norms and values than those they themselves hold.

Third, there are substantial numbers of people who are not aware of official departmental policy in relation to misconduct. For the cases considered least serious, only 50% of the officers were aware that there was a violation of official policy. For seven out of the eleven cases, at least one in five officers did not perceive a violation of policy to exist or were not sure if there was one. Once again, this finding shows that there are serious shortcomings in the police organization's ability to ensure that its rules and regulations are fully understood.

Fourth, there are considerable differences of perceptions among officers about the internal disciplinary system. The spread of answers in relation to discipline for each of the cases reveals that there is not a consistent understanding of the system. The system has changed twice since 1994, and indications are that there remains a lack of clarity about how it operates and an inconsistency of understanding as to what constitutes serious or less serious misconduct. Indeed, most police officers at this station have not had disciplinary steps taken against them and would not be aware of what kinds of sanctions would be imposed for specific violations. Generally, police officials do not consider the disciplinary system effective or a real deterrent to misconduct. This has significant implications for attempts to combat corruption and criminality within the South African Police Service.

Fifth, it is clear that the code of silence is a strong characteristic of the police culture at this station. While respondents generally indicate a willingness to report only the most serious of offenses, even then there is an indication that the officers have little faith that their colleagues would report such incidents. This relates to the previous point. If most police officers do not believe that reporting the misconduct of colleagues will result in adequate disciplinary action being taken, then they are less likely to report misconduct themselves.

## CONCLUSION

The reform process of the SAPS has come a long way since the advent of democracy in 1994. The political landscape within which a negotiated settlement was reached precluded a radical approach to developing a police service based on liberal democratic values. Racial and ethnic differences also contribute to undermining the establishment of a common set of values and standards within the police. At the same time, the crime wave that struck the country during the latter part of the 1990s resulted in much of the reform process focusing on the operational dimensions of policing at the expense of organizational culture. These factors, combined with a diffuse organizational culture, low morale, and inadequate systems of control, have resulted in the significant integrity problem confronting the SAPS.

The integrity-measuring instrument used in the study discussed here reflects many of the cultural characteristics that have an impact on the integrity of the police organization as a whole. In particular, the lack of adherence to positive organizational values, inadequate systems of internal control, and a strong code of silence characterized by police officers being unwilling to report misconduct, contribute to the high levels of corruption and criminality prevalent in the SAPS. Indeed, it could be argued that so far the organization's attempts to combat corruption have been very weak. Clear ethical standards are not being adequately communicated to and encouraged in South Africa's police officers. Many officers are not fully aware of the rules and regulations governing misconduct and, even if they are aware of them, do not see the organization as able to take appropriate or adequate disciplinary action if violations come to light. As a result, those officers who are frustrated by corruption would be very hesitant to report violations by their fellow officers.

It needs to be recognized that the reform process is far from over. Crime remains one of the biggest challenges facing South Africa's democracy, and there will continue to be public and political pressure on the police to improve their performance and behavior. Although at a policy level the response to police corruption has so far been inadequate, combating and preventing corruption remains an official national policing priority. There are indications that a new strategic approach is being developed in this regard and that, in addition, many of the other systemic and institutional reforms that have been instituted since democracy should have a positive impact on police integrity in South Africa in the long run. Hopefully, the day will arrive in the not-too-distant future where, as far as police integrity is concerned, the SAPS learn to march in step.

## NOTES

1. "Homelands" or "Bantmustans," as they were also known, were politically autonomous geographical areas within the borders of South Africa established by the apartheid regime as a scheme to strip black South Africans of their citizenship. Millions of black South Africans were forcibly moved into these areas according to which "ethnic group" they were deemed to belong. While each homeland had its own government and police force, it was largely economically dependent on the apartheid state. The homelands were disbanded with the advent of democracy.

2. These included a number of loosely constituted government protection structures, such as the "municipal police" and the "railway police."

3. The two main unions are the South African Police Union (SAPU) and the Police and Prison Officials Civil Rights Union (POPCRU). One crucial issue on which the unions have had an impact is through resisting lateral-entry recruitment as a strategy for ensuring "new blood" at management level. The unions were concerned that their lower ranking members be promoted into management posts as part of the affirmative action policy.

4. As a result, South Africa currently has 1 sworn police officer for every 424 citizens. This translates into a ratio of 236 police officers per 100,000 people, which is less than England, with 347 officers, or the United States, with 300 officers, but more than other similarly developed countries (such as Turkey, with 190 officers).

5. A constable after a year's training would take home between R800 (US$72) and R1200 (US$109) per month after taxes and other deductions.

6. The private security industry has experienced phenomenal growth since 1994 and presently employs more than 216,000 people, whereas the SAPS employs 121,000 people (Schonteich, 2000).

7. There were no new police recruits for approximately 3 years following the 1994 elections. As a result, constables and sergeants make up approximately 30% of the total staff of the SAPS as opposed to Australia where they make up 94% or 91% in Britain.

8. There were four official racial classifications during apartheid: White, Indian, Colored, and African. These classifications are still in use today for affirmative action purposes. Generally, the "Black" category includes "Coloureds" and "Indians" and refers to all people not classified "White."

9. Statistics for August 31, 2001, from the SAPS National Head Office.

10. By the end of 2000, the total crime incidents recorded were 2,479,700, which was 481,000 more crimes than were recorded during 1994. In particular, violent crime had increased by 33.6% during this period. Statistics from the South African Crime Information Analysis Centre can be accessed at http://www.saps.org.za/8_crimeinfo/bulletin/index.htm.

11. Statistics from the South African Crime Information Analysis Centre can be accessed at http://www.saps.org.za/8_crimeinfo/bulletin/index.htm.

12. Commanders are now required to formally record verbal and written warnings and to engage in counseling sessions following each incident of less serious misconduct. More serious disciplinary action (i.e., a hearing) can be initiated for repeated offenses considered less serious only if these other steps have been taken.

13. Between the end of March and the end of August of 2001, 7,045 new disciplinary cases had been registered and only 3,718 had been

finalized. These backlogs reflect the extent to which the system cannot cope with the number of cases it has to deal with. (These statistics were obtained from the SAPS national Head of Discipline management on October 15, 2001.)

14. This figure represents a substantial increase from the yearly average between 1995 and 1999 of 1,320 convictions. This could be as a result of the massive increase in the number of complaints against the police—from 11,495 in 1996 to 17,526 by the end of 1997. Criminal cases against the police typically take much longer than a year to finalize.

15. Figures obtained from the South African Police Services Annual Report for 2001 to 2002.

16. The ACU receives cases from all sources, including citizens complaints, other police units, the Independent Complaints Directorate, and even members of criminal syndicates who get into a dispute with the police officers they are working with.

17. At the time of this writing, a new Anti-Corruption Bill is being considered in parliament that provides clearer definitions of corrupt incidents. It is expected that this legislation, if passed, will significantly enhance the ability of prosecutors to obtain convictions for corruption.

18. For instance, while the ACU was responsible for 9% of the convictions against police officials in 1999, only 3% were officially recorded as corruption.

19. Although immunity from prosecution may be offered for testimony, it is not guaranteed until the completion of the trial that this will be the case. Recently however, a system for plea-bargaining been introduced which may assist in prosecutions against corruption.

20. Interview with Director Stef Grobler, national Head of the SAPS Anti-Corruption Unit, June 21, 2001.

21. According to Director Stef Grobler, national Head of the SAPS Anti-Corruption Unit, it takes an average of 18 months to complete such a "project" (Interview, June 21, 2001).

22. This speech was the Safety and Security Budget Vote and Independent Complaints Directorate Appropriation Bill Address by Minister S.V. Tshwete, which was presented in the National Assembly on June 7, 2001.

23. For instance, SAPS officials would generally not stop a motorist for speeding, as in Case 6 (this is the responsibility of Traffic Department officials), but they would stop a motorist for driving under the influence of alcohol, what is commonly referred to as "reckless and negligent" driving.

## REFERENCES

Brogden, M., & Shearing, C. (1993). *Policing for a new South Africa*. London: Routledge.

Chan, J. B. L. (1997). *Changing police culture. Policing in a multicultural society*. Cambridge, UK: Cambridge University Press.

Frič, P., & Waleck, C. (2001). *Crossing the thin blue line: An international annual review of anti-corruption strategies in the police*. Prague: Transparency International.

Goldsmith, A. (1990). Taking police culture seriously: Police discretion and the limits of the law. *Policing and Society, 1*, 91-114.

Greybe, D. (2000, March 2). SAPS Streamlines its approach to policing. *Business Day*, p. 4.

Hartley, W. (2001, November 21). MPs want to close loopholes. *Business Day*, p. 3.

Kessel, I. van. (2001, July 1-4). *Transforming the South African Police Service (SAPS): The changing meaning of change*. Paper presented at the annual conference of the South African Sociological Association, "Globalisation, Inequality and Identity," University of South Africa (UNISA).

Kirk, P. (2001, March 16). Top cop accused of extortion quits. *The Mail and Guardian*, p. 12.

Klockars, C. B., Kutnjak Ivkovich, S., Harver, W., & Haberfeld, M. R. (2000). *The measurement of police integrity*. National Institute of Justice Research Brief. Washington DC: Office of Justice Programs, U.S. Department of Justice.

Lamberti, T. (2000, March 16). Crackdown targets 124 crime hot spots. *Business Day*, p. 3.

Laufer, S. (2001). The politics of fighting crime in South Africa since 1994. In J. Steinberg (Ed.), *Crime wave: The South African underworld and its foes* (pp. 14-23). Johannesburg: Witwatersrand University Press.

Louw, A., & Pelser, E. (2001). *Community policing and police service improvement study. A project report*. Pretoria: Institute for Security Studies.

Mabuza, E. (2001, August 27). Good economy can help fight crime. *Business Day*, p. 12.

Masuko, S. (2001). Policing the police: SAPS members charged and convicted of crime. *Nedbank/Institute for Security Studies Crime Index*, 5(2), 13-16.

Naude, B. (2000, Spring). To catch a cheat: Comparing corruption and fraud victimisation data. *Crime and Conflict*, 21, 21-25.

Newham, G. (2000). *Transformation and the internal disciplinary system of the South African Police Service*. Johannesburg: Centre for the Study of Violence and Reconciliation.

Palmer, M. (1992). Controlling corruption. In P. Moir & H. Eijkman (Eds.), *Policing Australia: Old issues, new perspectives*. Melbourne: The Macmillan Company of Australia.

Rauch, J. (2000). *Police reform and South Africa's transition*. Johannesburg: Centre for the Study of Violence and Reconciliation.

Schonteich, M. (2000). Guarding the guardians: New regulations for the private security industry. *Nedbank/Institute for Security Studies Crime Index*, 4(3), 13-16.

Shaw, M. (2001). *Crime and policing in transitional societies*. Seminar report 2001, No 8. Johannesburg: Konrad-Adenauer-Stiftung/Ins.

Sherman, L. (1983). Scandal and reform. In C. B. Klockars (Ed.), *Thinking about police: Contemporary readings*. New York: McGraw-Hill.

Smit, B. (1999, September 22-25). *Investigating morale amongst police detectives*. Paper presented at the 1999 World Conference on Modern Criminal Investigation, Organized Crime and Human Rights held at Sun City, South Africa.

South African Police Service (SAPS). (2000). *Policy document for anti-corruption units*. Pretoria, South Africa: Divisional Commissioner Detective Services (SAPS).

Statistics South Africa. (1998). *Victims of Crime Survey*. Pretoria: Statistics South Africa.

Syed, T., & Bruce, D. (1998). Inside and outside the boundaries of police corruption. *African Security Review*, 7(2), 3-21.

The Truth and Reconciliation Commission. (1998). *Truth and Reconciliation of South Africa Report*, 2. Cape Town: Juta and Co.

United Nations Office on Drugs and Crime. (2003). *Country Assessment Report. South Africa*. Pretoria: United Nations Office on Drugs and Crime, Regional Office for Southern Africa.

# CHAPTER 14

# Homogeneity in Moral Standards in Swedish Police Culture

MARIE TORSTENSSON LEVANDER

BÖRJE EKENVALL

## INTRODUCTION

This chapter will give a brief overview of the current status of police integrity in Sweden. It is based on a study conducted in Sweden in 1999 (Ekenvall, 2000; 2002). According to Klockars, Kutnjak Ivkovich, Harver, and Haberfeld (2000), *police integrity* can be defined as "the normative inclination among police to resist temptations to abuse the rights and privileges of their office" (p. 10). All human behavior can be described from both an individual and a contextual perspective. We are born as unique individuals, shaped by our experiences (including education), and controlled by the structure around us.

A primary objective of this chapter is to discuss whether police recruits are initiated into a culture that accepts or rejects norm-violating behavior and whether the police force recruits people with a high propensity to violate the rules. An important question,

therefore, is whether the ability of police officers to resist temptations is to be looked upon as an individual problem (the "bad apple" theory) or as an educational, organizational, or cultural issue. A marked shift in the orientation of research on this issue took place in the early to mid-1970s. Until then, the main focus of debate was on bad apples (i.e., odd, maladjusted individuals within the police force). The idea was that better recruitment would lead to a reduction in the intake of such people. This approach was apparently endorsed by the U.S. police service as a way to explain and to some extent mitigate the impact of various internal scandals (Simpson, 1977; Stoddard, 1968). The bad apple is blamed when the integrity of a department can no longer be defended and administrators need a scapegoat to provide an excuse and explanation for a bad situation.

However, this approach has attracted increasing criticism (see, e.g., Bordua,

1967; Goldstein, 1975, 1977; The Knapp Commission, 1972; Reiss, 1971). A leading alternative to this approach is the hypothesis that corrupt behavior in a police force is socially conditioned and shaped by the "code of silence" rather than by individuals (Stoddard, 1968). "It is the barrel that needs the examination, not the apples" (Burnham, 1973, p. 93, quoted in Simpson, 1977). Thus, the focus has switched from regarding the problem as the individual to regarding the problem as occupational and/or organizational (see, e.g., Klockars et al., 2000; Sherman, 1974).

Sweden's experience of integrity with regard to corruption in public and municipal administration is very limited. A small number of incidents have been noted in the police force, though all were of a fairly minor nature. The Swedish parliamentary ombudsman keeps an eagle eye on every official in law enforcement and criticizes any lapse. According to our experience, the most common infringements are related to acceptance of inducements such as small discounts on the cost of lunches, coffee, and the like. There have been a few cases of senior officers accepting offers of discounts on new cars bought privately. Corruptive tendencies appear to be more prevalent in local government, where during the past 10 years there have been repeated instances of municipal politicians abusing the rights and privileges of office.

This chapter will first give a brief overview of the Swedish Police Service in terms of its organization, training, and career system. Second, it will present and discuss the results of the study conducted in Sweden in 1999. Two important issues to consider are to what extent there is a unified view among police officers on the corruption issue and what happens to a police officer's attitude toward corruption during the course of a professional career. As Sherman (1999) stated, police work involves a professional career and a moral career.

## THE SWEDISH POLICE SERVICE: A BRIEF OVERVIEW

### Careers

As of the end of 2001, the Swedish Police Service is comprised of about 16,120 police officers, of whom 18% are women. Its organization and system of rank differs somewhat from those in many other countries. At a general level, there are only four main categories in the ranking hierarchy. *Assistant* is the lowest rank and includes newcomers from the National Police Academy and line officers. After a number of years on the job, most assistants generally become *inspectors*. Some will, in turn, be promoted to become *chief inspector* (*kommissarie*). The fourth category is *police chiefs* (*commissioners*), who have until recently been recruited more or less straight from their law studies. However, this policy has changed and nowadays chief inspectors may be promoted to police chief rank after completing complementary law studies.

There is a political ambition in Sweden that the police force should mirror Swedish society. For this reason, efforts are made to recruit more students with an immigrant background to the National Police Academy. However, there are difficulties attached to fulfilling this goal and the rather few police students recruited from immigrant ranks have been second-generation immigrants (i.e., individuals born in Sweden).

### Organization

Since 1965 the Swedish Police Service has been organized as a national police force, and since 1992 it has consisted of 21 local districts (1 per county). Each district has a police authority headed by a County Police Chief with responsibility for police work in the region. The police authority is managed by a board—the National Police Board (NPB)—appointed by the government. The NPB is headed by the National Police Commissioner and is the central administrative and supervisory authority of the police service. The NPB is also responsible for developing new work methods and technological support. Through the National Police Academy it is also responsible for training police officers.

Sweden's police force has been built up around its main duty of "maintaining order and safety" (The Police Act 1984). This can be expressed as the objective that people should, insofar as is possible, be able to live in society without being exposed to crime or experiencing fear of crime. A constitutional framework regulates the police's work more directly. It is rather broad and encompasses a wide variety of duties. The first section of the Police Act states that the work of the police is part of society's efforts to promote justice and safety. The purpose of police work is to maintain public order and safety and to provide the public with protection and other assistance. The Act's second section lists the main duties of the police as being to "prevent crime and other disturbances to public order and safety" and to "supervise public order and safety, prevent disturbances, etc." The third section of the Act states that the police shall cooperate with public prosecution authorities, the social service, and other authorities.

## Training

Police officers' basic training spans 2 years, during which shorter periods of work experience are undertaken. Prior to 2000, all police officers in Sweden were trained at the Swedish National Police Academy in Stockholm, which may imply that past recruits were socialized into a quite similar culture of norms and values, at least as long as they remained at the Academy. Today, training is also conducted at two subsidiaries of the Academy at universities in Umeå and Växjö. The decision to decentralize training reflects a proposed effort to link

practical elements of police training with various academic disciplines.

Nowadays, the training follows identical study plans in all locations, but it may be executed differently depending on local policies, teachers' competencies, and local educational interests and models. The main focus of the basic training is "police science," which includes the main duties and basic work methods of the police and relevant legal rules. Law and behavioral science also form part of the syllabus. Ethics is not taught as an individual course subject like criminology or the handling of weapons. Instead, the aim is that ethical discussions should permeate the entire curriculum, although the quantity and quality of such ethical content may depend on individual teachers.

Further training beyond the mandatory 2 years is not compulsory and is at the discretion of local police forces. This means that competency levels can vary on account of economic conditions, commanders' training preferences, or individual police districts' policy on training at a given point in time. The content of additional training is determined to a great extent either by the local police commander or other local representatives or by the National Police Academy (with respect to the courses it offers). Certainly, curricula may vary according to the organizing body.

## THE STUDY

### The Main Study and the Reference Groups

The Swedish study was mainly conducted as a postal survey (with two reminders) sent to residential addresses over the 5 months from April to August of 1999 (Ekenvall, 2000). An attempt was made to compare two different methods of administering the questionnaire in the main study. One method was to send them by post to police officers' home

**Table 14.1**    Distribution of Responses in the Main Study by Rank, Age, and Gender (N = 1,560)

| | Age 26-35 | | Age 36-50 | | Age 51-65 | | |
| | *Male* | *Female* | *Male* | *Female* | *Male* | *Female* | *Total* |
|---|---|---|---|---|---|---|---|
| Assistants | 161 | 73 | 114 | 42 | 52 | 6 | 448 |
| Inspectors | 51 | 19 | 427 | 96 | 383 | 20 | 996 |
| Chief Inspectors | — | — | 29 | — | 59 | 2 | 90 |
| Police Chiefs | — | 1 | 5 | 2 | 17 | 1 | 26 |
| Total | 212 | 93 | 575 | 140 | 511 | 29 | 1,560 |

Note: There were 19 cases that could not be classified according to age and gender.

addresses to be filled in individually; the other was to have them filled in by officers while they were on duty (at a certain time and place at their respective stations).

For practical and financial reasons, only 82 police officers in two rural police departments were able to take part in sessions organized for on-duty officers to fill in the questionnaire. No significant differences were found in the answers submitted from the two different environments, except with regard to one case (that of an officer's running a private business alongside—and potentially in some conflict with—his work as a police officer).

The main study sample contained a group of 2,109 police officers. The Swedish version of the survey also involved an effort to compare the main study sample with all instructors in police ethics (N = 80) and with a class of recently graduated police cadets (N = 64). The reason for including the comparison groups was the hypothesis that the ethical instructors, with responsibility for ethics in the police organization, ought to have a higher level of integrity and that the police cadets (who probably were still not fully socialized into the police culture) ought to reject rather than accept corrupt behavior.

*Sampling*

A two-step sampling process was conducted. First, 9 of Sweden's 21 police departments were selected. Three of these were departments in Sweden's largest cities (Stockholm, Gothenburg, and Malmö), together accounting for 58% of the national police force. The remaining 18 departments—here referred to as mid-sized or rural departments—do not vary greatly in size and are similar in a number of other ways. Two departments were therefore chosen at random from northern Sweden, two from the central part of the country, and two from the south.

Second, 2,109 police officers were chosen proportionally at random (1,200 or 58% from the big city departments and 909 or 42% from mid-sized or rural departments) and included in the main study, along with the 80 ethics instructors and 64 police cadets, respectively, in the two reference groups.

Of the 2,109 officers in the total sample, 1,590 answered the questionnaire (see Table 14.1). After correction for 11 questionnaires (which the respondents admitted contained false answers), the final response rate was 76% (*n* = 1,579), although it was significantly lower in metropolitan areas (69%-72%) than it was in rural districts (79%). In a few regions, an introductory letter from the Chief Superintendent was attached to the questionnaire. The response rate was somewhat higher for this group.

The nonresponse rate varied according to age and was significantly higher among the youngest respondents (26-35 years of age) and the oldest respondents (50 years of age and over). The nonresponse rate also varied according to region and was significantly lower in urbanized areas than in rural areas (83% and 70%, respectively; $p < .001$). No differences in response rate were found with respect to gender. The distribution of answers according to rank is shown in Table 14.1. A majority of the respondents were assistants and inspectors ($n = 448$ and $n = 996$, respectively). For 19 participants, data on age, gender, and/or rank were missing.

### The Reference Groups

As a comparison to the main sample, the questionnaire was distributed to 80 ethics instructors in the Swedish police force and to all 64 police cadets in their final semester at the National Police Academy during the spring of 1999.

Of the ethics instructors, 74% ($N = 59$, 36-50 years of age, 40% female) answered the questionnaire. All the cadets answered the questionnaire ($N = 64$, 26-30 years of age, 42% female).

### The Questionnaire

The questionnaire is based on questions asked in a study of police integrity initiated at the University of Delaware by Klockars and colleagues (2000). It consists of 11 scenarios for the respondent to consider. For each scenario, the respondent is given identical questions (with five or six options on a Likert scale; see Exhibit 1.1).

Four scenarios were added to the final section of the Swedish version of the questionnaire that were assumed to reflect particular aspects of the Swedish police system and culture. The four scenarios are as follows:

Case A - An officer accepting a Sunday dinner for himself or herself and his or her spouse (This is a variation on the scenario in Case 9, an officer's accepting a few drinks in the bar,

which was considered too alien to the "Swedish police mentality" and was consequently rephrased.)

Cases B and C - Two variations on the same theme: An officer using a police car to be picked up from home when going to work either during the day or at night (when public transportation is unavailable). (This is a matter that is frequently discussed in police circles, and also a matter that has required discipline in some cases.)

Case D - An officer inaccurately filling out time sheets with regard to his or her working hours (This, like the case above, deals with the issue of the personal responsibility of the police officer.)

## STUDY RESULTS

### Officers' Acceptance or Rejection of the Misconduct in the Scenarios

Overall, the results indicate a high level of integrity in the respondents with regard to conduct violating norms and rules. Table 14.2 presents the mean values and standard deviations for each scenario. The mean values clearly illustrate that the respondents strongly distance themselves from the conduct in the majority of the scenarios and that deviations from the mean values are very low.

However, there are some variations according to the perceived seriousness of the misconduct. The respondents accord the least acceptance to behavior that clearly violates the law—crime scene theft (Case 5) and bribe for not reporting the speed limit violation (Case 3). All or almost all the respondents regard such misconduct as serious or very serious.

The respondents express a low acceptance of behavior such as accepting kickbacks and bribes (e.g., receiving a commission for recommending people to a certain auto body shop [Case 6], a free Sunday dinner for the family for not reporting a bar that stayed

**Table 14.2** Officers' Views of the Seriousness of the Misconduct in the Scenarios

| Case Number | Mean | Standard Deviation | Range* |
|---|---|---|---|
| 1 | 1.51 | 1.34 | 0-4 |
| 2 | 3.10 | 0.98 | 0-4 |
| 3 | 3.98 | 0.16 | 2-4 |
| 4 | 3.07 | 1.02 | 0-4 |
| 5 | 3.99 | 0.08 | 3-4 |
| 6 | 3.73 | 0.55 | 0-4 |
| 7 | 3.82 | 0.44 | 1-4 |
| 8 | 3.73 | 0.58 | 0-4 |
| 9 | 3.72 | 0.57 | 0-4 |
| 10 | 3.36 | 0.87 | 0-4 |
| 11 | 3.96 | 0.2 | 2-4 |
| A | 3.72 | 0.55 | 0-4 |
| B | 1.24 | 1.11 | 0-4 |
| C | 0.77 | 1.02 | 0-4 |
| D | 1.72 | 1.26 | 0-4 |

Note: 0 = Not at all serious, 4 = Very serious

open late [Case 9], or repairing the boss's car in return for time off from work [Case 7]. A high percentage of the respondents (96%-98%) regard such misconduct as serious or very serious. Not reporting a drunk driving colleague (Case 8) also fell into this category.

The respondents express low to medium acceptance for conduct like receiving holiday gifts (Case 4) and the use of excessive force on a captive car thief (Case 10). The percentages were 76% and 85%, respectively, for these scenarios.

On the other hand, a great majority of the respondents strongly accept the notion of getting a free ride to work in a police car (Cases B and C). Only 14% report that being picked up and driven to work by a colleague instead of using public transportation is serious misconduct (Case B) and only 8% think it is serious misconduct to be picked up at night after public transportation has stopped running (Case C). It is somewhat astonishing that almost half of the respondents show a strong acceptance of inaccurately filling out time sheets (Case D).

It comes as no surprise that respondents strongly accept the running of a private business selling security devices during off-duty hours (Case A). More than half of the respondents (53%) respond positively to the idea. In Sweden, at least, it is apparently quite common for police officers to run private businesses, often in security. Such sideline occupations are not prohibited, but a Swedish police officer is supposed to inform his or her employer if he or she intends to take such a job. In general, a police officer must observe three considerations in this context. First, the extra work should not be regarded as a (physical) obstacle and thereby impede the officer from carrying out his or her police duties. Second, the extra job should not compete with the primary job (policing). Third—and the trickiest to evaluate—is that the person cannot take extra work that could undermine confidence in his or her role as a police officer.

Partial employment in a shop might be considered acceptable, but it is considered a much greater conflict of interest for the police officer to run a business, though it is not specifically prohibited. The police carefully examine every such case and if confidence in the officer is questioned, he or she will not be permitted to continue with the work. (However, examples have been recorded of police officers who, to avoid being sanctioned, name their spouses as formally responsible for the business.)

### Gender and Age Differences

Regarding gender differences, the results show quite small variations between males and females. There is one significant exception to this, namely, that females strongly reject the use of excessive force in Case 10 (90% for female officers and 84% for male officers; $X^2 = 15.928$, $df = 4$, $p < .003$). Thus, female police officers exhibit a stronger stance against using violence in the course of their work than do male officers. This could possibly reflect a "softer" attitude or illustrate a "social desirability," whereby women ought to think less positively about and be less inclined to violence than are men.

The effect of the officers' age on their responses to the individual scenarios is generally quite small. However, a correlation analysis shows that age has significant ($p = < .001$) positive effects on four attitudes: acceptance of running a private security business (Case 1) (gamma = 0.23), of the two scenarios involving getting a free ride in a police car (gamma = 0.19 in both Cases, B and C), and of inaccuracies with time sheets (Case D) (gamma = 0.16).

Obviously, rank correlates strongly with age (gamma = 0.63), and we therefore get the same significant correlations between rank and acceptance of scenarios as between age and acceptance. The higher integrity the older police officers display with regard to certain types of conduct may be a consequence of the socialization process that is likely to occur within the profession; in other words, the ability to resist temptations and negative influences in the police culture increases with age.

There is a relatively small "urbanization effect" in respondents' acceptance of various scenarios. Police officers working in big cities (in Stockholm, Gothenburg, and Malmö) respond more positively than those in less urban areas to the scenarios of an officer's running a private business (Case 1) (gamma = 0.16), receiving gifts (Case 4) (gamma = 0.11), and being picked up in a police car when the officer is unable to use public transportation (Case C) (gamma = 0.14). The results also show a weak but significant correlation ($p = < .01$) between the responses to scenarios of receiving a free meal (Case A) and driving a drunken police officer home instead of booking him for drunk driving (Case 8). There is, therefore, a slight indication that metropolitan police officers exhibit a lower level of integrity toward such conduct than do nonmetropolitan police. A difference between police in metropolitan and other areas also emerged in a

previous Swedish study (Torstensson, 1996) over officers' willingness to change and their attitudes toward various types of police work. Metropolitan police express greater intolerance toward organizational changes and are more inclined to define reactive, incident-based police work as "real policing."

Even though the results show some significant effects according to age, rank, and police department location, the most striking finding is the officers' similarities rather than dissimilarities across gender, age, rank, and geographical location when it comes to acceptance or rejection of moral code infringements.

## Officers' Willingness to Report a Colleague for Rule Violations

Respondents were asked first about their willingness to report a colleague for any of the listed rule violations and second about their perceptions of their colleagues' willingness to report violations committed by others. Table 14.3 illustrates the distribution of mean values and standard deviations for each scenario.

With respect to the officers' willingness to report a colleague, the results show significant correlations between the perceived seriousness of the violation and the willingness to report it. The correlations vary in strength between 0.72 and 0.93 (gamma), being weakest for Case A (an officer accepting Sunday dinner for himself or herself and his or her spouse) and strongest for Case C (an officer using a police car to get picked up from home when going to work late at night).

The proportion of those who profess a willingness to report a colleague for a breach of conduct is lower for certain scenarios. For some scenarios, a significant proportion of officers state they would be unwilling to report a colleague. Almost all the respondents believe that they would report a colleague in the stolen watch situation (Case 5), a colleague who stole the money from the

**Table 14.3**   Officers' Views of Own Willingness to Report a Colleague

| Case Number | Mean | Standard Deviation | Range* |
|---|---|---|---|
| 1 | 1.05 | 1.23 | 0-4 |
| 2 | 2.06 | 1.27 | 0-4 |
| 3 | 3.60 | 0.78 | 0-4 |
| 4 | 2.25 | 1.29 | 0-4 |
| 5 | 3.85 | 0.49 | 0-4 |
| 6 | 3.21 | 0.99 | 0-4 |
| 7 | 3.02 | 1.08 | 0-4 |
| 8 | 3.15 | 1.05 | 0-4 |
| 9 | 2.95 | 1.10 | 0-4 |
| 10 | 2.61 | 1.22 | 0-4 |
| 11 | 3.68 | 0.68 | 0-4 |
| A | 2.82 | 1.12 | 0-4 |
| B | 0.67 | 0.96 | 0-4 |
| C | 0.47 | 0.87 | 0-4 |
| D | 0.93 | 1.15 | 0-4 |

Note: 0 = Definitely not, 4 = Yes, definitely

wallet he or she found in a public parking lot (Case 11), and a colleague prepared to take a bribe for not reporting a speed violation (Case 3) (97%, 94%, and 91%, respectively). By contrast, only just over half of respondents (57%) think that they would be likely to report a colleague for using excessive force on a captive car thief (Case 10).

There is an extremely low propensity among the respondents to report a colleague for running a private business (Case 1), doctoring time sheets (Case D), or being given a free ride in a police car during the day or late at night (Cases B and C). The proportions of those who think that they would report their colleague in these instances are 16%, 12%, 6%, and 5%, respectively.

By classifying officers' willingness to report the misconduct in the various scenarios, it is possible to identify a group of 91 police officers (5.8% of the respondents) who express unwillingness to report a colleague regardless of the seriousness of the misconduct. This group can be characterized as young to middle-aged (60% are 45 years of age or under), of low rank (98% are inspectors or lower), and working in big city departments (64%).

Gender has no significant ($p < .001$) effect on officers' willingness to report a colleague, with one exception: the scenario in which the police officer neglects to report a drunk driving colleague involved in a car accident (Case 8). Female respondents are less prone to report the colleague in such a situation, with 13% of female officers and 9% of male officers saying they would not do so.

Age and rank correlate significantly with officers' willingness to report a colleague for misconduct in the majority of scenarios; that is, the older the officer, the greater the propensity to report misconduct. With regard to two scenarios, age has no significant effect on the responses: Case 8 (the cover-up for a drunk driving fellow police officer) and Case 10 (the use of excessive force on a car thief).

Also, the size and location of the respondents' police department correlated positively and significantly in their responses to most of the scenarios. In general, the results imply that police officers working in small to mid-sized departments or in less urbanized areas are more willing to report a colleague for misconduct. Exceptions to this were the responses to the scenarios involving an officer accepting a bribe from a speeding motorist (Case 3), stealing a watch from a crime scene (Case 5), and accepting a ride to work in police car (Cases B and C), where no differences were found.

Do the results support the hypothesis that a code of silence exists in the Swedish police? Integrity can be said to be generally high among the respondents, although there is a small group that is more inclined to turn a blind eye to misconduct or to cover up for colleagues. The results also reveal that lower levels of integrity are more widespread in metropolitan areas and among younger police officers.

The results show a very high correlation between respondents' willingness to report a colleague and their opinion of what their colleagues would do in the same circumstances. The correlations (gamma) are seldom lower than 0.85, and the lowest correlation is seen for Case 2 (an officer accepting free meals and discounts on beat). However, when the mean values (Table 14.4) for each scenario are compared, the respondents score somewhat higher than they believe their colleagues would.

Here, too, the results show a relatively high level of homogeneity in the Swedish police service when it comes to assessing moral rights and wrongs in a professional context. There is, admittedly, a small element of "ego defense," whereby the subject regards himself or herself as somewhat more morally upstanding than his or her colleagues are. Notwithstanding this, the picture in this study of a homogenous profession holds firm.

The respondents were highly consistent in their attitudes toward misconduct sanctions: The more serious they regard the behavior, the more severely they believe it should and would be punished, and the more they believe they and other officers would be willing to report it. For example, 87% of the respondents state that dismissal is a proper punishment for theft, but only 1% believe that running a private business while off duty warrants dismissal. The results strongly suggest major similarities between what the respondents believe is the appropriate punishment for each offense and the corresponding departmental policy. The responses to three scenarios differ from this pattern: the cases involving an officer fixing his superior's car (Case 7), two officers' use of excessive force on a captive car thief (Case 10), and an officer's getting a ride to work in a police car (Case B). Regarding Case 7, the tolerance of respondents appears to be lower than that they expect of their employers: 21% of the respondents think dismissal is the appropriate discipline for the offense in the case, but only 14%

**Table 14.4** Officers' Views of Their Colleagues' Willingness to Report the Misconduct

| Scenario | Mean | Standard Deviation | Range* |
|---|---|---|---|
| 1 | 0.91 | 0.98 | 0-4 |
| 2 | 1.77 | 1.09 | 0-4 |
| 3 | 3.29 | 0.83 | 0-4 |
| 4 | 2.01 | 1.16 | 0-4 |
| 5 | 3.61 | 0.64 | 0-4 |
| 6 | 2.93 | 0.97 | 0-4 |
| 7 | 2.79 | 1.05 | 0-4 |
| 8 | 2.9 | 1.01 | 0-4 |
| 9 | 2.67 | 1.04 | 0-4 |
| 10 | 2.18 | 1.1 | 0-4 |
| 11 | 3.46 | 0.77 | 0-4 |
| A | 2.53 | 1.05 | 0-4 |
| B | 0.58 | 0.82 | 0-4 |
| C | 0.42 | 0.75 | 0-4 |
| D | 0.82 | 1.99 | 0-4 |

Note: 0 = Definitely not, 4 = Yes, definitely

believe that the police department would impose this sanction.

In contrast, respondents express a more tolerant attitude than that they expect of their employers toward the use of excessive force on a captive car thief. This pattern was mirrored in the officers' responses to the scenario involving an officer riding to work in a police car (Cases B and C) and the one in which an officer is doctoring duty lists (Case D).

## Further Analysis of the Data

Preliminary inspection of the data set suggested much covariance among the responses to the 15 scenarios. The seven questions for each of the scenarios were analyzed for homogeneity (Cronbach's alpha). Mean values, standard deviations (*SD*), and homogeneity coefficients are provided in Table 14.5. Nine items were excluded because of low variance. All were items 1 to 3 within scenarios, pertaining to the perceived seriousness of the violation rather than to sanctions or officers' willingness to report a colleague. Some scenarios received high acceptance (Cases 1, B, C, and D), and others received low acceptance (Cases 3, 5, 6, 8, and 11). There was no consistent relationship between mean values and standard deviations in relation to acceptance (i.e., there was disagreement among participants even when there was a strong overall lack of acceptance or vice versa).

The homogeneity of the various items within each scenario suggested that a factor analysis was a proper way to reduce the data set. A principal component analysis with a promax solution yielded three factors, reflecting 23%, 8%, and 5% of the total variance. The distribution of the 15 scenarios to the three factors is displayed in Table 14.5. The three factors correlated in the interval 0.31 to 0.49.

The three factors were regarded as the main dependent variables and subjected to an analysis of variance for repeated measures, with age (eight categories), department size (four categories), and gender as independent variables. The overall analysis was significant. There were no significant interaction effects, but there was a simple main effect of age ($F = 2.39$, $p < .01$) . Even if gender was not revealed as significant in the multivariate analysis, we performed $t$ tests for gender differences in the three factors. Women were more accepting according to factor 1, interpreted to reflect more serious irregularities (0.31 $z$ points difference, $t = 4.44$, $df = 1443$, $p < .001$). Women were also more accepting according to factor 2, interpreted to reflect the "Swedish situation" (0.14 $z$ points difference, $t = 1.98$, $df = 1,443$, $p < .05$). The difference for factor 1 is characterized as small according to conventions regarding "clinical significance." The difference for factor 2 is minuscule and barely significant.

### Additional Results

The Swedish version of the survey also involved additional efforts to compare the main study sample with a group of instructors in police ethics ($N= 80$) and with a class of recently graduated police cadets ($N = 64$). The group of ethics instructors was too small (59 respondents) to permit any definitive conclusions about their responses, but their responses differ only slightly from those of the main group. Later interviews indicated that one explanation for this is that the instructors were recruited from ordinary rank-and-file officers with the express intention of avoiding the recruitment of "know-it-alls" (*Besserwissers*).

Nor do the police cadets' attitudes differ in any significant way from those of the main group. This may also be considered a little surprising since they, in their role of "freshmen," were expected to show a little more intolerance compared with their (mostly) older colleagues.

## CONCLUSION

The results suggest the following main conclusions:

> Swedish police officers seem to have a high level of integrity because they generally do not accept violations of the moral or legal code.

> There is strong homogeneity between respondents' attitudes and their perceptions of their colleagues' attitudes and departmental policy.

> Age has a significant effect on acceptance of the moral and legal codes, in that acceptance of the codes increases linearly with age.

> Gender has a small impact on acceptance of the moral and legal code, suggesting that female police officers are slightly more intolerant in some respects of more serious irregularities as the use of excessive force (Case 10).

The results of the study reflect a uniform and stable moral code in the police organization and appear to define the existence of a moral subculture within it. The finding that age and a higher moral standard covaried may be interpreted as the unfolding of a

**Table 14.5**  Mean Values, Standard Deviations (*SD*), and Homogeneity Coefficients of 7 Items Within the 14 Scenarios

| Case Number and Description | Mean ± SD value | Homogeneity | Comments |
|---|---|---|---|
| Case 1 - Off-Duty Security System Business | 9.86 ± 7.02 | .92 | |
| Case 2 - Free Meals and Discounts on Beat | 18.1 ± 6.03 | .90 | |
| Case 3 - Bribe From Speeding Motorist | 27.4 ± 6.78 | — | Items 1-3 low *SD* |
| Item 1-3 | 11.9 ± 0.49 | — | |
| Item 4-7 | 15.5 ± 6.70 | .78 | |
| Case 4 - Holiday Gifts From Merchants | 19.0 ± 6.76 | .93 | |
| Case 5 - Crime Scene Theft of Watch | 27.0 ±1.80 | — | Items 1-3 low *SD* |
| Item 1-3 | 12.0 ± 0.26 | — | |
| Item 4-7 | 17.0 ± 1.72 | .74 | |
| Case 6 - 5% Kickback From Auto Repair Shop | 24.9 ± 4.50 | .88 | |
| Case 7 - Supervisor Grants Holiday in Exchange for Car Tune-Up | 24.0 ± 4.35 | .82 | Items 1-3 rather low *SD* |
| Case 8 - Cover-Up of Police DUI Accident | 25.0 ± 4.30 | .86 | Items 1-3 rather low *SD* |
| Case 9 - Free Drinks to Ignore Late Bar Closing | 23.5 ± 4.50 | .86 | Items 1-3 rather low *SD* |
| Case 10 - Excessive Force On Car Thief | 21.7 ± 5.58 | .88 | |
| Case 11 - Theft From Found Wallet | 26.8 ± 2.67 | — | Items 1-3 low *SD* |
| Item 1-3 | 11.8 ± 0.59 | — | |
| Item 4-7 | 16.0 ± 2.43 | .80 | |
| Case A - Free Dinner to Ignore Late Bar Closing | 23.1 ± 4.45 | .85 | Items 1-3 rather low *SD* |
| Case B - Ride to Work in Police Car—During the Day | 7.34 ± 5.75 | .92 | |
| Case C - Ride to Work in Police Car—at Night | 5.07 ± 5.55 | .93 | |
| Case D - Doctoring time sheets | 9.96 ± 6.84 | .93 | |

Note: Higher numbers reflect lower acceptance.

moral career during the occupational one (Sherman, 1999). As Sherman (1999) puts it: "Should the rookies follow the formal rules of society or the informal rules of the senior colleagues?" (p. 301). However, we cannot rule out that the finding simply reflects the fact that older people in general develop more rigorous moral standards. The study did not include any group that could serve as a comparison group (e.g., judges or forensic

**Table 14.6**  Summary Table: Distribution of the 15 Scenarios to the Three Promax Rotated Factors

---

*Factor 1 (Interpreted as "More serious violations of the moral code")*
*Case Number and Description*
Case 3 - Bribe From Speeding Motorist
Case 5 - Crime Scene Theft of Watch
Case 6 - 5% Kickback From Auto Repair Shop
Case 7 - Supervisor Grants Holiday in Exchange for Car Tune-Up
Case 8 - Cover-Up of Police DUI Accident
Case 9 - Free Drinks to Ignore Late Bar Closing
Case 10 - Excessive Force on Car Thief
Case 11 - Theft From Found Wallet
Case A - Free Dinner to Ignore Late Bar Closing
*Factor 2 (Interpreted as "Specific Swedish items")*
*Case Number and Description*
Case B - Ride To Work In Police Car—During the Day
Case C - Ride To Work In Police Car—at Night
Case D - Doctoring Time-Sheets
*Factor 3 (Interpreted as "Less serious offenses")*
*Case Number and Description*
Case 1 - Off-Duty Security System Business
Case 2 - Free Meals and Discounts on Beat
Case 4 - Holiday Gifts From Merchants

---

psychiatrists, who in some ways have to perform duties similar to the police).

In a Swedish study (Levander, Ivarsson, Lichtenstein, & Weiss, 1996), a questionnaire aimed at assessing moral competency was administered to 297 subjects working in government or private enterprises, 233 students at the Stockholm Police Academy, and 321 prison inmates. The questionnaire included a set of short stories each describing a moral dilemma. Also included was a set of solutions to the dilemmas, to which each participant was to respond "right" or "wrong." A factor analysis suggested a three-factor solution. The factors were interpreted as "rule knowledge," "rule adherence," and "utilitarianism." In addition to the moral dilemma items, items from a standardised personality inventory—the Karolinska Scales of Personality—were included.

Prisoners differed markedly from well-adjusted subjects, in terms of their responses to both the moral dilemma items and the personality items. A discriminant analysis yielded 85% correct classifications. Individual comparisons among the mean values showed the police academy students to be most different from the other socially well-adjusted groups (25 of 40 comparisons were significant, far more than for any other group). The differences were mainly in a prosocial direction (e.g., they were higher in skills such as social desirability and socialization), but they were also higher in the moral factor scale "rule adherence." In a separate analysis it was shown that police academy freshmen were more "prosocial" than final-year students, suggesting that the curriculum and experiences provided by college modified the overly idealistic and rule-adherent moral conceptions that characterized freshmen.

Thus it appears that the recruitment factor (who wants to become a police officer) favors rule adherence, and that confrontation with the police academy curriculum modifies that moral stance in a liberal direction—but not so much as to conform with the moral stance of the white-collar Swedish workforce in general. However, it should be noted that among the police academy students there were a few individuals who displayed personality traits and moral attitudes well into the criminal realm (bad apples).

From the Swedish study by Levander and colleagues (1996), we can assume that freshmen at the Swedish National Police Academy are more "prosocial" according to societal norms and values than are "normal subjects" and students who graduate from the academy. Interestingly, the current study shows that moral standards seem to change over time, as expressed by the finding that greater age and nonacceptance of rule-breaking go together: Older police officers are less tolerant of such behavior.

The results illustrate to some extent the existence of a code of silence (i.e., an unwillingness to report a colleague for rule-violating behavior). According to Sherman (1999), loyalty to colleagues is an essential feature of police culture, together with the assumption that the world outside the police organization is the "enemy." It is noteworthy that this attitude has its parallel in the criminal subculture. Another finding of some interest is that the items reflecting the officer's own moral standards are numerically larger, and have less variance, than items reflecting their perceptions of the attitudes of others (colleagues or the department). Put more simply, subjects regard themselves as morally more conscientious than are their colleges and the department—a kind of self-enhancement or ego defense.

The study has some limitations. It is a cross-sectional piece of work that combines age effects with societal changes in values and attitudes over time. There was no control group, which would have made it possible to say something about the prevalence of low tolerance of professional misconduct in other occupations.

The first problem can be rectified by conducting longitudinal studies, which could have been done by extending the study and retesting the same subjects (e.g., 5 years later). That would potentially have provided important data on reliability, validity, and development over time. Unfortunately, the Research Department at the Stockholm Police Academy was closed at the start of the study. The second problem will probably make it necessary to modify the questionnaire instrument if it is going to be used with other professional groups. This will create a new problem, however, because such an instrument will not be well suited to the type of work and inducements to nonprofessional conduct that are relevant in a police context. Summing up, Swedish police officers display a uniform and high standard of moral and professional integrity. With increasing professional experience, police officers become still more intolerant of misconduct within the organization.

## REFERENCES

Bordua, D. (Ed.). (1967). *The police: Six sociological essays.* New York: John Wiley.

Ekenvall, B. (2000). *Attityder kring polisintegritet. Delaware-projektet. Den svenska enkätundersökningen.* Solna, Sweden: Polishögskolan.

Ekenvall, B. (2002). *Om oegentliga beteenden hos poliser.* Stockholm: Kriminologiska Institutionen, Stockholms Universitet.

Goldstein, H. (1975). *Police corruption: Perspectives on its nature and control.* Washington, DC: The Police Foundation.

Goldstein, H. (1977). *Policing a free society.* Cambridge, MA: Ballinger.

Klockars, C. B. (1969). The Dirty Harry problem. In C. B. Klockars & S. Mastrofski (Eds.), *Thinking about police. Contemporary readings.* Boston: McGraw-Hill.

Klockars, C. B., Kutnjak Ivkovich, S., Harver, W. E., & Haberfeld, M. R. (2000, May). *The measurement of police integrity: Final report to the National Institute of Justice.* Research in Brief. Washington, DC: U.S. Department of Justice, National Institute of Justice.

The Knapp Commission. (1972). *The Knapp Commission Report on Police Corruption.* New York: George Braziller.

Levander, S., Ivarsson, K., Lichtenstein, P., & Weiss, P. (1996). *Development and validation of a moral questionnaire* (Report No. 87, Vol. 19). Trondheim, Norway: Department of Psychiatry and Behavioral Medicine, University of Trondheim.

The Police Act. (1984). Stockholm: National Swedish Police Board.

Reiss, A., Jr. (1971). *The police and the public.* New Haven, CT: Yale University Press.

Sherman, L. (1974). *Police corruption: A sociological perspective.* New York: Doubleday.

Sherman, L. (1999). Learning police ethics. In L. K. Gaines & G. W. Cordner (Eds.), *Policing perspectives.* Los Angeles: Roxbury.

Simpson, A. E. (1977). *The literature of police corruption.* New York: The John Jay Press.

Stoddard, E. R. (1968). The informal "code" of police deviancy: A group approach to "blue-coat crime." *Journal of Criminal Law, Criminology and Police Science, 59,* 201-213.

Torstensson, M. (1996). *Problem-oriented policing: The R&D approach.* Unpublished manuscript, Swedish National Police College, Solna.

# CHAPTER 15

# Police Integrity in the United States of America

Carl B. Klockars

Sanja Kutnjak Ivković

Maria R. Haberfeld

The single most distinctive feature of policing in the United States is the extent to which it is decentralized. The best information available suggests that as of 1997, some 741,000 sworn police officers were employed by 18,700 independent U.S. towns, cities, counties, states, and special entities such as transit systems, schools, and airports (U.S. Department of Justice, 2000). We may add to these state and local totals an additional 75,000 police officers employed in 31 federal agencies. Although the exact number of police officers and police agencies is unknown—even the 1997 figure was based on a sample—it is a reasonable estimate that in 2002 policing in the United States consisted of approximately 19,000 independent police agencies employing about a million sworn officers.

U.S. citizens endorse this radical decentralization of policing with two arguments. The first argument is a reflection of the distrust of the power of a national government. This distrust is embodied in their belief in the concept of "limited government" and the host of republican procedural and structural arrangements—federalism, checks and balances, separation of powers, legislative confirmation, bicameralism, referendum, the right to keep and bear arms, and a profoundly decentralized police—that are thought to serve to promote it.

The second argument is the belief that local police will be most responsive to local needs when under the control of local government. Indeed, there is ample historical evidence that U.S. police have long responded obediently to local concerns. However, it is more accurate to characterize the American police agency as an instrument for partisan political ambitions. To quote the classic study, *American Police Systems*, by Fosdick (1920/1972):

> There is scarcely a city in the United States in which the police department has not been

used as a ladder by which the political organization has crawled to power. . . . The struggle for party dominance, the desire of jobs for the faithful, the determination to control the machinery of elections were the contributing motives in the principal alterations. (in police organizations). . . . The department has been stunted and dwarfed, with no opportunity for rational development. It has been shaped as a tool of party success rather than as an instrument of public service. Regarded as the legitimate spoils of the victory at the polls, it has been prostituted to base and selfish purposes. (pp. 115-117)

One thus turns from the history of our municipal departments with the wish that most of its sordid history could be blotted out. The sorry history of the American police is a well-established historical fact. Moreover, the process of reform of the American police is a story that has been told in many versions, and retelling it in terms of the reforms of *legalization, militarization,* and *professionalization* would take us over well-traveled territory and far beyond the space and scope of this chapter.[1] Suffice it to say that the American experience with police corruption and misconduct is extensive. From this sorry history, Americans have learned some basic propositions about police corruption, brutality, misconduct, and their control that guide contemporary thinking.

## BASIC PROPOSITIONS ABOUT POLICE CORRUPTION

### Police Corruption is the Abuse of the Police Office "for Gain"

Although the concept of *corruption* has recently grown to include nearly all forms of real and imagined misconduct, making a distinction between corrupt acts "for gain" and other misconduct is critical and worth preserving because it separates misconduct

police engage in because it is profitable to do so from misbehavior motivated by other factors. Corruption is not necessarily better or worse or more of less harmful than are other forms of misconduct. However, making a distinction between corrupt acts committed for gain and those committed for other reasons is practically crucial because it bears explicitly on both the potential distribution of corruption and the potential for its control. U.S. police agencies have learned through experience that certain divisions within police agencies (e.g., vice, drugs, and detectives) and certain police assignments (e.g., undercover operations, licensing, and inspections) are particularly vulnerable to the temptations of misconduct for gain that may be presented to them. In response, many U.S. police agencies have developed special devices to monitor and control the behavior of officers in those assignments. (e.g., random drug testing, rotating assignments, integrity testing). Other forms of police misconduct, such as discourtesy to citizens, use of excessive force, arriving late to work, and spending too much time on ("milking") calls for service, are typically motivated by factors other than gain and usually require interventions that take account of other motives.

### Police Misconduct Varies in Magnitude—Over Time, in Intensity, Across Organizations

The experience in the United States demonstrates that police agencies can differ in the extent of corruption that characterizes them, with a number of departments reversing their once-corrupt reputations. Kansas City, Missouri, and Oakland, California, for instance, once regarded as profoundly corrupt and brutal departments, today enjoy reputations as agencies of integrity. Since the 19th century, the New York City department has gone though repeated episodes of scandal and reform, periodically shutting down corrupt practices only to have them return within a few years. Likewise, there are some U.S. departments that have maintained nearly uniform reputations for honesty throughout their existence (e.g., those in Berkeley, California, and Madison, Wisconsin) and others that have enjoyed persistently unsavory reputations (e.g., those in Key West, Florida, and New Orleans, Louisiana).

We have also learned from the U.S. experience that corrupt practices, even when they are widespread in a police department, can differ markedly among individual police officers. According to the Knapp Commission report on New York City:

> Corrupt policemen have been described as falling into two basic categories: "meat eaters" and "grass eaters." As the names might suggest, the meat eaters are those policemen who . . . aggressively use their police powers for personal gain. The grass eaters simply accept the payoffs that the happenstances of police work throw their way. (New York City Commission, 1972, p. 4)

While such distinctions mark agencies in which corruption is widespread, far more common are agencywide differences in tolerance of low levels of corruption. In some agencies officers may regularly "badge" their way into movies and other entertainments, receive what are euphemistically called "ministerial discounts" on consumer merchandise, and regularly expect half-price or free meals, while in other agencies such practices are strongly condemned.

*Misconduct Is Better
Understood as an Organizational
and Administrative Problem of
Police Agencies Than as a Problem of
Defective Individual Police Officers*

While corrupt police officers have often received detailed press coverage of their criminal exploits and have been identified by police administrators as morally defective officers who slipped through the agency's screening system, most police misconduct is better understood as an organizational or agency problem rather than as a defect of individual police officers. It is in the very nature of police work that its practitioners are regularly exposed to temptations to abuse their office. It is the obligation of the police agency to specify the behavior it expects from its officers, to train them to exhibit the behavior it expects, to detect occasions when officers fail to comply with agency expectations, and to discipline officers who fail to comply with agency expectations. In short, the administrative obligation is to create an agency culture that is intolerant of misconduct.

The evidence from the U.S. history of corruption and brutality demonstrates that agencies are reformed not by weeding out bad apples but by creating an occupational and organizational environment in which they cannot survive. Moreover, the history of scandal and reform in American police agencies and the history of departments transformed from agencies that are thoroughly corrupt into agencies that are revered for their honesty is evidence that the administrative and organizational tools for effecting such transformation are in the hands of police administrators—if they are willing and able to use them.

*Police Officers, Police
Administrators, and Citizens
Are Often Reluctant to Disclose
the Misconduct of Police Officers*

While there are certainly accounts of morally courageous police officers who blew the whistle on rampant corruption (Maas, 1973), police officers who confessed their own shameful careers (Daley, 1978), and police administrators who were distinguished by their efforts to expose and suppress corruption (Bratton, 1998), one of the distinguishing features of police corruption is the extent to which it is likely to be concealed by police officers, police administrators, and citizens alike.

Most police corruption is a "victimless crime," meaning that, like drug use, gambling, and prostitution, however harmful it may be in its consequences, it normally lacks an immediate complainant. The police officer who accepts a bribe to permit a bar to stay open past its designated closing time, to serve teenagers alcohol, or to allow gambling on its premises is unlikely to be reported by the bar owner who paid the officer or the customers who patronize the establishment. Even less likely to be reported is the police officer who accepts a kickback to refer a crime victim to a lawyer or refer an auto accident victim to an auto repair shop or a towing service.

The "code of silence," the informal prohibition among police officers against disclosing the misconduct of fellow officers, may also shield corruption and other forms of police misconduct. The code of silence tends to grow among police officers as an extension of the support police officers come to expect of their fellow police officers. As Bittner (1975) has observed,

> Policing is a dangerous occupation and the availability of unquestioned support and loyalty is not something officers could readily do without. In the heat of action it is not possible to arrange, from case to case, for the supply of support, nor can the supply of such support be made dependent on whether the cooperating agents agree on abstract principles. The governing consideration must be as long as "one of us" is in peril, right or wrong, he deserves help. (p. 22)

Like line officers, police administrators, even if they are personally committed to honesty, are reluctant to disclose corrupt practices, particularly if corruption is pervasive. Exposing corruption may bring outside investigators into the department, call press attention to the corruption issue, and subject the full range of police practices (e.g., acceptance of free meals, rewards, and holiday gifts; off-duty employment; and special arrangements involving ambulance services, lawyers, bail bondsmen, auto repair shops, sales of tickets to police events, and advertisement in police journals) to public scrutiny. The decision to disclose corrupt practices may come to define the administration of a police leader. He or she often will not find support from the community for anticorruption efforts, can expect opposition from some political sources, and can almost always anticipate vigorous opposition from police unions.

We will also add that under these conditions, measuring the amount of corruption within any police agency is beyond the capacities of social science. The forces barring police administrators and police officers from knowing the extent and location of corruption and inclining them to keep what they know secret are also formidable obstacles to social science measurement of corruption. Under these conditions, students of police misconduct must rely on the information that surfaces in scandals, is generated in official inquiries, or focuses on the "reputations" of the character of individual agencies.

## METHODOLOGICAL ISSUES IN THE STUDY OF POLICE CORRUPTION

Because of these insurmountable obstacles to the measurement of police corruption we decided to measure its conceptual opposite: police integrity. *Police integrity* is a concept we have defined as "the normative inclination among police to resist temptations to abuse the rights and privileges of their occupation" (Klockars, Kutnjak Ivkovich, Harver, &

Haberfeld, 2000). In contrast to the limitations on the direct study of corrupt behavior, the major propositions of an organizational or occupational approach to the study of police integrity involve questions of *fact* and *opinion* that can be explored directly and without anything like the resistance that direct inquiries about corrupt *behavior* are likely to provoke. It is, for example, possible to ask nonthreatening questions about officers' *knowledge of agency rules* and questions about officers' *opinions* about the seriousness of the violation, the punishment it deserves or is likely to receive, and their willingness and that of other officers to report such behavior—without asking them directly about their own or others' corrupt *behavior*.

Finally, very different goals and visions of police integrity characterize the individual approach and the occupational or organizational culture approach to the understanding of corruption. The individual approach envisions the police agency of integrity to be one from which all morally defective individual officers have been removed and in which the agency remains vigilant in preventing their entry or emergence. By contrast, the occupational or organizational culture approach envisions the police agency of integrity to be one in which the culture of the agency is highly intolerant of corruption.

Methodologically, the consequences of these different visions are critical. Measuring the level of corrupt behavior, the number of morally defective police officers, and agency vigilance in their discovery may not be impossible, but the obstacles to it are enormous. Measuring how seriously officers regard misconduct, how willing they are to support the punishment of it, and how willing they are to tolerate it in silence—the components of the occupational culture of police integrity—is well within the capacities of modern social science.

In an effort to measure the occupational culture of police integrity in American police officers in a systematic, standardized, and quantitative manner, we designed a questionnaire that probes the dimensions of an organization's culture of integrity. It targets officers' support for agency rules, familiarity with the disciplinary threat the police agency is making, perceptions of disciplines' fairness, and expressed willingness to report the misconduct of their fellow police officers.

The questionnaire presents police officers with 11 short hypothetical case scenarios (see Exhibit 1.1 in Chapter 1 of this volume). While the primary focus of the questionnaire is on corrupt behavior, the scenarios cover a range of activities, from those that merely give an appearance of conflict of interest (Case 1 - Off-Duty Security Business) to incidents of bribery (Case 3 - Bribe From Speeding Motorist), theft (Case 5 - Crime Scene Theft of Watch and Case 11 - Theft From Found Wallet), and kickback (Case 6 - 5% Kickback From Auto Repair Shop). Only one scenario (Case 10 - Excessive Force on Car Thief) does not involve an officer engaging in a corrupt act for gain.

The respondents were asked to evaluate each scenario by responding to the same set of six questions. Two questions pertained to their own and other officers' perceptions of the *seriousness* of each case, two pertained to the severity of *discipline* it *should* and *would* *receive*, and two to their own and other officers' *willingness to report* it (see Exhibit 1.2 in Chapter 1 of this volume).

## The Sample of American Police Officers

The overall sample consisted of 3,235 officers from 30 U.S. police agencies. Although these agencies were drawn from across the nation and the sample is quite large, it was nonetheless a nonrandom, convenience sample resulting in the overrepresentation of particular types of police agencies and particular regions of the country.

**Table 15.1**     Characteristics of the Police Agency Sample

| Agency Type | Percentage of National Sample | Sample Size | Percentage Supervisory | Percentage Patrol/Traffic | Mean Length of Service |
|---|---|---|---|---|---|
| All Agencies | 100% | 3235 | 19.8% | 63.1% | 10.30 years |
| Very Large (500+ Sworn Officers) | 59.9% | 1937 | 14.8% | 64.2% | 9.18 years |
| Large (201-500 Sworn Officers) | 19.7% | 638 | 23.2% | 60.3% | 12.05 years |
| Medium (76-200 Sworn Officers) | 9.0% | 292 | 29.9% | 59.0% | 12.29 years |
| Small (25-75 Sworn Officers) | 8.5% | 275 | 30.8% | 66.1% | 11.70 years |
| Very Small (< 25 Sworn Officers) | 2.9% | 93 | 35.9% | 64.8% | 11.29 years |

Not all the agencies we asked to participate in the study accepted the invitation. One of the reasons that we opted to study integrity rather than police corruption was precisely to weaken the reluctance of police agencies to participate in the study. However, some agencies declined to participate despite assurances that their participation in the survey would be kept confidential, that all individual responses would remain anonymous, and that respondents would be asked only about their opinions and not about actual misconduct. Our assumption is that many if not all of the agencies that refused to participate did so because they believed they had something to hide. Nevertheless, the sample includes some seriously troubled police agencies. We have key contacts in a number of such agencies, including senior officers and high-ranking union officials, who exercised sufficient influence to arrange the participation of these agencies in the survey.

Response rates among the agencies varied from 16% to 93%.[2] However, in over one half of the agencies in the sample (57%), the majority of police officers employed by the agency participated in the study. Furthermore, in an additional one quarter of the agencies (23.3%), between 40% and 50% of the police officers participated, and in only 20% of the agencies was the response rate lower than 40%. The analyses indicate that (1) the variation in response rates had no significant effect on the ranking of the agencies on our integrity scale, and (2) the representation of supervisors among the respondents from each agency is not related to the response rates.

As Table 15.1 shows, the majority of the surveyed police officers were employed in patrol or traffic units (63.1%). The overwhelming majority of our respondents were line officers; only one in five respondents was a supervisor. The mean length of service for the entire sample was 10.3 years, and it varied from 9.18 years in the very large agencies to 12.29 years in the medium-sized agencies.

Table 15.2    Spearman Correlation Coefficients—U.S. Police Officer Rank Ordering of Their Own and Others' Views of Misconduct's Seriousness, the Punishment It Should and Would Receive, and Their Own and Others' Willingness to Report It

| | Own View of Seriousness | Others' View of Seriousness | Punishment It Should Receive | Punishment It Would Receive | Own Willingness to Report It | Others' Willingness to Report It |
|---|---|---|---|---|---|---|
| Own View of Seriousness | | | | | | |
| Others' View of Seriousness | 1.00 p < .001 | | | | | |
| Punishment It Should Receive | .973 p < .001 | .973 p < .001 | | | | |
| Punishment It Would Receive | .973 p < .001 | .973 p < .001 | 1.00 p < .001 | | | |
| Own Willingness to Report It | .973 p < .001 | .973 p < .001 | .982 p < .001 | .982 p < .001 | | |
| Others' Willingness to Report It | .980 p < .001 | .980 p < .001 | .989 p < .001 | .989 p < .001 | .998 p < .001 | |

## THE CONTOURS OF U.S. POLICE INTEGRITY

In spite of the limitations of our sample, a picture of the integrity of U.S. police agencies emerges from the officers' responses to our questions about the seriousness of the misconduct in the cases, the appropriate discipline for it, and their and others' willingness to report it. First, we should note that the rank order of the cases on all three measures of the contours of integrity was exceptionally high (see Table 15.2). The more serious police officers regarded a behavior, the more severely they thought it should and would be punished, and the more willing they were to report it. This high correlation between rank order scores suggests that the three scales all measure the same phenomenon—the degree to which misconduct is tolerated.

Despite the fact that the relative, rank ordering of the scores on the measures of seriousness, discipline, and willingness to report were highly correlated with one another, the absolute scores on each of these scales were very different. For example, the surveyed police officers evaluated the cases described in the questionnaire to vary from a mean score of 1.45 for the least serious case, Case 1 (Off-Duty Security System Business) to a score of 4.95 for the most serious case, Case 5 (Crime Scene Theft of Watch), to scores ranging from 1.37 to 3.07 for the same cases on the willingness to report scale.

These very high rank-order correlation estimates suggest that all three scales are but different measurements of the same underlying dimension—integrity—while the substantial differences in absolute scores suggest that each of the scales is subject to different error properties. For example, there is a real question of what "seriousness" means to our police officer respondents. Unlike the evaluations of the appropriate discipline for misconduct and officers' willingness to report it, the perceived "seriousness" of the misconduct has no direct behavioral implications. Officers were "free" to estimate "seriousness" however they wished. At best, the evaluation of some behavior as "serious" or "very serious" implies that it is more objectionable or more harmful, in terms of some normative dimensions, than some behavior officers designate as "less serious" or "not serious at all." We do not know whether that dimension is moral, professional, organizational, occupational, reputational, or some combination of these or other values.

In contrast, officer estimates of expected and appropriate discipline were questions with at least indirect behavioral consequences. An estimate of the expected discipline for misconduct is a measure of an officer's experience and organizational knowledge—it reflects an officer's competence. An estimate of the appropriate discipline for misconduct is a reflection of the disciplinary environment to which officers want to be subjected. Estimating it either too high or too low may have consequences for the lives of police officers when police administrators learn the results of the survey. Finally, the question asking about the willingness to report misconduct tests officers knowledge of the unwritten norms of the agency and their willingness to depart from them. Given these considerations, we should not be surprised to find that in some departments some officers found certain types of misconduct "very serious" but reported that they would be unlikely to report them and that they neither expected nor supported the severe punishment of such misconduct.

We may also add to our discussion the measures of seriousness, discipline, and willingness to report that while seriousness is highly correlated with discipline and willingness to report, we cannot assert the directionality of that relationship. While we might be tempted to assert that most officers believe that *because* certain misconduct is very serious, it should be punished severely, it is equally likely that they find it serious because it is punished severely. Likewise, officers may refuse to report certain misconduct because it will not be punished.

## The Seriousness of the Misconduct

The police officers' evaluations of the cases described in the questionnaire vary substantially on our scale of seriousness, from the least serious case, Case 1 (Off-Duty Security System Business) to the most serious, Case 5 (Crime Scene Theft of Watch). Such a large latitude in evaluations of seriousness allows us to classify cases into three categories based on their mean values: the least serious cases, cases of intermediate seriousness, and the most serious cases.

The means for four cases (Case 1 - Off-Duty Security System Business, Case 2 - Free Meals and Discounts on Beat, Case 4 - Holiday Gifts From Merchants, and Case 8 - Cover-Up of Police DUI Accident) are below or just around the midpoint of the seriousness scale (3.0) (see Table 15.3), indicating that our respondents did not evaluate those cases as serious. Several cases with a corrupt quid pro quo arrangement providing a direct benefit for the police officer (Case 6 - 5% Kickback From Auto Repair Shop, Case 7 - Supervisor Grants Holiday in Exchange for Car Tune-Up, and Case 9 - Free Drinks to Ignore Late Bar Closing), the only case of excessive force (Case 10 - Excessive Force on Car Thief), and the case of internal corruption involving a supervisor (Case 7) were perceived as more serious (see Table 15.3). Finally, the three cases perceived most serious (Case 3 - Bribe From Speeding Motorist, Case 5 - Crime Scene Theft of Watch, and Case 11 - Theft From Found Wallet) all uniformly have mean

**Table 15.3** Police Officers' Views of the Misconduct's Seriousness, the Punishment It Should and Would Receive, and Officers' Willingness to Report It

| Case Number and Description | Seriousness | | | | Discipline | | | | | | Willingness to Report | | | |
| --- | --- | --- | --- | --- | --- | --- | --- | --- | --- | --- | --- | --- | --- | --- |
| | Own View | | Other Officers' View | | Should Receive | | | Would Receive | | | Own View | | Other Officers' View | |
| | $\bar{x}$ | Rank | $\bar{x}$ | Rank | $\bar{x}$ | Rank | Mode | $\bar{x}$ | Rank | Mode | $\bar{x}$ | Rank | $\bar{x}$ | Rank |
| Case 1 - Off-Duty Security System Business | 1.46 | 1 | 1.48 | 1 | 1.34 | 1 | None | 1.51 | 1 | None | 1.37 | 1 | 1.46 | 1 |
| Case 2 - Free Meals and Discounts on Beat | 2.60 | 2 | 2.31 | 2 | 2.13 | 2 | Verbal Reprimand | 2.37 | 2 | Verbal Reprimand | 1.94 | 2 | 1.82 | 2 |
| Case 3 - Bribe From Speeding Motorist | 4.92 | 10 | 4.81 | 10 | 4.92 | 9 | Dismissal | 4.86 | 9 | Dismissal | 4.19 | 9 | 3.92 | 9 |
| Case 4 - Holiday Gifts From Merchants | 2.84 | 3 | 2.64 | 3 | 2.53 | 3 | Verbal Reprimand | 2.82 | 3 | Written Reprimand | 2.36 | 4 | 2.28 | 3.5 |
| Case 5 - Crime Scene Theft of Watch | 4.95 | 11 | 4.88 | 11 | 5.66 | 11 | Dismissal | 5.57 | 11 | Dismissal | 4.54 | 11 | 4.34 | 11 |
| Case 6 - 5% Kickback From Auto Repair Shop | 4.50 | 7 | 4.26 | 7 | 4.40 | 8 | Suspension Without Pay | 4.46 | 8 | Suspension Without Pay | 3.95 | 8 | 3.71 | 8 |
| Case 7 - Supervisor Grants Holiday in Exchange for Car Tune-Up | 4.18 | 6 | 3.96 | 6 | 3.59 | 5 | Written Reprimand | 3.43 | 5 | Written Reprimand | 3.45 | 6 | 3.29 | 6 |
| Case 8 - Cover-Up of Police DUI Accident | 3.03 | 4 | 2.86 | 4 | 2.81 | 4 | Suspension Without Pay | 3.21 | 4 | Suspension Without Pay | 2.34 | 3 | 2.28 | 3.5 |
| Case 9 - Free Drinks to Ignore Late Bar Closing | 4.54 | 8 | 4.28 | 8 | 4.02 | 7 | Suspension Without Pay | 4.08 | 7 | Suspension Without Pay | 3.73 | 7 | 3.47 | 7 |
| Case 10 - Excessive Force on Car Thief | 4.05 | 5 | 3.70 | 5 | 3.76 | 6 | Suspension Without Pay | 4.00 | 6 | Suspension Without Pay | 3.39 | 5 | 3.07 | 5 |
| Case 11 - Theft From Found Wallet | 4.85 | 9 | 4.69 | 9 | 5.09 | 10 | Dismissal | 5.03 | 10 | Dismissal | 4.23 | 10 | 3.96 | 10 |

values very close to the serious end of the scale (see Table 15.2), indicating that the police officers evaluated them as very serious both in absolute terms and in comparison with other cases in the questionnaire. These three cases describe either opportunistic theft (Case 5 and Case 11) or classic bribery (Case 3).

## The Appropriate and Expected Discipline for the Misconduct

Because estimates of the seriousness of misconduct and opinions about the appropriate discipline for it are both measures of the same underlying phenomenon—police integrity—estimates of the misconduct's seriousness are positively related to the opinions about the appropriate discipline for it. There are three features of our respondents' opinions about the expected and appropriate discipline for the misconduct that merit special comment. The first is that the respondents evaluated three cases as among the "most serious" and as deserving and likely to receive the most severe modal discipline— dismissal. Similarly, the respondents evaluated three cases as the least serious and as deserving and likely to receive the least severe modal discipline—no discipline at all or a verbal warning.

A second feature of the officers' disciplinary responses is that in all four of the cases the officers regarded as the most serious, the officers endorsed a slightly more severe discipline than they expected the organization would deliver. Similarly, in the remaining seven cases, which the officers regarded as less severe, they endorsed a slightly less severe discipline than they expected the organization would deliver.

Third, and most important, it must be said that the overall opinion of U.S. police officers is that the discipline they are subject to by their employers is fair. In only one out of the eleven scenarios does the modal discipline that officers expect differ from that which they believe is appropriate. And in that case (Case 4 - Holiday Gifts From Merchants), the difference is between the expected discipline of a written reprimand and what they believe is the appropriate discipline—a verbal reprimand.

## The Willingness to Report the Misconduct

The final dimension of integrity asked about in our survey was officers' willingness to report the misconduct. We asked the respondents to tell us whether they and their fellow officers in their agency would be willing to report police colleagues who engaged in the behaviors described in the questionnaire. With regard to the four least serious cases (Case 1 - Off-Duty Security System Business, Case 2 - Free Meals and Discounts on Beat, Case 4 - Holiday Gifts From Merchants, and Case 8 - Cover-Up of Police DUI Accident), the respondents say they would be unlikely to report the misconduct (the means are all below the midpoint and toward the nonreporting side of the scale) (see Table 15.3). The respondents were somewhat more likely to say that they would report the cases of intermediate seriousness (Case 6 - 5% Kickback From Auto Repair Shop, Case 7 - Supervisor Grants Holiday in Exchange for Car Tune-Up, Case 9 - Free Drinks to Ignore Late Bar Closing, and Case 10 - Excessive Force on Car Thief). The means are closest to the reporting side of the scale for the most serious cases (Case 3 - Bribe From Speeding Motorist, Case 5 - Crime Scene Theft of Watch, and Case 11 - Theft From Found Wallet), indicating that the police officers would be most likely to report cases of such severity. Furthermore, when police officers' own willingness to report misconduct is compared to what they estimate is the willingness of most police officers in their agencies to report it, the differences are rather small[3] (see Table 15.3).

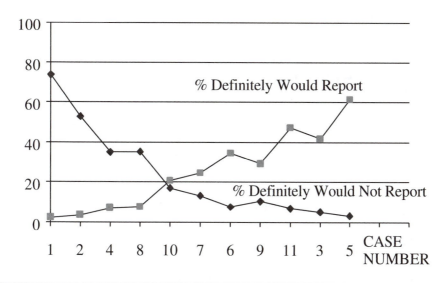

**Figure 15.1**  Percentage of Police Officers Who Said That Other Police Officers Would Report/Would Not Report Misconduct, by Case

The code of silence—the informal prohibition of reporting the misconduct of fellow police officers—can be traced more directly by examining the percentage of police officers who say that other police officers definitely would and definitely would not report (see Figure 15.1). Those percentages are not the same across all the cases (see Figure 15.1); rather, they are related to the respondents' perceptions of the seriousness of each case. The more serious respondents perceived the case to be, the less likely they were to say that other police officers definitely would not report it. Moreover, the more serious they perceived the case to be, the more likely they were to say that other police officers would definitely report it.

However, these two extremes—those who say that they definitely would not report the misconduct and those who say that they definitely would report it, regardless of the circumstances—represent the two ends of the integrity distribution. The reality in each police agency is that there is a substantial proportion of police officers who have the "swing votes"—those who are in the middle and whose decision whether to report

misconduct or not depends on a number of factors (ranging from the circumstances of a particular case to the extent of peer pressure in their informal group and the perceptions about the seriousness of the disciplinary threat by their immediate supervisors), quite a number of which can be affected by a police administrator's words and conduct.

## CONTRASTS IN AGENCY CONTOURS OF INTEGRITY

One of the most dominant features of U.S. policing is its decentralized character. Thus, we would expect differences in the environments of integrity across various police agencies, not only because these agencies are separate entities entitled to regulate the behavior of their employees within the larger legally established boundaries, enforce agency standards of acceptable behavior, and punish violators of official rules, but also because of the divergent social and political environments in which they operate. We next examine the degree to which these environments of integrity differ across the 30 police agencies in our sample.

## The Seriousness of the Misconduct

In order to compare environments of integrity, we calculated a mean value for each case, based on police officers' individual estimates of the seriousness of the misconduct, for each of the 30 agencies in the sample. The means were then ranked for each agency from the least serious to the most serious. The distribution of case rankings indicates that the respondents across 30 agencies evaluated the relative case seriousness (i.e., each case in comparison with every other case in the questionnaire) in very similar terms. Thus, police officers from all 30 agencies shared a very similar understanding of the relative seriousness of acts of police corruption.

Although the relative rankings of the cases are very similar across the 30 agencies, the absolute degree (means) of seriousness (i.e., estimates of how serious the case itself is on our seriousness scale) were somewhat different from agency to agency. Moreover, as can be seen in Table 15.4, the degree of difference of seriousness estimates varied the least for the three most serious cases (Case 3, Case 5, and Case 11), while the estimates of the misconduct's seriousness exhibited the greatest variability in Case 4 (Holiday Gifts From Merchants), Case 8 (Cover-Up of Police DUI Accident), and Case 10 (Excessive Force on Car Thief).

## Expected Discipline for the Misconduct

To detect the differences in the disciplinary environments of the 30 agencies, we used the mode as the average estimate of expected discipline. A common picture emerges across the 30 agencies—the average estimates of expected discipline across eleven cases followed the average estimates of case

seriousness; the more serious a case is perceived to be, the more severe the selected punishment (see Table 15.4); nevertheless, these agencies display rather different disciplinary environments. Although the disciplinary expectations across the majority of agencies are similar for a number of cases (see Table 15.4), extensive differences in disciplinary expectations surface for as many as six cases. Particularly striking is the response to the misconduct in Case 8 (Cover-Up of Police DUI Accident), which police officers state that their agencies would not punish at all or would discipline by using a variety of disciplinary options (i.e., a verbal reprimand, a written reprimand, or suspension).

## Willingness to Report the Misconduct

The greatest variation across agencies appears for the police officers' expressed willingness to report misconduct; the code of silence appears to vary *enormously* across the agencies in our sample (Table 4). Even for the three most serious cases (Case 3 - Bribe From Speeding Motorist; Case 5 - Crime Scene Theft of Watch; Case 11 - Theft From Found Wallet), the mean values for a number of agencies are around the mid-point, indicating, at best, that the respondents would be as likely to report as they would be not to report.

## AGENCY CONTRASTS IN CONTOURS OF INTEGRITY

To illustrate the degree to which the environments of integrity differ across U.S. police agencies, it is helpful to contrast the differences in two agencies: Agency 2 and Agency 23 (see Table 15.5). Both are large municipal police agencies. Agency 2 is extremely receptive to research, is often promoted as a model of innovation, and enjoys a local and national reputation for integrity. Agency

Table 15.4   Distribution of Mean and Modal Values Across 30 Police Agencies

| Case Number and Description | Own Seriousness | | | | Expected Discipline | | | Own Willingness to Report | | | |
|---|---|---|---|---|---|---|---|---|---|---|---|
| | 1st Q | Median | $\bar{x}$ | 3rd Q | 1st Q | Median | 3rd Q | 1st Q | Median | $\bar{x}$ | 33rd Q |
| Case 1 - Off-Duty Security System Business | 1.19 | 1.41 | 1.40 | 1.58 | 1 | 1 | 1 | 1.09 | 1.25 | 1.29 | 1.37 |
| Case 2 - Free Meals and Discounts on Beat | 2.69 | 2.87 | 2.90 | 3.09 | 2 | 2 | 2 | 1.70 | 2.00 | 2.09 | 2.39 |
| Case 3 - Bribe From Speeding Motorist | 4.89 | 4.95 | 4.92 | 5.00 | 4 | 4 | 6 | 3.41 | 4.09 | 3.97 | 4.59 |
| Case 4 - Holiday Gifts From Merchants | 2.56 | 2.98 | 2.97 | 3.36 | 2 | 3 | 3 | 1.91 | 2.31 | 2.44 | 2.91 |
| Case 5 - Crime Scene Theft of Watch | 4.95 | 5.00 | 4.95 | 5.00 | 6 | 6 | 6 | 3.81 | 4.54 | 4.35 | 4.86 |
| Case 6 - 5% Kickback From Auto Repair Shop | 4.23 | 4.59 | 4.50 | 4.74 | 4 | 4 | 4 | 3.08 | 3.88 | 3.76 | 4.38 |
| Case 7 - Supervisor Grants Holiday in Exchange for Car Tune-Up | 4.01 | 4.22 | 4.21 | 4.40 | 3 | 3 | 4 | 2.91 | 3.51 | 3.43 | 3.74 |
| Case 8 - Cover-Up of Police DUI Accident | 2.63 | 3.00 | 2.94 | 3.22 | 1 | 2.5 | 4 | 1.83 | 2.18 | 2.16 | 2.42 |
| Case 9 - Free Drinks to Ignore Late Bar Closing | 4.42 | 4.62 | 4.50 | 4.76 | 4 | 4 | 4 | 2.95 | 3.72 | 3.53 | 4.14 |
| Case 10 - Excessive Force on Car Thief | 3.00 | 3.27 | 3.38 | 3.80 | 3 | 4 | 4 | 2.36 | 2.76 | 2.88 | 3.21 |
| Case 11 - Theft From Found Wallet | 4.72 | 4.89 | 4.80 | 4.94 | 4 | 6 | 6 | 3.36 | 4.05 | 3.94 | 4.61 |

**Table 15.5**  U.S. Police Agencies 2 and 23—Reports of the Misconduct's Seriousness, the Expected Discipline For It, and Their Willingness to Report It

| | Own Perceptions of Seriousness | | | Expected Discipline | | Own Willingness to Report | | |
|---|---|---|---|---|---|---|---|---|
| | A2 | A23 | A2 – A23 | A2 | A23 | A2 | A23 | A2 – A23 |
| Case 1 - Off-Duty Security System Business | 1.57 | 1.36 | 0.21 | None | None | 1.57 | 1.22 | 0.35 |
| Case 2 - Free Meals and Discounts on Beat | 3.04 | 2.85 | 0.19 | Written Reprimand | Verbal Reprimand | 2.42 | 1.75 | 0.67 |
| Case 3 - Bribe From Speeding Motorist | 4.94 | 4.78 | 0.16 | Dismissal | Suspension | 4.67 | 3.02 | 1.65 |
| Case 4 - Holiday Gifts From Merchants | 3.07 | 2.79 | 0.28 | Written Reprimand | Verbal Reprimand | 2.74 | 2.05 | 0.69 |
| Case 5 - Crime Scene Theft of Watch | 4.97 | 4.79 | 0.18 | Dismissal | Dismissal | 4.92 | 3.36 | 1.56 |
| Case 6 - 5% Kickback From Auto Repair Shop | 4.58 | 4.02 | 0.56 | Suspension | Suspension | 4.38 | 2.71 | 1.67 |
| Case 7 - Supervisor Grants Holiday in Exchange for Car Tune-Up | 4.16 | 4.05 | 0.11 | Written Reprimand | Suspension | 3.68 | 2.66 | 1.02 |
| Case 8 - Cover-Up of Police DUI and Accident | 3.16 | 2.68 | 0.48 | Suspension | None | 2.67 | 2.03 | 0.64 |
| Case 9 - Free Drinks to Ignore Late Bar Closing | 4.68 | 3.77 | 0.91 | Suspension | Suspension | 4.21 | 2.48 | 1.73 |
| Case 10 - Excessive Force on Car Thief | 4.45 | 3.49 | 0.96 | Suspension | Suspension | 4.02 | 2.53 | 1.49 |
| Case 11 - Theft From Found Wallet | 4.94 | 4.55 | 0.39 | Dismissal | Suspension | 4.74 | 2.95 | 1.79 |

23 has a long history of scandal and, despite various reform efforts, continues to carry a reputation as an agency with persistent corruption problems. Although a local newspaper once labeled it "the most corrupt police department in the country," half a dozen other departments in our sample appear to have an integrity environment that is as poor or worse.

As is the case for all 30 agencies, in both of these agencies there was a very high correlation between the rank ordering of scores in each category. In almost every case, the mean rank order officers awarded a scenario for seriousness was almost identical to the rank order they awarded the seriousness with which officers would judge it, the severity of discipline it should and would receive, and the likelihood that they and other officers in their agency would be likely to report it. There was also little difference between the two agencies in the rank ordering of the scenarios. While these differences in the within-agency and between-agency rank ordering of the scenarios were minimal, discrepancies between the agencies' absolute scores reflect the wide differences between them. Likewise, the estimates of the seriousness of the misconduct in the cases were consistently higher for Agency 2 than for Agency 23. Comparison of modal discipline scores shows that, although the modal values are the same for five cases, for five other cases the police officers in Agency 2 expected more severe discipline for the misconduct than did the officers in Agency 23. For some of these cases, the contrast between the agencies regarding the expected discipline for the misconduct is dramatic. For example, in Case 8 (Cover-Up of a Police DUI Accident) police officers from Agency 2 expected the police officer who engaged in such conduct to be suspended, while the police officers from Agency 23 expected there to be no discipline whatsoever.

The differences in discipline were also substantial for the cases describing the most serious types of corruption, such as Case 3 (Bribe From Speeding Motorist), Case 5 (Crime Scene Theft of Watch), and Case 11 (Theft From Found Wallet). While the officers in Agency 2 think that dismissal would be meted out for all three of these most serious cases, the officers in Agency 23 expect that the discipline of dismissal would follow in only one case—Case 5.

Clearly, the most dramatic differences between Agencies 2 and 23 were found in their attitudes toward the code of silence; with the exception of Case 1 (Off-Duty Security System Business), the police officers in Agency 23 are consistently more likely to say that they would not report corruption than are the police officers in Agency 2 (see Figure 15.2). Since the means are below the midpoint of the scale (see Table 15.5), in both agencies the officers are unlikely to report any of the least serious types of corrupt behavior (Case 1 - Off-Duty Security System Business, Case 2 - Free Meals and Discounts on Beat, Case 4 - Holiday Gifts From Merchants, and Case 8 - Cover-Up of Police DUI Accident). The means above the midpoint indicate that the officers from Agency 2 would be likely to report the misconduct described in all the other cases. In stark contrast, there is only a single case— Case 5 (Crime Scene Theft of Watch)—that the officers from Agency 23 say that they would report. In sum, while Agency 2 is a police agency in which the code of silence seems to be under control, the results indicate that the code is very strong in Agency 23 and provides an environment in which corrupt behavior could easily flourish.

## CONCLUSION

Despite the large number of officers surveyed, we cannot specify the general integrity levels of police agencies in the United States. Only a probability sample would permit that. We can,

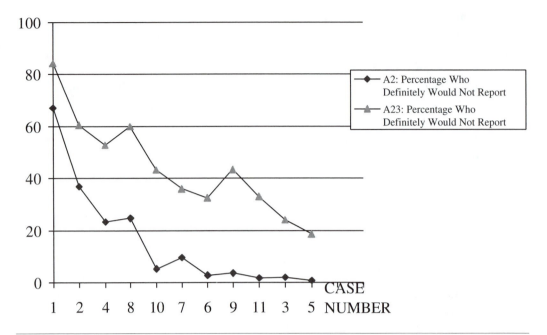

**Figure 15.2**    Percentage of Police Officers Who Said That Other Police Officers Definitely Would Not Report Misconduct, for Agencies 2 and 23

however, make some statements about police integrity in general and in the United States in particular that it previously was not possible to make. We have demonstrated that, unlike corruption, police integrity lends itself to measurement. It is possible to measure the environment of integrity in a police agency by measuring the extent to which officers resist temptations to abuse their office. Indicators of this resistance are the officers' perceptions of the seriousness of the offense, the extent to which it should be punished, and their willingness to report it. As we have shown in our U. S. study, all of these dimensions are measurable in themselves, are subject to different error properties, and are highly correlated with one another.

This capacity to measure integrity makes it possible to compare agencies with one another in terms of integrity. In the United States, we were able to identify both agencies of stellar integrity and those whose integrity environments were seriously deficient. This capacity to measure integrity also makes it

possible to measure changes in agency integrity over time and across divisions. It even makes it possible, as other essays in this volume illustrate, to measure the condition of integrity in police agencies of different nations and to measure as well in what specific areas integrity differs among them.

Finally, we have established that the "culture of integrity" in a police agency is measurable in three dimensions: officers' estimates of misconduct's seriousness, its appropriate discipline, and their willingness to report it. The rank order in which the officers rate these three dimensions is extraordinarily high, even though the absolute rankings differ sharply among the agencies surveyed. Moreover, in individual agencies, the scores on each dimension are highly correlated. That is, in agencies that rank a situation as very serious, officers endorse and expect a high level of discipline for it and are willing to report it.

According to the individual approach, the key to creating an environment of integrity in a police agency is to persuade officers to believe that misconduct is serious and they will therefore support discipline for it and come forward to report it. Our research is consistent with such an interpretation. However, another explanation is even more plausible. This explanation holds that officers believe misconduct to be "serious" based on how the organization that employs them punishes it and the willingness of most officers to report it. This view of things holds out the hope that agencies of integrity are not necessarily those with persuasive teachers of individual ethics, but those whose administrators and managers have been able and willing to employ effective technologies of discipline and reporting.

## NOTES

1. On the legalization of police see Mark Haller's (1976) *Historical Roots of Police Behavior, 1890–1925*, and, more generally, Egon Bittner's (1975) *The Functions of Police in Modern Society*, particularly Chapter 4, The Courts and the Police, and Chapter 5, The Institutional Independence of the Police. On militarization, Robert Fogelson's (1977) *Big City Police* is a good guide (see especially Chapter 2, The Military Analogy). Finally, see O. W. Wilson's *Police Administration* (1950) for his view of the meaning of the professionalization of the police.

2. If our sample were a probabilistic sample, we could try to determine the sampling error. However, the chances of error cannot be calculated for a convenience sample such as ours (see Weisberg, Krosnick, & Bowen, 1976).

3. The rather small difference may be due entirely to the form of the questions asked. When officers are asked "How likely would YOU be to report this behavior?" a proportion of those responding will be supervisors or administrators, who have a formal responsibility to take action when they learn of misconduct. By contrast, the question "How likely would MOST POLICE OFFICERS IN YOUR AGENCY be to report this behavior?" focuses on line officers and probably does not include supervisors in the mind of most respondents.

## REFERENCES

Bittner, E. (1975). *The functions of police in modern society*. New York: Jason Aronson.

Bratton, W. (1998). *Turnaround: How America's top cop reversed the crime epidemic*. New York: Random House.

Daley, R. (1978). *Prince of the city*. New York: Grenada.

Fogelson, R. (1977). *Big city police*. Cambridge, MA: Harvard University Press.

Fosdick, R. B. (1972). *American police systems*. Montclair, NJ: Patterson-Smith. (Original work published 1920)

Haller, M. (1976). Historical roots of police behavior, 1890-1925. *Law and Society Review, 10*(2), 303-323.

Klockars, C. B., Kutnjak Ivkovich, S., Harver, W. A., & Haberfeld, M. (2000, May). *The Measurement of Police Integrity*. A National Institute of Justice Research in Brief. Washington, DC: National Institute of Justice.

Maas, P. (1973). *Serpico*. New York: Viking.

New York City Commission to Investigate Allegations of Police Corruption and the City's Anti-Corruption Procedures. (1972). *Commission Report* (Whitman Knapp, Chairman). New York: Bar Press.

U.S. Department of Justice. (2000, November). *Law Enforcement Management and Administrative Statistics, 1999, Data for Individual State and Local Agencies of 100 or More Officers* (NCJ 184481). Washington: U.S. Department of Justice, Bureau of Justice Statistics.

Weisberg, H. F., Krosnick, J. A., & Bowen, B. D. (1976). *An introduction to survey research, polling, and data analysis.* Beverly Hills, CA: Sage.

Wilson, O.W. (1950). *Police administration.* New York: McGraw-Hill.

# Index

# About the Editors

**Maria (Maki) R. Haberfeld** is Professor of Police Science in the Department of Law, Police Science, and Criminal Justice Administration at the John Jay College of Criminal Justice in New York City. She was born in Poland and immigrated to Israel as a teenager. She holds two bachelor's degrees, two master's degrees, and a Ph.D. in criminal justice. During her army service in the Israel Defense Force, in which she earned the rank of sergeant, she was assigned to a special counter-terrorist unit that was created to prevent terrorist attacks in Israel. Prior to coming to John Jay, she served in the Israel National Police, in which she earned the rank of lieutenant. She has also worked for the U.S. Drug Enforcement Administration, in the New York Field Office, as a special consultant.

Haberfeld has taught at Yeshiva University and New Jersey City University. Her research interests and publications are in the areas of private and public law enforcement, specifically training, police integrity, and comparative policing (her research involves police departments in the United States, Eastern and Western Europe, and Israel). She has also done some research in the area of white-collar crime, specifically organizational and individual corruption during the Communist era in Eastern Europe. For 3 years (from 1997 to 2000), she was a member of a research team, sponsored by the National Institute of Justice, studying police integrity in three major police departments in the United States. Between 1999 and 2002, she was also a Principal Investigator on a research project in Poland, sponsored by the National Institute of Justice, where she studied the Polish National Police and its transformation to community-oriented policing. She has received additional grants from the PSC-CUNY Research Foundation to continue her research in Poland, with particular focus on the balancing act between the public perceptions of the new police reform and rampant accusations of police corruption and lack of integrity.

Haberfeld has recently published a book on police training, *Critical Issues in Police Training* (2002), presented numerous papers on training-related issues during professional gatherings and conferences, and written a number of articles on police training, specifically on police leadership, integrity, and stress. In addition, she has been involved in active training of police officers on issues related to multiculturalism, sensitivity, and leadership, as well as provided technical assistance to a number of police departments in rewriting procedural manuals. She is a member of a number of professional police associations, such as the International Association of Chiefs of Police, International Police Association, and American Society of Law Enforcement Trainers. For the last 2 years (from 2001 to 2003), she has been involved in developing, coordinating, and teaching in special training program for the NYPD. She has developed a graduate course titled "Counter-Terrorism Policies for Law Enforcement," which she teaches at John Jay to the ranking officers of the NYPD. Her most recent involvement in Eastern Europe includes redesigning the basic academy curriculum of the Czech National Police, with the emphasis on integrity-related training. She is currently writing the book *Police Leadership*. (forthcoming).

**Sanja Kutnjak Ivković** is Assistant Professor of Criminology and Criminal Justice at Florida State University. She received her LL.B. degree from the University of Zagreb, Croatia, a Ph.D. in criminology from the University of Delaware, and a S.J.O. degree from Harvard Law School. She is a member of the Croatian bar. Kutnjak Ivković has been pursuing a variety of topics in criminology, criminal justice, and the sociology of law. Her particular area of interest and expertise is policing. Jointly with Carl Klockars, she initiated a cross-cultural study of police corruption that, over time and with support from colleagues from a number of countries, has grown into a project including more than 13,000 police officers from 14 countries. The results of this unique cross-cultural research, the largest and most comprehensive empirical study of police corruption to date, are outlined in the present volume. Kutnjak Ivković has also been a Senior Research Associate on the related project *Enhancing Police Integrity* (funded by the National Institute of Justice, U.S. Department of Justice). In her current work in progress, *The Fallen Blue Knights: Controlling Police Corruption*, she explores police corruption and the mechanisms of its control.

Her interests also include the court system and legal decision making. Kutnjak Ivković has studied participation of lay persons (jurors, lay judges) as decision makers in criminal and civil cases, both in the United States and abroad. In the arena of international jurisprudence, she undertook a project focusing on the delivery of justice by the International Criminal Tribunal for the Former Yugoslavia to the victims of war crimes.

Kutnjak Ivković has published a book, book chapters, and numerous journal articles in the areas of policing, comparative criminology/criminal justice, and sociology of law. Her work has appeared in journals such as the *Journal of Criminal Law and Criminology, Law and Social Inquiry, Stanford Journal of International Law, Law & Policy, International Journal of Comparative and Applied Criminal Justice, International Criminal Justice Review, Journal of Crime & Justice, Police Practice and Research: An International Journal,* and the *International Journal of the Sociology of Law*. She is currently writing the book *The Fallen Blue Knights: Controlling Police Corruption* (forthcoming).

**Carl B. Klockars** was Professor of Criminal Justice and Sociology at the University of Delaware. He was a graduate of the University of Rhode Island, where he earned his bachelor's degree in sociology, and the University of Pennsylvania, where he earned his master's and doctoral degrees. A criminologist with more than 30 years of experience, Klockars authored five books, more than 50 scholarly articles, and numerous professional papers. He served as nationally elected Vice President of the Police Section of the Academy of Criminal Justice Sciences and was three times elected by the members of the American Society of Criminology to serve on its Executive Board. He also served as a lobbyist for the Maryland Sheriff's Association and as an expert witness in cases of alleged police misconduct. Klockars was a pioneer in building collaborative research relationships between police and academics. He wrote extensively on professional crime, criminological theory, the moral dilemmas of policing, and police use of force. With colleagues, he had recently completed a study, titled *Enhancing Police Integrity*, with three police agencies—in Charleston, South Carolina; Charlotte-Mecklenburg, North Carolina; and St. Petersburg, Florida—that seeks to understand the mechanisms through which police agencies may create organizational environments that enhance and encourage integrity.

# About the Contributors

**Marc Alain** was born in Quebec City, Canada, in 1961. Alain completed undergraduate studies in ethnology, psychology, and criminology. After completing a bachelor's degree in humanities, he opted for graduate studies in criminology. His master's thesis is still considered one of the first academic efforts in criminology devoted to the understanding of police responses and police strategies aimed at the biker gang phenomenon. His doctoral research embraced a much larger sociological perspective as he studied the cross-border smuggling of tobacco products into Canada between 1985 and 1994; he proposed that such a phenomenon be considered a vast social response designed to reestablish an equilibrium once broken by the state. This work lead to the publication of a book and numerous articles in specialised journals. He earned his Ph.D. in criminology in 1997 from the Université de Montréal. Afterwards, Alain was awarded a postdoctoral fellowship at the Catholic University of Leuven, Belgium, to study the complex field of transnational police cooperation in Europe and in North America; in this domain, he was one the earliest researchers to study these mechanisms not from the more traditional perspective of treaties and legal agreements but, rather, from the perspective of police officers in the field, who have to work on a daily basis with sometimes awkward policies. This research lead to specialized publications and scientific conferences in Europe, North America, and Australia. Alain was then offered a tenure-track position at the University of Sherbrooke, where he studied the management and the division of security mandates between public, private, and semipublic agencies. He also conducted research on the difficulties encountered by police organizations when they depart from more traditional policing methods in favor of community and problem-oriented policing. At the University of Sherbrooke, Alain taught the sociology of organizations, macroeconomy, and case studies in the management of security organizations. After 2 years at the University of Sherbrooke, he was hired at the École nationale de police du Québec in 2000, with a mandate of creating its first research unit. Alain is now the head of the Centre for Research in Police Activities of the École nationale de police du Québec. His recent work pertains to the sociology of security organizations and policing. More recently, he has been interested in ethical issues in police work as well as police attitudes and culture.

**Zubair Nawaz Chattha** joined the Pakistan Air Force as a cadet in its Aeronautical Engineering branch and obtained an F.Sc. degree (with a major in aero sciences). On resigning from the Air Force in 1986, he continued his education at the Government College, Lahore, and majored in economics and political science. He then attended the Punjab University Law College, where he obtained a law degree in 1989.

On passing the provincial services examination in 1991, Chattha joined the Excise and Taxation Department, where he worked as District Excise and Taxation Officer of Attock. He subsequently joined the Pakistan Police Service in 1995. As part of his duties, he was a member of the team responsible for developing Pakistan's first Motorway and National Highway Police in 1997, which developed high standards of efficiency and service with a low number of corruption and misconduct complaints. He was transferred to the Punjab police in 1998 and served in Lahore as Assistant Superintendent of Police in Naulakha and Iqbal Town. During his service in the Lahore Police, apart from policing activities, he also conducted research on the patterns of modern crime and the efficiency of the police organization.

In 2001, he obtained an LL.M. degree from Harvard Law School. While a student at Harvard, he authored research papers on a variety of topics, including police misconduct, cybercrime, and the Kashmir issue. He also arranged a 1-day conference on prospects of peace in Kashmir. When he returned to Pakistan from the United States in June of 2001, he was promoted to Superintendent of Police Headquarters, Lahore. As part of his duties, he arranged many courses on human rights. During this period, he was closely associated with the members of National Reconstruction Bureau responsible for police reforms. After the promulgation of the Police Order of 2002, he finalized the plan to reorganize the Lahore Police (the second largest police department in Pakistan). He is currently serving in the newly formed Provincial Investigation Branch as a crime analyst.

**Maximilian Edelbacher** was born in 1944 in Vienna, Austria. Between 1963 and 1968, he studied law at the University of Vienna. After performing a 1-year traineeship at court as an attorney candidate and having worked in the documentary L/C department of a bank, in 1972 he became a legal expert in the Bundespolizeidirektion Vienna, the headquarters of the Federal Police. Between 1976 and 1986, he was an expert on burglary, fraud, forgery, and prostitution with the Viennese Major Crime Bureau. From 1986 to 1988, he was the head of the homicide squad. From 1988 to 2002, Edelbacher was the chief of the Major Crime Bureau. Since November of 2002, he acts as chief of the Criminal Investigation Department South of Vienna. He has been working for the Federal Police Department for more than 30 years. In addition, Edelbacher is involved in the training of criminal investigators and executives. He is trainer in the leadership education of the Federal Police for the whole Austria, teacher in the Middle European Police Academy, and lecturer at the Vienna University of Economics and Business Administration. Since 1995, he has been a member of the Academy of Criminal Justice Sciences (ACJS) and the International Association of Financial Crime Investigators (IAFCI). Since 1998, he has been

Vice President of the IPES (International Police Executive Symposium). He has also been editor for Europe of the *International Journal of Police Practice and Research*. Between 2001 and 2003, he acted as President of the International Chapter of the ACJS.

He was selected seven times as an expert for the Council of Europe in Prague in the Czech Republic, in Tilburg in The Netherlands, in Banská Bystrica in Slovakia, in Strasbourg in France, in Tallinn in Estonia, in Priština in Kosovo, and in London, in Brussels, and in Moscow. He was also engaged three times as a consultant of the United Nations—in Skopje in Macedonia, in Bishkek in the Republic of Kyrgyzstan, and in Vienna at the 10th congress of the Crime Prevention Center.

Edelbacher's publications include *Viennese Criminal Chronicle* (1993), *Applied Criminalistics* (3 vols., 1995), *History of Insurance Fraud in Austria* (1997), *Organized Crime in Europe* (1998), *Security Management* (1999), *Fraud in the European Union* (2001), and *Crime Scene Vienna* (2003). He has also written several book chapters in books published in the United States, Israel, Japan, and Hungary and various technical articles regarding police and criminalistic subjects.

**Börje Ekenvall** has recently retired from his post as lecturer in law at the Swedish National Police Academy in Stockholm, where he taught for the past 25 years. During this time, he also lectured at Stockholm University´s Faculty of Law. He began studying criminology some years ago, and has developed an interest in, among other things, the redistribution of drug offending in Stockholm (hot spots) as a result of various police measures. His research into police attitudes toward misconduct has to date resulted in the publication of two books and an article. He has also been inspired to continue research into the attitudes of both police cadets and other groups toward different forms of police misconduct. Börje Ekenvall has a master's degree in humanities from the University of Uppsala, a law degree from the University of Lund, and a postgraduate (licentiate) degree in criminology from the University of Stockholm.

**L.W.J.C. (Leo) Huberts** is Professor in Police Studies and Criminal Justice and senior lecturer in Public Administration at the Department of Public Administration and Organization Science at the Faculty of Social Sciences of the Vrije Universiteit Amsterdam in The Netherlands. He teaches courses in decision-making theory, public integrity, police studies and criminal justice, police management, and police integrity.

Huberts has done research on political and administrative decision making and power, on public power and power abuse (including an international expert survey on corruption and fraud), on police integrity, and on police administration. He is director of the research program on "Integrity of Governance" of his department. The program includes projects on the amount of political and administrative corruption in The Netherlands, the history of public integrity, law- and rule-breaking by governmental actors, police corruption and integrity, the strategies to protect organizational integrity (including the importance of leadership), and the relationship between public and business ethics and values.

He is author or editor of books on influence on governmental policy, on social movements, on public corruption and fraud, and on the Dutch police and police integrity. With Hans van den Heuvel he edited *Integrity at the Public-Private Interface* (1999), and with Cyrille Fijnaut he edited *Corruption, Integrity and Law Enforcement* (2002). For a Transparency International research project, Huberts did evaluation research on the National Integrity System of The Netherlands. His articles in English about public integrity have been published in *Crime, Law and Social Change,* the *European Journal on Criminal Policy and Research,* and *Public Integrity.* Huberts is a fellow of the International Institute for Public Ethics, and he cochairs the Study Group on Ethics and Integrity of Governance of the European Group of Public Administration.

**David T. Johnson** is Associate Professor of Sociology and Adjunct Professor of Law at the University of Hawaii at Manoa. He is the author of *The Japanese Way of Justice: Prosecuting Crime in Japan* (2002), which won the best book award from the American Society of Criminology's Division on International Criminology. Johnson has studied at Bethel College in Minnesota, the University of Chicago, the University of California at Berkeley, and Harvard University. He has lived in Japan for 5 years, has received two Fulbright grants to do research in Japan, and has lectured and studied at universities in Kobe and Tokyo. Johnson's current research is about corruption control in Japan, the United States, Italy, and South Korea, capital punishment in Japan, and law and social change in Japan. In 2000, he won the Regents Award for Excellence in Teaching, the University of Hawaii's highest honor for teachers.

**Ferenc Krémer** is Associate Professor of Sociology and Political Science at Police College, Budapest, Hungary. He has been a consultant to the police since 2000. He received a Ph.D. in ancient Greek and Roman history and a Ph.D. in sociology from ELTE (Eötvös Loránd Tudományegyetem) in Budapest, Hungary. Krémer is the author of 20 scholarly articles, a sociology textbook for law enforcement students, and a book on police subculture and police corruption.

His first steps in studying police and policing were supported by ECESP (East-Central European Scholarship Program of USAID). Then in 1996 he was a visiting scholar at George Washington University, Washington, D.C. for a semester. These studies formed starting points for Krémer's research of the Hungarian police.

In the last few years, Krémer's domain has been police subculture and police corruption, especially with regard to identifying the police reform that is necessary in Hungary. His recent research is oriented to the problem of prejudice in policing and to a theoretical view of changing conditions and the role of social control.

**M.E.D. (Terry) Lamboo** is a doctoral student researcher at the Department of Public Administration and Organization Science at the Faculty of Social Sciences of the Vrije Universiteit Amsterdam in The Netherlands. She holds a master's degree in sociology and American studies, with a minor in criminology and policy analysis, from the

University of Amsterdam. As an exchange student, she studied American studies and criminology at the University of Minnesota in Minneapolis for a year.

Currently, Lamboo is concluding her dissertation on the content and effectiveness of the integrity policies of the Dutch police and the Dutch Ministry of the Interior. For this research, she has conducted extensive case studies on three police forces, holding interviews with both management and street cops. Her research will result in a book to be published in 2004.

A separate project has been Lamboo's analysis of the internal investigations of the Dutch police over the years 1997 and 1999, with Andrea Nieuwendijk and Magrete van der Steeg. Subsequently, this has lead to the development of a Monitor Internal Investigations Police. This Monitor has been applied to the internal investigations of the Dutch police over the years 1999 and 2000. The results have been published and received wide attention in the media. Further publications (in English) will be forthcoming from Lamboo.

She also joined professors Maurice Punch and Leo Huberts in surveying Dutch police to measure their integrity by analyzing their perceptions of the misconduct in specific scenarios. The survey was undertaken in cooperation with Carl Klockars and his colleagues, and its results are the topic of their chapter in this volume. Her research interests include integrity and integrity policies for the public sector and most specifically for the police, police reform, and the cooperation between police and other institutions in the performance of police duties.

**Marie Torstensson Levander** is Associate Professor in Sociology at Vaxjo University and Lund University, Sweden. She received her Ph.D. in sociology from Stockholm University.

Torstensson Levander is interested in several topics in criminology and criminal justice. She has studied the etiology of drug abuse, female criminality, fear of crime, and community crime prevention. Her particular area of interest is policing strategies, and during the 1990s she made several studies of the implementation of problem-oriented policing in Sweden. At that time, she was also the head of the Research unit of the Swedish Police College.

Torstensson Levander has published books, book chapters, and journal articles in the areas of policing, drug abuse and crime, female criminality, fear of crime, and crime prevention. Her work has appeared in journals such as the *British Journal of Criminology*, *Journal of Quantitative Criminology*, *European Journal on Criminal Policy and Research*, and the *International Review of Victimology*.

**Branko Lobnikar** received his degree in sociology in 1993 from the University of Ljubljana, Slovenia. He completed a master's degree in human resource management (HRM) at the University of Maribor, Slovenia, in 1999. He started his doctoral study in HRM at the same university in 2000, which he will complete in 2003 with his thesis, *Aggressive and Violent Behavior Management in the Workplace*.

Lobnikar is the Vice Dean and the Head of Police Administration and Management Department at the College of Police and Security Studies, where he is also a Senior Lecturer in theories of police work and sociology. He is also a Senior

Lecturer of Human Resource Management at the College of Entrepreneurship in Piran, Slovenia. In addition to his academic positions, Lobnikar is an employee of the Ministry of the Interior of the Republic of Slovenia, in the rank of an Adviser to the Government. During his career, Lobnikar has been an Assistant Chief of Police and Police Inspector. He has published over 15 scientific and professional journal articles, presented papers at over 20 international and domestic conferences, and coauthored or edited some books and book chapters. His work has appeared in *Security Journal*, *Kriminalistik*, and the *International Journal of Police Science and Management*, among others.

His current research interests are in the areas of police deviance, studies of aggressive behavior and violence in the workplace, the nature of human resources in public and private sector, and applications of management and organizational psychology in police organizations.

**Gareth Newham** joined the Centre for the Study of Violence and Reconciliation (CSVR) in August of 1998 as a researcher. He currently holds the position of Project Manager for the policing projects of the Criminal Justice Programme (CJP). The CSVR is a nonprofit, public interest organization that was initially established in 1989 to study the affects of apartheid state-sponsored violence on South African society. Today it is an organization consisting of approximately 65 people who work in six program areas dedicated to building a democratic society dedicated to human rights.

Presently, Newham is managing a team of four researchers working in the following three areas: tackling police corruption, promoting police accountability, and improving witness management. The aim of the research is both to develop policy-relevant knowledge for police reform and to understand the requirements for culture change amongst police officers at station level in the South African context.

During 1999, Newham started working with a large inner-city police station in Johannesburg that recorded one of the highest levels of serious and violent crime in South Africa. As a result of this work, he has managed to build a healthy working relationship with senior police managers who are dedicated to building a professional police agency able to combat crime and deliver police services effectively and equitably in a democratic society.

He is also interested in training and was contracted as a facilitator by a consortium of universities to train senior station-level commanders throughout the country. Toward this end, he has helped develop and facilitate modules dealing with leadership, performance management, and the management of police corruption.

Newham's other main area of interest in the criminal justice field is witness management and security. Consequently, he designed and managed the first independent research project on the country's National Witness Protection Programme. Prior to this, he researched and developed a policy document for the establishment of a witness protection programme for the Truth and Reconciliation Commission. Before joining the CSVR, he spent a few years working for the Institute for Democracy in South Africa (IDASA), where he conceptualized, developed, and coordinated the Provincial Parliamentary Monitoring Project that worked toward facilitating public understanding of and access to the country's newly established provincial legislatures.

Newham holds a bachelor of social sciences degree and a postgraduate honors degree in political studies from the University of Cape Town, a postgraduate diploma in applied research methodology from the University of Stellenbosch, and a master's degree in public and development management from the University of the Witwatersrand.

**Milan Pagon** got his doctorate (Sc.D.) in organizational sciences in 1990 at the University of Maribor, Slovenia. In the period between 1990 and 1994, he was a Fulbright Scholar to the University of Arkansas, Fayetteville, where he both studied and taught at the College of Business Administration. In 1994 he was awarded a Ph.D. in management.

During his police career, Pagon has been an Educator at the Police High School, a Detective, a Deputy Commander and a Commander of Police Station, a Police Inspector, and a State Undersecretary at the Ministry of the Interior. Outside the police, he has been an Assistant Director of the Personnel Agency of Slovenia, a Human Resource Manager at a chemical company, a Teaching Assistant, an Assistant Professor, and an Associate Professor. In 1995, he was elected Dean of the College of Police and Security Studies, a duty that he initially performed for 3 years. In 2001, he was again elected Dean, the position that he is currently holding. In 2003, Pagon was elected to the rank of Full Professor. In addition to his administrative and teaching duties at the College of Police and Security Studies, he is also Professor of Organizational Behavior at the Faculty of Organizational Sciences, University of Maribor.

Pagon was invited in the summers of 1996, 1997, 1998, and 1999 to serve as a Visiting Professor at the University of Arkansas, Fayetteville, where he taught the courses "Concepts of Management and Organizational Behavior" and "Human Resource Management" at the Sam M. Walton College of Business.

Pagon is a member of the following professional and scientific associations: the Academy of Management, Honorary Management Fraternity Sigma Iota Epsilon, International Society for Human Resource Management, Society of International Scholars Phi Beta Delta, American Psychological Society, American Society for Criminology, Academy of Criminal Justice Sciences, American Association of University Professors, International Police Association, and the Association of Professors of the University of Maribor.

He was a founding father and the Chairman of the Program Committee of the International Biennial Conference "Policing in Central and Eastern Europe," of which there have been four, with the following subtitles: "Comparing Firsthand Knowledge with Experience From the West" in 1996, "Organizational, Managerial, and Human Resource Aspects" in 1998, "Ethics, Integrity, and Human Rights" in 2000, and "Deviance, Violence, and Victimization" in 2002.

In his research, Pagon has collaborated with some of the top international researchers in the fields of management and police work: Daniel C. Ganster, Paul E. Spector, and Carl B. Klockars from the United States and Cary L. Cooper from the United Kingdom. These cooperative efforts have produced papers at scientific conferences and publications in the best international journals.

Pagon was also appointed to the editorial board of two international and one domestic journal, namely *Stress & Health* and the *International Journal of Police Science and Management* and *Varstvoslovje: Journal of Security Theory and Praxeology.*

He also serves as a reviewer for one international and two domestic journals, namely *Stress & Health* and *Varstvoslovje*, and *Organization: Journal of Management, Informatics, and Human Resources.*

**Maurice Punch** studied at the universities of Exeter, London, Cambridge, and Essex, earning an M.A. in 1966 and a Ph.D. in 1972. He has worked at Essex University, University of Utrecht, S.U.N.Y. Albany, and Nyenrode University (The Netherlands Business School) and has given numerous lectures, seminars, and courses in several countries (including Spain, Italy, and Finland). In the United Kingdom, he specialized in the sociology of education, and in The Netherlands (where he has lived since 1975), he has researched corporate crime, regulation, and control in business and also deviance, corruption, integrity, and reform of the police organization. He has published in English, Dutch, French, and American journals and has written several books, including *Dirty Business: Exploring Corporate Misconduct* (1996). His latest book, with Jim Gobert (of the University of Essex), is *Rethinking Corporate Crime* (2003). After 16 years as Professor of Sociology at Nyenrode, where he performed many administrative functions and set up the International M.B.A. Programme, he became an independent researcher and consultant in 1994. Since then he has researched crises in policing in Britain, Belgium, and The Netherlands; taught in the National Police Training (Bramshill) and University of Cambridge program in applied criminology for senior police officers in the United Kingdom; and taught in various executive programs for managers, bankers, and consultants—including seminars on ethics, integrity, and control. In 1999, he became Visiting Professor at the Mannheim Centre for the Study of Criminology and Criminal Justice, London School of Economics, where he teaches primarily in the areas of policing and corporate crime. In The Netherlands he was on the board of R.B.C. Network for several years and, with colleagues from R.B.C. Network, he engaged in studies of organizations that led to strategic interventions. He has been involved in numerous conferences as presenter, organizer, and chair, including contributions for the Council of Europe, United Nations, and National Institute of Justice; he organized and chaired panels at the Global Forum on Fighting Corruption and Safeguarding Integrity II in The Hague and at the International Anti-Corruption Conference in Prague in 2001.

**Anne Puonti** has a master's degree in education and she is finishing her doctoral dissertation on the collaboration among authorities (such as the police, the tax authority, the enforcement authority, and the prosecutor) in economic crime investigation. Her research focuses on how collaboration and a shared investigation process are constructed between the authorities in practice when their organizational tasks and goals are so divergent. She worked as a researcher and a doctoral student at the Center for Activity Theory and Developmental Work Research (National Center for Excellence 2000-2005) from 1999 to 2002. Currently, she works as a development manager at the National Bureau of Investigation, Finland.

**Sami Vuorinen** is a licentiate of public administration. He worked as a criminologist researching economic crime at the National Research Institute of Legal Policy, Finland, between 1997 and 2002. His latest study describes police practice in the investigation of economic crime and suggests factors that affect the success and length of investigations. Currently, he is employed as a senior auditor at the State Audit Office, Finland. In addition to this, he is currently working on a doctoral thesis on how Finnish economic life prevents the development of a gray economy and whether the measures carried out to ensure this economic life have taken or could conceivably take the place of official supervision to a certain degree.

**Louise Westmarland** is Lecturer in Criminology at the Open University in the United Kingdom. Her research interests include gender and policing, corruption, ethics, and integrity in the criminal justice system. She is also interested in ethnographic research methods in criminology, and in danger, fear, and ethics in situations where privileged access leads to dilemmas for researchers. Her recent key projects have included the first published ethnography of gender and policing conducted in the United Kingdom and research on police informers and how they are regulated—and the effect of this on rights and justice. Her first degree was a bachelor's with honors in sociology from the University of York (in the United Kingdom). She then studied for a Ph.D. in sociology and social policy at the University of Durham, supervised by Professor Dick Hobbs. The title of her thesis was *An Ethnography of Gendered Policing.* Prior to her current employment as Lecturer in Criminology at the Open University in Milton Keynes, Westmarland held a research post at the University of Durham and was a Research Fellow in Department of Sociology, University of York. She has held lectureships at University College Scarborough, Teesside University, and the Scarman Centre, University of Leicester. In her current post at the Open University, she is Course Chair of an undergraduate criminology degree course titled "Crime, Order and Social Control."